Novel Approaches to Anthropology

Novel Approaches to Anthropology

Contributions to Literary Anthropology

Edited by Marilyn Cohen

LEXINGTON BOOKS
Lanham • Boulder • New York • Toronto • Plymouth, UK

Published by Lexington Books
A wholly owned subsidiary of The Rowman & Littlefield Publishing Group, Inc.
4501 Forbes Boulevard, Suite 200, Lanham, Maryland 20706
www.rowman.com

10 Thornbury Road, Plymouth PL6 7PP, United Kingdom

British Library Cataloguing in Publication Information Available

Library of Congress Cataloging-in-Publication Data
Novel approaches to anthropology : contributions to literary anthropology / edited by
Marilyn Cohen.
    pages cm
  Includes bibliographical references and index.
  ISBN 978-0-7391-7502-6 (cloth : alk. paper) — ISBN 978-0-7391-7503-3 1.
Literature and anthropology. 2. Fiction—History and criticism. I. Cohen, Marilyn,
1952– editor of compilation.
  PN51.N66 2013
  809'.93358—dc23   2013014086

™
⊖ The paper used in this publication meets the minimum requirements of American
National Standard for Information Sciences—Permanence of Paper for Printed Library
Materials, ANSI/NISO Z39.48-1992.

Printed in the United States of America

Contents

Figures and Photograph

Acknowledgments

The successful completion of this book was made possible by a Kenny Summer Fellowship through Saint Peters University that provided funding for the book's Introduction, the chapter on Harriet Martineau written by the editor, Marilyn Cohen, and for preparing the manuscript. Richard Blot is credited with the title for the book. The editor thanks all of the contributors to the book for their assistance with formatting their chapters and commitment to the project. Finally, the editor thanks Alan Serrins for his support and Lissadell and Julian Cohen-Serrins for their patient instruction in the use of MS Word that saved her sanity.

Chapter One

Introduction: Anthropological Aspects
of the Novel

MARILYN COHEN

I have chosen the title "Aspects" because it is unscientific and vague, because it leaves us the maximum of freedom, because it means both the different ways we can look at a novel and the different ways a novelist can look at his work.[1]

Interdisciplinarity consists in creating a new object that belongs to no one.[2]

The inspiration for this volume is a long-standing reading group comprised largely of anthropologists interested in literature, most of whom were graduate students at the Graduate Faculty/The New School for Social Research during the 1970s and 80s. Elizabeth Long argues that the image of the solitary writer and reader has blinded us to the essentially social nature of reading and writing in the past and present, and renders invisible to scholarship "groups of readers and their modes of textual appropriation." "Textual communities," which require joint decisions about the reading program, are empowering because they establish social spaces that create community among people with shared values, sustain collective memory, challenge tradition, and nurture new interpretations and ideas through conversations with the authorial "other" and each other.[3] Similarly, for Wolfgang Iser, literary texts are a form of communication that has meaning only when read. Textual communities bring texts to life by sharing the individual imaginative process of reading. Through the process of reading both text and reader are set in motion realizing in multiple ways the author's artistic creation. When a world created by an author comes to life through reading, "we are able to experience things that no longer exist and to understand things that are totally unfamiliar to us."[4] This imaginative motion is further developed and accelerated by discussion.

According to Raymond Williams, literary texts represent a perspective of the social and cultural world constructed by authors through language. Like language and culture, literature or "the process and the result of formal composition within the social and formal properties of a language," is historical and processual, "evidence of a particular form of the social development of language." Literature did not fully emerge until the nineteenth century when its original fourteenth century meaning of an ability to read and level of educational achievement shifted to sensibility as a criterion defining literary quality.[5] Literary criticism, or commentaries on literature within learned criterion, is a socially constructed process involving ideas of taste and discrimination. The process through which a text is then translated into the reader's consciousness reflects his/her own social context and interests. This volume showcases the myriad ways that anthropologists bring their disciplinary perspectives and theoretical concepts to interpreting fiction mostly written in the past. Anthropologists explore and explain how other people live in the world and are often encouraged by the fact that there are alternatives to patriarchal sex/gender systems and the western capitalist way of life. Anthropologists typically learn about themselves and their own culture and society as they encounter and attempt to interpret others.

In cultures that produce written literature, dimensions of plasticity in human nature are illuminated. The aesthetic experience of reading literary works of art activates the imagination to visualize other worlds existing in the past, present, or future blurring binary oppositions between reality/fiction, objective/subjective, or logic/affect. These dichotomies, along with the bourgeois separation of the individual from society, are transgressed in artistic production. Literature stimulates a critical sociological imagination by allowing readers to take a fresh look at social norms in their own culture that they have taken for granted. It also can enlist the reader in the process of willing self-transformation through education.[6]

As a product of its time, the contributors to this volume reflect the neo-modernist search for an intermediate space between the meta-theories of modernism and the relativism of postmodernism. We integrate theoretical insights from the reflexive deconstructive postmodern turn in anthropology while maintaining a critical Marxist and feminist perspective that emphasizes global capitalist political economy. A significant insight of postmodernism was that language and ethnographic writing are political acts and that subjective interpretation cannot be eliminated from anthropological analysis. Cultural accounts by ethnographers are culturally constructed and contested. As Clifford Geertz states: "ethnography is a second-order interpretation; it is our own interpretation of their interpretation of their experience." [7]

The self-reflexive moment in anthropology, when traditional modes of representation in the discipline were being questioned, had much to gain from feminist theory. For fifty years feminist discourse explored how culture and language were composed of contested gendered codes of meaning and how constructions of the "Other" entailed relations of domination.

> Unlike postmodernism, feminist theory is an intellectual system that knows its politics, a politics directed toward securing recognition that the feminine is as critical an element of the human as the masculine and this a politics skeptical and critical of traditional "universal truths" concerning human behavior. Similarly, anthropology is grounded in a politics; it aims to secure a recognition that non-Western is as crucial an element of the human as the Western and thus is skeptical and critical of Western claims to knowledge and understanding.[8]

This volume contributes to the interdisciplinarity that began in earnest during the late 1960s. All of the contributors to this volume are interdisciplinary scholars, and several are historical anthropologists. Since ethnography is impossible for historical anthropologists, research is conducted "along the archival grain," reconstructing ways of life from primary archival sources including various nominal lists, letters, diaries, and when possible, oral histories and intensive interviews.[9] To construct a sense of place, considered fundamental to ethnography, historical anthropologists "read the scene," observing and interpreting where possible the built environment (factories, housing, shops, houses of worship, community institutions, modes of transportation) and other artifacts of past ways of life to provide the essential empathy that anthropologists bring to their fieldwork and interpretations of cultures. Finally the contributors are drawn to dialectical material approaches that ground interpretation in the worldliness and events of human life. Following Edward Said:

> Each essay in this book affirms the connection between texts and the existential actualities of human life, politics, societies and events. The realities of power and authority—as well as the resistances offered by men, women and social movements to institutions, authorities and orthodoxies—are the realities that make texts possible, that deliver them to their readers, that solicit the attention of critics.[10]

Members of this textual community yearned to move beyond social science scholarship to fiction, particularly that written during the long nineteenth century, a historical period extending from the late eighteenth century to World War I. Unlike historians who typically become familiar with fiction written during the time periods in which they specialize, social scientists do not as typically turn to fiction as sources of information relating to social life in the past or present. One reason is that fiction, as a form of artistic expression and aesthetic response, lies outside of the scientific epistemology grounded in empiricism. From its inception in the works of Bacon and Locke, the empirical tradition relegated the imagination to an inferior rank compared with reason.[11] The sharp bourgeois dichotomies between fact and fiction and objective/subjective were the historically specific theoretical starting point for literary criticism during the nineteenth and early twentieth centuries.

The contributors to this volume share the view that fiction, like all artistic expression, is rooted in historically and culturally specific contexts. We assume it can provide a rich source of information about societies that can or cannot be investigated through traditional ethnographic methods. Writers of fiction combine keen observations of their society, scholarly research, self-consciousness, and poetics in their constructed interpretations of meaning as recognized by the quintessential historical materialist Friedrich Engels: "[Balzac] gives us a most wonderfully realistic history of French 'Society'... from which ... I have learned more than from all the professed historians, economists and statisticians of the period together."[12]

Contributions to Literary Anthropology

This volume reflects the current stage of play among anthropologists who read and use fiction with "veracious imaginations." Fiction as an art form offers a rich interpretive source about social life and culture in the past or present, especially when written by authors whose repertoire reflects an imagination. A prime example of a veracious imagination is George Eliot who first described its components:

> By veracious imagination, I mean the working out in detail of the various steps by which a political or social change was reached, using all extant evidence and supplying deficiencies by careful analogical creation. How triumphant opinions originally spread; how institutions arose; what were the conditions of great inventions, discovered or theoretic conceptions; what circumstances affecting individual lots are attendant on the decay of long-established systems ... I want something different from the abstract treatment which belongs to grave history from a doctrinal point of view, and something different from the schemed picturesqueness of ordinary historical fiction. I want briefly, severely conscientious reproductions, in their concrete incidents, of pregnant movements in the past.[13]

The theoretical premise that literature, like any art form, is rooted in a particular historical and social context, originated in the late eighteenth century when materialist explanations about the forces governing the natural and social world began to be formulated challenging religious world views. By the nineteenth century, Marxist scholars, committed to historical materialism, the heuristic value of social class and class struggle, and to "considering the intrication of power in symbolic systems" were among the first to theorize connections between material life and symbolic systems such as art.[14] Classical Marxist literary theory accepted the determining force of the economic base as an ontological model which often relegated literature to ideological (mis)representation of the world. Although the mode of determination has since been conceived by Marxists in different ways (base/superstructure, determination, mediation, typification), all challenge the separation of areas of consciousness from real human activities and power relations.

The Frankfurt School, for example, addressed the Marxist theme of the dependence of consciousness on social being and the materialist premise.

> For critical theory the materialist premise operates as a limiting horizon with which any interpretive formulation must come to grips if it is to avoid mystification. It is not a dogmatic assertion that culture "reflects" social relations in any simple sense, nor that culture is an epiphenomenon of technology, economics, or any other historical force. The importance of the materialist presupposition is rather its insistence on the inerradicable tension between human urges for coherent life and thought and the limitation forced on us by our involvement in bodily, social, historical existence.[15]

Georg Lukacs postulated a small number of literary genres, each determined by a recognizable set of laws and he compared the material historical conditions from which the epic and the novel emerged.[16] "The epic hero is, strictly speaking, never an individual ... One of the essential characteristics of the epic is the fact that its theme is not a personal destiny but the destiny of a community." In the bourgeois age of the novel, this previous unity or mechanical solidarity between human beings and their social world is lost. "The novel is the epic of an age in which the extensive totality of life is no longer directly given, in which the immanence of meaning in life has become a problem, yet which still thinks in terms of totality." The hero, rather than a representative of a totality or collective social life is an estranged seeker of the meaning of existence.[17]

Raymond Williams built on the Frankfort School's insistence on art as an active process mediating social reality and imaginative creativity and on Antonio Gramsci's holistic hegemony concept. Hegemony is a whole lived social experience organized by specific and dominant meanings, values, expectations, and practices that constitute a perceived reality or way of life for most people in a society. A lived hegemony is a process, not a structure that must be reproduced, modified, challenged, altered over time. Art, itself a formative process within a specific social reality, is included within an effective hegemony.[18]

Beginning in the twentieth century, sociologists and anthropologists began to mine the rich source of evidence about social life contained in literature. Sociologist Joan Rockwell built on Lukács' insight regarding the novel as the "prototypical bourgeois art form" highlighting how its themes correspond to the principle bourgeois values of individualism and profit, particularly crucial during the formative years of young adulthood. "The preoccupation of the novel with the period of settling in life, is due to the fact that with the new sets of behavioral patterns associated with the breakdown of traditional society and the gradual establishment of one far more open, mercantile and mobile, it became an ever more strict social imperative that young people find their own way in life" whether this means moving away, making a living, and choosing their own marriage partners. Thus, success is individually achieved rather than ascribed by family or class.[19]

In 1974 Rockwell was using fiction to teach sociology to her students. Since literature is an integral part of society like other institutions, it provides descriptive information about the social structure and organization of a society including the existence of social institutions and customs and information about values and norms that may be inferred for the characters and their behavior. Literature is both a product of and reproduces society due to its normative function, particularly as an agent of socialization and social control. It can also be a force for social change by mobilizing public opinion or changing accepted norms and values. Through personification fictional characters are regularly used as prototypes of social roles and values by the distribution of rewards such as wealth, power, or marriage. "It is astonishing what a seepage there is of the values of a society into the depiction of the social, physical, and even sexual characteristics of persons in narrative fiction. The norms of sexual attraction are an indicator of what the society counts as desirable." Fiction can be influential because "reading fiction includes a psychological sense of participation" of living in the story, of "participating in communal existence." Since human beings are never fully defined by historically or socially constructed roles, aesthetic experiences like reading literature allow for questioning accepted norms, and imagining new identities, social relationships, and possible worlds.[20]

Questions probing the relationship of art to social life or "reality" continue to engage our speculation. Although the spectrums of social science and art are equally broad, the whole of human life, neither art nor science can present total reality. A selection of "aspects" of human life is inevitable as is a selection of how to order these so that we can comprehend the presentation. Novels, like social science and history, seek to describe, explain, and interpret social life and behavior through actual and imaginary events, characters, and commentary that can illuminate myriad social theories, themes, and issues. A resemblance to truth freed novelists from strict adherence to facts and liberated them to portray experience based on the imagination, to use the truths of history to transcend it.

According to sociologist Morroe Berger, the earliest modern novelists sought to give the status of truth and historicity to their new art form. The French novelists of the seventeenth and eighteenth centuries "solved" the issue of fit by devising the notion of "verisimilitude" or closeness to the truth. Probability, the likelihood that an event or a character could be found in real life, was another way novelists stayed close to social facts. Readers grant novelists their "willing suspension of disbelief" because novels dealt with ordinary people, true to life events, developing verisimilitude, to accept as true something that was not actual fact. Quoting Henry James: "It is impossible to imagine what a novelist takes himself to be unless he regarded himself as an historian and his narrative is a history." For James, the "supreme virtue of a novel" is "the air of reality."[21]

Norms or "conventional form" in literature create "expectancy" in the reader even before he/she experiences a novel or poem. To Iser: "A piece of fiction devoid of any connections with known reality would be incomprehensible."[22] The novelist constructs his characters to conform to normative expectations to a degree credible to the reader.

> Fictional conventions involve two social conventions that the novelist must attend to: the expectations which the reader brings to a novel from his own life and experience—that is, the writer must understand his audience; and the expectations which the reader acquired from the novel itself—that is, the writer must persuade the reader that a given character is constructed so consistently that the reader can believe in him both as a type (doctor, plumber, dressmaker) and an individual."

These conventions, like all norms, allow for prediction of what might happen in a story.[23]

In the nineteenth century some writers in the realist tradition (i.e., Balzac, Eliot, Drieser) claimed that their novels were objective reports on human behavior. Realist fiction achieved an intimacy among life, art, and the reader by attempting to portray life factually by creating worlds that the reader will empathize with even if the place, time, and characters are unfamiliar. Domestic realism in particular, an essentially bourgeois genre, rejected the romantic and aristocratic in favor of the local and provincial community; the details of daily life spent at home with family. George Eliot's scientific interests brought her, more than any other novelist, to the point of anticipating the notions and even the language of the social sciences that reproduced the dichotomy between objectivity and subjectivity. Drawn to the air of truth in Dutch realist paintings, Eliot and other Victorian novelists sought to create subjects and a way of life that their readers could recognize and verify through their experiences. The substance and meaning of community was central to Victorians at a time of rapid social change. Realist novels critique the weaknesses and strengths, "grandeur and tragedy" of human beings and social life, institutions, cultural ideas through characters and story emplotment or through "authorial intrusions." It is in the comments by authors or authorial intrusions that novelists come closest to social scientists. From the time of Henry Fielding, authors have used various strategies including intrusions in the novel: to edify, to guide the reader's mental images, attitude toward the characters, and to explain the characters on the basis of general ideas about human nature and social institutions. Intrusions are frequently related to sociopsychological insights on a wide range of topics bringing the novel close to social science.[24]

The connections between social life and literature were also being theorized by anthropologists in the nineteenth century beginning with scholars who focused on folklore and literature rooted in specific locales. Brad Evans examined the developing ethnographic imagination in American literature between 1865-1920. Influenced by George Stocking, a historian among the anthropologists, Evans focused on the prehistory of the culture concept, a concept that "became useful when race no longer described type but denoted biology."[25] Evans identified the source of the anthropological idea of culture in the humanistic realm of nineteenth-century folklore and literary objects seen as a reflection of a particular people rooted in time and place.

The conflation of folklore and racial or national character dated at least from the eighteenth century. For Johann Gottfried Herder, folklore was evidence of *Volksgeist* or folk spirit. Thus literature was ethnological material, evidence of the character of the person who wrote it and the society behind the individual. "One read it, rather circularly, to elucidate the nature of English literature in terms of English national character and, in turn, to elaborate English character by its literature. It was not of interest for what it said about a culture, but for what it could not help but say, suspended as it was in a web of meanings unique to a particular place, time, and people." In the1860s the perspectives of French philosophy and literary history were similar in that, "literature was the direct product of its race, moment, and milieu."[26] Thus, literature was subject to the same elemental causes as are other aspects of society and could serve as sources of evidence.

Evans located the origins of the ethnographic imagination in the literature of the Gilded Age when three "artistic impulses crystallized around notions of society attuned to localized populations, a deep knowledge of everyday life, and the vitality of

folk(loric) environments." By the 1880s folklore was a field organized institution-
ally. Comparisons discovered similar tales among different people challenging the
folk spirit argument. The initial move to view folklore as circulating culture carried
the antiessentialist, "antiracist, antievolutionary charge" since there was nothing to
suggest that members of the same race living apart developed the same folklore and
members of different races living even in remote contiguity shared folktales. Folklore was instead circulating culture that traveled widely "across any number of imagined categorical boundaries ... They become vehicles for the articulation and
disarticulation of different systems of meaning across discontinuous geographies and
temporalities." Debates among American folklorists centered on folklore as evidence
of social evolution or proof of the historical diffusion of cultural traits from a common source.[27]

Several students of anthropologist Franz Boas, including Alfred Kroeber, Ruth
Benedict, Margaret Mead, and Zora Neale Hurston, transferred to anthropology from
the discipline of English acquiring "habits of mind" trained in literary criticism.[28]
Those concerned with folklore, such as Benedict, clearly recognized the connection
between anthropology and the humanities. In her 1947 address to the American Anthropological Association, Benedict acknowledged that for centuries before Anthropology "great men" had derived their cross-cultural insights from literature. She
considered autobiographies, memoirs, and life histories to be essentially ethnographic reporting because they reflect how ideational culture is constructed in historically and culturally specific contexts.[29] Benedict, editor of the *Journal of American Folklore* between 1920-1940, stated that: "people's folktales are their
autobiography and the clearest mirror of their life" serving to "crystallize and per-
petuate the forms of culture that it has made articulate."[30] Although Benedict's anthropological writings conformed to the parameters of objective factual social science, she was a life-long poet as were her contemporaries Margaret Mead and
Edward Sapir. These anthropologists experienced and anticipated how "the range of
writing in most forms crosses the artificial categories" of subjective and objective.[31]

The link between anthropology and the humanities recognized by Benedict was
illustrated in a 1973 volume, *Anthropology Through Literature*, where the editors,
James Spradley and George McDonough aimed "to help readers understand the
concepts and data of anthropology through the medium of literature."[32] Structured as
an introductory cultural anthropology text, the volume incorporated a myriad of literatures from around the globe, some written by anthropologists, some not, to illustrate typical anthropological topics such as human nature and culture, subsistence
and economics, social organization and kinship, politics, religion, language, and
culture change. The editors included literature that possessed the "sensitivity that
was often missing in conventional anthropological writing." They sought engaging
writing grounded in the "language of experience" rather than in the process of ab-
straction, that is integral to scientific description and generalizations. They encouraged the application of anthropological concepts and categories used in the interpretation of social and cultural behavior to literature. In their selection process, the
editors were drawn to writings that promote self-reflection along with learning about

an "other," examples that provided a sense of people, place and time ("we wanted to be there, wherever there was; we wanted to be with them, whoever they were"), and to examples that challenged "the cult of objectivity" that falsely denied the subjective presence of the author.[33]

Jane Austen's ethnographic insights about England in the early nineteenth century were tapped by anthropologists Richard Handler and Daniel Segal who "recognize Austen as someone doing something like ethnographic writing in a different time and place."[34] As students of anthropologist David Schneider, the authors approached Austen's writing as a source for interpreting the cultural ideology of courtship, marriage, kinship, and social rank in late eighteenth early nineteenth century England and drew comparisons between her findings and other societies.

Arguing against the conventional reading of Austen as a portrayer and upholder of a well-ordered society, Handler and Segal evaluate the rhetorical techniques that make Austen an effective ethnographer of diverse, intertwined social realities. David Schneider insisted on the contingency of cultural principles even those constructed as natural by natives. Cultural systems are made-up, or fictions, and remain open to being challenged and re-made. Austen repeatedly made visible the fictional status of social conventions. In Austen's fiction of culture, social rules do not determine the characters' conduct or ensure the reproduction of the established social order. They give significance and value to pragmatically pursued social action. Although the authors assume that human acts are structured and learned they challenge the search for "singular social totalities." Opposition and unrealized alternatives are part of cultural principles and social relations as are hierarchical distinctions including gender, class, and age. "Austen's narrative techniques privilege multiplicity rather than unity; they create conversations, negotiations, and confrontations in which any voice or perspective can call into question the completeness of any other."[35]

Other anthropological approaches to analyzing literature recognize the link between oral and written traditions. John Stewart applied Victor Turner's concept of "social drama" where the "dialectic between persistence and change in social life is highlighted."[36] In societies with underdeveloped social science traditions, literary texts are a key source of information. The literature that anthropologists have traditionally mined (folklore, myths, tales, legends) are both oral and dramatic linking the story to other elements of a cultural complex and linking the social group to its spiritual and environmental context through ritual. Written imaginative work such as fiction has been less used because it stands apart from the social group assuming no clear role in a group ritual. However, as "the universe of man's interiority" is appreciated these works are increasingly turned to as sources. Prose fiction and social realism, "reconstructs how disruptive tensions emerge and are resolved in the posited social existence of identifiable characters." Fiction documents and stores repertories of social strategies and values that are integral to the nature of social process. Once written, fiction encloses dramatic situations that remain fixed and dated, but the experiences simulated are vicariously available for as long as the fiction itself survives. The "details of character, action, and setting are organized in a manner analogous to the case study. Significant relationships between a selected number of individuals are focused, as are relationships between them and the social environment, to which, and for which, they are responsible." Analysis reveals the social principles of interaction allowing readers to judge the quality and desirability of social life.[37]

Kathleen Ashley's 1990 volume also approached the link between literature and anthropology through the interdisciplinary lens of Victor Turner. Breaking from classical Marxist literary theorists who treated literature as "superstructure" or epiphenomenon, Turner viewed ritual and literary forms as "metalanguages" for discussing sociality because they are society talking about itself.[38] Writers are often liminal figures because writing itself is a liminal activity. The attributes of liminality are necessarily ambiguous and indeterminate, conservative and freeing. "Liminality offers an escape from the current structures of society, or at least from one's place in them."[39]

The concept of interpretation has provided a fertile theoretical juncture among fiction, history, and anthropology since the 1970s. Anthropologists and sociologists who focus on symbolic meaning follow Max Weber who argued that culture consists of the webs of significance spun by human beings and the analysis of culture is, therefore, not an experimental science in search of law but an interpretive one in search of meaning. The consequence for Clifford Geertz is "blurring genres":

> If [social scientists] are going to develop systems of analysis in which such conceptions as following a rule, constructing a representation, expressing an attitude, or forming an intention are going to play central roles—rather than such conceptions as isolating a cause, determining an variable, measuring a force, or defining a function—they are going to need all the help they can get from people who are more at home among such notions than they are.[40]

As Benedict understood, the human mind is rooted in shared patterned symbolic systems that can be interpreted. Literary critics are among those who can pave the way for anthropologists since ethnographic description is essentially interpretive and culture is a "context, something within which they can be intelligibly—that is thickly—described." Thus ethnographies are fictions; fictions in the sense that they are "something made," "something fashioned"—the original meaning of fiction—not that they are false, unfactual, or merely "as if" experiments."[41]

Similarly, for Hayden White in *Tropics of Discourse*, interpretation provides the common ground between history and fiction in the construction of their stories. Facts cannot be separated from the fictional representation (emplotment) or symbolic interpretations of their meaning. "Histories, then, are not only about events but also about the possible sets of relationships that those events can be demonstrated to figure. These sets of relationships are not, however, immanent in the events themselves; they exist only in the mind of the historian reflecting on them."[42] Events occur, but their meanings and consequences are constructed by people who live in specific historical and cultural contexts. White anticipated by two decades the theoretical argument by James Clifford and George Marcus about the poetics of writing culture and ethnography. Although White does not include the political argument that domination/subordination is built into the conceptual language used by anthropologists and the importation of scientific objectivity and methods that removes them from engagement with the subjects of their research, he clearly demonstrates the "fictions of factual representation." Fiction involves imaginative constructions that are embedded in historical and cultural contexts while history and ethnography construct stories about real events mediated by their interpretations. The similarities between novels and history exist because their aims, to provide a verbal image of "reality" are the same.[43]

Prior to the French Revolution, historiography was conventionally regarded as a literary art or branch of rhetoric that "recognized the inevitability of a recourse to fictive techniques in the representation of real events in the historical discourse ... truth was not equated with fact ... the imagination no less than the reason had to be engaged in any adequate representation of the truth." In the nineteenth century, with the advancement of empiricism, it became conventional among historians to identify truth with fact and to regard fiction as the opposite of truth, a hindrance to the understanding of reality rather than as a way of apprehending it. History came to be set over against fiction and especially the novel, as the representation of the "actual." The aim of the nineteenth century historian, that continued well into the twentieth century, was to "expunge every hint of the fictive or merely imaginable from his discourse."[44]

> Most 19th century historians did not realize that ... the facts do not speak for themselves, but that the historian speaks for them, speaks on their behalf, and fashions the fragments of the past into a whole whose integrity is—in its representation—a purely discursive one. Novelists might be dealing only with imaginary events whereas historians are dealing with real ones, but the process of fusing events, whether imaginary or real, into a comprehensible totality capable of serving as the object of a representation is a poetic process.[45]

Since the 1986 publication of *Writing Culture: The Poetics and Politics of Ethnography* by James Clifford and George Marcus, anthropologists have recognized that ethnography is "a strange cross between the realist novel, the travel account, the memoir, and a scientific report."[46] Thereafter, ethnographic texts were understood to be as much about poetics and politics as objective scientific analysis of a society and its culture. James Clifford analyzed the long tradition of dichotomized representations of the fragmentation and social dislocation associated with the rise of capitalism. Echoing Lukacs, lost are the pastural wholeness and viable collective ties of the precapitalist past. George Eliot's *Middlemarch* situated in 1830 England, developed this

> style of sociological writing that will describe whole cultures (knowable worlds) from a specific temporal distance and with a presumption of their transience. This

will be accomplished from a loving, detailed, but ultimately disengaged stand-point. Historical worlds will be salvaged as textual fabrications disconnected from ongoing lived milieux and suitable for moral, allegorical appropriation by read-ers.[47]

Clifford Geertz, whose early ambition was to be a novelist, also considered ethno-graphic writing and the strategies for establishing authority. Ethnographic descrip-tion is highly situated—"this ethnographer, in this time, in this place, with these in-formants, these commitments, and these experiences, a representation of a particular culture, a member of a certain class." Kirin Narayan, an anthropologist who writes both ethnographies and novels, states that although ethnography and fiction are "his-torically contingent categories," the border between these genres is essential to both, grounded in distinctions of disclosure of process, generalization, the uses of subjec-tivity, and accountability.[48]

Attempts by anthropologists to blur genres began in the 1920s, when Franz Boas' students, who conducted ethnographic studies among Native Americans, were blurring the boundaries between fiction and anthropology as writers of fiction. In *American Indian Life*, edited by Elsie Clews Parsons, anthropologists presented ethnographic information in literary form rather than the "forbidding monographs" that few would read. Parsons sought to provide a volume "for anyone who just wants to know more about Indians."[49] In the introduction A. L. Kroeber sought to authenti-cate and distinguish the contributions of anthropologists to the fictional genre by stressing the advances of the American cultural approach under Boas: inductive dif-fusion, culture areas, ethnography—compared with the speculative deductive evolu-tionary perspective of nineteenth century anthropologists. "It [fiction] has been very little formulated by the very men who know most, who have given a large block of their lives to acquiring intensive and exact information about the Indian and his cul-ture." Although it was important that the stories written about Indian cultures were grounded in reliable cultural and social facts, Kroeber drew a sharp distinction be-tween objective science, assumed to be devoid of subjective interpretation, and fic-tion. Echoing Forster, Kroeber argued that the fictional form or historical novel al-lows for "a freedom in depicting or suggesting the thoughts and feelings of the Indian, such as is impossible in a formal scientific report."[50]

The fiction and ethnographic writings of two of Boas' women students, Ella Cara Deloria, a Dakota Sioux who worked closely for Boas, Benedict and Mead on a freelance basis and Zora Neale Hurston, an African American contributor to the Harlem Renaissance, illustrate sharply how the prevailing social science writing genres, the subjective/objective binary, and the predominantly white mentors and audiences available to them in academic anthropology and in American society dur-ing the early twentieth century were culturally inappropriate for what they were try-ing to accomplish. Deloria and Hurston were "cultural brokers," insider/outsiders who were both "othered" and mentored by anthropology and were required to "other" their cultures of origin due to the confines of scientific writing, and prevail-ing structures of inequality including patronage, class, race, and gender.[51]

Ella Deloria's 1947 novel, *Waterlily*, was half the length of her unpublished "The Dakota Way of Life," an ethnographic manuscript that reflected a decade of research between 1927-1937. Deloria's motivation to research and write about Sioux culture for a white audience was a survival strategy: if whites could understand their way of life, based on extended kinship relations, a strong work ethic, hospitality, and sexual morality, the Sioux's future would be less uncertain. Deloria, directly raised the question about which genre, fiction or ethnography, was better suited to tell the "truth" about Native American culture and "challenge the histories of misrepresentation by dominant groups."[52] Through fiction Deloria sought to enlighten readers about "a way of life that worked" at a time when Anglos removed Native children from their families and placed them in adoptive homes and boarding schools. *Waterlily*, written from a Dakota woman's perspective, provides a detailed account of women's work, knowledge, artistry, and the centrality of kinship obligations. The largely autobiographical novel, based on the life-long experiences of a woman, was a safer genre for writing about her own people since she could speak about the Sioux through fictional characters without betraying anyone's confidentiality. As an insider, Deloria "struggled all her professional life with having to squeeze Sioux narrative styles and values into a EuroAmerican epistemological framework." Instead Deloria wrote about the Dakota as a storyteller: "Hers was a conversational anthropology and many autobiographical comments (spanning several generations of her family) disrupted the linear scientific narrative expected of her."[53]

The "highly experimental discursive style" of Zora Neale Hurston's writings "defy disciplinary frameworks" and obliterate subjective/objective binaries. Irma McClaurin refers to Hurston as one of the "warrior women unafraid to cross literary and anthropological borders simultaneously."[54] Hurston, an African American woman raised in Eatonville, Florida, was concerned about vanishing Southern Negro folklore, songs, music, and West Indian Voodoo practices and introduced these to a wider audience through research patronized by the controlling "Godmother" of the Harlem Renaissance Charlotte Osgood Mason and her academic mentor at Barnard College, Franz Boas. This material, much of it "autoethnographic," was "vividly connected in her mind to habits of being and ways of life."[55] Hurston understood, after a disappointing initial six months of research, that collecting folk tales (locally referred to as lies) involved transgressing several dichotomies: researcher/object of research, white/black, and poor/elite. Hurston first adjusted her approach:

> The glamour of Barnard College was still upon me. I dwelt in marble halls. I knew where the material was all right. But, I went about asking, in carefully accented Barnardese, 'Pardon me, but do you know any folk tales or folk songs?' The men and women who had whole treasuries of material just seeping through their pores, looked at me and shook their heads. No, they had never heard of anything like that around here. [In her hometown of Eatonville, Florida], I was just-Lucy Hurston's daughter, Zora [and she knew that] the best source of folk-lore is where there are the least outside influences and these people being underprivileged, are the shyest. They are most reluctant at times to reveal that which the soul lives by. And the Negro, in spite of his open-faced laughter, his seeming acquies-

cence, is particularly evasive.[56]

Folklore was performance bound to a particular time and place. It is the act of speech, the telling, that defines structures of feeling and "beingthereness."[57]

Hurston also adjusted her writing strategies, the end products of which—books—never fully satisfied her. "I wish I could write it again. In fact, I regret all of my books."[58] She created highly inventive literary harmonics that combined the ethnographic data, the storyteller, writer, and reader in the interpretations of the folktales. Hurston's novels provide rich ethnographic information on gender conceptions and the role of community in shaping cultural norms in rural southern black communities. Similarly at this time, "local color fiction was written around the subject of a particular place, usually in dialect, with a narrator who was an outsider directing an ethnographic gaze on a peripheral community." Local color fiction was not simply about local places and peoples but re-imagined as being fundamentally representative of them.[59]

In 1989 a volume of essays, *Literature and Anthropology*, continued the theme of anthropologists as writers. Editors Philip Dennis and Wendell Aycock emphasized that anthropologists have used literature as a source of data to be analyzed, have used works of literature as a teaching tool and have produced literature of their own including poetry, mystery literature, novels, and ethnographic novels. Many anthropologists would agree with Kurt Vonnegut, at one time a graduate student in anthropology at University of Chicago, that anthropology is a "science that is mostly poetry."[60]

An ethnography from the reflexive 1990s that weaves the perspectives, writing genres and responses of an anthropologist and novelist is *Parallel Worlds*, co-authored by anthropologist Alma Gottlieb and novelist Philip Graham. Gottlieb's fieldwork among the Beng of the Ivory Coast is the obvious weft providing the book's core themes: research interests, establishing rapport with the villagers, learning the language, managing culture shock, and physical ailments. Their alternating responses and intellectual creativity provide the weft. These responses are reflected in their writing styles. Gottlieb's personal style and non-authoritative voice blur the subjective/objective binary, but her analytic purpose is firmly rooted in interpretive social science. Still, when her husband Philip reads his latest draft of a story to her she questions: "Yet were the differences between Philip's work and mine really so stark? For as much as I tried to remain true to what I saw, I knew that it was I who decided what to take notes on and what to leave unsaid, I who sketched out my own analyses of all I heard and witnessed—like Philip's stories, the characters populating my notebooks were, at last to some extent my inventions too." Graham's engaging painterly style of writing similarly reflect his attempts to interpret Beng culture. However, he also invites the reader into his creative imaginative process of fiction writing while in the field. "For months I'd struggled to maintain a kind of amphibious consciousness, trying to fuse the insistent call of my stories with the call of the odd and exciting events around me." His insight that the Beng create situated fictions of culture would have resonated with Jane Austen. [61]

For Elizabeth Fernea, ethnographic novels are "texts that in the course of telling a fictional story, creates setting, characters and action that the audience judges to be authentic in terms of a particular cultural, social, or political situation."[62] She drew a distinction between an ethnographic novel written by an outsider about others, and an ethnographic novel written by an artist from within the culture. The latter is referred to as the auto-ethnographic novel as illustrated by Ella Deloria. The ethnographic novel has some advantages over the ethnography since the author has more freedom to become involved without violating scientific norms of objectivity.

A recent example of ethnographic novel writing is Camilla Gibb's *Sweetness in the Belly* where Gibb recognizes how closely related fiction writing and anthropology are. "Later when I became a writer, I realized that in choosing anthropology I really hadn't strayed all that far from fiction—anthropology is about people's stories, their experiences of being in the world, their relationships, and the myriad and diverse ways we create meaning in our lives." She argues that fiction should matter to anthropologists "because it offers us intimate insight into the heads of others, allows us to feel a certain empathy, allows us to recognize the parallels in our basic human struggles to create meaning and attachment in our lives."[63]

The contributors to this volume agree that fiction should matter to anthropologists. It begins with two chapters that analyze eighteenth century fiction. The first chapter by Ray McDermott, "A Shandean Description of Frakean 'Ethnographic Behavior,'" is an adaptation from the classic 1964 paper by Charles Frake, "A Structural Description of Subanun 'Religious Behavior.'" The substitution of "Shandian" for "structural" and "Frakean 'ethnographic behavior'" for "Subanun 'religious behavior'" highlights the differences between two kinds of description: Frake's formal/structural and Sterne's anti-structural/emergent. McDermott argues that at first glance nothing could be more obviously different from Sterne's mad-house peek-a-boo relation to structure than an early Charles Frake paper. Sterne's is an ungainly, confusing, earthy, disruptive treatment of eighteenth century English rural life where almost nothing happens, while Frake reports on people in the island of Mindinao in the Southern Philippines in a style that is short, elegant, formal, methodic, with linguistic details tied precisely to conditions of elicitation. Sterne promises and Sterne flees. Frake promises and Frake delivers.

Nevertheless, McDermott demonstrates how Frake and Sterne have much in common and how the stereotypical dichotomy of approach reinforces the opposition between ethnography and literature, science and art, structure and emergence, measurement and insight, and social and individual. New modes of inquiry and presentation are as integral to ethnography as they are to literature. Both Sterne and Frake confront some of the same demons, however differently placed, and offer some of the same well intended roads to escape and liberation, however differently partial.

Mary-Elizabeth Reeve's chapter, "Reading Defoe, the Eighteenth Century Master Story-teller" focuses on the travel narrative that has fascinated generations of audiences. It is not surprising that when Defoe published his first novel, *Robinson Crusoe*, it was an instant sensation. *Robinson Crusoe* was followed in quick succession by a number of novels that have made their mark on English literature. Defoe has been described as the first English novelist, an interesting distinction for a man who spent the majority of his career as a pamphleteer and newspaper writer. However, it is precisely the fine tuned eye for a "story" that marks Defoe's genius, and why an anthropologist would find his work of genuine interest, beyond simple pleasure reading generally associated with novels.

Reeves examines three of Defoe's major works: *Robinson Crusoe* (1719), *Moll Flanders* (1722), and *A Journal of the Plague Year* (1722) for what they tell us not only of English urban and sea-faring life during the mid-seventeenth to early eighteenth centuries, but what they also tell us about the worldview of the writer. Defoe wrote in plain, unvarnished prose. His novels are devoid of literary artifice and read instead like memoirs and documentaries. If we read him unaware that we are reading a newspaperman's story we can dig easily into the facts and situations, as representative of the life as it was truly lived at the time; in a sense, an ethnography really written down almost 300 years ago. Yet, as with modern ethnography, the voice of the author comes through, as much as Defoe tried to distance himself from his writing, the stories that he chose to tell, and the order of their telling, gives voice to a view of the world that was at once liberal and deeply religious, pragmatic, and yet humane—the voice of an emerging middle class sensibility that was to storm old Europe and new America, culminating in the American and French revolutions. Defoe was a thinker of his time; and his worldview is surprisingly modern. We are inheritors of that worldview, which produced the social upheavals that shook the old European social order to its foundations. For this reason, Defoe speaks to us from another world in a language that we understand which makes reading his works so pleasurable. What Defoe addresses in all three works is the indomitable human spirit, the will to survive, if not thrive, through adversity by its own wits, a thoroughly modern idea.

The next two chapters examine fiction written during the nineteenth century. The chapter by Marilyn Cohen, "'A Genuine Victorian Oddity': Harriet Martineau's Fiction," focuses on selected fiction and travel writing by Harriet Martineau, England's premier woman of letters in the nineteenth century and a founder of sociology before the letter. Cohen's chapter argues that Martineau should also be recognized as a founder of radical, critical, feminist anthropology. Martineau's renown as a writer is attributed to her prolific writing at a time when few women earned their living in the public domain by writing, even fewer used their feminine given names, and fewer still addressed the substantive political and economic issues of the time.

Cohen examines Martineau's two novels, *Deerbrook* and *The Hour and the Man: An Historical Romance*, her travel writing, *Society in America* and selections from her early didactic stories for children and fictionalized *Illustrations of Political Economy*. Martineau used realist fiction to reflect on and criticize the limitations of the prevailing ideologies concerning class relations, sex/gender systems, and slavery. In fact, her fiction anticipated several genres that flourished in the 1840s and 50s including the sociological novel that focused on the significance of the community and its dense web of social connections; the social problems novel that focused on the degradation faced by the poor; and domestic realism that celebrated the values of home and family.

Martineau was a founder of qualitative research methods, anticipated cultural relativism, and addressed several relevant anthropological issues including the significance of work, race, class, gender, and their myriad intersections in the public and private domains. Martineau dedicated much of her life to the abolitionist movements in Great Britain and the United States. She anticipated the contemporary anthropological perspective on race as a social construction and the intersections among race, gender, sexuality, and colonialism. Martineau was equally convinced that gender was a social construction and her work explored the mediations among gender, waged work, and unpaid domestic reproductive work. Her writings continue to have relevance for global feminism since she stated that one key determinant in estimating the degree of social justice and freedom in a society is the status of women.

David Surrey's chapter, "Mark Twain's Weapon of Mass Destruction: 'The Human Race Has Only One Really Effective Weapon and that Is Laughter,'" addresses how fiction can be valuable in the anthropological classroom. Surrey has used literature for thirty years with his students to engage them with specific eras and cultures and to link past insights with current social issues. Literature provides insights into the cultural context of the society that it describes. With great literature these insights endure partly because many of the issues addressed endure. Surrey finds that fiction is a more effective means of initially captivating students than traditional ethnographic monographs because of the art form: the scenery is often "painted" brighter and the emotions conveyed more fully.

Surrey's chapter focuses on selected writings of Mark Twain to demonstrate their effectiveness in entering the worlds of racism and imperialism at the end of the nineteenth and beginning of the twentieth centuries and illustrates their usefulness as a heuristic classroom tool on many levels. For example, Surrey uses Twain's *Pudd'nhead Wilson* to introduce Social Darwinism and race and to introduce nature verses nurture and to demonstrate its relevance to the contemporary "no child left behind" policy. Twain is at his sharpest when discussing imperialism and several works including *King Leopold's Soliloquy*, reveal how he challenged prevailing normative ideologies and paid dearly both financially and personally.

The final three chapters analyze fiction written in the twentieth century. John W. Pulis' chapter "The Creole Speaks: Daniel, Sandi, and the Other in *Wide Sargasso Sea*" shifts the geographic focus to Jamaica through Jean Rhys' novel. Set in Jamaica, the crown jewel of the British empire, in the decade following Emancipation (1830-1840), Rhys crafted what has been acclaimed as a pioneering work of West Indian literature, prefiguring in many ways post-colonial, feminist, and more recent trends in literary studies. She herself was a white creole, born on the island of Dominica (1890-1979) and her language, tone, and dialogue is rich and descriptive expressing an intimacy born out of an "insider's point of view." Conceived as a prequel to Charlotte Bronte's *Jane Eyre*, scholars have discussed the inter-textual, post colonial, and feminist aspects of the novel, but have glossed the creole or insular aspects exemplified by figures such as Christophine, Daniel, Sandi, and others. Although they are introduced as "colored, half-caste, black," racial classifications tend to flatten the subtleties and nuances of ethnic, insular, and class distinctions. Pulis' chapter approaches *Wide Sargasso Sea* much like an anthropologist encountering a new different society. It focuses primarily on Parts One and Two that are set in Jamaica and interprets Daniel, Sandi, and other characters as insiders whose subject positions open a window on a critically important juncture in the formation of creole society.

In Ireland, the literary movement was a major force in the political process towards national independence. Building on a rich literary tradition with classic writers such as James Joyce and Samuel Beckett, there is now an acclaimed generation contemporary Irish writers. Like other artistic accounts, these literary stories are not direct reflections of what is happening around the writers, they are intricate commentary, frequently focusing on social relations and Irish society. Helena Wulff's chapter, "Ethnografiction and Reality in Contemporary Irish Literature," explores literary accounts, primarily novels but also short stories and travel writing by Éilís Ní Dhuibhne and Colm Tóibín, in terms of "ethnografiction," a genre she contextualizes in a discussion of the role of literature in anthropology, anthropology versus art and science, and ethnography versus fiction.

While researching dance and culture in Ireland, Wulff started reading contemporary Irish novels as one way to learn about the society. She discovered the short stories *Midwife to the Fairies* (2003) and novels *The Bray House* (1990); *The Dancers Dancing* (2007); *Fox, Swallow, Scarecrow* (2007) of Éilís Ní Dhuibhne, who is an astute observer of social life, especially from a woman's perspective both historically and in the new Ireland. Many of Ní Dhuibhne's characters are struggling to combine contradictory ideals of what a woman should be: traditional wife and mother or successful professional?

Colm Tóibín often sets his stories in Ireland, discussing issues ranging from exile and immigration to homosexuality, as in Tóibín's novels *Brooklyn: A Novel* (2009) and *The Master* based on the life of the American writer Henry James, where the role of his hidden homosexuality is key. With his background in journalism, Tóbín has also been a prolific travel writer in a fictionalized form in such works as *A Walk along the Irish Border* (2001), *The Sign of the Cross* (2001), *Homage to Barcelona*, and *Homage to Catalonia*. As writers of ethnografiction, Ní Dhuibhne and Tóibín prepare their fiction writing through research, even ethnographic observations, interviews, and archival work.

Particularly since the publication of *Writing Culture*, anthropologists have had to reflect on the ethics of communicating to their readers about other people without claiming to speak for those people. At the same time, like writers in any genre, they have had to think about what kind of material would best hold their readers' attention while they, as scholars, convey the kinds of information about their subject that they think really matter. Ward Keeler's chapter "Engaging Students with Fiction, Memoirs, and Film," argues that teaching poses some of the same problems. Keeler has found one solution to these two challenges, when teaching undergraduate students about Southeast Asia, by having them read fiction and memoirs, rather than more conventional ethnographic material. For the most part, the readings he assigns are written by authors who are themselves Southeast Asian. Some of the texts, such as Mai Elliott's gripping memoir of growing up in Vietnam before and during the American War in Vietnam, *The Sacred Willow*, were written in English. Others, such as the nostalgia-filled Thai historical novel, *Four Reigns*, by Kukrik Pramoj, and the bitterly satirical Indonesian novel, *Durga Umayi*, by Mangunwijaya, were written in a Southeast Asian language and later translated into English. In either case, students are led to see what matters to Southeast Asians as they describe what the world looks like from their perspective, whether they are recounting their own life experiences or creating stories about fictional characters.

The real advantage of this method is that it draws upon what is, for many people, anthropology's greatest allure: its capacity to address an intense interest many of us share in other people's lives. If reality television is the most debased genre to play upon this curiosity, fiction and memoirs can grant us richly contextualized stories about people from culturally and/or historically distant places. The stories keep us engaged; the thoughts, decisions, actions, goals, feelings, set-backs, and successes of the people involved teach us much about the societies in which they live. Attending to the entertainment value of readings to be assigned does mean diminishing students' awareness of the latest in anthropology's theoretical evolution. But only anthropology majors are likely to regret the trade-off. For the far more numerous students who sign up for a course about Southeast Asia out of a general interest in the region, well-told stories will be more thought-provoking, because so much more vivid, than most academic prose. As a result, they will come away with a deeper empathy for people they might otherwise find inscrutable, or simply odd.

This interdisciplinary volume of chronotopic essays confirms that anthropological analysis and writing are essentially hybrid activities. We hope that it serves as a model for hybrid or collaborative and expansive research and classroom teaching. Such collaboration provides both faculty and students with a deeper understanding of the subject, invigorates and sharpens critical thinking by approaching a subject from a variety of disciplinary angles. Students in particular and all readers can benefit from experiencing knowledge as holistic rather than compartmentalized into bounded disciplines.

Notes

1. E. M. Forster, *Aspects of the Novel* (New York: Harcourt, Brace & World, 1955), 24.

2. Roland Barthes, quoted in James Clifford, "Introduction: Partial Truths," in *Writing Culture*, eds. James Clifford and George E. Marcus (Berkeley: University of California Press, 1986), 1.

3. Elizabeth Long, "Textual Interpretation as Collective Action," in *The Ethnography of Reading*, ed. Jonathan Boyarin (Berkeley: University of California Press, 1992), 193, 194, 197.

4. Wolfgang Iser, *The Act of Reading* (Baltimore: Johns Hopkins University Press, 1980), 9.

5. Raymond Williams, *Marxism and Literature* (Oxford: Oxford University Press, 1978), 6-47, 53.

6. Iser, *Reading*, 70; Brook Thomas, "The Fictive and the Imaginary: Charting Literary Anthropology, or, What's Literature Have to Do with It?" *American Literary History* 20, no. 3, (Fall, 2008): 625; Shelagh Hunter, *Harriet Martineau: The Poetics of Moralism* (Aldershot: Scolar Press, 1995), 56.

7. Quoted in Edward Bruner, "Introduction: The Ethnographic Self and the Personal Self," in *Anthropology and Literature*, ed. Paul Benson (Urbana: University of Illinois Press, 1993), 19.

8. Frances Mascia-Lees, Patricia Sharpe, and Colleen Ballerino Cohen, "The Feminist Turn in Anthropology: Cautions from a Feminist Perspective," in *Anthropology and Literature*, ed. Paul Benson (Urbana: University of Illinois Press, 1993), 225, 227.

9. Ann Laura Stoler, *Along the Archival Grain* (Princeton: Princeton University Press, 2009).

10. Edward W. Said, *The World, the Text, and the Critic* (Cambridge: Harvard University Press, 1983), 5.

11. Wolfgang Iser, *The Fictive and the Imaginary: Charting Literary Anthropology* (Baltimore: Johns Hopkins University Press, 1993), 115-118.

12. Friedrich Engels quoted in Morroe Berger, *Real and Imagined Worlds: The Novel and Social Science* (Cambridge: Harvard University Press, 1977), 1

13. George Eliot, "Historic Imagination," in *Essays of George Eliot*, ed. Thomas Pinney (New York: Columbia University Press, 1963), 243-245.

14. John Frow, *Marxism and Literary History* (Oxford: Blackwell Press, 1986), vii.

15. Paul Rabinow and William M. Sullivan, "The Interpretive Turn: Emergence of an Approach," in *Interpretive Social Science: A Reader*, ed. Paul Rabinow and William M. Sullivan (Berkeley: University of California Press, 1979), 15.

16. Frow, *Marxism*, 9.

17. György Lukács, *The Theory of the Novel* (Cambridge: MIT Press, 1971), 56, 66.

18. Williams, *Marxism*, 110-112.

19. Joan Rockwell, *Fact in Fiction: The Use of Literature in the Systematic Study of Society* (London: Routledge & Kegan Paul, 1974), 91-93.

20. Rockwell, *Fact in Fiction*, vii-viii, 40, 43-44 (quote), 60-61 (quote), 117.

21. Berger, *Real and Imagined*, 130 (quote), 171-185; Vineta Colby, *Yesterday's Woman: Domestic Realism in the English Novel* (Princeton: Princeton University Press, 1974), 23.

22. Iser, *The Fictive*, 1.

23. Berger, *Real and Imagined*, 180.

24. Berger, *Real and Imagined*, 4-6, 119, 153; Colby, *Yesterday's Woman*, 4, 10-18.

25. Brad Evans, *Before Cultures: The Ethnographic Imagination in American Literature, 1865-1920* (Chicago: University of Chicago Press, 2005), 6.

26. Evans, *Before Cultures*, 13.

27. Evans, *Before Cultures*, 10 (quote), 15, 52-53, 57, 69 (quote).

28. Ruth Benedict quoted in Margaret Mead, *An Anthropologist at Work* (Boston: Houghton Mifflin, 1959), 467.

29. Benedict quoted in Mead, , 463-470.

30. Barbara A. Babcock, "Not in the Absolute Singular: Rereading Ruth Benedict," in *Women Writing Culture*, eds. Ruth Behar and Deborah A. Gordon (Berkeley: University of California Press, 1995), 112.

31. Williams, *Marxism*, 148.

32. James P. Spradley and George E. McDonough, eds. *Anthropology Through Literature* (Boston: Little, Brown and Co., 1973), xii.

33. Spradley and McDonough, *Anthropology*, xii-xvi.

34. Richard Handler and Daniel Alan Segal, *Jane Austen and the Fiction of Culture* (Lanham: Rowman & Littlefield, 1999), xii.

35. Handler and Segal, *Jane Austen*, xiv-xv, 7, 10 (quote), 19.

36. John Stewart, "The Literary Work as Cultural Document: A Caribbean Case," in *Literature and Anthropology*, eds. Philip A. Dennis and Wendell Aycock (Lubbock: Texas Tech University Press, 1989), 97.

37. Stewart, "Literary Work," 99, 111-112.

38. Kathleen M. Ashley, "Introduction," in *Victor Turner and the Construction of Cultural Criticism*, ed. Kathleen M. Ashley (Bloomington: Indiana University Press, 1990), xix.

39. Robert Daly, "Liminality and Fiction in Cooper, Hawthorne, Cather and Fitzgerald," in *Victor Turner and the Construction of Cultural Criticism*, ed. Kathleen M. Ashley (Bloomington: Indiana University Press, 1990), 71.

40. Clifford Geertz, *The Interpretation of Cultures: Selected Essays* (New York: Basic Books, 1973), 23.

41. Geertz, *Interpretation*, 10, 14, 15.

42. Hayden V. White, *Tropics of Discourse: Essays in Cultural Criticism* (Baltimore: Johns Hopkins University Press, 1985), 94.

43. White, *Tropics*, 121-122.

44. White, *Tropics*, 123.

45. White, *Tropics*, 125.

46. Ruth Behar, "Introduction: Out of Exile," in *Women Writing Culture*, eds. Ruth Behar and Deborah A. Gordon (Berkeley: University of California Press, 1995), 3; Kirin Narayan, *Alive in the Writing: Crafting Ethnography in the Company of Chekhov* (Chicago: University of Chicago Press, 2010).

47. James Clifford, "On Ethnographic Allegory," in *Writing Culture*, eds. James Clifford and George E. Marcus (Berkeley: University of California Press, 1986), 114-115.

48. Clifford Geertz, *Works and Lives: The Anthropologist as Author* (Stanford: Stanford University Press, 1989), 5; Ruth Behar, "Believing in Anthropology as Literature," in *Anthropology Off the Shelf*, eds. Alisse Waterston and Maria D. Vesperi (West Sussex: Blackwell Publishing, 2011), 108; Kirin Narayan, "Ethnography and Fiction: Where Is the Border," *Anthropology and Humanism* 24 (2): 139-144.

49. Elsie Worthington Clews Parsons, ed. *American Indian Life* (New York: B. W. Huebsch, Inc., 1922), 1.

50. A. L. Kroeber, "Introduction," in *American Indian Life*, ed. Elsie Worthington Clews Parsons (New York: B.W. Huebsch, Inc., 1922), 13.

51. Susan Gardner, "Introduction," in *Waterlily*, Ella Cara Deloria (Lincoln: University of Nebraska Press, 1988), vii-xiv.

52. Janet L. Finn, "Ella Cara Deloria and Mourning Dove: Writing for Cultures, Writing Against the Grain," in *Women Writing Culture*, eds. Ruth Behar and Deborah A. Gordon (Berkeley: University of California Press, 1995), 133.

53. Gardener, "Introduction," ix-xi.

54. Graciela Hernandez, "Multiple Subjectivities and Strategic Positionality: Zora Neale Hurston's Experimental Ethnographies," in *Women Writing Culture*, eds. Ruth Behar and Deborah A. Gordon (Berkeley: University of California Press, 1995), 151, 160; Irma McClaurin, "Walking in Zora's Shoes or 'Seek[ing] Out de Inside Meanin' of Words': The Intersections of Anthropology, Ethnography, Identity, and Writing," in *Anthropology Off the Shelf*, eds. Alisse Waterston and Maria D. Vesperi (West Sussex: Blackwell Publishing, 2011), 121.

55. bell hooks, *Yearning: Race, Gender and Cultural Politics* (Boston: South End, 1990), 140-141; McClaurin, "Walking in Zora's Shoes," 125.

56. Zora Neale Hurston, *Folklore, Memoirs, and Other Writings* (New York: Literary Classics of the United States, 1995), 10, 687.

57. Evans, *Before Cultures*, 11; Behar, "Believing," 108.

58. Hurston, *Folklore*, 217.

59. Evans, *Before Cultures*, 11, 83-86; McClaurin, "Walking in Zora's Shoes," 121.

60. James S. Whitlark, "Vonnegut's Anthropology Thesis," in *Literature and Anthropology*, eds. Philip A. Dennis and Wendell Aycock (Lubbock: Texas Tech University Press, 1989), 77.

61. Alma Gottlieb and Philip Graham, *Parallel Worlds* (Chicago: University of Chicago Press, 1993), 202, 250.

62. Elizabeth Fernea, "The Case of Sitt Marie Rose: An Ethnographic Novel from the Modern Middle East," in *Literature and Anthropology*, eds. Philip A. Dennis and Wendell Aycock (Lubbock: Texas Tech University Press, 1989), 153, 154.

63. Camilla Gibb, "Interview," In *Sweetness in the Belly* (New York: Penguin Books, 2005), 4, 8.

References

Ashley, Kathleen M.
1990 *Victor Turner and the Construction of Cultural Criticism: Between Literature and Anthropology.* Bloomington: Indiana University Press.
Babcock, Barbara A.
1995 "Not in the Absolute Singular: Rereading Ruth Benedict." In *Women Writing Culture.* Eds. Ruth Behar and Deborah A. Gordon. Berkeley: University of California Press, Pp. 104-66.
Banner, Lois W.
2004 *Intertwined Lives: Margaret Mead, Ruth Benedict, and Their Circle.* New York: Vintage.
Behar, Ruth
1995 "Introduction: Out of Exile." In *Women Writing Culture.* Eds. Ruth Behar and Deborah A. Gordon. Berkeley: University of California Press, Pp. 1-29.
2011 "Believing in Anthropology as Literature." In *Anthropology Off the Shelf.* Eds. Alisse Waterston and Maria D. Vesperi. Sussex: West Publishing, Pp. 106-16.
Behar, Ruth and Deborah A. Gordon, Eds.
1995 *Women Writing Culture.* Berkeley: University of California Press.
Benson, Paul, Ed.
1993 *Anthropology and Literature.* Urbana: University of Illinois Press.
Berger, Morroe
1977 *Real and Imagined Worlds: The Novel and Social Science.* Cambridge, MA: Harvard University Press.
Boyarin, Jonathan
1992 *The Ethnography of Reading.* Berkeley: University of California Press.
Bruner, Edward M.
1993 "Introduction: The Ethnographic Self and the Personal Self." In *Anthropology and Literature.* Ed. Paul Benson. Urbana: University of Illinois Press, Pp. 1-26.
Clifford, James
1986 "On Ethnographic Allegory." In *Writing Culture: The Poetics and Politics of Ethnography.* Eds. James Clifford, and George E. Marcus. Berkeley: University of California, Pp. 98-122.
Clifford, James, and George E. Marcus
1986 *Writing Culture: The Poetics and Politics of Ethnography.* Berkeley: University of California.
Colby, Vineta
1974 *Yesterday's Woman: Domestic Realism in the English Novel.* Princeton: Princeton University Press.
Collins, James, and Richard K. Blot
2003 *Literacy and Literacies: Texts, Power, and Identity.* Cambridge, UK: Cambridge University Press.
Daly, Robert
1990 "Liminality and Fiction in Cooper, Hawthorne, Cather and Fitzgerald." In

Victor Turner and the Construction of Cultural Criticism, Ed. Kathleen M. Ashley. Bloomington: Indiana University Press, Pp. 70-85.

Deloria, Ella Cara
1988   *Waterlily*. Lincoln: University of Nebraska Press.

Dennis, Philip A. and Wendell Aycock
1989   *Literature and Anthropology*. Lubbock: Texas Tech University Press.

Eliot, George
1963   "Historic Imagination." In *Essays of George Eliot*. Ed. Thomas Pinney. New York: Columbia University Press.
1990   *Selected Essays, Poems and Other Writings*. London: Penguin Classics.

Evans, Brad
2005   *Before Cultures: The Ethnographic Imagination in American Literature, 1865-1920*. Chicago: University of Chicago.

Fernea, Elizabeth
1989   "The Case of Sitt Marie Rose: An Ethnographic Novel from the Modern Middle East," In *Literature and Anthropology*, Eds. Philip A. Dennis and Wendell Aycock. Lubbock: Texas Tech University Press, Pp. 153-164.

Finn, Janet L.
1995   "Ella Cara Deloria and Morning Dove: Writing for Cultures, Writing Against the Grain." In *Women Writing Culture*. Eds. Ruth Behar and Deborah Gordon. Berkeley: University of California Press, Pp. 131-147.

Forster, E. M.
1955   *Aspects of the Novel*. New York: Harcourt, Brace & World.

Fox, Richard Gabriel.
1989   *Recapturing Anthropology: Working in the Present*. Santa Fe, NM: School of American Research.

Frow, John
1986   *Marxism and Literary History*. Oxford: Blackwell.

Gardner, Susan
1988   "Introduction." In *Waterlily*. Ella Cara Deloria. Lincoln: University of Nebraska Press, Pp. v-xxviii.

Geertz, Clifford
1973   *The Interpretation of Cultures: Selected Essays*. New York: Basic Books.
1986   *Works and Lives: The Anthropologist as Author*. Stanford: Stanford University Press.
2000   *Local Knowledge: Further Essays in Interpretive Anthropology*. New York: Basic Books.

Gibb, Camilla
2005   *Sweetness in the Belly*. New York: Penguin Books.

Gottlieb, Alma, and Philip Graham
1993   *Parallel Worlds*. Chicago: University of Chicago Press.

Handler, Richard, and Daniel Alan Segal
1999   *Jane Austen and the Fiction of Culture*. Lanham, MD: Rowman & Littlefield.

Hernandez, Graciela
1995   "Multiple Subjectivities and Strategic Positionality: Zora Neale Hurston's Experimental Ethnographies." In *Women Writing Culture*. Eds. Ruth Behar and Deborah Gordon. Berkeley: University of California Press, Pp. 148-165.

hooks, bell
1990 *Yearning: Race, Gender, and Cultural Politics.* Boston: South End.
Hunter, Shelagh
1995 *Harriet Martineau: The Poetics of Moralism.* Aldershot: Scolar Press.
Hurston, Zora Neale
1995 *Folklore, Memoirs, and Other Writings.* New York: Literary Classics of the United States.
Iser, Wolfgang
1980 *The Act of Reading: A Theory of Aesthetic Response.* Baltimore: Johns Hopkins University Press.
1993 *The Fictive and the Imaginary: Charting Literary Anthropology.* Baltimore: Johns Hopkins University Press.
Kroeber, A. L.
1922 "Introduction." In *American Indian Life.* Ed. Elsie Worthington Clews Parsons. New York: B. W. Huebsch, Inc., Pp. 5-16.
Long, Elizabeth
1989 "Textual Interpretation as Collective Action." In *The Ethnography of Reading.* Ed. Jonathan Boyarin. Berkeley: University of California Press, Pp. 180-211.
Lukács, György
1971 *The Theory of the Novel.* Cambridge, MA: MIT Press.
1983 *The Historical Novel.* Lincoln: University of Nebraska Press.
Mascia-Lees, Frances E., Patricia Sharpe, and Colleen Ballerino Cohen
1990 "The Feminist Turn in Anthropology: Cautions from a Feminist Perspective." In *Anthropology and Literature.* Ed. Paul Benson. Urbana: University of Illinois Press, Pp. 225-48.
McClaurin, Irma
2011 "Walking in Zora's Shoes or 'Seek[ing] Out de Inside Meanin' of Words': The Intersections of Anthropology, Ethnography, Identity, and Writing." In *Anthropology Off the Shelf.* Eds. Alisse Waterston and Maria D. Vesperi. Sussex: West Blackwell Publishing, Pp. 119-33.
Mead, Margaret
1959 *An Anthropologist at Work.* Boston: Houghton Mifflin.
Narayan, Kirin
2010 *Alive in the Writing: Crafting Ethnography in the Company of Chekhov.* Chicago: University of Chicago Press.
1999 "Ethnography and Fiction: Where Is the Border?" *Anthropology and Humanism.* Vol. 24, No. 2, Pp. 134-147.
Parsons, Elsie Worthington Clews
1922 *American Indian Life.* New York: B.W. Huebsch, Inc.
Rabinow, Paul and William M. Sullivan
1979 "The Interpretive Turn: Emergence of an Approach." In *Interpretive Social Science: A Reader.* Eds. Paul Rabinow and William M. Sullivan Berkeley: University of California Press, Pp. 1-24.
Rockwell, Joan
1974 *Fact in Fiction: The Use of Literature in the Systematic Study of Society.* London: Routledge & Kegan Paul.
Said, Edward W.
1983 *The World, the Text, and the Critic.* Cambridge: Harvard University Press.

Shumaker, Wayne
     1960 *Literature and the Irrational.* New York: Washington Square Press.
Spradley, James P., and George E. McDonough, Eds.
     1973 *Anthropology Through Literature.* Boston: Little, Brown and Co.
Stewart, John
     1989 "The Literary Work as Cultural Document: A Caribbean Case," In *Literature
            and Anthropology.* Eds. Philip A. Dennis and Wendell Aycock. Lubbock:
            Texas Tech University Press, Pp. 97-112.
Stoler, Ann Laura
     2009 *Along the Archival Grain: Epistemic Anxieties and Colonial Common Sense.*
            Princeton: Princeton University Press.
Thomas, Brook
     2008 "The Fictive and the Imaginary: Charting Literary Anthropology, or, What's
            Literature Have to Do with It?" *American Literary History.* Vol. 20, No. 3,
            Fall, Pp. 623-28.
White, Hayden V.
     1985 *Tropics of Discourse: Essays in Cultural Criticism.* Baltimore: Johns Hopkins
            University Press.
Whitlark, James S.
     1987 "Vonnegut's Anthropology Thesis." In *Literature and Anthropology.* Eds.
            Philip A. Dennis and Wendell Aycock. Lubbock: Texas Tech University
            Press, Pp. 77-86.
Williams, Raymond
     1978 *Marxism and Literature.* Oxford: Oxford University Press.

Chapter 2

A Shandean Description of Frakean "Ethnographic Behavior"

RAY McDERMOTT

We are tormented with the opinions we have of things, and not by the things themselves.

> Epictetus, c. 55-135 C.E. (title page epigraph for *Tristram Shandy*)

The test of descriptive adequacy must always refer to informants' interpretations of events, not simply to the occurrence of events.

> Charles Frake, "A Structural Description of Subanun 'Religious Behavior'"[1]

It is for this reason, an' please your Reverences, That key-holes are the occasions of more sin and wickedness, than all other holes in this world put together.

> Laurence Sterne, *Tristram Shandy* (9.1.546-7)[2]

My title is adapted from a classic paper by Charles Frake on "religious behavior" in Eastern Subanen mountain villages on the island of Mindinao in the southern Philippines.[3] The new title makes three changes: from "A Structural Description of Subanun 'Religious Behavior'" to "A Shandean Description of Frakean 'Ethnographic Behavior.'" The first change substitutes Shandean for structural to signal the easy to overstate difference between two kinds of description: one formal in commitment and style, the other—the Shandean kind—overwhelmed by emergence and mayhem. The other changes highlight Frakean ethnographic behavior as a style of disciplined work that contrasts with the wild Shandean fashion.

Substituting Shandean for structural could invite the structure vs. emergence contrast that divides much modern social research, but the Shandean innovation took place in 1759, when a northern English clergyman (though Irish born and reared for a decade) named Laurence Sterne (1713-1768) published the first two (of nine) small volumes of a rule defying, structure-be-damned, bawdy[4] novel called

27

Tristram Shandy. Sterne could not have been clearer, or more frequent, in his call to charms over the demands of form, wit over logical exposition, and disruption over sequential progress:

> *Digressions incontestably, are the sun-shine;—they are the life, the soul of reading;— take them out of this book for instance,—you might as well take the book along with them;—one cold eternal winter would reign in every page of it; restore them to the writer;—he steps forward like a bridegroom— bids All hail; brings in variety, and forbids the appetite to fail.* (1.22.64)

Imagine a novel without a beginning, middle, or end. Does *Tristram Shandy* have a beginning? One appears on the first page, but others are formally announced along the way. Dedications occur a few times, and an Author's Preface is deep in the third volume. Mostly there are transitions and promises. Sterne wrote under threat of death from consumption, and every entry is written as if it were his last, his last past, only then to rise again. If the end is a death that never arrives, the beginning is correspondingly obstetric and also almost without end. The opening pages announce the conversational conditions of Tristram's conception and move quickly to his mother's labor, but delivery does not happen for hundreds of pages. In between, chapters come and go only sometimes in relation to anyone's conception, labor, or birth. Edmund Burke reviewed the first two volumes as having "uncommon merit" despite being "a perpetual series of disappointments."[5] Sterne invites his readers into the story and throws them out, in and out: *joinus interruptus*.

At first glance, nothing is more different from Sterne's mad-house peek-a-boo relation to structure than a Frake paper: short, elegant, formal, methodic, showing linguistic detail tied to the conditions of their elicitation, and describing people through the words they use to make their world. Sterne goes to the opposite side from Frake: ungainly over short, confusing over elegant, earthy over formal, disruptive over methodic, displaying linguistic detail only to complain about the constraints of language, and describing people through the conversations they use to limit their world.

By the standards of fine ethnography, Frake promises and delivers. Frake is rule defining. He describes the rules people follow, invoke, bend, and ignore.

By the standards of fine fiction, Sterne promises and digresses. Sterne is rule defying. He displays the rules people follow by breaking them himself.

Their visuals highlight the contrasting styles. A description of Frake's every stop and go while gathering data in the field might look like the ups and downs of topics in Sterne's first four volumes (Figure 1), but Frake's data display (Figure 2) shows no such mayhem. Compiling a list of characters engaging "Subanen 'religious behavior'"—many of them invisible in our mortal world—is no small feat, and Frake likely tried many misleading connections before presenting the list. In contrast, Sterne would play with the ambiguity and temporality of the categories. Then he would do it again. First glance differences between Shandean and structural description seem profound.[6]

Figure 1: Sterne's Famous Depiction of the Serpentine Logic of His First Four Volumes

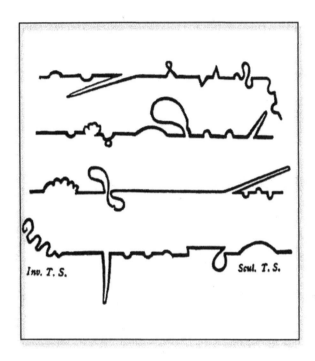

Inv. T. S.

Scul. T. S.

Figure 1: Reprinted with permission of the University Press of Florida.

At second glance, Frake and Sterne have more in common. Contrast sets opposing science to art, ethnography to literature, structure to emergence, measurement to insight, or description to critique are overstated. The search for new modes of inquiry and presentation—beyond numbing and dumbing dualisms—is integral to both ethnography and literature. Frake and Sterne share an enemy. Whether building representations of far off or forgotten others with details on what they know how to do, like Frake, or inventing hard to forget fictional others with loose footing and word play, like Sterne, their works deliver us from evil of similar kinds and grinds. They mistrust snobbery and abhor arrogance. Down with the all balls know-it-alls!

The first glance stereotypes of Frake's formal and Sterne's fevered descriptions are limited and limiting. Frake's work over sixty years grows what was there from the start: a nice mix of fine-grained empiricism, an appreciation for the ingenuity of the people studied, and a nervous concern for the delicacy, hilarity, and occasional cruelty of the situations in which they must make their lives. Or is this Sterne? Including the empiricism?[7]

Figure 2: The Structure of Data in an Early Frakean Ethnography

Categories of Participants of Subanun 'Offerings'
'persons' *getaw*:

*1. 'supernaturals' *kanaq kilawan*
1.1. 'souls' *gimuud*
1.2. 'spirits' *mitubuq*
1.3. 'demons' *getau-telunan*
1.3.1. 'ogres' *menemad*
1.3.2. 'goblins' *memenwa*
1.3.3. 'pygmies' *menubuq*
1.4. 'gods' *diwata*
1.4.1. 'sky gods' *getau-laŋit*
1.4.2. 'raw-food-eating gods' *kemunluq, menilaw*
1.4.2.1. 'sunset gods' *getau-slndepan*
1.4.2.2. 'sea gods' *getau-dagat*
1.4.2.3. 'ocean gods' *getau-laud*
1.4.3. 'sunrise gods' *getau-sehanan, turmlag*
1.4.4. 'underworld gods' *getau-bayaq*

2. 'mortals' *kilawan*
*2.1. 'functionaries' *sug mikanu dun*
2.1.1. nonprofessional functionaries
2.1.2. 'professional functionaries *belian*
2.1.2.1. 'invocators' *bataq belian*
2.1.2.2. 'mediums' *gulan belian*
2.1.2.2.1. 'shamans' *guleligan*
2.1.2.2.2. 'interviewers' *meninduay*
2.2. 'assistants' *gimpaŋ*
*2.3. 'beneficiaries' *sug pikanuan dun*
2.4. 'audience' *sug suminaup dun*

*Marks categories which must be represented at any offering

Figure 2: Reprinted with permission of McGraw-Hill Education.[8]

Neither Frake nor Sterne allow named structural inequalities—"your fat king and your lean beggar"[9]—to hide how perfectly ordinary and, in that same way, how mutually special people are. Both authors emphasize how people handle, mishandle, and manhandle each other, and they insist that writers and readers examine their own place in the struggle. As Frake might have said, as Sterne did say, "*my purpose is to do exact justice to every creature brought upon the stage of this dramatic work*" (1.10.18). As Sterne might have said of the data of experience, as Frake did say of the data of ethnography, "one cannot find new truths behind the walls of pre-definition ... Formal instruments are for playing with data, not for discovering them."[10]

To approximate telling the truth, they have both had to observe and comment on their own process of apprehending it and writing it down. They both fear mistaking the fashions and mystifications of stated opinion for reality. They worry that the press of reality is both ordered and distorted by words and opinions and are wise in knowing that realities are not easily available for the asking. Words and opinions must be found in action: getting dressed, addressed, and redressed with lives caught and bought in the balance.

Sterne complained that, "*A man cannot dress but his ideas get clothed at the same time*" (9.13.561), and Frake suggested "one look upon the task of getting names for things ... as a way of finding out what are in fact the 'things' in the environment of the people being studied."[11] Both lines have a glorious before and after, some listed in Figure 3.

Figure 3: Speaking Relatively about Relatively Speaking

> Po chu-I: "He has gradually vanquished the demon of wine/And he does not get wildly drunk//But the karma of words remains."
>
> Francis Bacon: "Certain it is that words, as a tartar's bow, do shoot back upon the understanding of the wisest, and mightily entangle and pervert the judgment."
>
> John Locke: "*Custom* [language] settles habits of thinking in the understanding, as well as of determining in the will, and of motions in the body: all which seems to be but trains of motions in the animal spirits, which, once set a going, continue in the same steps they have used to; which, by often treading, are worn into a smooth path, and the motion in it becomes easy, and as it were natural."
>
> Johann Wolfgang von Goethe: "It's just when sense is missing that a word comes pat and serves one's purposes most conveniently." [Marx borrowed this with slight changes.]
>
> William Butler Yeats: "All one's life one struggles toward reality, finding always but new veils. One knows everything in one's mind. It is the words, children of the occasion, that betray."
>
> Franz Boas: "in the peculiarities of the grouping of ideas in different

languages an important characteristic is the history of the mental development of the various branches of mankind."

Benjamin Lee Whorf: "Our behavior ... can be seen to be coordinated in many ways to the linguistically conditioned microcosm ... people act about situations in ways which are like the ways they talk about them."

T. S. Eliot: "One has only learnt to get the better of words for the thing one no longer has to say."

Edward Sapir: "Three-term sets do not easily maintain themselves because psychology, with its tendency to simple contrast, contradicts exact knowledge, with its insistence on the norm, the 'neither nor.'"

Hugh MacDiarmid: "If we think that any feature of our language and/Thought is absolutely necessary, this is nearly/Always because we have not made the effort of/Imagination needed in order to project/Ourselves outside our habits. A language is/A form of life; but there are many forms of life."

Ferruccio Rossi-Landi: "The linguistic worker lets himself be dragged on by the 'spontaneous' motion of the great machine of language. In a sense which is fundamental because it is constitutive of what is human, he no longer thinks about what he is doing when he speaks."

Edward Said: "In language as in families ... the past weighs heavily on the present, making more demands than providing help. The direct genealogical line is parenthood ... [F]iliation ... will produce a disguised quasi-monstrous offspring, that is farce or debased language, rather than a handsome copy of the precursor or parent—unless the past is severely curtailed in its powers."[13]

Doing justice means taking everyone seriously in the full play of the contexts they inhabit and inhibit with each other. For Sterne, this means exploring structural resources at every turn as if, as is so, without the weight of structure, there is neither mayhem nor humor. For Frake, this means capturing as much life as possible in formal presentations directed to further inquiry and play, as if, as is so, without play and realignment, appeal to structure flattens reality. People at Subanen ceremonies did not hand Frake a playbill. His *dramatis personae* of those visible and invisible was an ongoing achievement requiring careful attention to Subanen "religious behavior"—and to whatever that might mean to the Subanen under conditions of their own making.

However differently directed, Frake and Sterne toy with the same demons: human frailty, false hierarchy, and distorted knowledge.

However differently played, they rely on the same daemons (the guardian spirit kind): surprise and ironic humor in resistance to received conditions.

However differently partial, they share overlapping pathways to reformation and liberation: ethnography and novels.

Posner says Sterne "writes so as to experience himself as a writer—and the reader's most suitable reaction is to read so as to experience himself as a reader."[12] Snobbery and arrogance can only get in the way. Frake also shares what he is doing, how he is doing it, and what difference it makes. His objectivity is impressive, notoppressive. His empiricism is disruptive for inviting readers into sensitivities shared with those he studies. His precision is convincing, because it does not interfere with his honesty, just as Sterne's *sotto voce* disruptive confidences with the reader make his accounts of people's behavior more realistic. Fiction delivers surprise by playing with what we know all too well; ethnography delivers surprise by documenting what we hardly know at all. Every reading of Sterne and Frake must begin with their wildly different styles, but their similarities reveal that fiction and science are badly paired opposites.

I proceed in three sections. The first asks what Sterne did and who has noticed. The second asks what Frake has been doing and why we should notice. The third experiments with melding Frake's findings and Sterne's windings with a hodgepodge of hard facts in a mock history of the world from 1759 to 1959. The conclusion uses Sterne and Frake to insist that the differences between retailed fiction and detailed ethnography are both overrated and underutilized in claims to method and style of presentation in anthropology.

The Influence of Shandean Description

Lawrence Sterne published little before 1759 and a great deal in his nine remaining years. The authoritative edition of his works lists three volumes for *Tristram Shandy*, two each for sermons and letters, and one for journals covering his last lost love and a small travel novel called *A Sentimental Journey through France and Italy*.[14] Twentieth-century scholarship has discussed those who enchanted him and an ever-growing number enchanted by him. Of those he played with, played on, and borrowed from,[15] Rabelais, Montaigne, Cervantes, Burton, "*the sagacious Locke*," Pierre Bayle, and Swift are enough to put him in a two-century street corner society of Western letters. Those who follow are no less distinguished and/or controversial. His influence on great thinkers goes beyond technical experiments. Consider the endorsements listed in Figure 4.

In *Tristram Shandy*, four men talk endlessly with each other and their visitors about everything and nothing. They talk around and about each other and their versions of things. Think phatic communication: polyphonic and multivocalic, for sure, but phatic, /fæʃæ/. Reality is mailed in, usually by women, and so: femaled in and maled out by opinions stated and overstated, the sort of thing men of station insist on while shielded from the consequences. The men know exit at every turn to talk. *Tristram Shandy* is a speech act convention gone almost purposeless: circumlocutions, drive by mootings, sit down mutings, and requests for inaction abound and rebound, bind and double bind.[16] Sterne's speakers are up to their rears in *in situ* recourse and miscourse analysis.

Figure 4: Admiration and Imitation for Laurence Sterne

Denis Diderot (1713-1784): so excited by the book—"am reading the maddest, the wisest, the gayest of all books"—he set to work on a stunning shadow novel, *Jacques, the Fatalist.*

Johann Wolfgang von Goethe (1749-1832): "as years went on my admiration for [*Tristram Shandy*] seems increased, and is still increasing, for who, in the year 1759, saw through Pedantry and Philistinism so well or described it so cheerily. As yet I have not found his equal in the wide world of letters."

Heinrich Heine (1797-1856): Sterne "reveals to us the remotest abysses of the soul. He tears a rent in the soul, permits a glance into its abysses, paradises ... attained a consciousness of the infinite and the poetic ... of equal birth with Shakespeare."

Honoré de Balzac (1799-1850): calls Sterne's letter on marriage from Walter Shandy to Uncle Toby (8.33.536-538) "one of the most famous masterpieces of the human mind...most original of English writers."

Nikolai Gogol (1809-1852): adapted Sterne's "Slawkenbergius's Tale" of the man with a prodigious proboscis; in *The Nose,* Gogol turns a man into a full-bodied nose walking around St. Petersburg in a military uniform.

Karl Marx (1818-1883): at age 19 wrote an un-stunning and short shadow novel, *Scorpion and Felix.*

Virginia Woolf (1882-1941): "Sterne's eyes were so adjusted that small things often bulked larger ... In his preference for the windings of his own mind to the guide-book and its hammered high road, Sterne is singularly of our own age. In this interest in silence rather than in speech Sterne is the forerunner of the moderns."

Bertrand Russell (1872-1970): named a logical infinity paradox "the Tristram Shandy."

Robert K. Merton (1910-2003): "the non-linear, advancing-by-doubling-back Shandean Method of composition" shows "the course taken by history in general, by the history of ideas in particular, and, in a way, by the course taken in scientific inquiry as well." This Shandean social history of genius emulates more than it critiques pomposity. Shandean fiction and academic diction are a difficult mix.

Italo Calvino (1923-1985): Sterne is "the undoubted progenitor of all the avant-garde novels of our century."

Other admirers and/or imitators include: Voltaire, Hume, Jefferson, Austen, Coleridge, Melville, Freud, Joyce, Lukács, Nabokov, Beckett, Flann O'Brien, Márquez, Kundera, Fuentes, Updike, Ginzburg, Josipovici, Rushdie, and Nicholson Baker (whose *Mezzanine* is a Frake favorite). [17]

Frake's speakers are more muscular and require a dissed-course analysis; they litigate, diagnose, ask for drinks, get stuck and struck by speech, and make more requests for faction; they define borders—formally and formidably—and then they devise, enforce, and reinforce ways of crossing these borders: quietly shifting, shifty borders. In the "peripheral places" of the Sulu Sea where Frake worked, people transgress borders across both land and sea, and border tensions reach all the way down, embodied down, into their vocal cords. /gulp/!

Sterne's four men are: young Tristram, our hero, conceived, born, misnamed, variously maimed, and forgotten in later volumes but to narrate everyone else's story; Walter, Tristram's father, a master of philosophizing with well-seasoned and ill-reasoned opinions on everything but reality; Uncle Toby, a gentle retired soldier preoccupied with military fortifications on mock-up battle-grounds that are in turn his grounds for entry to any conversation except the one others share about his groin wound; and Corporal Trim, Toby's dedicated servant in offensives and defenses real and imagined. The scene rarely leaves the parlor, nothing happens over and over, and the conversations, especially the conversations about the conversations, are delightful.

In *Tristram Shandy*, no detail is too small to be pushed aside, recovered, and pushed aside again. In an early scene, Sterne has Uncle Toby take his pipe from his mouth before the narrator introduces a digression (1.21.56); one volume later (2.6.88), he returns to the scene, reminds us of Toby taking his pipe from his mouth, and allows him to speak until he is quickly ... (Sterne might ask readers to complete the end of this sentence). Sterne is forceful about his right to proceed this way, or any way he pleases. First, he says he will follow Horace's recommendation to get to the bottom of things from the beginning, "*Ab ovo*," but even Horace, almost from the beginning, gets pushed aside:

> *Horace, I know, does not recommend this fashion altogether: But that gentle-*
> *man is speaking only of an epic poem or a tragedy;—(I forget which —besides,*
> *if it was not so, I should beg Mr. Horace's pardon;—for in writing what I have*
> *set about, I shall confine myself neither to his rules, nor to any man's rules that*
> *ever lived. (1.4.8)*

Seven volumes and many beginnings later, Sterne comes clean on his method: "*That of all the several ways of beginning a book which are now in practice throughout the known world, I am confident my own way of doing it is best—I am sure it is the most religious—for I begin with writing the first sentence—and trusting to the Almighty God for the second*" (8.2.490). Sterne's God delivers more delight than factual precision, and readers must learn to live without normal concerns for character and event chronologies.[18] Parson Yorick enters early in the first volume and is quickly put in his grave—complete with two black pages *en memoriam*. Sterne then reinserts Yorick for cameos so widely dispersed across reality's calendar that he would have had to be a century old by the time Sterne gives him the lead in *A Sentimental Journey*.[19]

For outwitting clock and calendar, Sterne was hailed early in the twentieth century as "the playwright of impressionism"[20] and later in the century as a pre-modern postmodernist. The point: when a new generation tries to rewrite the world, Sterne comes into fashion. He leaves linear time to his readers, and we can never be sure how he is toying with reality. Nietzsche warned that "the reader who demands to know exactly what Sterne really thinks of a thing, whether he is making a serious or laughing face, must be given up for lost: for he knows how to encompass both in a single facial expression; he likewise knows how, and even wants to be in the right and in the wrong at the same time, to knot together profundity and farce."[21]

The Shandy four have to go nowhere to do the nothing that they do together. They rarely work or eat. Money is important only for an occasional discussion of rights and duties. They live on words. Sterne's characters have only to get dressed in the morning that their conversations, however much linguistic work and ingenuity they exhibit, are at the same time set to an agreed upon finish line that, Zeno-like, is never reached.

Sterne's characters are not unique. People talking to each other are a primary site for social life most everywhere, and a fundamental assumption of Frakean ethnographic behavior is that people living together must regularly keep each other informed about what is going on and how it might be consequential. How the Shandean four—or their counterparts in the southern Philippines or the English countryside—make sense of each other just might reveal the shape and extent of the forces organizing their lives. How Frake does that work will have to wait for the next section, *"dear reader,"* for we must first examine how Sterne, while seemingly telling us little about the harsh realities of life tells us nonethemore enough to work responsibly on imagining them. I will go as quickly as I can—just a few paragraphs, you can't begrudge me that.

Along with extending Sterne's genealogy, recent scholarship has documented lateral connections between the non-events and strong opinions in his novels and sweeping political and economic changes shaping his characters from markets and war zones far far away.[22] Sterne wrote his characters into existence while living through the Seven Years War (1756-1763), the first war fought across "the four quarters of the world."[23] Sterne's characters give little direct notice of how much their *"life and opinions"* are changing under their noses, the latter topic—*nasutus bulbus et proborsus*—on which, by the way, by the weigh, Sterne has much to say. We will have to touch, I mean touch upon, Sterne's noses later in the paper—or not, depending on how Shandean this thing gets. We might also connect the extension of the Seven Years' War to the Philippines in 1762 to Frake's arrival there almost 200 years later: from chitchat in the Shandy parlor, or in villages of the Sulu Zone, to more global events. Beyond, behind, right through, and around Sterne's talk about noses and Frake's analyses of ethnonyms, there are the intrusions and delusions of global capitalism.

If Sterne's characters live on talk, where have their words been before landing on their tongues? This core question for Frakean ethnography is a background consideration for Sterne, although even when he is mostly quiet on money and power machinations, his words—and his characters' words—have had their own life in the marketplace.

Three questions help move Sterne's words from hints to possible facts. First, what does Sterne complain about? An early inquiry into Sterne's political economy focused on *Tristram Shandy* as a pastoral set far from the push and pull of urban markets. The pastoral setting was not incidental. Sterne wrote, said Anderson, to establish "the vital lives of ordinary men, and he is explicit in his attacks on those who live only for themselves."[24] *A Sentimental Journey* is more in the world and gives occasion for direct complaints about the *"base, ungentle passion"* guiding life in the market:

> *It must needs be a hostile kind of a world, when the buyer (if it be but of a sorry post-chaise) cannot go forth with the seller thereof into the street to terminate the difference betwixt them, but he instantly falls into the same frame of mind, and views his conventionist with the same sort of eye, as if he was going along with him to Hyde-park corner to fight a duel ... —base, ungentle passion! thy hand is against every man, and every man's hand against thee ...*[25]

Sterne rejects the public benefits of private interests in Mandeville's beehive.[26] Whether sitting in a parlor or riding a road to Paris and moving an occasional coin to whatever purpose, Sterne's charges reject turning greed into a virtue.

Second, what do Sterne's characters worry about? Recent work has been aggressive in using his characters' situated opinions on local topics to conjure their opinions on more worldly topics like the Seven Years' War, gender and labor arrangements, and slavery.[27] Sterne could not have planned to say all that has been ascribed to him, but his characters' subliminal reactions to the world have given a glimpse of their ongoing connections.

One intermingling of a local and international sore spot occurs on the map that Uncle Toby and Corporal Trim have been using to build a replica of their battlefield experiences. The fortifications record the place where Toby received a groin wound: a constant source of intrigue and gossip for the rest of the village. Having toyed for six volumes with the what, where, and extent of the wound, Sterne has his readers attentive to every possible outcome. Speculation reigns. Even Mrs. Shandy wants at their conversation through a keyhole (the context for Walter's rebuke in the third epigraph starting this paper).

While fielding a marriage proposal from Uncle Toby, the Widow Wadman asks, *"a little categorically,"* where exactly he received his *"sad blow."* Toby promises she *"shall see the very place,"* but questions only sometimes get the answers they seek:

Mrs. Wadman blush'd—look'd towards the door—turn'd pale—blushed
slightly again—recovered her natural color—blush'd worse than ever; which
for the unlearned reader, I translate thus—
"L—d! I cannot look at it—
What would the world say if I look'd at it?
I should drop down, if I looked at it—
I wish I could look at it—
There can be no sin in looking at it
—I will look at it." (9.20.567)

> *... In asking this question, Mrs. Wadman gave a slight glance towards the*
> *waistband of my uncle Toby's red plush breeches, expecting naturally, as the*
> *shortest reply to it, that my uncle Toby would lay his fore-finger upon the*
> *place—It fell out otherwise.* (9.26.580)

Toby leads Mrs. Wadman to the very place on the map where he received his wound and puts her forefinger upon it. Mrs. Wadman seeks exact bodily data on a war wound of unspecified dimensions and consequences, and Toby gives exact geographic data on where he was wounded in a war of unspecified dimensions and consequences. This cute mix-up engages both the source of his wound in international battles of armies and economies and the source of their confusion in the attractions and distractions of men and women.

Their interests and worries—their possible marriage and progeny—have to go a-progress through battles fought around the globe. Intentions and extensions pass each other by. Walter Shandy offers a comment wide enough to include, if he were to think about it, the political economy of Toby's "*sad blow*": "*Love, you see, is not so much a SENTIMENT as a SITUATION*" (8.34.535). By 1767, their "*SITUATION*" had expanded to the four corners of the globe.[28]

Third, what might have Sterne been thinking about in his own life that he does not put in his books? Sterne was an accomplished self-promoter, and he paid careful attention to the book market.[29] The content and style of his novels were tuned to his expectations of the purchasing public. Even while claiming fame over money as his goal, Sterne missed few chances to advance the profit potential of his books. He spiced them with current events and fashions to entice sales. His own survival strategies—the ones he shared with a growing number of people in the 1760s—have been read for ideas about the material conditions he had written into his characters. Even if he was mostly concerned with "the underlying morality of his art," market strategies may have sometimes dominated his mind.[30]

If spotting the play of political economy in Shandean chitchat has required analytic intervention, imagine Frake sorting out group identities while sailing across the idyllic Sulu Sea. What could seem further from global capitalism or even the Siege of Manila at the end of the Seven Years' War, but they are as connected as the sore spots shared by Uncle Toby and Widow Wadman.

The key to Sterne is the surprise we experience when he puts fact and tact together for a delicious misunderstanding, for what James Joyce calls an "astewte use of endadjustables."[31] Frake's detailed empirical ethnographies rely on a more factual sense of surprise.

Sterne makes us laugh at ourselves by creating silly situations that people take all too seriously.

Frake makes us laugh at ourselves by showing that people in serious situations can laugh at themselves.

The Ironic Excellence of Frakean Ethnography

Frakean ethnography delivers situations and their rules as performed and interpreted by people interacting with each other and with the things that make their lives go: rice, kin, ghosts, and beer among the Subanen; kin, languages, ladders, sultans, violence, but less beer among the mostly Muslim peoples of the Sulu Sea; tides, clocks, hedges, Roman roads, and more beer along the English North Sea. In each case, Frake delivers both the know-how and the now and not-now for its portrayal under conditions always, however partially, however desperately, under local control. Behind all the rules, there are self-important rule-makers, chest-beating rule-breakers, slippery rule-fakers, and some of Frake's favorite people, the data rich rule-benders.

Frake has proposed the term "fine description" for the kind of work he and Harold Conklin have been doing.[32] Fine description develops facts that are relational: dependent not just on each other, but on the activities that brought them together with the interpretations that move them forward. There is a long tradition of noticing that facts are not stand-alone realities. About midway between Sterne and Frake, Ralph Waldo Emerson, as if he were reading Epictetus (he probably was), noted that a lone fact is nothing more than "the rumor of some fact."[33] Without careful inquiry, rumored facts are like those gained through "*key-holes*": they are "*occasions of more sin and wickedness, than all other holes in this world put together*" (9.1.546-7). Rumored facts and "*key-hole*" wisdom are the topics of good ethnography, but they should not determine its categories of analysis.[34]

Frake's version of Emerson would ask: What is a fact, but a series of interpretations set against fast-action realities? What is a Subanen "sunrise god"—or an Uncle Toby war wound—but interpretations made relevant and consequential to their persons across time. The terms rumor and interpretation should not invite the knee-jerk diminutives: unimportant, fanciful, or just ideological. Instead, as next moves in a sequence, interpretations move facts from past to future and back again, each time with a slight reshaping of the world. Emerson again: "A fact is only a fulcrum of the spirit. It is the terminus of past thought, but only a means now to new sallies of the imagination and new progress of wisdom."[35]

Fine description requires a deep empiricism that admits no facts to a data corpus without someone specifying the place of the facts in the sequential organization of behavior over some relevant period of time. In Frakean inquiry, facts have to be treated, like the people engaging them, with respect for their complexity. Easily obscured by routine and artifice and invariably on the move, the relevant facts of a situation can be hard to find. Empiricism is not easy, but it is as worth the effort as it is dangerous when done badly or not at all. Balancing on Emerson's "fulcrum"—the pin-point of competence, desire, knowledge, devotion, neurosis—invites a constant shaping of reality and leads sometimes to confusion, surprise, and humor for participants and their ethnographers; together, they get to cringe and/or laugh with the unexpected.

Too positive positivists finish their work just as Frake gets focused; they don't cringe or laugh enough. Postmodern anti-positivists cringe well and laugh occasionally, but rarely in tune with a relentless search for the facts. Frakean descriptions find fact-filled structures everywhere—in languages, houses, border arrangements, and instruments—and ask how people work with them, around them, and against them. Frakean ethnographers follow the cringing and laughing.[36]

Frake plied his trade on intensive field trips to the southern Philippines from 1953 to 1972 when martial law made the area too dangerous. Through the 1980s, he studied the ingenuity of medieval navigators and the creation of European tools—tidal charts, sundials, clocks, the compass—for reckoning time, space, and direction. Since 1990, he has resumed fieldwork with a few months every year on England's eastern shores and follow-up visits to the Philippines.[37]

The ethnographic attitude he developed in the Philippines has fitted well his historical inquiries. Even old tools can be explored for how things work on the ground. Whether in a Subanen swidden, on a Yakan porch, with a medieval sundial, near an English landmark church, or across an international border, his studies describe how people make their things and what they make of them: the sort of things they have names for, even if they are not available to the senses.

Frake makes visible the complex problems people solve with the resources at hand. He works on deep problems: people staying alive and fashioning identities to negotiate their way. He also works on seemingly mundane problems, but mines them for accounts of the larger forces at work: how to ask for a drink, identify an ogre, enter a house, read a dial, or describe the history of a road, all the while asking how many people are involved, to what extent, within what hierarchy, across what range of time and space, and with what consequences.

The lives he studies are recognizable. He does not study exotic peoples: only people under conditions not yet understood. He does not study extraordinary people: only ordinary people doing the ingenious things ordinary people sometimes do. Yakan and Zamboangan farmers and traders have to out-maneuver each other and the treachery of a badly divided political economy; medieval seafarers have to overcome the nasty tides and shifting sands of the North Atlantic with instruments that demand as much intelligence as they make available; and English villagers must make their way through a thicket of stories bringing contested multilayered histories into the present. The ethnographer's job is to describe where the problems come from and how they are handled.

Frake's descriptions are mostly soothing and encouraging. People in his papers—his "natives": once a complimentary term, now suspect, like everything naming others—are generally smart about their situation even when it brings them crushing troubles. Fools and knaves, however foreground important, are moved analytically to the background; they are not the news. The excitement is that wherever Frake looks, as if he were Sterne, people are overall wide awake, doing their best, laughing at themselves, and toying with the self-important. Bullies, blowhards, and tyrants can dominate social life, but Frake has generally preferred studying those outwitting problems to those causing them. Even beyond the reach of evil, life is filled with binds, conundrums, foibles, and quandaries. The people in Frake's papers recognize such difficulties, and how they respond with humor, pride, and/or violence is the rich stuff of ethnographies—and the stuff of novels, too.

It is difficult to appreciate examples of Frakean irony without examining the details. James Boon has warned us what to expect: "Irony doesn't exactly grow, does it? ... [It] may be intrinsically implicit, obtaining from human negativities and multiplicities."[38] Ironies, like gods and devils, exist in the details. Ethnic group relations in the southern Philippines deliver rich occasions for cringing, laughing, and plunging, however implicitly, into irony. Negativities and multiplicities abound.

Around 1970, long before multi-sited ethnography took center stage in anthropological theory, Frake began a life-long project on "the genesis of kinds of people in the Sulu Sea." His first success is to have shown that, whatever the current divisions among kinds of people, they are the systematic result of previous arrangements across hundreds of years and thousands of miles of islands, languages, religions, trade sites, and colonial campaigns. His second success is to have placed the facts against current interpretations of ethnic variation and to show how opinions and perspectives have been consequential to the people talked about, talked for, talked up, and talked down.

In Figure 5, Frake shows fifteen names for interacting groups in the southern Philippines. Frake presents them not as a fixed structure for calculating or predicting intergroup relations, but as a list of slippery resources people can use to negotiate their respective identities from multiple perspectives tuned to ever emergent purposes. By local calculations, the first two (Tausug, Yakan) and the last (Subanen) are "unproblematic ethnonyms" and easily differentiated by five criteria (Figure 6). The other twelve groups are less clearly defined, and Frake has had to add a few more considerations people might employ to keep themselves in "rough rank order," for example: the notoriety of a group's place of origin (real or imagined) or the vantage point and language of the people doing the defining.[40]

At the top of ethnic power and prestige, the Tausug are Muslim, centrally located, fierce, stratified, and supported by a strong historical narrative (however opportunistically connected to historical facts). Because "there is a structure to discern in practice as well as discourse," the Tausug are privileged to claim that they deserve to be all that they are.[41]

Figure 5: Some Ethnonyms of Sulu and Zamboanga
(in rough rank order)

```
Tausug
Yakan

(sama) balangingiq
sama + 'place name'
"Samal"
"'floater'"
sama + 'true'
sama + 'sea'
"Sama(l) 'to be spit on'"
"Bajao"
sama + 'land'
"         "

"Kalibugan"
kalibugan

Subanun
```

Figure 5: Reprinted with permission from Australian National University.[39]

The Yakan are in second place by being Muslim and fierce, but less centrally located and stratified. Their "notoriety is geographically restricted, their politicalintegration more feeble, their claim to titles on shakier grounds." Being less than Tausug even "casts suspicion on the purity of their Islam."[42]

At the bottom of ethnic identities, the Subanen are pagan, upstream, pacifist, egalitarian, and lacking a strong historical narrative. Being less than Tausug in all five ways, by local values, the Subanen deserve to not be all they are not.[43]

By Frake's explanation of the terms in Figure 5, the middle twelve ethnonyms must be sorted further by the identities of those using the terms and whether by:

self identification [*sama*, for example]
"attributed identification" ["Bajao," for example]
"English gloss of local term" ["land," for example]
"English gloss of local attributed identification" ["floater," for example].

With twelve groups marked by five characteristics and four finer grained criteria of use, this arrangement gives enough structure and wiggle-room for both practice and discourse to adapt to emerging circumstances, enough structure and mayhem for play, constraint, and violence depending on the politics at work.

One irony apparent in the details is almost cute. The Tausug were not really the original civilizers of the area. The various "*sama*" groups were not really followers of the Tausug lead. The historical record has them in reverse roles. Up and down are temporary positions in ethnic politics, and for the last twenty years, a new group has been taking shape through the area. The new group is called the indigenous. The last group to take the spotlight goes by a word that describes them as the originals, and the criteria for indigeny are increasingly defined, refined, and redefined by NGOs according to needs better fitting NGO organizational fads and pressures than any historical facts. The oldest are the newest, and the newest are made by those least connected to local contingencies, no matter how far wither and whence.[44] Now that's funny.

A second and related irony leads to more cringing than laughing, except sometimes. They are both sad situations, but the second is more deadly, sometimes viciously so. Frake asserts that the individuals he knows in the Sulu Sea area are wonderfully kind, and so a question can be asked about why they are so adept at killing each other. We can take the proposition about nice and kind on Frake's testimony: "Philippine Muslims (like all Filipinos) are as hospitable, friendly, kind, cheerful, and helpful on most occasions (outside government offices and combat zones) as one could possibly desire."[45]

Figure 6: Dimensions of High (Tausug, Yakan) and Low (Subanen) Ethnic Prestige among Mostly Muslim Groups in the Southern Philippines

	Tausug	Yakan	/ Subanen
Religion	Muslim	Muslim	/ Pagan
Location	Central	Inland	/ Up-stream
Ferocity	Fierce	Less fierce	/ Pacificist
Internal Hierarchy	Formal	Less Formal	/ Egalitarian
"Keyhole" Narrative	Founders of civilization	Users of civilization	/ Without ties to civilization

Proof of the violence is available in body counts and terrifying reports in Manila newspapers. How does violence come so easily to nice people? Coleridge once defined a sin as "an evil which has its ground or origin in the agent, and not in the compulsion of circumstances."[46] The question from the southern Philippines can be rephrased: What circumstances might lead nice people to compulsive violence? The answer requires a history of states and colonies run against the intricacies of on the ground actions and interpretations. Frake would be interested in all sides of the problem, but his ethnographic work reports on the ground actions and interpretations.

> It is in the everyday repetitive application of interpretative procedures by ordinary people advancing pressing agendas, in the face of deadly indifference, and within constraining contexts of prevailing violence that results in the proliferation of contested identities among those who most need unity. In a world where one is continually redefined as nobody, one can only keep trying to be somebody.[47]

The irony of good people doing bad things is not lost on the participants. Anxious to work against the most local injustices, they invoke the wrath of international armies. It is as if street gangs from the Bronx were spotlighted as a threat to Western civilization and bombed by NATO forces. That the situation is well organized does not reduce the irony. That local conditions are full fact systematic products of wider developments makes their suppression by state and international forces fully ironic. That the situation is in no way funny does not stop Philippine insurgents from laughing.

Remember Nietzsche appreciating Sterne for confounding "whether he is making a serious or laughing face ... for he knows how to encompass both in a single facial expression; he likewise knows how, and even wants to be in the right and in the wrong at the same time, to knot together profundity and farce."[48] Running violent insurgencies against state militias is serious business and expanding them against other locals, against those with the temerity to be called something else on Frake's list, gets close to seriously wrong. So the people of the Sulu Sea grimace, arm themselves, and sometimes murder, but when their insurgent groups are headed by "Kumander Toothpick" or "Kumander James Bond," they get to laugh as well. As Frake notes, even "vicious violence cannot kill Filipino humor."[49] The wider world that has thrown the groups against each other, like the wider world that brought Uncle Toby and the Widow Wadman to a different kind of sore spot, is occasionally made available. The ironies are noted, and the people laugh.

Given the ironic complexities of everyone's situation, Frake has worried often about questions of method. There should be some rough principles and procedures for figuring out what is surprising about being ordinary. Good ethnography requires an eye for what people do and an ear for what they make of their doings. Years ago, Frake and I sat next to each other at an all night Native American ghost dance. Around 3:00 a.m., with exhaustion setting in and our eyes stinging from the smoke and dust, he asked me what I was "researching." I was following the dancers: seven steps to the right, six to the left, five right, seven left. I couldn't get a pattern. He said he was counting the beams in the lodge's ceiling. There we were, momentary visitors in search of patterns in a world specifically designed to keep outsiders at bay, counting whatever we could, filling our empty minds with likely useless facts, each, by Emerson's imagery, a "terminus" of only recent thought and each an unlikely means to any "new progress of wisdom" (particularly if a new wisdom would require insight into why we were there or how we were perceived). In a longer visit, we might have learned what is important to the dancers and lodge builders. We might have learned to look more carefully and to ask better questions. We might have learned the interpretations of the people at the ceremony. We might have learned if we were an imposition.

Frake, as if he were reading Epictetus and Sterne, specified the differences between counting possible events and knowing one's way around a social scene:

> a failure of an ethnographic statement to predict correctly does not necessarily imply descriptive inadequacy as long as the members of the described society are as surprised by the failure as the ethnographer. The test of descriptive adequacy must always refer to informants' interpretations of events, not simply to the occurrence of events.[50]

Events, interpretations of events, anticipation of and surprise at how events unfold, these are the specific foci of Frakean ethnographic behavior.[51] How to get at them? Watch carefully, of course, and ask carefully, too. Frake worried most about how to ask carefully. He thought of ethnography as a systematic search for right questions.[52] His method is more a "sculptor's reduction" than a inductive accumulation or deductive expansion: more a chipping away of preset—as if in stone—questions, so that a more accurate, more life-like, object might emerge.[53]

To the standard fieldwork manual of British social anthropology, *Notes and Queries in Anthropology*, Frake pressed an alternative approach with a paper called, "Notes on Queries in Ethnography."[54] In Frakean ethnography, the unit of analysis is not a set of answers to standard questions, nor even question-answer pairs, but questions-answer pairs tuned to the contexts that make them informative, that make people ask them and make their answers consequential.

There is no greater source of misinformation, or even oppression, than wrong questions asked in exactly the wrong way or at the wrong time. Plato had Meno make the case: "And how will you inquire, Socrates, into that which you do not know? What will you put forth as the subject of inquiry? And if you find what you want, how will you ever know that this is the thing which you did not know?"[55]

Like Meno, like all people, Philippine villagers were fussy about the questions they were asked. In the same way of speaking—silently speaking—so were the materials used by medieval navigators. For both inquiries, Frake had to learn a few languages to get right questions, a situation that made the interactive life of question-answer pairs more difficult, but when carefully examined, more revealing. In English villages, the language was easy, but productive questions and their contexts were still difficult to discern.

Remember that ethnic groups in Figure 5 could enhance their standing by tying their identities to a place of notoriety. The right origin story might make a difference, and questions about provenance helped to create what Frake called "query-rich settings."[56] Who could resist talking about the origins of "*sama*" from near an oil storage facility outside Zamboanga City who identify as—surprise!—"*sama mobilgas?*"[57] In "query rich settings," simple questions can reveal complex issues, and so simple questions about space and place put to people interested in such things, to the *sama mobilgas*, for instance, can deliver a well structured and always emergent system of group identities and territorial circumstances existent across hundreds of years and thousands of miles. Recently, Frake has reported a new "rumor ... that the '*sama mobilgas*' may soon be replaced by the '*sama 7-Eleven.*' They keep longer hours."[58] As an ethnonym, "*sama 7-Eleven*" may or may not bring more prestige, but it will definitely be good to interpret and discuss.

Questions of origin are less telling in other situations. In American chitchat, "Where ya from?" queries make good conversational openers, but they are rarely as consequential as "*sama*" maneuvers. Suppose, because it is true, Frake has to *self identify* as coming from "*Utah,*" while I can say I grew up near a train yard in New York City. "*Irish thirdrail*" should win, but nothing is at stake.

Frake had to adjust his questions about origins in the English countryside where talk about place and identity are less welcome. Inappropriate questions, if carefully tracked, can lead to better questions. After bumpy conversations about provenance, Frake came to appreciate how often the English prefer a more secluded identity. "If one comes from a posh place, it is rather unsightly to proclaim it; if your conversation partner comes from a common place, it is unkind to ask about it. Better not to ask or be asked at all. One does not intrude."[59] Question-answer exchanges about "pleasant places" were more productive. Questions about "a church too far near a bridge oddly placed"—a church built long ago and since contested as a cornerstone of local history[60]—just might reveal how a place can be converted into the past, present, and future of a local English identity.

It takes time and struggle to get good questions. It requires a deep empiricism to figure out how a question fits a situation of use well enough that its answer can be read for an account of what people are doing together. Query-rich settings in which people have to ask each other what is going on, in which people have to deal with their own surprise, in which people have to recover from their own laughing and crying, such settings are the stuff of great ethnography. Anthropologists have always been interested in what people know how to do, but Frake pushed the question further by focusing on what people do when they are not sure of what is happening, when they have to talk with each other about what is surprising, upsetting, insightful, or funny.

Sterne illustrated how much a bad question can disrupt "a query rich setting" in his account of Uncle Toby disrupting Walter's philosophizing with a question too far off and oddly placed in Walter's mind:

> *Nothing should prove my father's mettle so much or make his passions go off so like gun-powder, as the unexpected strokes his science met with the quaint simplicity of my uncle Toby' questions.—Had ten dozen of hornets stung him behind in so many different places all at one time,—he could not have exerted more mechanical functions in a few seconds,—or started half so much,*

as with one single quaere of three words unreasonably popping in full upon him ... (3.41.216)

Questions and answers are a social relationship. They must take their place among the rituals of life. Timing and calibration are crucial. Like Uncle Toby, ethnographers cannot ask questions however and whenever they like. Knowing what people ask and when gets ethnographers closer to what people need to know from each other.

Windings and Findings: An Exercise in Historical Narrative with Sterne and Frake, 1759-1959

"In a word, my work is digressive, and it is progressive too,— and at the same time" (1.23.64).

How can I recommend Sterne and Frake without offering my own surprise? I would love, like Sterne, to use story fragments picked from whence and whither to hint at enough structure to allow a reader to persevere long enough to be surprised. The problem: without nine volumes to build an emergent order in wild repetition, how can structure and mayhem get sequenced in the same text?

I would love, like Frake, to develop an empirical focus on language use in litigation or border crossings in other cultures. The problem: without integrated facts and interpretations about farming, kin, trade, and war, how can unexpected events and structure get ordered in the same text enough to surprise the reader?

A make-shift solution: I combine bits from Sterne's chaotic novels and Frake's careful reports in ten tiny Shandean chapters. *"The two stories reflect light upon each other—and tis a pity they should be parted."*[61]

A make-shifty solution: I resort to a sorta sordid method that mixes excerpts from both authors with a preselected list of facts—a sorta sorted list—marking situations and ideas that might connect their writings.

Figure 7 introduces authors, writings, and events from 1759 and 1859 that helped set the scene in 1959. Keep it nearby; its facts, like the ethnonyms of the Sulu Sea, are the spine of both continuity and surprise in this exercise. Births, writings, inventions, and interventions are listed by exact date, but their effects are more Shandean: more rounded than grounded.

In this section, I take license to round Sterne's nine years of writing to 1759 and all of Frake's sixty years of writing to 1959. This allows a Shandean-laced, Frakegraced history of people, capital, and colony limited to three leaky calendar years and a focus on the cultural work of ... surprise: pockets and ladders. Neither as fictive as Sterne, nor as factual as Frake, I miss the mark twice in order to explore the mutual necessity of structure and disruption.

I hope my effort amuses "*your reverends and worships*." Remember that "*I did jest—but was not paid for it—'twas entirely at my own expense.*"[62]

Don't try to stop me, "*—for in writing what I have set about, I shall confine myself... not to any man's rules that ever lived*" (1.1.8).

Skip the footnotes for a while.[63]

Chapter I: Hand to Pocket

While waiting for his wife to give birth, Walter Shandy chats with Uncle Toby and Dr. Slop in the parlor. The latter is a science fielding, forceps wielding, damage yielding backup midwife. Dr. Slop raises an obstetric topic—"*All hail and flail well*

Figure 7: Facts and Opinions Connecting Sterne and Frake?

1759
Born:
      William Willburforce, successful advocate for the abolition of slavery (offended by *Tristram Shandy*)
      Mary Wollstonecraft, advocate for women's rights, blamed culture, not biology, for inequities (influenced by *A Sentimental Journey*)
Published:
      Adam Smith, *The Theory of Moral Sentiments*
      Voltaire (a *Shandy* fan), *Candide*
      Samuel Johnson (a *Shandy* not fan), *Rasselas*
      Edmund Burke (a *Shandy* fan), "The Present War" and "Introduction on Taste"
      Thomas Sheridan, *A Course of Lectures on Elocution*
      Edward Young, *Conjectures on Original Composition*
Benchmarks:
      "The Year of Victories" for England in the Seven Years' War, 1756-1763

1859
Born:
      Henri Bergson, John Dewey, Arthur Conan Doyle, Edmund Husserl, Georges Seurat (pointillist)
Published:
      Charles Darwin, *On the Origin of Species*
      Karl Marx, *Introduction to a Critique of Political Economy*
      Charles Dickens, *Tale of Two Cities*
Benchmarks:
      Successful drilling for oil (Titusville, PA), first internal combustion engine (Lenoir, France), Suez Canal breaks ground, French capture Saigon, first steamroller

ab ovo"—and Uncle Toby razes it for an obscure bridge to his own hobby-horse: "*the prodigious armies we had in Flanders.*" Annoyed with his brother, Walter takes off his wig and goes for a handkerchief to wipe sweat from his head and military operations from his mind. In Sterne's hands, the tiniest plans can go awry, and so then in Walter's hands. Walter removes his wig with his right hand and has to use his left hand to get to his right hand pocket.

Martin Rowson shows the problem in eight frames: one for Toby's favoritetopic, five for Dr. Slop's confusion, and two for Walter's response (Photo 2.1, page 72).[64] Sterne's version is equally evocative.

> *As my father's India handkerchief was in his right coat pocket, he should by no means have suffered his right hand to have got engaged: on the contrary, instead of taking off his wig with it, as he did, he ought to have committed that entirely to the left; and then, when the natural exigency my father was under of rubbing his head, call'd out for his handkerchief, he would have had nothing in the world to have done, but to have put his right hand into his right coat pocket and taken it out;—which he might have done without any violence, or the least ungraceful twist in any one tendon or muscle of his whole body ... Now as my father managed this matter,—consider what a devil of a figure my father made of himself* (3.2.143).

If Walter's predicament reminds you, "*dear reader*," of the trouble I am having engaging mayhem and structure while recommending an engagement with mayhem and structure, then I can beg your understanding.

Chapter II: Knowledge to Action

The best laid plans—wig off, handkerchief to head—are rarely the best played plans. Laid and played can work more at odds than at ends whether in Shandy Hall in 1759 or traditional Philippine societies in 1959. People go off to do something and invariably find impediments along the way. Action is rarely an affair of just knowing—or unjust knowing—going along automatically. One thing leads to another. Events drive off "*zig-zagery*" and "*hey-go-mad*" and invite the opinions and interpretations of others.

Action is more like Tristram's life: going forward and backward simultaneously.

Action is more like Sterne's writing: "*digressive ... and progressive too—,and at the same time*" (1.22.64).

Frake could have learned to theorize the hard work of sequencing life in interaction with others by reading Sterne. Or he could have read the time-sensitive writings of the 1859-born Henri Bergson, John Dewey, Edmund Husserl, the pointillist painter Georges Seurat, or the pointillist detective writer Arthur Conan Doyle. For Bergson, Dewey, and Husserl, there are no lone things: only things in relation to other things constantly refigured in real time. Our 1859-born philosophers (see Figure 8) and 1859-published Charles Darwin and Karl Marx articulated a world of

emergence in which structure and continuity are an ongoing achievement—a result
in parts fragile and determinative, in parts *"digressive and ... progressive too."*

I'll explain Seurat and Doyle to *"your honors and reverences"* later. Or it might
just as well be now (neither will be, nor was, is now). Or we can split the difference.
I tell you about Seurat, for whom all colors live only in relation to other colors, and
we can skip Sherlock Holmes, even if he too knew all facts live only in relation to
other facts.

Because Seurat painted with autonomous dots, some might take him for an
atomistic thinker, but his pointillism fits his birth group as an experiment with colors changing by context.[66] As a relational thinker, Seurat would have loved color
categories in the Philippines, where "both the Hanunóo and the Subanen have a
word and the same word ... for 'yellow.' The difference is structural. Hanunóo
'yellow' is a kind of red; Subanen 'yellow' is not a kind of any color. It is a basic
term."[67] Imagine Seurat's delight with the Ifugao weaver's explanation of off-blue:
"because its blackness is white."[68] Action invariably outruns its vocabulary.

Figure 8: 1859-Born Thinkers Reorganize Time

Henri Bergson: "Action is discontinuous, like every pulsation
of life; discontinuous, therefore, is knowledge."

John Dewey: "Time ... is the organized and organizing medium
of the rhythmic ebb and flow of expectant impulse, forward and
retracted movement, resistance and suspense, with fulfillment and
consumption."

Edmund Husserl: "... even in the content of that which is per-
ceptually given as itself, there is, on closer inspection, an element
of anticipation. In fact, nothing in perception is purely and adequately perceived."[65]

Chapter III: Knowledge and Self-Congratulation

Samuel Johnson was less disruptive than Sterne in 1759 or Bergson, Dewey,
Husserl, or Seurat in the years after 1859. For Johnson, knowledge works on a pli-
able world for productive results. Knowledge comes first in the order of progress.
Best results belong to persons and countries most informed by reason and science.
His answer to a question about European dominance, scripted as a voice from outside, fits better from atop a colonial system: "They are the more powerful, Sir, than
we, answered Imlac, because they are the wiser; knowledge will always predominate over ignorance, as the man governs the other animals."[69]

This position makes predictive good sense when knowledge supports an arrogant colonialism tied to military advances. England was the center of progress and
intelligence in 1759. To Johnson's vision of predominating "over ignorance," add

the industrial revolution, ever-expanding markets, and British domination around the world (even to the Philippines). Only a few people born in 1759, William Will-burforce and Mary Wollstonecraft among them, could resist the side effects of Johnson's instinctive superiority. Now add facts from 1859: the steamroller (a totem for colonial desire), the promises of combustion engines, the Suez Canal, and the French takeover of Saigon. Traditional peoples and farmers were on the run while towns filled with factories. By 1959, colonial pipedreams from 1759 had downscaled to just oil pipe dreams.

Chapter IV: Knowledge and Other-Congratulation

Enter anthropology. *"But this is neither here nor there—why do I mention it?— Ask my pen,—it governs me,—I govern not it"* (6.6.375). My pen offers anthropology's anecdotal veto. To any generalization about differences and similarities across kinds of people, anthropology in 1959 offered a /mai pipl/ to disrupt easy conclusions. /mai pipl/ wisdom from the Philippines was extraordinary. Traditional botanists and farmers are more than smart; they are wise to their environments. The Hanunóo have a world champion 1625 items in their plant taxonomy, and the Subanen are not far behind; their agricultural systems are well-balanced marvels.[70] To know-it-alls trying to "predominate over ignorance," the Philippine refutation is chiseled into the terraced mountainsides of Ifugao.[71] Expanding markets are not the same as expanding brains. Knowledge is not just a commodity.

Anthropology is partly rooted in resistance to the 1759 colonial successes of the Seven Years' War, the justifications of Burke, and the imaginings of Johnson. Resistance from the same year includes Edward Young and Adam Smith downgrading the arrogance of showoff expertise and genius,[72] and the 1759-born Willburforce later turning his anti-slavery work over to the Aborigines Protection Society before it grew into the Royal Anthropological Institute.[73] Resistance in 1859 takes shape in Darwin and Marx celebrating the adaptive ingenuity of finch birds and workers, respectively and respectfully, too. By 1959, an appreciation of traditional know-how by anthropologists had become a necessity.

Chapter V: Still with the Pocket

By now, *"dear reader,"* you should be clamoring for word of Walter. We last saw him moving his left hand to his right pocket with his wig suspended midair. News from 1759, 1859, and 1959 should always be welcome, but even Sterne would return to the topic at hand, at Walter's hand—until something else would *"zig-zagery"* grab his attention. Zig-zag wins. Even if we never return to Walter, another side-story must be introduced. Fare well, Walter.

I have dropp'd a curtain over this scene for a minute... What I have to inform you, comes, I own, a little out of its due course;—for it should have been told a hundred and fifty pages ago, but that I foresaw then 'twould come in

pat hereafter, and may be of more advantage here than elsewhere.
(2.19.128-129)

Chapter VI: *"How to Enter a Yakan House"*
Side-story news comes from the Yakan, who show contrived and awkward situations with their feet more than their hands, and that, *your reverences*, while going in and out of houses. A Yakan house is well defended: a hobbyhorse shared with Uncle Toby. Entering
a house involves steps more complex than Walter's left hand to right pocket. Lives are at stake for persons who climb a ladder onto a Yakan porch without careful attention to the A, B, C, and D of things and their interpretation. There are four stages to an entrance (with 11 named steps of finer gradation): moving (A) from the vicinity to below the house, (B) from below the house to the ladder and porch, (C) from the ladder and porch to inside the house, and then (D) from inside the house to the "head zone" (the last step could require a marriage and another long wait). Each step requires a performance, and Frake lists a special vocabulary of 25 items used to evaluate one's progress. An entrance is scripted and emergent "—*and at the same time.*" A performance can be "appropriate, awkward, gracious, hostile, self-conscious, ridiculous, insincere, etc."[74] It can go badly or worse: from Walter's *"ungraceful twist"* to a Yakan ungraceful death. Best played is best delayed when the *"hey-go-mad"* tensions of Yakan life show up in the action/reaction sequencing of house entrance.

Chapter VII: *The World in Pockets*
Young Tristram understood how the social world disrupts simple steps between here and there. His birth had to go through wound-up clocks, mock-up marriage contracts, and heated-up negotiations on kinds of midwife. Big troubles can interfere with the smallest affairs and the smallest affairs with next events of the widest significance. Fine-grained descriptions of Walter's pockets or Yakan ladders show people working hard to create, maintain, and overcome their categories and divisions. Fine-grained descriptions are not about small things: neither micro-things over macro-things, nor irrelevant things over sites of power. As Frake might have said, as Sterne did say:

> *Matters of no more seeming consequence in themselves than, 'Whether my father should have taken off his wig with his right hand or with his left,—have divided the greatest kingdoms, and made the crowns of the monarchs who governed them, to totter upon their heads.—But need I tell you, Sir, that the circumstances with which every thing in this world is begirt, give every thing in this world its size and shape;—and by tightening it, or relaxing it, this way or that, make the thing to be, what it is—great—little—good—bad—indifferent or not indifferent, just as the case happens.* (3.2.142-3)

Walter's pockets, like Yakan ladders, are organized from on high: by gravity and the gravity of the situation.

> *In the latter end of Queen Anne's reign, and in the beginning of the reign of*
> *King George the first—'Coat pockets were cut very low down in the skirt.'—*
> *I need say no more—the father of mischief, had he been hammering at it a*
> *month, could not have contrived a worse fashion for one in my father's situa-*
> *tion.* (3.2.143)

Among good reasons for pockets *"cut very low down,"* the Shandy family could keep their rears close to the ground.

Chapter VIII: Pockets in the World

Daniel Defoe (born likely in 1659, to keep our 1659 string alive) also described the social
structure of pockets in his story of young Colonel Jack getting acquired by a money economy. Jack was a street waif. He begged successfully by day and slept peacefully over a glass works by night until recruited by pickpockets to steal from the rich. He soon acquired a fistful of coins, but had no place to keep them. He lost a night of sleep—*"But pray, Sir, what was"* Colonel Jack doing all night—*"Why, Madam,—he was all that time"* holding on to his money. The next morning he bought a pair of pants—with pockets—and started a life of dangerous work: getting enough money to buy what was needed to meet the demands of having money. Life be damned. "I knew not what Money was, or what to do with it; and never knew what it was not to sleep, till I had Money to keep, and was afraid of losing it."[75] Money is all that counts. It's coins in, coins out, in and out: *coinus interruptus.*

Walter Shandy's pockets, set for 1718, were in the right place for his life; his only problem was trying to do two things at once. Nor did his son need ready pockets. When Walter decides to move the fast growing Tristram from vests and tunics into breeches, he says to the ever-agreeable Mrs. Shandy:

> *I am resolved, however, quoth my father, breaking silence the fourth time, he*
> *shall have no pockets in them,*
> *—There is no occasion for any, said my mother. —*
> *I mean in his coat and waistcoat,—cried my father.*
> *—I mean so too, replied my mother.*
> *—Though if he gets a gig or a top—Poor souls! It is a crown and sceptor to*
> *them, —they should have where to secure it.* (6.18.396)

Tristram would eventually have more occasions for pockets. The English economy was increasingly showing up in pockets, and, like Colonel Jack, he would need them *"to secure it."*

Fast-forward a century from Defoe and young Tristram, and pockets have a regular place in biographies and novels, enough for one critic to write of nineteenth century English literature that "money as a medium of exchange has found precisely the level (the pocket level) that will enable it to become the chief social force in people's lives."[76]

In the eighteenth century, pockets move up and away from the private concerns they invited when women wore them under their garments —where there were no undergarments, not then—and the word "purse" was slang for female genitalia, there to receive the male "crown."[77] In the eighteenth century, pockets move up and closer to the public concerns of economic exchange. After Sterne, pockets were more for men of market action than men of leisure retrieving their handkerchief from a sitting position. Men were up to their arrears when going to their pockets.

By 1768, Sterne compared the French—for their entrepreneurship and "*urbanity*"—to coins worn down as "*smooth as glass ... by jingling and rubbing one against the other for seventy years together in one body's pocket or another's*" and leaving them, both coins and the French, without edge or humor.[78] A century later, Charles Baudelaire portrayed a many-pocketed waistcoat: a separate pocket for each denomination of coin.[79] In 1922, Joyce has Molly Bloom restricting her husband's night crawling by searching his pockets for a condom. Pockets had become a repository of the market's extension to hand and gland, or, as Molly says of her husband: "I suppose he thinks I don't know deceitful men all their 20 pockets aren't enough for their lies."[80]

When asked about Yakan pockets, Frake replied that it would require "a long answer—the world has changed from worrying where to keep your betel nut ingredients to where to keep your cellphone so you can talk to your friends, lovers, co-conspirators, and enemies (to lure them into an ambush)."[81] By content and function, pockets are a possible good beginning point for a fine description of the world brought down on the peoples of the Sulu Sea.

Chapter IX: The World around the Yakan

Pockets and opinions change together. Take selfishness: an occasion of sin and condemnation in medieval Christianity, the motivational engine of a moral society for Smith in 1759, critiqued as competitive bile by Dickens and Marx in 1859, and a reason anthropologists had to defend people without coin-filled pockets in 1959. A great deal of selfishness can be fitted into a pocket.

Ladders and pockets among the Yakan are organized, like Tristram's pockets, by the complicities of circumstance; it's politics and economics all the way up. In 1975, Frake pointed to the wider world of "endemic" warfare in the Southern Philippines: Yakan vs. Yakan, Yakan vs. other Muslim groups, and Yakan, other Muslim groups, and pagans vs. Christians. "The weaponry includes not only locally made spears, swords, and shotguns but also the latest in U.S. military small arms—a fact not without relevance to the construction of a Yakan house."[82] Later papers added local militia, martial law from Manila, and post-9/11 CIA inquiries into the newly notorious group of Abu Sayyaf terrorists.[83] From pockets and ladders in face-to-face interaction, a Frakean ethnography can move to large-scale events like the expansion of capitalism during the Seven Years' War and the rearrangement more than 200 years later of core/periphery relations in a southern Philippines caught in the shadow of global terrorism. With borders reinvented and reinforced by ethnic, linguistic, religious, and political identifications—all "*at the same time*" posed, imposed, and opposed, from local ladders and pockets to national and international hierarchies—the necessity of a defensive structuring of life around the Sulu Sea comes into focus.

Chapter X: "We're both still alive."

In Sterne's novels and Frake's later ethnography sits the threat of death. Sterne was writing while facing his own end,[84] and many Subanen and Yakan have faced violent deaths over the past fifty years. When Frake returned to the Sulu area in the early 1990s, he ran into an old friend: "As we stared at each other in mutual recognition, then hugged one another, his first words were: '*ellum pe kita*' 'We're both still alive.'"[85]

The good news: Sterne and Frake have offered ways of resisting—with style and some assurances, with wit and the promise of renewal—the less dramatic but often destructive slow deaths latent in received categories. As Sterne said, as Frake would agree, "*Everything in this world ... is big with jest,—and has wit in it, and instruction too, —if we can but find it out*" (5.32.470). Reading Sterne's theology through Derrida, Karen Prior uses the term "incarnation" to capture how Sterne balances the disappointments of life with renewal.[86] Incarnation is too theological for Frake's view of renewal, but he does believe in ethnographic, linguistic, and historical inquiry to help the world along. When I saw him in England in 2011, he was planning his next field trip to the Philippines and reading Herodotus in Greek. Renewal reigns. Works by Sterne and Frake continue to instruct.

Conclusion

Frake would sometimes tell students that ethnographers were novelists who did not have the imagination to make up the complex details of a narrative. He would alternately say that not even novelists could imagine the richness and complexity ethnographers must try to describe.[87] He was right twice. The excitement is not to argue one side over the other, or worse, to mix them without responsibility (but for fun, as in the previous section), but to know how to read the promises and problems of various kinds of description.

Writing this chapter has made me struggle with my divided loyalties to the pizzazz of fiction and to the promises of responsible ethnographic description and analysis. While writing about Sterne, I have a responsibility to the play of his words and what scholars have said about them. While writing about Frake, I have a responsibility to his words and the lived facts of the Subanen and Yakan. The only thing wrong with these loyalties is that they have been divided. Mainstream social sciences argue for one over the other: science vs. art, empiricism vs. interpretation, and, in the silliest format, quantitative vs. qualitative. These are delusive either/ors. I would prefer both/and, or better, as Joyce said, "one aneither."[88] I would prefer research agendas in which they are not pitted against each other—neither paired up, nor pared down; neither mixed, nor mixed up—but more orchestrated by the demands of purpose, honesty, depth, and validity.

Put the facts in Figure 7 on a conveyor belt, and Sterne would pick one here, one there, and make of them, it seems, whatever he might in the course, and off-course, of his story. When Corporal Trim begins to tell "*the story of the king of Bohemia*" and has trouble getting his dates together, Uncle Toby sets Trim's mind at ease: "*take any date in the whole world thou choosest, and put it to—thou art heartily welcome.*" The constraints close in quickly when Trim begins again and picks, says Uncle Toby, "*the very worst year of the whole bunch.*" So he tries again, is interrupted again, and then set free with better advise:

> To tell thee truly, Trim, quoth my uncle Toby, any other date would have pleased me much better, not only on account of the sad stain upon our history that year ... but likewise on the score, Trim, of thy own story ... Leave out the date entirely,
>
> Trim, quoth my uncle Toby, leaning forwards ... a story passes very well without these niceties, unless one is pretty sure of 'em. (8.19.510-511)

Even Sterne cannot play with facts anyway he chooses. Their well-structured coherence held enough sway in his fiction that generations of scholars have used his dating games to conjure the alignments of his world.

Put the same dates on a conveyor belt for Frake, and the contexts are more immediately in demand. He would worry instantly about why the facts got organized by date, by whom, how, under what circumstances, and with what consequences for the "*life and opinions*" of those who would interpret them. By what logic, and with whose permission, can a line get drawn from Johnson or Smith in 1759 to the steamroller and the discovery of oil in 1859? Is it a tragedy or a farce that 98 years later the Suez Canal is the center of a world crisis, or that 50 years later again the battle over the control of oil should show up in the Philippines as an Islamic insurgency?

For Sterne, established facts are playthings with constraints; for Frake, they are proposals about the world that must be investigated in relation to each other as they are interpreted by their constituents. Whether as disease among the Subanen, litigation among the Yakan, or formality conventions everywhere, facts mean things only in relation to each other in the organization and interpretation of behavior in situations over time.

Novelists rarely worry about facts the way a Frakean ethnographer might. Ethnographers, in turn, rarely morph facts the way a novelist might. In my exercise with Sterne and Frake, the facts were allowed to stand both tall and short, both disconnected and reconnected, both responsibly and in jest. Put that in your pocket. Or better, notice that novels can be mined for their facts, and ethnographies, even "a structural description" of, say, "Subanun 'religious behavior,'" can be read as playful, artful and well tuned to the experiences of real people, to their questions and answers, to their problems and responses.

Novels are methodic, but it is usually the critics of future generations who sort out the systematics in what the novelist has accomplished. Most social scientists, in contrast, like to define their methods up front, as if they might know, with no apologies to Meno, what they have to know before making an inquiry. Sterne and Frake challenge both ends of the extremes: Sterne because he shows how he is proceeding; Frake because he shows how he is finding the things that organize how he is proceeding. As Frake says, as Sterne would agree, "comparability is something to be discovered ... you can't legislate it;"[89] and so generalizations—about people, language, writing, time, courtship, and warfare—come "not through comparison but from learning to describe and inscribe."[90]

To enhance the study of Sterne, wouldn't it be good to have recordings and deep empirical analyses of a few real conversations from London, Yorkshire, and Calais in 1759—the very stuff of Sterne's account of the world. To enhance ethnography, wouldn't it be fine to have a fuller stream of consciousness version of only a few days of Frake's fieldwork—the very stuff underlying his data displays. And wouldn't it be great to have many kinds of partial description moving in and out of each other in ways responsible to the complexities of experience.

The goals of ethnography should be broad and self-conscious: from technical and precise when possible, to political when necessary, or to playful when either delightful or desperate. We should strive to write reports that are deeply empirical, deeply imaginative, deeply emotional, deeply disruptive "—and at the same time."

Notes

Acknowledgments

Richard Blot twice gave amazingly helpful comments. He and John Willinsky offered the same pun—from rears to arrears—for me to exploit. Penny Eckert supplied the phonetics of Valley Girl "for sure," and Roy Pea alerted me to the Sherlock Holmes text. Shelley Goldman listened to a year of Shandy talk. John Hitchman took me to Wigtown, Scotland, where he found the Hugh MacDiarmid volumes I had been wanting. Thanks to them all.

Bibliographic Note

References listed in the Footnotes give the year of publication for editions used to prepare this paper. References in the Bibliography use, if possible, the original date of publication. The same copy of Sterne's *A Sentimental Journey*, for example, is dated 1928 in the Footnotes and 1768 in the References. This allows the reader to follow more easily the logic of highlighting the years 1759, 1859, and 1959.

1. Charles O. Frake, "A Structural Description of Subanun 'Religious Behavior,'" in *Explorations in Cultural Anthropology*, ed. Ward H. Goodenough (New York: McGraw-Hill, 1964), 112.

2. Laurence Sterne, *The Life and Opinions of Tristram Shandy, Gentleman* (London: Penguin, 1997). All quotes from *Tristram Shandy* are in italics. Substantial passages, but not small phrases, are cited in the text by volume, chapter, and page. The "key-hole" passage, for example, is from Volume 9, Book 1, and Pages 546-547. I have tried to preserve Sterne's punctuation.

3. Except when quoting early Frake, I use Subanen, not Subanun. The new spelling conforms to NGO—and so Subanen—ideas about what makes an indigenous group. Charles Frake, "How to Be a Tribe In the Southern Philippines during the Advent of NGO's and the Invention of the Indigenous" (unpublished ms., 2012).

4. Bawdy is naughty in 1759 (especially for a clergyman!), a scandal in 1859, an intellectual puzzle in 1959, and now a critical issue. Bergin Evans has a mid-century view: "It is plainly not the prurience of the jest that really tickles him, but the reconditeness of the lore that carries it and the unexpectedness of the juxtaposition that produces it." Evans, "Introduction," in *Tristram Shandy* (New York: Modern Library, 1950), xv.

5. Edmund Burke, "Review of *Tristram Shandy*," in Laurence Sterne, *Tristram Shandy*, ed. Howard Anderson (New York: Norton, 1980), 481.

6. Whatever structuralism was, it has given way rhetorically to a post-structuralism that emphasizes agency over institutional roles and statuses, insight over formal operations, and the patterned, put upon, but lived experience of people over concretized social structures measured and distorted by the causal claims of distant social scientists. The overall trend has been mostly liberating, but unfortunate if detailed ethnographic description is bypassed for post-structural depiction. Among post-structuralists, Pierre Bourdieu found Frake's activity driven accounts of structure exemplary, this from an interview reported in a book of essays on Bourdieu, but to quote Sterne citing Horace, "—*I forget which.*" Although I really can't find the book, Sterne was likely at play: citing Horace for the opposite of what Horace had said; see Adam Thirlwell, "Reproduction," *The Shandean* 21, (2010), 25.

7. I might say more about Sterne's encyclopedic natural history later, or not, but with no reason to believe me now, see Peter Anstey, "The Experimental History of the Understanding from Locke to Sterne," *Eighteenth-Century Thought*, 4, (2009), 143-169; and Jack Lynch, "The Relicks of Learning: Sterne among the Renaissance Encyclopedists," *Eighteenth-Century Fiction* 13, (2000), 1-20.

8. Frake, "A Structural Description," 118.

9. Hamlet: "Your worm is your only emperor for diet. We fat all creatures else to fat us, and we fat ourselves for maggots. Your fat king and your lean beggar is but variable service—two dishes, but to one table" (4.2.22-25); William Shakespeare, *Hamlet* (New York: Modern Library, 2008), 94.

10. Frake, "Notes on the Formal" *TEXT* 3, (1983), 302.

11. Frake, "The Ethnographic Study of Cognitive Systems," in *Anthropology and Human Behavior*, eds. Thomas Gladwin and William Sturtevant (Washington: Anthropological Society of Washington, 1962), 74.

12. Roland Posner, "Semiotic Paradoxes in Language Use, with Particular Reference to *Tristram Shandy*," *The Eighteenth Century* 20, (1979), 162.

13. Po Chu-I, quoted in Arthur Waley, *The Life and Times of Po Chu-I, 772-846 A.D.* (London: Allen & Unwin, 1949), 207; Francis Bacon, *The Advancement of Learning* (Oxford: Oxford University Press, 1974), 128; John Locke, *An Essay Concerning Human Under-*

standing. Fifth edition. (London: Penguin, 2004), 335; Johann Wolfgang von Goethe, *Faust, Part One* (Oxford: Oxford University Press, 1987), 60; Karl Marx, *Capital* (London: Penguin, 1976), 161; William Butler Yeats, "Letter to Horace Mason Reynolds," in *The Collected Works of W.B. Yeats*, vol. 7: *Letters to the New Island*, eds. George Bornstein and Hugh Witemeyer (New York: Macmillan, 1989), xviii; Franz Boas, "Introduction," in *Handbook of American Indian Languages*, vol. 1, ed. Franz Boas (Washington, DC: Bureau of American Ethnology, 1911), 71; Benjamin Lee Whorf, "The Relation of Habitual Thought and Behavior to Language," in *Language, Thought, and Reality* (Cambridge: MIT Press, 1956), 148; T. S. Eliot, *Four Quartets* (San Diego: Harcourt Brace Jovanovich, 1971), 30; Edward Sapir, "Grading," in *Selected Writings of Edward Sapir*, ed. David Mandlebaum (Berkeley: University of California Press, 1949), 133; Hugh MacDiarmid, "In Memoriam James Joyce," in *The Complete Poems of Hugh MacDiarmid*. Vol. 2, eds. Michael Grieve and W.R. Atkin (London: Martin Brian & O'Keefe, 1978), 799; Ferruccio Rossi-Landi, *Ideologies of Linguistic Relativity* (The Hague: Mouton, 1973), 75-76; the last phrase is capitalized in the original); Edward Said, "On Repetition," in Angus Fletcher (ed.), *The Literature of Fact* (New York: Columbia University Press, 1976), 155.

14. Sterne hardly touches events in Italy. Illness shortened his life more than his title.

15. Sterne thought of plagiarism as play. He condemned plagiarism (5.1.310) with lines plagiarized from Robert Burton's *Anatomy of Melancholy*; in 1798, John Ferriar called the play on Burton a "characteristic example of Sterne's roguishness"; quoted in Alan Howes, *Sterne: The Critical Heritage* (London: Routledge & Kegan Paul, 1974), 283-292; Melvyn New, "Notes," in Laurence Sterne, *The Life and Opinions of Tristram Shandy, Gentleman* (London: Penguin, 1997), 673.

16. Another list of "Sterne's love for disruptive, interruptive, and confounding rhetorical devices—hyperbation, aposeiopesis, innuendo, catachresis, aporia, ellipsis, pleonasm, pun." Scott MacKenzie, "*Homunculus Economicus*: Laurence Sterne's Labour Theory of Literary Value," *Eighteenth-Century Fiction* 18, (2005), 63.

17. Denis Diderot, quoted in Ian Ross, *Laurence Sterne: A Life* (Oxford: Oxford University Press, 2001), 285; see also David Coward, "Introduction," in Denis Diderot, *Jacques, the Fatalist* (Oxford: Oxford University Press, 1999); Goethe, from a diary kept in 1830; in Howes, *Sterne,* 435; Heinrich Heine quoted in Peter Conrad, "Introduction," in Laurence Sterne, *Tristram Shandy* (New York: Everyman's Library, 1991), xxii; Honoré de Balzac, *The Physiology of Marriage* (Baltimore: Johns Hopkins University Press, 1997), 65; Nikolai Gogol, see Neil Stewart, "Notes on Noses: Laurence Sterne and Nikolai Gogol," *Arcadia* 36, (2001), 143-155; Marx, see Francis Wheen, *Karl Marx: A Life* (New York: W.W. Norton, 1999); Virginia Woolf, "Introduction," in Laurence Sterne, *A Sentimental Journey through France and Italy* (Oxford: Oxford University Press, 1928), ix-x; Bertrand Russell, *The Principles of Mathematics* (London: Allen & Unwin, 1903); Robert K. Merton, *On the Shoulders of Giants: A Shandean Postscript.* Post-Italianate edition (Chicago: University of Chicago Press, 1993), xix; Italo Calvino, quoted in Ross, *Laurence Sterne*, 429.

18. Duncan Patrick, "Character and Chronology in *Tristram Shandy* (1)," *The Shandean* 14, (2003), 39-70.

19. Sterne's nonchalance is belied by extensive editing in his manuscripts. Virginia Woolf finds his final texts marked by "extreme art and extraordinary pains." See Woolf, "Introduction," in Laurence Sterne, *A Sentimental Journey through France and Italy* (Oxford: Oxford University Press, 1928), vii.

20. Walter Sichel, *Sterne: A Study* (New York: Haskell House, 1971), 49.

21. Friedrich Nietzsche, *Human, All Too Human*. Second edition. (Cambridge: Cambridge University Press, 1996), 239.

22. See Thomas Keymer, *Sterne, the Moderns, and the Novel* (Oxford: Oxford University Press, 2002).

23. So said Edmund Burke, *The Complete History of the Recent War, or the Annual Register of its Rife, Progrefs, and Events, in Europe, Afia, Africa, and America*. Fourth edition. (Dublin: John Exshaw, 1766), 2. Burke documented all seven years in all four corners, including the Siege of Manila; Burke, *The Complete*, 513-524. The rest of his title is revealing: ... *and Exhibiting the State of the Belligerant Powers at the Commencement of the War; their Interests and the Objects in its Continuance: Interfperfed with The Characters of the able and difinterefted Statesmen, to Whofe Wisdom and Integrity, and of the Heroes, to whofe Courage and Conduct we are indebted for that NAVAL and MILITARY Succefs, which is not to be equaled in the Annals of this or any other Nation.*

24. Howard Anderson, "A Version of Pastoral: Class and Society in *Tristram Shandy*," *Studies in English Literature, 1500-1900*, 7, (1967), 526.

25. Sterne, *A Sentimental Journey*, 23-24.

26. Bernard Mandeville, *The Fables of the Bees: Or, Private Vices, Publick Benefits*. 2 vols. (Oxford: Oxford University Press, 1924).

27. See Thomas Keymer, *Sterne, the Moderns*; Ross, *Laurence Sterne*; MacKenzie, "*Homunculus Economicus*"; Ann Campbell, "*Tristram Shandy* and the Seven Years War: Beyond the Borders of the Bowling Green," *The Shandean* 17, (2006), 106-120; Carol Watts, *The Cultural Work of Empire: The Seven Years' War and the Imagining of the Shandean State* (Toronto: University of Toronto Press, 2007).

28. Two more comments on Sterne's below the belt embodiment of the global "*SITUATION*": "All manifestations of male sexuality in *Tristram Shandy* fall prey to economics ... The rake's drive towards novelty and the moment of release burns in the Shandy Loins, but the capacity for satisfaction fails"; see MacKenzie, "*Homunculus Economicus*," 80; and "Toby's affective, bodily language appears to be a sensitive litmus test of the ravages of the 'scurvy, disasterous world' [1.5.10], its modest blushes a passive register of external forms of violence: historical, sexual, social"; see Watts, *The Cultural Work*, 75.

29. Especially Keymer, *Sterne, the Moderns*.

30. Parnell offers a gentler view of Sterne's market savvy; "Introduction," in Laurence Sterne, *A Sentimental Journey and Other Writings* (Oxford: Oxford University Press, 2002), ix. On a disappointing note, at a demanding moment when landlords were enforcing the enclosure movement against his parishioners, Sterne might have used a "*base, ungentle passion*" to enhance his own situation; see Anne Leonard, "Sterne, Sutton, and Bohemia," *The Shandean* 21, (2010), 35-45. Sterne's silence on economics contrasts with, say, Defoe, Balzac, Dickens, Trollope, Wharton, and Hemingway, who feature financial negotiations throughout their work. Novelists who write about the disenfranchised are often more sensitive to human ingenuity in the face of economic constraints than their social science counterparts; see Ray McDermott, "The Passions of Learning in Tight Circumstances," *National Society for the Study of Education* 109, no. 1, (2010), 144-159; Ray McDermott and Jason Raley, "Looking Closely: Toward a Natural History of Human Ingenuity," in *The Sage Handbook of Visual Research Methods*, eds. Eric Margolis and Luc Pauwels (Thousand Oaks, CA: Sage, 2011).

31. Joyce, *Finnegans Wake* (New York: Viking, 1939), 256.

32. Frake, "Fine Description," in Harold C. Conklin, *Fine Description: Ethnographic and Linguistic Essays*, eds. Joel Kuipers and Ray McDermott. Monograph 56 (New Haven:

Yale Southeast Asia Studies, 2007). What can be said in praise of Frake has been said in praise of Conklin; see Joel Kuipers and Ray McDermott, "Ethnographic Responsibility," in Conklin, *Fine Description.* In their different ways, they set the bar for excellent fieldwork. Are Conklin and Frake empirical scientists? Unabashedly so. Are they concerned with the human relations underlying their empirical investigations? They would have nothing to report, but for people making their activities visible and consequential to each other. Do they resist the imposition of essentialist terms in their inquiries? Nothing enters their analytic field without a specification of how the people studied worry about their behavior—and interpretations of their behavior—in particular contexts. Essentialist assumptions are never precise enough. Michael Dove's appropriately radical anti-essentialist reading of Conklin's scientism applies perfectly to Frake; see "Kinds of Fields," in Conklin, *Fine Description.* By force of field situation, Frake has reported more than Conklin on colonial intrusions; by dint of personality, he has appealed more to humor and irony. They can be compared totemically to different novelists: Frake:Sterne :: Conklin:Joyce; see McDermott, "Conklin Joyce, and the Wannaknów," *American Anthropologist* 99, (1997), 257-260. If Frake picked his own avatar, it would be Geoffrey Chaucer.

33. Ralph Waldo Emerson, *Representative Men* (New York: Marsilio, 1995), 177.

34. For the distinction between research topic and analytic resource, see Harold Garfinkel, *Studies in Ethnomethodology* (Englewood Cliffs: Prentice-Hall, 1967). Garfinkel was an early influence on Frake; see Frake, "A Conversation with Charles O. Frake at the Laboratory of Comparative Human Cognition" (unpublished ms, 1977); for commentary, see D. Lawrence Wieder, "On Meaning by Rule," in *Understanding Everyday Life*, ed. Jack Douglas (Chicago: Aldine, 1970).

35. Emerson, *Representative*, 177.

36. Recent calls for an ethnographic focus on the "precarious" or for a disruptive "kinky empiricism" that "takes seriously the situated nature of what all thinkers do"—who could argue with that—have a deeper past than is currently acknowledged; see, for example, Kathleen Stewart, "Precarity's Forms," *Cultural Anthropology* 27, (2012), 518-526; Danilyn Rutherford, "Kinky Empiricism," *Cultural Anthropology* 27, (2012), 465-479. In the hands of great ethnographers, structural—and even functional—frameworks have been used to deliver what is precarious, transient, and sensuous.

37. Early essays were collected in Frake, *Language and Cultural Description*, ed. Anwar Dil (Stanford: Stanford University Press, 1980); papers from the last thirty years will appear in Frake, *The Cultural Work of Borders: Essays in the Ethnographic Study of Cognitive Systems in Action* (in preparation, 2013).

38. James A. Boon, *Verging on Extra-vagance* (Princeton: Princeton University Press, 1999), 8.

39. Frake, "The Cultural Construction of Rank, Identity, and Ethnic Origins in the Sulu Archipelago," in *Origins, Ancestry, and Alliances*, eds. J.J. Fox and Clifford Sather (Canberra: Australian National University, 1996), 321.

40. Frake, "The Cultural Construction," 318.

41. Frake, "The Cultural Construction," 319.

42. Frake, "The Cultural Construction," 320.

43. Frake, "The Cultural Construction," 322.

44. Frake, "How to Be a Tribe in the Southern Philippines during the Advent of NGO's and the Invention of the Indigenous." Unpublished ms, 2012.

45. Frake, "Abu Sayyaf: Displays of Violence and the Proliferation of Contested Identities among Philippine Muslims," *American Anthropologist* 100, (1998), 48.

46. Samuel Taylor Coleridge, *Aids to Reflection* (London: John Grant, 1905), 48.

47. Frake, "Abu Sayyaf," 51.

48. Nietzsche, *Human*, 239.

49. Frake, "Abu Sayyaf," 48.

50. Frake, "A Structural," 112.

51. In Frake's hands, even the invention and adoption of precise calculating instruments—the very hallmark of the Western mind—"have been motivated as much by the symbolic power of these displays of their modernity as by their technical superiority:" see Frake, "A Reinterpretation of the Micronesian 'Star Compass,'" *Journal of the Polynesian Society* 104, (1995), 147; and "Dials: A Study in the Physical Representation of Cognitive Systems," in *The Ancient Mind: Elements of Cognitive Archaeology*, eds. Colin Renfrew and Ezra Zubrow (Cambridge: Cambridge University Press, 1994).

52. Early in the anti-behaviorist meaning revolution that swept the social sciences a half-century ago, eliciting conditions were a focal concern for what became known as cognitive anthropology. Frake wrote the signature paper for that field, "The Ethnographic Study," but his use of the term cognitive thankfully bears little resemblance to how most surviving versions of cognitive anthropology or cognitive psychology have developed; see Frake, "A Conversation"; "Plying Frames Can Be Dangerous: An Assessment of Methodology in Cognitive Anthropology," *Quarterly Newsletter of the Laboratory of Comparative Human Cognition* 1, no. 3, (1977), 1-7; "Cognitive Anthropology: An Origin Story," in *The Making of Psychological Anthropology II*, eds. Marcelo Suárez-Orosco, George Spindler, and Louise Spindler (Fort Worth: Harcourt Brace, 1994). Sources for Frake's concern for question-answer pairings include Conklin, "Hanunóo Color Categories," *Southwestern Journal of Anthropology* 11, (1955), 339-344; Ward Goodenough, "Residence Rules," *Southwestern Journal of Anthropology* 12, (1956), 22-37; Duane Metzger and Gerald Williams, "Tenejapa Medicine I: The Curer," *Southwestern Journal of Anthropology* 19, (1963), 216-234; Roy D'Andrade, "Trait Psychology and Componential Analysis," *American Anthropologist* 67, no. 5, (1965), 215-258.

53. The "sculptor's reduction" image is from Gertrude Hughes in her account of Emerson's method; *Emerson's Demanding Optimism* (Baton Rouge: Louisiana State University Press, 1984), 37.

54. Royal Anthropological Institute, *Notes and Queries in Anthropology*. Sixth edition. (London: Routledge and Kegan Paul, 1951); Frake, "Notes on Queries in Ethnography," *American Anthropologist* 66, no. 3(2), (1964), 132-145.

55. Plato, *Meno* (New York: Liberal Arts Press, 1949), 36.

56. For "query rich settings," see Frake, "Notes on Queries"; "Plying Frames"; and "Cognitive Anthropology."

57. Frake, "The Cultural Construction," 320.

58. Email from Charles Frake, 20 December 2012.

59. Frake, "Pleasant Places, Past Times, and Shared Identity in Rural East Anglia," in *Senses of Place*, eds. Steve Feld and Keith Basso (Santa Fe: School of American Research, 1996).

60. Frake, "A Church Too Far Near a Bridge Oddly Placed: The Cultural Construction of the Norfolk Countryside," in *Beyond Nature and Culture*, eds. Roy Ellen and Katsuyoshi Fukui (Oxford: Berg, 1996).

61. Sterne, *A Sentimental Journey*, 148.

62. Sterne, *A Sentimental Journey*, 161.

63. Frake always reads footnotes first. Hi Chuck! His explanation: "It's all in the epigraphs and footnotes—just like life" (from a scribbled note on one of his manuscripts). Politically, footnotes mimic the interpretative affordances of Sulu Sea ethnonyms. Anthony Grafton says footnotes "buttress and undermine, at one and the same time," and he offers Edward Gibbon's extensive footnotes as an example of profound scholarship, biting humor, and, as a critic complained in 1778, "'a good artifice ... to escape detection'"; *The Footnote* (Cambridge: Harvard University Press, 1997), 32, 100. Sterne loved footnote mischief.

64. Martin Rowson, *The Life and Opinions of Tristram Shandy, Gentleman* (London: SelfMadeHero, 2010).

65. Henri Bergson, *Creative Evolution* (New York: Holt, Rinehart, and Winston, 1969), 307; John Dewey, *Art as Experience* (New York: Perigree, 1980), 23; Edmund Husserl, quoted in Zahavi, *Husserl's Phenomenology* (Stanford: Stanford University Press, 2003), 96. James Joyce played with the temporal import of the 1859-born philosophers: "the races have come and gone and Thyme, that chef of seasoners, has made astewte use of endadjustables and whatnot willbe isnor was"; *Finnegans Wake*, 256, for a possible translation, from gustatory to temporal semes and seams, try: ... Time, that chief of seasons, has made astute use of endless adjustments and whatnot will be, is, nor was; see Claudette Sartillot, *Citation and Modernity: Derrida, Joyce, and Brecht* (Norman, OK: University of Oklahoma Press, 1995). Joyce tied modern time to Swift and Sterne and "swiftly sterneward!" toyed with the reflexivity of past, present and future: "one yeastyday he sternely struxk his tete in a tub for to watsch the future of his fates"; *Finnegans Wake*, 4, 236.

66. On Seurat's interest in psychophysics, see Robert Herbert, *Seurat and the Making of La Grande Jatte* (Chicago: The Art Institute of Chicago, 2004).

67. Frake, "Conklin on Color," in *Fine Description*, 158.

68. See Conklin, "Color Categorization," *American Anthropologist* 73, (1973), 936; and the commentary by Frake, "Conklin," 158.

69. Samuel Johnson, *The History of Rasselas, Prince of Abissinia* (Oxford: Oxford University Press, 2009), 30. By the rules of Frakean ethnographic behavior, answers cannot enter a data set without their questions; see "The Ethnographic Study"; "Notes on Queries"; "Plying Frames"; and "Cognitive Anthropology." Here is Johnson's query that gets Imlac's answer: "'By what means,' said the prince, 'are the Europeans thus powerful? [sic], or why since they can so easily visit Asia and Africa for trade or conquest, cannot the Asiaticks and Africans invade their coasts, plant colonies in their ports, and give laws to their natural princes?'" A note on Johnson's query: Don't ask. Knowledge politics aside, Johnson was a strong critic of Western colonialism; see Keymer, "Introduction," in Samuel Johnson, *The History of Rasselas, Prince of Abissinia* (Oxford: Oxford University Press, 2009), xxviii.

70. Conklin, *The Relation of Hanunóo Culture to the Plant World* (Unpublished dissertation, Department of Anthropology, Yale University, 1954); *Hanunóo Agriculture* (Rome: FAO, 1957); Frake, *Social Organization and Shifting Cultivation among the Sindangan Subanun* (Unpublished dissertation, Department of Anthropology, Yale University, 1955).

71. Conklin, *Ethnographic Atlas of Ifugao* (New Haven: Yale University Press, 1980); *Fine Description*.

72. Young insisted on the separation of genius from any cheap display of learning that "is a great lover of rules, and boaster of famed examples ... [that] inveighs against natural unstudied graces, and small harmless inaccuracies, and sets rigid bounds to the liberty"; *Conjectures on Original Composition* (Manchester: Manchester University Press, 1918), 13. Smith agreed in sentiment, and said so seventeen years later: "The difference in natural talents in different men is, in reality, much less than we are aware of; and the very different

genius which appears to distinguish men of different professions, when grown up to matur-
ity, is not upon many occasions so much the cause as the effect of the division of labor";
The Wealth of Nations (New York: Random House, 1994), 14. See McDermott, "Materials
for a Confrontation with Genius as a Personal Identity" *Ethos* 32, (2004), 278-288.

73. George Stocking, "What's in a Name? The Origins of the Royal Anthropological
Institute (1837-1871)," *Man* 6, (1971), 369-390.

74. Frake, "How to Enter a Yakan House," in *Sociocultural Dimensions of Language
Use*, eds. Ben Blount and Mary Sanches (New York: Academic Press, 1975), 25, 39-40.

75. Daniel Defoe, *Colonel Jack* (Oxford: Oxford University Press, 1989), 40.

76. John Vernon, *Money and Fiction: Literary Realism in the Nineteenth and Early
Twentieth Century* (Ithaca: Cornell University Press, 1984), 16. Vernon put the pocket in
parentheses.

77. So said Sterne, *A Sentimental Journey*, 121; see also, Barbara Burman, "Pocketing
the Difference: Gender and Pockets in Nineteenth-Century Britain" *Gender & History* 14,
(2002), 447-469; Christopher Nagle, "Sterne, Shelley, and Sensibility's Pleasures of Proximity," *English Literary History* 70 (2003), 813-845; Ariane Fennetaux, "Women's Pockets
and the Construction of Privacy in the Long Eighteenth Century," *Eighteenth Century
Fiction* 20, (2008), 307-334.

78. Sterne, *A Sentimental Journal*, 165.

79. Charles Baudelaire, *Paris Spleen and the La Fanfarlo* (Indianapolis: Hackett, 2008),
58.

80. Joyce, *Ulysses* (New York: Modern Library, 1961), 772.

81. An email from Charles Frake, 16 December 2012.

82. Frake, "How to Enter," 26.

83. Frake, "Abu Sayyaf," 41-54.

84. Rowson describes *Tristram Shandy* as "an accurate portrayal of life as it truly is,
with the compensating factor of making us laugh ... into the grinning face of Death ... and
kicking the old bastard in the cobblers before making as quick a get away as you can for as
long as you
can get away with it." See Rowson, "A Comic Book Version of *Tristram Shandy*," *The
Shandean* 14, (2003), 119-120.

85. Frake, "Cultural Anthropological Studies of Muslim Societies of the Philippines,"
Pilipinas 21, (1993), 3.

86. Karen Prior, "*Embawdiment: Tristram Shandy* and the Paradox of Incarnation," *The
Shandean* 22, (2011), 116-131.

87. Okay, okay, I can deliver now on the connection with Arthur Conan Doyle, who
celebrated what cannot be described by any ethnographer short of Sherlock Holmes: "...
life is infinitely stranger than anything which the mind of man could invent ... If we could
... peep in at the queer things which are going on, the strange coincidences, the plannings,
the cross-purposes, the wonderful chains of events, working through generations, and leading to the most *outré* results, it would make all fiction with its conventionalities and fore-
seen conclusions most stale and unprofitable" (2009:47).

88. Joyce, *Finnegans Wake* (New York: Viking, 1939), 101; see McDermott, "'One
aneither': A Joycean Critique of Educational Research," *Journal of Educational Controversy* 5, (2010).http://www.wce.wwu.edu/Resources/CEP/eJournal/v005n001/

89. Frake, "A Conversation," 7.

90. Frake, "Cognitive Anthropology," 246.

References

Anderson, Howard
 1967 "A Version of Pastoral: Class and Society in *Tristram Shandy.*" *Studies in English Literature, 1500-1900* 7: 509-529.

Anstey, Peter
 2009 "The Experimental History of the Understanding from Locke to Sterne." *Eighteenth-Century Thought* 4: 143-169.

Bacon, Francis
 1623 *The Advancement of Learning.* Oxford: Oxford University Press. [1974]

Balzac, Honoré de
 1829 *The Physiology of Marriage.* Baltimore: Johns Hopkins University Press. [1997]

Baudelaire, Charles
 1869 *Paris Spleen and the La Fanfarlo.* Indianapolis: Hackett. [2008]

Bergson, Henri
 1911 *Creative Evolution.* New York: Holt, Rinehart, and Winston. [1969]

Boas, Franz
 1911 "Introduction." In *Handbook of American Indian Languages*, vol. 1. Franz Boas, ed. Pp. 1-83. Washington, DC: Bureau of American Ethnology.

Boon, James A.
 1999 *Verging on Extra-vagance.* Princeton: Princeton University Press.

Burke, Edmund
 1760 Review of *Tristram Shandy.* In Laurence Sterne, *Tristram Shandy.* Howard Anderson, ed. Pp. 481-482. New York: Norton. [1980]
 1766 *The Complete History of the Recent War, or the Annual Register of its Rife, Progrefs, and Events, in Europe, Afia, Africa, and America.* Fourth edition. Dublin: John Exshaw.

Burman, Barbara
 2002 "Pocketing the Difference: Gender and Pockets in Nineteenth-Century Britain." *Gender & History* 14: 447-469.

Campbell, Ann
 2006 "*Tristram Shandy* and the Seven Years War: Beyond the Borders of the Bowling Green." *The Shandean* 17: 106-120.

Coleridge, Samuel Taylor
 1824 *Aids to Reflection.* London: John Grant, 1905.

Conklin, Harold C.
 1954 *The Relation of Hanunóo Culture to the Plant World.* Unpublished dissertation, Department of Anthropology, Yale University.
 1955 "Hanunóo Color Categories." *Southwestern Journal of Anthropology* 11: 339-344.
 1957 *Hanunóo Agriculture.* Rome: FAO.
 1973 "Color Categorization." *American Anthropologist* 73: 931-942.
 1980 *Ethnographic Atlas of Ifugao.* New Haven: Yale University Press.
 2007 *Fine Description: Ethnographic and Linguistic Essays.* Joel Kuipers and Ray McDermott, eds. Monograph 56. New Haven: Yale Southeast Asia Studies.

Conrad, Peter
 1991 "Introduction." In Laurence Sterne, *Tristram Shandy.* Pp. v-xxiv. New York:

Everyman's Library.
Coward, David
    1999   "Introduction." In Denis Diderot, *Jacques, the Fatalist.* Pp. vi-xxxi. Oxford: Oxford University Press.
D'Andrade, Roy
    1965   "Trait Psychology and Componential Analysis." *American Anthropologist* 67(5): 215-258.
Defoe, Daniel
    1722   *Colonel Jack.* Oxford: Oxford University Press. [1989]
Dewey, John
    1934   *Art as Experience.* New York: Perigree. [1980]
Dove, Michael
    2007   "Kinds of Fields." In *Fine Description: Ethnographic and Linguistic Essays of Harold C. Conklin.* Joel Kuipers and Ray McDermott, eds. Pp. 411-427. Monograph 56. New Haven: Yale Southeast Asia Studies.
Eliot, T. S.
    1943   *Four Quartets.* San Diego: Harcourt Brace Jovanovich. [1971]
Emerson, Ralph Waldo
    1850   *Representative Men.* New York: Marsilio. [1995]
Evans, Bergen
    1950   "Introduction." In *Tristram Shandy.* Pp. v-xvii. New York: Modern Library.
Fennetaux, Ariane
    2008   "Women's Pockets and the Construction of Privacy in the Long Eighteenth Century." *Eighteenth Century Fiction* 20: 307-334.
Frake, Charles O.
    1955   *Social Organization and Shifting Cultivation among the Sindangan Subanun.* Unpublished dissertation, Department of Anthropology, Yale University.
    1961   "Diagnosis of Disease in Subanun." *American Anthropologist* 63: 113-132.
    1962   "The Ethnographic Study of Cognitive Systems." In *Anthropology and Human Behavior.* Thomas Gladwin and William Sturtevant, eds. Pp. 72-85. Washington: Anthropological Society of Washington.
    1964a   "How to Ask for a Drink in Subanun. *American Anthropologist* 66(6,2): 127-132.
    1964b   "Notes on Queries in Ethnography." *American Anthropologist* 66(3,2): 132-145.
    1964c   "A Structural Description of Subanun 'Religious Behavior.'" In *Explorations in Cultural Anthropology.* Ward H. Goodenough, ed. Pp. 111-129. New York: McGraw-Hill.
    1969   "Struck by Speech." In *Law in Culture and Society.* Laura Nader, ed. Pp. 147-167. New York: Academic Press.
    1975   "How to Enter a Yakan House." In *Sociocultural Dimensions of Language Use.* Ben Blount and Mary Sanches, eds. Pp. 25-40. New York: Academic Press.
    1977a   "A Conversation with Charles O. Frake at the Laboratory of Comparative Human Cognition" (with Michael Cole, John Dore, Jean Lave, David Roth, Sylvia Scribner). Unpublished ms.
    1977b   "Plying Frames Can Be Dangerous: An Assessment of Methodology in Cognitive Anthropology." *Quarterly Newsletter of the Laboratory of Com-*

parative Human Cognition 1(3): 1-7.

1980a   "The Genesis of Kinds of People in the Sulu Sea." In *Language and Cultural Description: Essays by Charles O. Frake.* Anwar Dil, ed. Pp. 311-332. Stanford: Stanford University Press.

1980b   *Language and Cultural Description: Essays Selected and Introduced.* Anwar Dil, ed. Stanford: Stanford University Press.

1983a   "Notes on the Formal." *TEXT* 3: 299-304.

1983b   "Did Literacy Cause the Great Cultural Divide?" *American Ethnologist* 85: 368-371.

1985   "Cognitive Maps of Time and Tide among Medieval Seafarers." *Man* 20: 254-270.

1992   "Lessons of the Mayan Sky: A Perspective From Medieval Europe." In *The Sky in Mayan Literature.* Anthony Aveni, ed. Pp. 274-291. Oxford: Oxford University Press.

1993   "Cultural Anthropological Studies of Muslim Societies of the Philippines." *Pilipinas* 21: 1-3.

1994a   Cognitive Anthropology: An Origin Story." In *The Making of Psychological Anthropology II.* Marcelo Suárez-Orosco, George Spindler, and Louise Spindler, eds. Pp. 244-253. Fort Worth: Harcourt Brace.

1994b   "Dials: A Study in the Physical Representation of Cognitive Systems." In *The Ancient Mind: Elements of Cognitive Archaeology.* Colin Renfrew and Ezra Zubrow, eds. Pp. 119-132. Cambridge: Cambridge University Press.

1995   "A Reinterpretation of the Micronesian "Star Compass." *Journal of the Polynesian Society* 104: 147-158.

1996a   "A Church Too Far Near a Bridge Oddly Placed: The Cultural Construction of the Norfolk Countryside." In *Beyond Nature and Culture.* Roy Ellen and Katsuyoshi Fukui, eds. Pp. 89-115. Oxford: Berg.

1996b   "The Cultural Construction of Rank, Identity, and Ethnic Origins in the Sulu Archipelago." In *Origins, Ancestry, and Alliances.* J.J. Fox and Clifford Sather, eds. Pp. 316-327. Canberra: Australian National University.

1996c   "Pleasant Places, Past Times, and Shared Identity in Rural East Anglia." In *Senses of Place.* Steve Feld and Keith Basso, eds. Pp. 229-257. Santa Fe: School of American Research.

1998   "Abu Sayyaf: Displays of Violence and the Proliferation of Contested Identities among Philippine Muslims." *American Anthropologist* 100: 41-54.

2007a   "Conklin on Color." In *Fine Description: Ethnographic and Linguistic Essays of Harold C. Conklin.* Joel Kuipers and Ray McDermott, eds. Pp. 155-159. Monograph 56. New Haven: Yale Southeast Asia Studies.

2007b   "Fine Description." In *Fine Description: Ethnographic and Linguistic Essays of Harold C. Conklin.* Joel Kuipers and Ray McDermott, eds. Pp. ix-xvii. Monograph 56. New Haven: Yale Southeast Asia Studies.

2011   "Lines across the Water: The Lasting Power of Colonial Borders in Maritime Southeast Asia." *NEAA (Northeastern Anthropological Association) Bulletin* (Fall): 7-17.

2012a   The Achievement of the Medieval Hour and the Alleged Emergence of the Modern Mind. Unpublished ms.

2012b   "How to Be a Tribe in the Southern Philippines during the Advent of NGO's

and the Invention of the Indigenous." Unpublished ms.
2013   *The Cultural Work of Borders: Essays in the Ethnographic Study of Cognitive Systems in Action.* (in preparation)
Garfinkel, Harold
1967   *Studies in Ethnomethodology.* Englewood Cliffs: Prentice-Hall.
Goethe, Johann Wolfgang von
1807   *Faust, Part One.* Oxford: Oxford University Press. [1987]
Goodenough, Ward
1956   "Residence Rules." *Southwestern Journal of Anthropology* 12: 22-37.
Grafton, Anthony
1997   *The Footnote.* Cambridge: Harvard University Press.
Herbert, Robert
2004   *Seurat and the Making of* La Grande Jatte. Chicago: The Art Institute of Chicago.
Howes, Alan, ed.
1974   *Sterne: The Critical Heritage.* London: Routledge & Kegan Paul.
Hughes, Gertrude
1984   *Emerson's Demanding Optimism.* Baton Rouge: Louisiana State University Press.
Iser, Wolfgang
1988   *Laurence Sterne: Tristram Shandy.* Cambridge: Cambridge University Press.
Johnson, Samuel
1759   *The History of Rasselas, Prince of Abissinia.* Oxford: Oxford University Press. [2009]
Joyce, James
1922   *Ulysses.* New York: Modern Library. [1961]
1939   *Finnegans Wake.* New York: Viking.
Keymer, Thomas
2002   *Sterne, the Moderns, and the Novel.* Oxford: Oxford University Press.
2009   "Introduction." In Samuel Johnson, *The History of Rasselas, Prince of Abissinia.* Pp. ix-xxxiv. Oxford: Oxford University Press.
Kuipers, Joel and Ray McDermott
2007   "Ethnographic Responsibility." In Harold C. Conkiln. *Fine Description: Ethnographic and Linguistic Essays.* Joel Kuipers and Ray McDermott, eds. Monograph 56. Pp. 1-24. New Haven: Yale Southeast Asia Studies.
Leonard, Anne
2010   "Sterne, Sutton, and Bohemia." *The Shandean* 21: 35-45.
Locke, John
1706   *An Essay Concerning Human Understanding.* Fifth edition. London: Penguin. [2004]
Lynch, Jack
2000   "The Relicks of Learning: Sterne among the Renaissance Encyclopedists." *Eighteenth-Century Fiction* 13: 1-20.
MacDiarmid, Hugh
1955   "In Memoriam James Joyce." In *The Complete Poems of Hugh MacDiarmid.* Michael Grieve and W.R. Atkin, eds. Vol. 2. Pp. 737-889. London: Martin Brian & O'Keefe. [1978]
MacKenzie, Scott

2005   *"Homunculus Economicus*: Laurence Sterne's Labour Theory of Literary Value." *Eighteenth-Century Fiction* 18: 49-86.
Mandeville, Bernard
1732   *The Fable of the Bees: Or, Private Vices, Publick Benefits*. 2 vols. Oxford: Oxford University Press. [1924]
Marx, Karl
1837   *Scorpion and Felix*. http://en.wikipedia.org/wiki/Scorpion_and_Felix
1867   *Capital*. London: Penguin. [1976]
McDermott, Ray
1997   "Conklin, Joyce, and the Wannaknów." *American Anthropologist* 99: 257-260.
2004   "Materials for a Confrontation with Genius as a Personal Identity." *Ethos* 32: 278-288.
2010   "The Passions of Learning in Tight Circumstances." *National Society for the Study of Education* 109(1): 144-159.
McDermott, Ray and Meghan McDermott
2010   "'One aneither': A Joycean Critique of Educational Research," *Journal of Educational Controversy* 5, no. 1, (2010).
http://www.wce.wwu.edu.Resources/CEP/eJournal/v005n001/
McDermott, Ray and Jason Raley
2011   "Looking Closely: Toward a Natural History of Human Ingenuity." In *The Sage Handbook of Visual Research Methods*. Pp. 272-291. Eric Margolis and Luc Pauwels, eds. Thousand Oaks, CA: Sage.
Merton, Robert
1993   *On the Shoulders of Giants: A Shandean Postscript*. Post-Italianate edition. Chicago: University of Chicago Press.
Metzger, Duane and Gerald Williams
1963   "Tenejapa Medicine I: The Curer." *Southwestern Journal of Anthropology* 19: 216-34.
Nagle, Christopher
2003   "Sterne, Shelley, and Sensibility's Pleasures of Proximity." *English Literary History* 70: 813-845.
New, Melvyn
1997   "Notes." In Laurence Sterne, *The Life and Opinions of Tristram Shandy, Gentleman*. Pp. 597-735. Second edition. London: Penguin.
Nietzsche, Friedrich
1886   *Human, All Too Human*. Second edition. Cambridge: Cambridge University Press. [1996]
Parnell, Tim
2003   "Introduction." In Laurence Sterne, *A Sentimental Journey and Other Writings*. Pp. vii-xxxiii. Oxford: Oxford University Press.
Patrick, Duncan
2003   "Character and Chronology in *Tristram Shandy* (1)." *The Shandean* 14: 39-70.
Plato
1949   *Meno*. New York: Liberal Arts Press.
Posner, Roland
1979   "Semiotic Paradoxes in Language Use, with Particular Reference to *Tristram*

Shandy." *The Eighteenth Century* 20: 148-164.

Prior, Karen
2011 "*Embawdiment: Tristram Shandy* and the Paradox of Incarnation." *The Shanean* 22: 116-131.

Ross, Ian
2001 *Laurence Sterne: A Life.* Oxford: Oxford University Press.

Rossi-Landi, Ferruccio
1973 *Ideologies of Linguistic Relativity.* The Hague: Mouton.

Rowson, Martin
1996 *The Life and Opinions of Tristram Shandy, Gentleman.* London: SelfMadeHero. [2010]
2003 A Comic Book Version of *Tristram Shandy. The Shandean* 14:104-121.
Royal Anthropological Institute
1951 *Notes on Queries in Anthropology.* Sixth edition. London: Routledge and Kegan Paul.

Russell, Bertrand
1903 *The Principles of Mathematics.* London: George Allen & Unwin.

Rutherford, Danilyn
2012 "Kinky Empiricism." *Cultural Anthropology* 27: 465-479.

Said, Edward
1976 "On Repetition." In *The Literature of Fact.* Angus Fletcher, ed. Pp. 138-158. New York: Columbia University Press.

Sapir, Edward
1944 "Grading." In *Selected Writing of Edward Sapir.* David Mandlebaum, ed. Pp. 122-149. Berkeley: University of California Press.

Sartillot, Claudette
1995 *Citation and Modernity: Derrida, Joyce, and Brecht.* Norman, OK: University of Oklahoma Press.

Shakespeare, William
1600 *Hamlet.* New York: Modern Library. [2008]

Sichel, Walter
1910 *Sterne: A Study.* New York: Haskell House. [1971]

Smith, Adam
1776 *The Wealth of Nations.* New York: Random House, 1994.

Sterne, Laurence
1759-1767 *The Life and Opinions of Tristram Shandy, Gentleman.* London: Penguin. [1997]
1768 *A Sentimental Journey through France and Italy.* Oxford: Oxford University Press. [1928]

Stewart, Kathleen
2012 "Precarity's Forms." *Cultural Anthropology* 27: 518-526.

Stewart, Neil
2001 "Notes on Noses: Laurence Sterne and Nikolai Gogol." *Arcadia* 36: 143-155.

Stocking, George
1971 "What's in a Name? The Origins of the Royal Anthropological Institute (183 1871)." *Man* 6: 369-390.

Thirlwell, Adam
2010 "Reproduction." *The Shandean* 21: 9-34.

Vernon, John
  1984   *Money and Fiction: Literary Realism in the Nineteenth and Early Twentieth Century*. Ithaca: Cornell University Press.
Waley, Arthur
  1949   *The Life and Times of Po Chu-I, 772-846 A.D.* London: Allen & Unwin.
Watts, Carol
  2007   *The Cultural Work of Empire: The Seven Years' War and the Imagining of the Shandean State*. Toronto: University of Toronto Press.
Wheen, Francis
  1999   *Karl Marx: A Life*. New York: W.W. Norton.
Whorf, Benjamin Lee
  1941   "The Relation of Habitual Thought and Behavior to Language." In *Language, Thought, and Reality*. John Carroll, ed. Pp. 134-159. Cambridge: MIT Press. [1956]
Wieder, D. Lawrence
  1970   "On Meaning by Rule." In *Understanding Everyday Life*. Jack Douglas, ed. Pp. 107-135. Chicago: Aldine.
Woolf, Virginia
  1928   Introduction to Laurence Sterne, *A Sentimental Journey through France and Italy*. Pp. v-xvii. Oxford: Oxford University Press.
Yeats, William Butler
  1934   "Letter to Horace Mason Reynolds." In *The Collected Works of W. B. Yeats*, vol. 7: *Letters to the New Island*. George Bornstein and Hugh Witemeyer, eds. Pp. xviii. New York: Macmillan, 1989.
Young, Edward
  1759   *Conjectures on Original Composition*. Manchester: Manchester University Press. [1918]
Zahavi, Dan
  2003   *Husserl's Phenomenology*. Stanford: Stanford University Press.

Photo 2.1. Walter Shandy Engages Structure and Emergence.
With permission of SelfMadeHero.

Chapter 3

Reading Defoe, the Eighteenth-Century Master Story-teller

MARY-ELIZABETH REEVE

The travel narrative has fascinated generations of audiences. When Defoe published his first novel, *Robinson Crusoe*, in 1719, this tale of sea voyage and survival was an instant sensation. *Robinson Crusoe* was followed in quick succession by a number of other memoir-style novels that have made their mark on English literature. Defoe has been described as the first English novelist, ushering in with his fiction a new reality-based story-telling style. Defoe spent the majority of his writing career as a pamphleteer and newspaper writer. It was not until he was almost sixty years old that he wrote *Robinson Crusoe*. However, it is precisely the finely tuned eye for a "story" that marks Defoe's genius, and why an anthropologist would find his works of genuine interest.

This chapter will examine three of Defoe's major works: *A Journal of the Plague Year* (1722), *Robinson Crusoe* (1719), and *Moll Flanders* (1722) for what they tell us not only of English urban and sea-faring life during the mid-seventeenth to early eighteenth centuries, but what they also tell us about the social values of the time, and the critical perspective of the writer. Defoe wrote in plain, unvarnished prose. His novels are devoid of literary artifice and read instead like memoirs and documentaries. If we read him aware that we are reading a newspaperman's story his realist writing allows us to dig easily into the facts and situations representative of life as it was truly lived at the time, in a sense, an ethnographic reality written down almost 300 years ago. Yet, as with modern ethnography, the voice of the author comes through. Defoe tried to distance himself from his writing, but the stories that he chose to tell, and the order of their telling, gives voice to a view of the world that was at once liberal and deeply religious, pragmatic and yet humane. In much of his writing, we hear the voice of an emerging middle class sensibility that was to storm old Europe and the new America, culminating in the American and French revolutions. Defoe was a thinker of his time—yet many aspects of his worldview are surprisingly modern. We are inheritors of that worldview, which produced the social upheavals that shook the old European social order to its foundations. For this reason, Defoe speaks to us from another world in a language that we understand, yet with enough distance in perspective and experience as to make reading his works intriguing, as well as pleasurable.

Defoe was the master of what I will refer to as the *epic survivor tale*, a fictional memoir that is both a thriller and a testimony to human ingenuity and the will to survive. Over the short period from 1719 through 1724, Defoe wrote six major epic survivor tales, beginning with his most famous: *The Life and Strange Surprising Adventures of Robinson Crusoe, of York, Written by Himself* (1719) and continuing with *The Life, Adventures, and Piracies, of the Famous Captain Singleton, Memoirs of a Cavalier*, (both 1720), *The History of Colonial Jack*; *A Journal of the Plague Year*; *The Fortunes and Misfortunes of the Famous Moll Flanders*, (all in 1722), and *The Fortunate Mistress: or, Roxanna* (1724). Both *Colonial Jack* and *Moll Flanders* are considered picaresque novels. Defoe's novels appeared between his work as an accomplished and influential pamphleteer and newspaper journalist, and his work as a writer of treatises on subjects ranging from moral conduct, such as his *The Family Instructor* (1715) and *The New Family Instructor* (1727); on trade, among which are his *A General History of Discoveries and Improvements* (1727); *A Tour Through the Whole Island of Great Britain* (three volumes—1724-27) and several works on the supernatural, among these: *The History of the Devil* (1726), and *An Essay on the History and Reality of Apparitions* (1727). Defoe's novelistic writing was influenced by his political, economic and social critiques—one of which, *The Shortest Way with the Dissenters* (1702), a satire, was received with such intense displeasure from the monarchy under Queen Anne that he was pilloried and then spent time in London's Newgate Prison. He was released only through the intercession of influential friends. Defoe was himself a survivor, his political, economic and religious treatises, and his vast personal experience combined to provide a wealth of material for his epic survivor tales.

Defoe wrote during a tumultuous time that spanned the religious struggles in England during the 1600s well into what is known as "the Long Eighteenth Century," the period of the Enlightenment.[1] As a young man he witnessed the "Glorious Revolution," the overthrow of Catholic King James and crowning of Protestant William and Mary in 1688. The Glorious Revolution ended Catholic power in England and "could be seen as rescuing all freeborn Englishmen from the threat of enslavement to popish tyranny."[2] This freedom was conceived as a basic human right and a fundamental element of civilization.[3]

This moment in history is associated with the origins of liberalism as espoused by John Locke, religious toleration of Protestant sects, and the creation of a new kind of modern state marked by a transformation for agrarian to manufacturing society.[4] Yet these social and intellectual stirrings germinated within the context of warfare. The Glorious Revolution was followed by two major wars in Europe: King William's War (1689-97) and the War of Spanish Succession (1702-14), and in England, major conflict between "Whigs" and "Tories" in which Defoe became embroiled by espousing Whig sentiments.[5] In Defoe's work we can also see the influence of the "religious enlightenment," that view espousing a middle way of reasonable belief, embracing toleration of competing religions and dissenting sects, but not Catholicism or Judaism.[6] The view rejected evangelical Protestantism and Counter-reformation Catholicism; both were regarded as driven by enthusiasm and superstition, rather than reason in which science could account for the "causal coherence of the providential order."[7]

The Emergence of the Realist Novel as a New Literary Form

Against the backdrop of the tumultuous "Long Eighteenth Century," Defoe, together with Richardson and Fielding created a new literary form, the novel. The development of the novel was an outgrowth of social changes taking place during the mid-seventeenth and eighteenth centuries, leading up to and encompassing the Enlightenment Period.[8] The novel broke with earlier literary tradition in that the plots were not taken from extant art forms such as mythology, legend, history, or earlier literature, but rather focused on individual lived experience as reality.[9] This early novel form became known as the Realist Novel. "Realism" was a product of a new way of looking at the world and at humanity, perhaps triggered in some fundamental sense by an attempt to assimilate a new world view following the era of discovery in the sixteenth and early seventeenth centuries, and expressed in the new philosophical realism that marked the Enlightenment Period. Realism was a product of a more detached scientific view of the world in which the truth about matter, nature, and humanity was discoverable through individual senses and reason, freed from traditional beliefs and assumptions.[10] Defoe achieved his realistic plots by focusing on individual lives, constructing purportedly autobiographical memoirs and allowing the plot to be shaped by the temporal trajectory of the lives thus portrayed, a portrayal drawn against a background of realistic physical and social environments. In this Defoe achieved "an important new tendency in fiction."[11]

The realism of Defoe's novels is of course why they are immediately appealing to twentieth century anthropologists. In a very real sense, the novels offer the anthropologist insights into social worlds of the past in the same way as archival materials may be studied, but with the added dimension of belief systems expressed in the thoughts and actions of the characters. In that sense, they are akin to oral tradition, in its aim to shape the listener's understanding of the world through the recounting of life stories and events in a way that both entertains and instructs. To set the stage for this instruction, Defoe created liminal characters—existing outside of the normal social sphere (e.g. Crusoe on a deserted island, Flanders as an orphan, and the city of London in the crisis of epidemic contagion), such that value systems are highlighted in the characters' struggles to re-integrate with society.

For the anthropologist, such epics are rich ethnographic material that can be mined for an understanding of daily life, knowledge, and values of mid-seventeenth to early eighteenth century England. Aside from the minute details of material culture, trade, shipping, financial, and legal practices, we also learn of the deep schism between Catholicism and Protestantism, especially in *Robinson Crusoe*, and between Dissenters and the Church of England in *A Journal of the Plague Year*. In *Robinson Crusoe*, we are given an unvarnished view of colonialism and the attitudes of European peoples toward both Sub-Saharan Africans and Native Americans. In *Moll Flanders*, we confront in gut-wrenching detail the plight of a lone woman attempting to achieve and maintain the status of a gentlewoman in mid-seventeenth century England. In *Robinson Crusoe* and *Moll Flanders*, we see clearly the high value that Defoe placed on a middle-class status, especially if it can be brought to the level of the life of a gentleman or gentlewoman. This is a time when the middle class was rapidly developing into a political and economic force beyond that of the medieval tradesman.

A Journal of the Plague Year, intended to read as a memoir of the Great Plague that hit London in 1665, is a carefully researched work that has been accredited as the most reliable record extant of the Great Plague. Here we see a society torn down to its elemental core through what is now an unthinkable event: an epidemic of bubonic plague in a major European city. Not only do we now understand the etiologic agent of plague and how it may be controlled, but we understand the mechanisms by which plague is spread and therefore how to prevent an isolated case from becoming an epidemic. Here it is modern science that separates us, and gives us an appreciation of the place from which the religious and moral concerns of the seventeenth and eighteenth century emanated.

Defoe's religiosity, and in particular his view of the importance of seeking redemption and forgiveness for misdeeds, permeates the novels. His is a very personal sort of belief between self and God, and as such was very much attuned to the religious thinking of the Dissenters. Coupled with this religiosity, what Defoe addresses in all three works is the indomitable human spirit, the will to survive, if not thrive, through adversity by its own wits; a force forged into timeless characters as appealing to the twenty-first century reader as they were to the readers of his own time.

In reading Defoe, I asked four questions of each novel: What can it tell us about how life was lived; what can it tell us about the values of the time as evinced by the author through his characters; what can it tell us about the motives of the author in writing the story; and how do these motives link into the wider social and political currents of the time of writing. These questions emerged from my work in analysis of historical documents and an awareness of the need to place such works of non-fiction within the wider social and political milieu of the time, in order to understand and respect the motives of the author in recording what he chose to record and conversely, what was not recorded, and thereby lost to time and memory.

A Journal of the Plague Year

Of the three novels under consideration, *A Journal of the Plague Year* comes closest to an historical document and was the first of Defoe's work to catch my attention. In this novel, Defoe employs the artifice of the narrator, a London merchant, presenting a journal of his year lived in London during the Great Plague. There is some indication that the journal which Defoe constructs may have been based on writings of his uncle, Henry Foe, as it is signed "HF."[12] However, it is clear that the narrative is founded on careful research into the plague utilizing medical texts and other records of the time, including parish records of numbers and causes of deaths.

The Journal is written against the long European experience of Bubonic plague epidemics. Bubonic plague epidemics started with the Black Death in the fourteenth century and continued through the eighteenth century, although the Levant suffered earlier with the Justinian plague which began in Egypt in c. 542 and ended in the eighth century.[13] Europeans were therefore familiar with epidemics when the Black Death appeared in 1347-48. The Black Death was chronicled by Italian luminaries from Petrarch, who described the death and desolation left by the plague to Boccaccio, who attributed the plague to either the influence of the stars, or the wrath of God.[14] Following the Black Death, there were at least seventeen outbreaks of bubonic plague in London between 1500 and the Great Plague of 1665.[15]

The writing in *A Journal* is intentionally unemotional, shifting like a drum beat between descriptions of the event and statistics on deaths. Defoe provides us with a description of the plague and its spread; presents ideas about infection and contagion; describes people's reactions; and dwells to a considerable extent on the official orders for control and management, with critical commentary (mostly supportive) of the effectiveness of these official orders. Yet, he digs deeper into the psyche of the people enduring the plague by examining the tension between understanding the plague as the hand of God versus astrological prediction, and its attendant, blind faith. Although he is less explicit, he also grapples with the tension between understanding the plague as a punishment sent from God and scientific reasoning as to its cause and spread.

The author's purpose in writing is clear. Through the narrator, he states that the reason for publishing a journal of the Great Plague is to provide advice in the event of another plague. Defoe timed his writing to appeal to the public, publishing during a scare in London (1720-22) when plague broke out in Marseilles.[16] The London city government proposed to move infected individuals by force to pest houses and to station troops around London with the purpose of shooting anyone who tried to escape to the countryside; a plan that produced a public outcry.[17] Defoe's *Journal* can be read as a response to this plan and an appeal for consideration of less violent control measures. His writing takes a pragmatic view, informed by the understanding that the plague has natural causes and therefore can be managed through appropriate government actions, a stance that places Defoe clearly within the reasoned thinking of his time.[18]

Defoe's aim was likely as much to produce a best seller, as to provide information for the public good. Defoe's narrator states clearly over and over that the intent is to describe events just as they occurred, without exaggeration, and the narrative holds to that promise. Yet, he uses the text as an opportunity for social criticism. He notes that at the height of the plague, people laid aside other concerns and Dissenters were able to preach to great crowds within the churches, due to a scarcity of Anglican preachers, as many had either died or fled into the country.[19]

> Indeed, the zeal which they showed in coming [to church], and the earnestness and affection that they showed in their attention to what they heard, made it manifest what a value people would all put upon the worship of God if they thought every day they attended at the church that it would be their last . . . Nor was it without strange effects, for it took away all manner of prejudice at or scruple about the person whom they found in the pulpit when they came to the churches … But as the terror of the infection abated, those things all returned again to their less desirable channel and to the course they were in before.[20]

In his dry, yet suspenseful descriptive style, Defoe details the first outbreak of plague in the winter, the first few deaths recorded, then the long months in which nothing more seems to happen, followed by the sudden reappearance of the plague in adjoining neighborhoods and its rapid spread as the weather warms in spring into summer. He details the peoples' reactions and the acts of civil authorities to control the population as the plague engulfs the city of London, and later spreads out into the countryside. For the epidemiologist, a close reading of the spread of the plague, the statistics and the treatment of the sick and dead is interesting, as are the various theories about disease etiology and spread presented by the narrator. For the student of government in crisis, the acts of city government and reactions of the people make sobering reading. For the historian, Defoe sets the story within the times, particularly the tension between the Church of England and the Dissenters. For the ethnographer, the descriptions of London itself, its social classes and the variation in options and beliefs open to people based on class, the details of trade, of life in the city and in the countryside, and of the ways in which a severe moral and civic crisis is handled overall provides a fine-grained glimpse into a past that is, over the roughly 350 years since the Great Plague, now part of another culture.

Defoe begins with a prosaic description of the first cases of bubonic plague, the efforts to cover up the deaths by assigning them to other causes, and the belief by Londoners far from the site of outbreak that they will be spared. As this belief crumbles, he details the flight of the wealthy and their servants out of the city. The narrator discusses the pros and cons of a requirement established by the city government that households stricken with the plague report this fact to local officials, who then quarantine the entire household for forty days and set guards, employing the poor for this task, to prevent the escape of "prisoners" (Defoe's characterization).

The control measures detailed by Defoe in his description of the Great Plague of London have long historical antecedents, and helped to shape not only local administrative structures of European towns and cities, but also laid a foundation for public health practice.[21] For example, by the mid-fifteenth century there existed in Florence and other major north Italian cities a system for recording all deaths and identifying the cause in each case.[22] Mass graves, house detention for infected persons, quarantine of populations and ships, and a public health magistracy were all established by the time of the plagues of the 1600s.[23]

Defoe describes the panic at the height of the plague, when travel from London was prohibited, and of people refused entry into towns and living in the fields, woods and abandoned barns; many he tells us simply dying of starvation. He describes how, despite the efforts of officials, at its height, the plague spread from the city into surrounding towns and outward into the countryside.

Throughout all of this we read the weekly death tolls for various neighborhoods, grim statistics that periodically remind the reader that this is no work of fiction. The narrator even provides us at one point with details of neonatal and maternal mortality, linking these higher than average statistics to the impact of the plague on the health of mothers. We are made to hear the rattle of the death cart, on its nightly rounds through each neighborhood, and to see the grisly lamp-lit scene of mass burial in the enormous pits dug for each neighborhood. To ward off a sense of the incredulous, the narrator details the exact dimensions of the pits, the way the bodies are dumped each night and then covered lightly with soil. He even tells us that some of the bodies wear charms meant to ward off the plague, and that all are dumped indiscriminately, mixing and mingling not just arms and legs, but the poor and wealthier classes together in the pit.

Using the statistics on deaths, he documents the increased virulence of the plague at its height and reduced virulence as the plague begins to abate and a greater percentage of people survive the infection. Rather than write a torrid, emotional account of the Great Plague, the narrator refers to his incapacity to convey to the reader the horror that he felt in all that he saw in the streets, his forays from his shut up house going about the city and, one night, following the death cart.

In dry, matter-of-fact tones, the narrator describes the options for survival of the wealthy, the merchant or middle class, and the poor. While the wealthy had options to leave, the merchants might or might not be able, but could at least provision themselves and their families and shut up their houses against visitors who might introduce the plague. The narrator, a merchant himself, details the difficult personal decision to stay in the city. The poor he tells us, had no capacity to provision themselves for more than a few days at a time, and, with the wealthy gone and trade all but collapsed, there was little work for the poor except that provided through the civil regulations created by civil authorities: work as house guards, nurses, or worse yet, bearers of the dead. The narrator describes the fatalism of the poor, the stark choice that they had between starvation from lack of wages, and work that put them at great risk of death from the plague. Defoe recognizes that social structures converge with the presence of plague to magnify risk for some and lessen it for others, what has been termed a "syndemic" approach.[24] He critiques social class barriers by demonstrating the higher risk of death born by the poor. He was also acutely aware of the role of social networks in the spread of disease, as the pattern of disease spread converged with these networks.

Reflecting Defoe's desire for scientific understanding of the plague, the narrator details attempts to prevent infection: of money dropped in a container of vinegar on its way between buyer and seller, of attempts to purify the air of a home by burning coal, to guard against inhaling the contagion. The narrator discusses the pros and cons of these approaches, referring to opinions held by his knowledgeable physician friend, Dr. Heath. He muses about various theories of contagion: that it is spread by invisible organisms in the air; that it is in the clothing of the people, and in bundles of cloth. He notes that there was greater risk of infection in the areas of the meat markets. He wonders about whether or not it is spread person to person or through some intermediary agent. Understanding of the route of bubonic plague infection was not achieved until the end of the nineteenth century. Belief in contagion via miasmas and fulminates (clothing and bedding) dictated many of the practices that Defoe details in the *Journal.*

More to his purpose, Defoe uses the plague narrative as a platform for telling morality tales, stories about individuals that illustrate examples he wishes his readers to heed. In classic Defoe style, he provides us, in the middle of the narrative, with an epic survival tale of three men who pool meager resources and set out for the countryside, surviving against all odds through their knowledge, their cunning and their leadership skills. Defoe uses the epic survival tale of the three men to heighten the drama of the narrative, and as a vehicle for moral instruction. "Their story has a moral in every part of it, and their whole conduct, and that of some whom they joined with, is a pattern for all poor men to follow, or women, either, if ever such a time comes again; and if there was no other end in recording it, I think this a very just one, whether my account be exactly according to fact or no."[25]

In the novel, Defoe combines his matter-of-fact descriptions as a guide for conduct in the event of another plague, with a liberal critique of society and his scientific curiosity about the epidemic. He leavens all of this with a strong religious perspective that considers the Great Plague as God's judgment of the city of London and its people, and God's vengeance on the city as a call to repentance. In exploring the moral dimension of the plague, Defoe provides evidence indicating that sinners and innocents alike fell to the plague, refuting the belief that individual deaths were a sign of earlier transgressions. Defoe instead writes of a punishment by God visited on an entire city. This was not original to Defoe. Europeans saw plague as part of the "providential order of things."[26]

The theme of God's judgment and repentance is characteristic of Defoe's novels. In focusing on individual acts of repentance, he first used it to great effect in *Robinson Crusoe*, and made it the central moral lesson of his later work, *Moll Flanders*.

The Life and Strange Surprising Adventures of Robinson Crusoe of York, Mariner, Written by Himself

Robinson Crusoe can be seen as belonging to the body of travel writing that emerged in the late seventeenth and eighteenth centuries. These stories are not simply a particular form of colonial discourse, but "as texts that are symptomatic of the changes in the perception of the world taking place in the sixteenth and seventeenth centuries and which constitute the 'modernity' of the early modern period."[27] In the Age of Enlightenment, these stories, of either real or imagined journeys, were a means to explore the self; subjectivity and identity at a personal and social level, through relating tales of exotic other places and peoples.[28] Equally, Defoe aimed to instruct his readers with the moral lessons derivable from the suffering, repentance, and deliverance of his character.[29] This travel account was written with "a deep sense of religious design."[30] For Defoe, the relationship of self to God was of paramount importance.[31]

In true journalist fashion, Defoe modeled the story of Robinson Crusoe on the account of a seaman, Alexander Selkirk, who spent five years (1704-1709) alone on the island of Mas-a-tierra, off the coast of Chile.[32] In adapting Selkirk's account to the novel, Defoe changed the name of the seaman, of course, but he also dramatically altered the location of the island, placing it instead off the coast of Venezuela. He altered other critical frames the story, most notably lengthening the seaman's stay to over twenty-eight years, and making him the sole survivor of a shipwreck, who managed to struggle on-shore to the island.

Defoe's work was an overnight success. It was his first novel, and launched a period of highly prolific writing. Using his fine sense of the dramatic, Defoe, at the end of *Robinson Crusoe*, left open the possibility that the reader would hear more of Crusoe's story. Defoe did follow up with two sequels, *Further Adventures of Robinson Crusoe* (1719), and *Serious Reflections during the Life and Surprising Adventures of Robinson Crusoe* (1720).

Robinson Crusoe can be read simply and enjoyably as the epic survivor tale that it is; a genre which continues to this day to be a highly popular form of entertainment. However, Defoe writes from the early 1700s and there is much that can be teased out from the narrative that provides the ethnographer with information about the material culture of the time, patterns of trade, legal frameworks for property acquisition and protection, and the values of the time. In that sense, the modern reader with an interest in history and ethnography may find the narrative even more fascinating than did Defoe's first audience.

In this story, we are treated to a description of material culture, family life, patterns of inheritance, trade and seafaring life, the fragility of communication consisting solely of letters and packets carried by ship or overland, the establishment of Brazilian plantations, as well as the hazards of both sea and overland travel. The reader gains insight into a wide swath of daily life, from family dynamics, to the details of handling a large sailing vessel in a storm; to how a young sea merchant could make money on trip to Africa, selling goods there with about a ten-fold profit; as well as the reality of piracy and slavery. Once Crusoe is shipwrecked, we are given, in minute detail, information about all of the items that he manages to take out of wreckage and their uses on shore. These descriptions would have been, on the one hand, familiar to the reader and less interesting than they are for us. But on the other hand, the moral lessons contained within the story are perhaps less accessible to the casual reader of today than they were to Defoe's contemporaries.

Crusoe is the quintessential survivor. Defoe introduces the character of the survivor as he describes Crusoe's escape after living as a slave for several years in North Africa. Crusoe's African adventure as a slave may seem surprising to us, as something hardly credible. However, it is a little known fact that there were a large number of Europeans, including citizens of England, enslaved by Muslims in North Africa during the seventeenth and eighteenth centuries.[33] We see Crusoe use cunning and trickery to aid in his escape from slavery, and when he is shipwrecked off the coast of Venezuela, he is the sole survivor in part because he figures out how to escape drowning by riding consecutive waves to shore.

The story is not only an epic survivor tale, but its focal narrative is that of a master-trope; the sea voyage, which touched the fancy of the people of Europe in what was still an age of discovery and colonization in far-off, exotic places; places with strange weather, plants, animals, and above all, with strange people who practiced cannibalism and other acts that lay, in their minds, outside the reach of God's grace. Defoe had much to work with as he wove his tale for the European imagination.

In the novel, we find three major themes that reappear in both *A Journal of the Plague Year* and *Moll Flanders*. These are: the desirability of belonging to the middle station (a gentrified middle class) rather than either extreme of wealth or poverty; the belief that hard work, diligence and ingenuity can overcome the greatest personal challenges integral to the epic survivor tale; and finally, that experience of such hardship can bring a person into discovery of God's grace in a highly personal and direct way.[34]

Crusoe takes to the sea as a young man in defiance of his parents' wish for him, which is that he should enter trade and carry on the middle class life into which he was born. While at first Crusoe does experience success as a merchant seaman, an attack by pirates reduces him to the status of a slave living in North Africa. At this point, he looked back to his father's advice as prophetic and he laments that "the hand of Heaven had overtaken me, and I was undone without redemption."[35] Defoe gives his character another chance. Escaping from slavery, Crusoe lands in Brazil, where he becomes a naturalized citizen and purchases land. Becoming a successful planter, he now has a chance to live as his father advised, comfortably in what Defoe refers to as the "middle station." Nevertheless, he abandons that chance for further adventure, foreshadowing the disaster of the shipwreck and life on the island. "I was still to be the willful agent of all my own miseries ... I had to leave the happy view I had of being a rich and thriving man in my new plantation, only to pursue a rash and immoderate desire of rising faster than the nature of the thing admitted."[36] Defoe's message to the reader is clear: that in an internal personal struggle of will against reason, if will triumphs over reason, the person is the agent of his or her own misfortune.

Once on the island, Defoe provides his character with plenty of leisure time to reflect on his follies, but it is only after falling very ill that he attempts to pray to God. Defoe is making the point that there is no religiosity in his character, being one who prays incoherently and only during times of severe fright. Crusoe reads a bible which he salvaged from the ship and finally awakens to the realization that he was "wicked and profane to the last degree" and had no knowledge of God.[37] Here Defoe clearly warns his readers of the miseries to be expected from such a condition, which he calls a "certain stupidity of soul" being unconscious of either good or evil.[38] Robinson Crusoe can also be read as a captivity narrative. Crusoe certainly laments his captivity on the island, isolated from the rest of the world, and rejoices in his eventual rescue by a European trading ship. In this reading, the story of captivity and rescue/freedom is the temporal and secular dimension of his spiritual journey from bondage in sin to repentance and deliverance.[39]

However, Defoe does not belabor the story with moral lessons. A major portion of the narrative is a description, in minute detail, of how Crusoe sets up his dwellings, learns to hunt and gather food, and his explorations around the island. Crusoe writes in his journal of his loneliness, measuring his good fortune at finding himself on an island where he could live comfortably against the reality of being entirely cut off from society.

All of this changes when, in the fifteenth year of his stay on the island while exploring an area remote to his dwelling, Crusoe is surprised to find a footprint on the beach. This revelation of possible other human occupation puts him into a panic, as he fears attack. Watchful, at last he observes a group of people he terms savages arrive in canoes and engage in cannibalism.

> my passions where at first fired by the horror I conceived at the unnatural custom
> of the people of that country; who, it seems, had been suffered by Providence, . . .
> to have no other guide than that of their own abominable and vitiated passions;
> and consequently, were left, . . . to act such horrid things, and receive such dread-
> ful customs, as nothing but Nature, entirely abandoned by Heaven, and actuated
> by some hellish degeneracy, could have run them into.[40]

Crusoe, horrified, wars within himself as to what his proper response should be in the event that they come back. Should he, as a European, kill the savages for their barbarous practices, or as a Christian, leave alone what does not concern him rather than to commit murder. He decides on the latter course, and in the end, saves one man—who becomes "Friday"—from being a victim. Defoe is making clear here the primacy of religious belief over the prevailing European social values. Defoe is equally clear that his religious belief is a very personal sort of Protestantism, in keeping with his Dissenter views. Crusoe, while musing on the religious beliefs and practices which Friday (who learns English) describes among his people, and in particular the existence of pagan priests, comments that the practice of making a secret of religion, which he terms "priestcraft," is followed not only by the Roman [Catholics] but also by the "most brutish and barbarous savages."[41] Crusoe's musings on the link between Catholic and pagan rituals was not original to Defoe. As early a figure as Luther regarded papism as another form of paganism. By the seventeenth and eighteenth centuries, Catholicism was critiqued by virtue of this perceived affinity to pagan religions, a critique in which pagan and Catholic practice were seen to converge under the umbrella of "paganopapism"[42] in contrast to Protestant belief and practice.[43]

For all of Crusoe's liberal view of human justice, he exhibits the European attitude prevalent at the time, an uncritical view of the superiority of European customs and material culture over that of native peoples. While Crusoe is inept at building a canoe, he nonetheless carries it out with an idea of improving the technique, using an axe to carve out the interior, rather than burning it out as he had seen done by native peoples. In the same vain, he is not happy with hand-shaped pottery, but must invent a pottery wheel. European attitudes are further evidenced in his choice of a name for the escaped native captive whom he helps rescue, calling him Friday. Friday is not granted the status of person by being given a person's name; he is simply named for the day of the week, according to Crusoe's reckoning, that they first met. In a direct reversal of the practical, but in keeping with Defoe's concept of European superiority over native peoples, it is Crusoe who instructs Friday how to live on the island, which is, of course, a foreign environment for Crusoe and not for Friday. The imposition of European practice on this foreign environment is completed by Crusoe himself, who is at pains to grow, from a few chance seeds scattered from a chicken feed bag that he salvaged from the ship, sufficient "corn" (probably barley) to feed himself and Friday. Having found early on a number of feral goats on the island, Crusoe also manages to develop animal husbandry so that by his eleventh year on the island, he has meat, milk, and most remarkably, cheese and butter as well.

In keeping with the imposition of a European worldview, Crusoe describes his "country seat," his "corn land," and his "enclosures for [his] cattle, that is to say, [his] goats," as if this was an estate in England.[44] Crusoe does not, however, construct a homestead, but rather a fortress, against the possibility of attacks by hostiles (native or other). After seeing the arrival of native peoples, he constructs a double fortification at his fortress in the event of an attack, taking, he tells us, five years to perfect this fortification. Crusoe's transformation of his island is "human landscape gardening."[45]

Crusoe's worldview is superimposed upon this tropical island not only in terms of subsistence and social relations with native peoples, but also with regard to the few Europeans who straggle onto the island. Defoe combines class and religion in Crusoe's musings about his island, once there are three additional inhabitants.

> My island was peopled, and I thought myself very rich in subjects . . . how like a king I looked . . . I had undoubted right of dominion [over the country] . . . my people were perfectly subjected . . . they owed their lives to me . . . I had but three subjects, and they were of three different religions . . . a Protestant . . . a pagan . . . and a Papist . . . However, I allowed liberty of conscience throughout my dominion.[46]

Defoe used the master-trope of sea voyage to explore and critically examine, through the eyes and life of his central character, the prevailing social order of early eighteenth century Europe. This is a world marked by rigid social class boundaries, a world in which he could detail the horrors of human cruelty while at the same time, provide insight into an emerging political economy that permitted a meteoric rise in fortune made possible through voyages to distant lands. The successful outcome of struggles experienced by Crusoe hinged on an emerging individualism and appreciation of the goodness of one's own labor. The world that Defoe described is distant, yet the character is familiar to us.

Robinson Crusoe has stood the test of time as a great novel, perhaps the first great novel. It has fired the imagination of many generations and inspired other writers to focus on the sea voyage as a vehicle for powerful storytelling. With Robinson Crusoe, Defoe pioneered the epic survivor tale, a story form that he deftly employed not only to entertain his readership, but also to instruct. Here we see Defoe most clearly, as a thinker rooted in the religious struggles dating from the fifteenth century; but also standing on the cusp of the modern era, at once deeply religious, while espousing new ideas that celebrated the emerging middle class and put a high value on individual freedom. The anthropologist has much to discover in a close reading, not only about life as it was lived by seafaring Europeans in the eighteenth century, but also about the intellectual currents then swirling about Europe, some of which were to define the Enlightenment, and ultimately become part of a modern ethos that is familiar to us.

The Fortunes and Misfortunes of the Famous Moll Flanders

In *Moll Flanders*, Defoe explored the feminine of the epic survivor tale. It is a credit to his versatility as a writer that he was able to do so convincingly. As in *A Journal of the Plague Year* and *Robinson Crusoe*, *Moll Flanders* is a first person narrative of harrowing life experience. In this narrative, the character (Moll Flanders) is telling not just about one year, or even of twenty-eight years, but of her entire life experience up to the date of her memoir, when she is almost seventy years old. On one level, Moll Flanders appears as the feminine version of a Robinson Crusoe type of character, suffering grave misfortunes and making sustained heroic efforts to overcome them. Flanders, like Crusoe, displays the qualities of intelligence, initiative, refusal to accept defeat, and cunning in dealings with others that mark the protagonists of the epic survival tale. Here, however, the similarities end, and we can begin an examination of the status of women in seventeenth century England, told from the perspective of a woman who has no claim to family, a profound social disadvantage.

The "central problem" of the narrative is the few opportunities available to women of any rank in seventeenth and eighteenth century England.[47] Flanders is seen to focus her efforts on managing her circumstances, and shows that good management can have a transforming power in a person's life, a viewpoint that Defoe introduced in *Robinson Crusoe*.[48] Defoe presents this optimistic view while at the same time, detailing a life story that exists both as a severe critique of social strictures, especially as they existed for women, orphans, and the poor, and also of the vast capacity for human failings and their attendant tragic consequences. This multifaceted story is at once difficult to read and highly revealing of life as lived by women in seventeenth century England.

A decline in the status and rights of women occurred in European society during the sixteenth and early seventeenth centuries. During the first half of the sixteenth century, a woman's right to hold and dispose of her own property was limited to what she could lay specific claim to in a marriage contract. Otherwise, all of her property was controlled by her husband.[49] Defoe used both *Moll Flanders* and a later novel, *The Fortunate Mistress: or, Roxanna* to explore the precarious status of women in seventeenth and eighteenth century England. Roxanna laments that through the marriage contract a wife was forced to "give up liberty, estate, authority, and everything to a man, and the woman was indeed a mere woman ever after—this is to say a slave!"[50] Here again Defoe is preoccupied with captivity and slavery. *Moll Flanders* is, in this sense, a captivity tale around a long struggle for emancipation, similar to that of *Robinson Crusoe.*

The character Moll Flanders is an orphan, born of a thief serving a term in London's Newgate Prison. Living in an orphanage at the age of eight, she is appointed by the local parish elders to become a house servant. She protests, and here we see the first indication of an indomitable spirit, and is finally given permission to remain in the orphanage until she is older. At about twelve years of age, when she again is appointed to become a house servant, she protests saying that she wishes to be a "gentlewoman" or provide for herself independently. Defoe is using irony here, something that his contemporary readers would not have missed. He plays with us, having his character, reflecting the child's partial understanding of a rigid society, insist that to provide for herself is not only far superior to serving in the household of another, but will allow her to gain the rank of gentlewoman. In fact, at the time, a woman who was not born into a gentile family could only hope to attain the status of gentlewoman through marriage to a gentleman. In the rigid social class system characteristic of seventeenth through nineteenth century England, such marriages were rare and were cause for disapprobation. For her insistence on wanting to become a gentlewoman, the child is given a second reprieve from household service, and in a few years is accepted into a gentile home as a kind of step-daughter. She becomes educated in the typically feminine arts of music, dance, and the French language, all of which she learns by observation of the instruction being given to the daughters of the family. So far, she has managed well.[51]

Moll Flanders makes her first serious mistake when she falls in love with one of the sons of the family and begins an affair that through complicated twists and turns, results in her becoming the wife of the other son whom she does not love. The family heartily disapproves of the union. Marriage was used by the urban merchant classes during the sixteenth and seventeenth centuries to solidify commercial relationships, a practice that began to weaken in the late eighteenth century.[52] Moll Flanders is in part a cautionary tale for merchant families against such weakening alliances and in part an exploration of the constraints placed on marriage choices of individuals (and their parents) compelled to consider marriage in terms of economic advantage. Sons were expected to marry a woman who had a large "portion settled on her" (similar to a dowry) given to her at marriage. This meant, in turn, that the only way for a woman to obtain a share of her natal family's wealth as an inheritance was to marry the person chosen for her. Although the poor were free to choose a marriage partner based on emotional preference, both men and women looked for a person who would be an asset to the household economy.[53]

That Defoe was highly critical of this form of marriage is evident in what his characters state "if a young woman has beauty, birth, breeding, wit, sense, manners, modesty, and all to an extreme, yet if she has not money, she's nobody—

nothing but money now recommends a woman; the men play the game all into their own hands."[54] Thus we are treated to not only a moral, but also a class-based gender dilemma.

The disaster of her first love and marriage results in Moll Flanders becoming self-interested and cunning in her affairs with men. She is widowed within five years and resolves to remarry well; to marry at least a tradesman who can pass himself off as a gentleman. Her attempts at a successful marriage lead to personal bankruptcy and she takes refuge in the Mint.[55] Yet she is undeterred in her approach to marriage as a business strategy, noting only that as such, women are at a serious disadvantage.

> I am far from granting that the number of women is so great or that the number of the men so small; but if they will have me tell the truth, the disadvantage of the women is a terrible scandal upon the men, and it lies here only; namely, that the age is so wicked and the sex so debauched that, in short, the number of such men as an honest woman ought to meddle with is small indeed, and it is but here and there that a man is to be found who is fit for an honest woman to venture upon . . . 'tis nothing but lack of courage . . . the fear . . . of that frightful state of life called the old maid. This, I say, is the woman's snare. [56]

The central narrative of the book, which covers some thirty years of Flanders' life, is a long tale of travels through parts of England and over the sea to Virginia; a tale of several husbands, a couple of lovers, and some seven children that she bears, all of whom appear and then disappear from the story. At a critical point in the story, she realizes that in order to marry a London banker who is divorcing a wife he believes is cheating on him, Flanders must abandon her newborn child begotten in her just previous marriage.

It is the abandonment of the child that finally stirs her consciousness to awareness of her past misdeeds. Mirroring Crusoe's awakening to his Godlessness, Moll Flanders lists all her sins saying: "And then it occurred to me: 'What an abominable creature am I! . . . And how is this innocent gentleman going to be abused by me! How little does he think that having divorced a whore, he is throwing himself into the arms of another!'"[57] She resolves to treat her new husband well and lives happily enough with this man until he becomes distressed by financial losses and dies. Moll Flanders is once again poor and begins to grow desperate.

Defoe at this point reminds his readers of the link between poverty and crime, as Moll Flanders remarks: "Let 'em remember that a time of distress is a time of dreadful temptation, and all the strength to resist is taken away; poverty presses, the soul is made desperate by distress, and what can be done?"[58] Being successful at her first attempt to steal, she bit by bit becomes a thief. Here the reader is initiated into the life of thieves, the information and the many stories that Defoe employs to illustrate their practices serving as a warning to honest readers as to how to protect themselves. She succeeds for five years operating as a thief. Five years is considered a long period of success, but she is finally caught and sent to Newgate Prison.

At this point Defoe really focuses on what he says in his preface is the most important part of the story: the act of repentance. Flanders repents in prison and through the influence of friends is granted a stay-of-execution, her punishment instead to be transported to Virginia as a convict. Even as a repentant criminal, Moll Flanders continues a survivor. Snatched from the gallows and transported with one of her former husbands, a fellow prisoner, she reconnects in Virginia with one of her sons born of an earlier marriage. This was a marriage that both parties entered into little knowing that they were half-brother and sister, making it an incestuous marriage. Defoe uses this element of the plot to once again mark Flanders as a sinner who does not realize that she has sinned. With the recognition of her sins and sincere redemption, and through her customary cunning management of those around her, Flanders at last finds peace and prosperity in her old age.

This story is not about Moll Flanders' travels, or about her husbands, lovers, and children. It is rather a story about social status and the struggles of one woman to become, outwardly at least, a gentlewoman against all odds, including some rather extreme misfortune. The outward appearance is a shell, hiding, Defoe repeatedly reminds us, a life of sin. The key turning point in the story occurs when Flanders truly repents her past life and is then graced with the opportunity to begin a new life in Virginia, where she eventually is reconciled to her natal family and becomes a comfortably wealthy planter.

As a survivor tale, *Moll Flanders* is not light reading; it does not have the glow of optimism and mastery over circumstances that we find in *Robinson Crusoe*. Rather than a romance, the story is a visceral sort of social commentary in which Defoe rails against class barriers, while he more than suggests that wealth and virtue may be inversely related. He demonstrates the links between poverty and crime, and details the plight of women hemmed in by rigid social and legal strictures. While Defoe presents sharp social criticism, the criticism nevertheless serves as context and backdrop. His characters are sinners. Defoe focuses on the value of finding God, of sincere repentance, and of redemption.

Of the three novels, *Moll Flanders* is the most densely difficult, and perhaps the most ambitious work. Defoe is bold in his efforts to provide us with insights into the challenges faced by women, orphans, and the poor at the time. Against these odds, the character Moll Flanders uses her beauty, wit, charm, strength of character, and boundless capacity for cunning manipulation of those around her as her survivor skills. The result is a dark survivor tale, which Defoe can lighten only with the promise of forgiveness of sins through true repentance.

Conclusion

The three novels, *A Journal*, *Robinson Crusoe*, and *Moll Flanders*, together provide a sweeping view of seventeenth and early eighteenth century English life. Focusing as he did on the middle class of merchants, and creating characters that overcome tremendous misfortune, Defoe stayed close to his own experience. His motivation is clear in writing these novels in the form of memoirs: to both entertain and to instruct. In this, he remained true to his life-long writing, having used it to mobilize public opinion with the hope of creating change. That we can still feel the power of his intent, after almost 300 years, is testimony to his capacity as a novelist. His characters, especially Crusoe and Flanders, are studies in resilience to adversity, providing the reader with portraits of epic survivors, and rather overt lessons in morality. Defoe did not abandon either his religiosity or his role as a social commentator and critic, which he had honed during his years as a pamphleteer and journalist. He provided the reader with an opportunity to critically examine accepted social norms. The narrator in *A Journal* possesses all of the characteristics of both observer and critic of citizens' conduct during the plague and the acts of civil authorities to maintain order within the city of London. Defoe used the story of *Moll Flanders* to write not just a morality tale, but a scathing critique of seventeenth century social norms with respect to women. He also painted a picture of the gentrified class that is pure satire. Defoe, one of the first novelists, was also among the influential thinkers of his time, a time in which intellectual ferment shaped the ideals of the Age of Enlightenment, ideals of which we are the inheritors.

Notes

1. Ruth Savage, "Introduction," in *Philosophy and Religion in Elightenment Britain*, ed. Ruth Savage (Oxford: Oxford University Press, 2012), 1.

2. Carla Gardina Pestana, *Protestant Empire: Religion and the Making of the British Atlantic World* (Philadelphia: University of Pennsylvania Press, 2009), 149.

3. Ole Peter Grell and Roy Porter, "Toleration in Enlightenment Europe," in *Toleration in Enlightenment Europe*, ed. Henricka Kuklick (Cambridge: Cambridge University Press, 2000), 1.

4. Steve Pincus, *1688: The First Modern Revolution* (New Haven: Yale University Press, 2009), 3-8.

5. Leon Guilhamet, *Defoe and the Whig Novel: A Reading of the Major Fiction* (Newark: University of Delaware Press, 2010).

6. David Sorkin, *The Religious Enlightenment: Protestants, Jews and Catholics from London to Vienna* (Princeton, Princeton University Press, 2008), 11.

7. Knud Haakonssen, "Enlightened Dissent: An Introduction," in *Enlightenment and Religion: Rational Dissent in Eighteenth Century Britain*, ed. Knud Haakonssen (Cambridge: Cambridge University Press, 2006), 2.

8. The chronology of the Enlightenment Period begins in 1674 with publication of Nicolas de Malebranche's "De la recherché de la vérité" and ends in 1814 with the publication of Francisco José de Goya y Lucientes, "Los desastres de la Guerra." It encompasses such world-changing events as the Glorious Revolution, the joining of England and Scotland to become Great Britain, and the founding by Peter the Great of the Russian Academy of Sciences in Saint Petersburg. It includes the publication of John Locke's "Letters on Toleration," "Essay on Human Understanding" and Two Treatises on Government"; Newton's "Opticks"; Berkeley's Treatise Concerning the Principle of Human Knowledge"; Pope's "Essay on Man"; and Hume's "A Treatise of Human Nature." See Ellen J. Wilson and Peter H. Reill, *Encyclopedia of the Enlightenment,* revised edition (New York: Book Builders Inc., 2004), xiv, xv.

9. Ian Watt, *The Rise of the Novel: Studies in Defoe, Richardson, Fielding*, 2nd edition (Berkeley: University of California Press, 2001), 14.

10. Watt, *The Rise of the Novel*, 11-12.

11. Watt, *The Rise of the Novel*, 15.

12. Anthony Burgess, "Introduction," in *A Journal of the Plague Year* (Harmondsworth, Middlesex, England: Penguin Books, Ltd., 1966), 15.

13. Patrice Bourdelais, *Epidemics Laid Low: A History of What Happened in Rich Countries*, translated by Burt K. Holland (Baltimore: Johns Hopkins Press, 2003), 8-10.

14. Suzanne E. and James Hatty, *The Disordered Body: Epidemic Disease and Cultural Transformation*, SUNY Series in Medical Anthropology (Albany: State University of New York Press, 1999), 84-87.

15. Paul Slack, "Responses to Plague in Early Modern Europe," in *In the Time of Plague: The History and Social Consequences of Lethal Epidemic Disease*, ed. Arien Mack (New York: New York University Press, 1991), 113.

16. In this time of international sea trade, it was considered quite possible that an infectious disease could spread to London from the French port of Marseilles. The Great Plague of London had spread from Holland via shipping.

17. Slack, "Responses to Plague," 129.

18. Guilhamet, *Defoe and the Whig Novel*, 133, 135.

19. Dissenter was a collective name for Protestant groups who separated from the Church of England. Critical of the hierarchical structure of the Church and its financial ties to secular government, they advocated for its reform during the sixteenth through the eighteenth centuries. Under Cromwell, Dissenters were granted the right to preach, however in 1662, the Act of Uniformity removed this right by requiring Anglican ordination of all clergy. Many clergy chose instead to preach outside of the Anglican Church.

20. Daniel Defoe, *A Journal of the Plague Year* (Harmondsworth, Middlesex, England: Penguin Books, Ltd., 1966 [1722]), 187-88.

21. See Guilia Calvi, *Histories of a Plague Year: The Social and the Imaginary in Baroque Florence,* translated by Dario Biocca and Bryant T. Ragan Jr. (Berkeley: University of California Press, 1989).

22. Hatty and Hatty, *The Disordered Body*, 145.

23. Calvi, *Histories of a Plague Year*, 1.

24. D. Ann Herring and Alan C. Swedlund, "Plagues and Epidemics in Anthropological Perspective," in *Plagues and Epidemics: Infected Spaces Past and Present*, eds. D. Ann Herring and Alan C. Swedlund (New York and Oxford: Berg Publishers, 2010), 5-6.

25. Defoe, *A Journal*, 137.

26. Slack, "Responses to Plague," 117.

27. The period between 1400 and 1800 is considered the "early modern" period, beginning with the Renaissance and Reformation and ending at the end of the Enlightenment. See Lisa Rosner and John Theibault, *A Short History of Europe 1600-1815: Search for a Reasonable World.* (Armonk, New York: ME Sharpe, Inc., 2000), 6.

28. Helga Quadflieg, "As mannerly and civill as any of Europe: Early Modern Travel Writing and the Exploration of the English Self," in *Perspectives on Travel Writing*, eds. Glenn Hooper and Tim Youngs (Burlington: Ashgate Publishing Co., 2004), 28.

29. Quadflieg, "As mannerly and civill," 29.

30. Robert Wokler, "Rites of Passage and the Grand Tour," in *Finding Europe: Discourses on Margins, Communities, Images*, eds. Anthony Molho and Diogo Ramada Curto (Oxxford: Berghahn Books, 2007), 207.

31. Harry Leibersohn, "Anthropology Before Anthropology," in *A New History of Anthropology*, ed. Henrika Kuklick (Oxford: Blackwell Publishing Ltd., 2008), 27.

32. Daniel Defoe, *Robinson Crusoe* (Ann Arbor; Ann Arbor Media Group LLC and Borders Classics, 2006 [1719]); publisher's comments.

33. Guilhamet, *Defoe and the Whig Novel*, 28.

34. Defoe's valuation of the "middle estate" has been linked to Whig tendencies in his thinking. Whigs valued hard work as a means to comfortable success, but deplored the accumulation of wealth to the extent of permitting a life of luxury. See Guilhamet, *Defoe and the Whig Novel*, 44.

35. Defoe, *Robinson Crusoe*, 19.

36. Defoe, *Robinson Crusoe*, 35.

37. Defoe, *Robinson Crusoe*, 78.

38. Defoe, *Robinson Crusoe*, 78.

39. Guilhamet, *Defoe and the Whig Novel*, 69, 71, 91, 93.

40. Defoe, *Robinson Crusoe*, 148.

41. Defoe, *Robinson Crusoe*, 189.

42. Peter Harrison, *Religion and the Religious in the English Enlightenment* (Cambridge: Cambridge University Press, 1990), 9.

43. In this view, Catholicism, in its rituals and priest class interceding between the individual and God, had an affinity with pagan religions.

44. Defoe, *Robinson Crusoe*, 132.

45. Larry Wolff and Marco Cipolloni, *The Anthropology of the Enlightenment* (Stanford: Stanford University Press, 2007), 329.

46. Defoe, *Robinson Crusoe*, 209.

47. Guilhamet, *Defoe and the Whig Novel*, 114.

48. Guilhamet, *Defoe and the Whig Novel*, 116.

49. Lawrence Stone, *The Family, Sex and Marriage in England 1500-1800* (New York: Harper and Row Publishers, 1977), 195.

50. Quoted in Stone, *The Family, Sex and Marriage*, 195.

51. Defoe considered the education of women as a high priority, in keeping with the view that women should have the right to be educated contributors to society. See Guilhamet, *Defoe and the Whig Novel*, 33.

52. Stone, *The Family, Sex and Marriage*, 132.

53. Stone, *The Family, Sex and Marriage*, 192-93.

54. Daniel Defoe, *The Fortunes and Misfortunes of the Famous Moll Flanders* (New York, Bantam Books, 1989 [1722]), 11.

55. The Mint referred to an area that in the time of Henry VIII had contained a mint, but by the late seventeenth and early eighteenth centuries, had become an area that offered debtors protection from prosecution because it was one of the "liberties," areas that were jurisdictional inter-zones and which were governed privately rather than under the king.

56. Defoe, *Moll Flanders*, 51-52.

57. Defoe, *Moll Flanders*, 135.

58. Defoe, *Moll Flanders*, 142.

References

Bourdelais, Patrice
  2003   *Epidemics Laid Low: A History of What Happened in Rich Countries*, trans-
          lated by Burt K. Holland. Baltimore: Johns Hopkins Press, 2003.
Burgess, Anthony
  1996   "Introduction." In *A Journal of the Plague Year*. Harmondsworth, Middlesex,
          England: Penguin Books, Ltd., Pp. 6-20.
Calvi, Giulia
  1989   *Histories of a Plague Year: The Social and the Imaginary in Baroque Flor-
          ence*, translated by Dario Biocca and Bryant T. Ragan Jr. Berkeley: Univer-
          sity of California Press, 1989.
Defoe, Daniel
  2006   *Robinson Crusoe*. Ann Arbor: Ann Arbor Media Group LLC and Borders
          Classics [1719].
  1989   *The Fortunes and Misfortunes of the Famous Moll Flanders*. New York:
          Bantam Books [1722].
  1966   *A Journal of the Plague Year*. Harmondsworth, Middlesex, England: Penguin
          Books, Ltd. [1722].
Grell, Ole Peter, and Roy Porter
  2000   "Toleration in Enlightenment Europe." In *Toleration in Enlightenment
          Europe*, edited by Henrika Kuklick. Cambridge: Cambridge University Press,
          Pp 1-22.
Guilhamet, Leon
  2010   *Defoe and the Whig Novel: A Reading of the Major Fiction*. Newark: Uni-
          versity of Delaware Press.
Haakonssen, Knud
  2006   "Enlightened Dissent: An Introduction." In *Enlightenment and Religion:
          Rational Dissent in Eighteenth Century Britain*, edited by Knud Haakonssen,
          Cambridge: Cambridge University Press [1996], Pp 1-11.
Harrison, Peter
  1990   *Religion and the Religious in the English Enlightenment*. Cambridge: Cam-
          bridge University Press.
Hatty, Suzanne E., and James Hatty
  1999   *The Disordered Body: Epidemic Disease and Cultural Transformation*.
          SUNY Series in Medical Anthropology. Albany: State University of New
          York Press.
Herring, D. Ann, and Alan C. Swedlund
  2010   "Plagues and Epidemics in Anthropological Perspective." In *Plagues and
          Epidemics: Infected Spaces Past and Present*, edited by D. Ann Herring and
          Alan C. Swedlund. New York and Oxford: Berg Publishers, Pp. 1-20.
Leibersohn, Harry
  2008   "Anthropology Before Anthropology." In *A New History of Anthropology*,
          edited by Henrika Kuklick. Oxford: Blackwell Publishing Ltd., Pp. 17-32.
Pestana, Carla Gardina
  2009   *Protestant Empire: Religion and the Making of the British Atlantic World*.
          Philadelphia: University of Pennsylvania Press.

Pincus, Steve
  2009   *1688 the First Modern Revolution.* New Haven: Yale University Press.
Quadflieg, Helga
  2004   "As mannerly and civill as any of Europe: Early Modern Travel Writing and
          the Exploration of the English Self." In *Perspectives on Travel Writing*, ed-
          ited by Glenn Hooper and Tim Youngs. Burlington: Ashgate Publishing Co.,
          Pp. 27-40.
Rosner, Lisa, and John Theibault
  2000   *A Short History of Europe 1600-1815: Search for a Reasonable World.*
          Armonk, New York: ME Sharpe, Inc.
Savage, Ruth
  2012   "Introduction." In *Philosophy and Religion in Enlightenment Britain*, edited
          by Ruth Savage. Oxford: Oxford University Press, Pp. 1-8.
Slack, Paul
  1991   "Responses to Plague in Early Modern Europe." In *In the Time of Plague:
          The History and Social Consequences of Lethal Epidemic Disease*, edited by
          Arien Mack. New York: New York University Press, Pp. 111-132.
Sorkin, David
  2008   *The Religious Enlightenment: Protestants, Jews and Catholics from London
          to Vienna.* Princeton: Princeton University Press.
Stone, Lawrence
  1997   *The Family, Sex and Marriage in England 1500-1800.* New York: Harper
          and Row Publishers.
Watt, Ian
  2001   *The Rise of the Novel: Studies in Defoe, Richardson, Fielding.* 2nd edition.
          Berkeley: University of California Press.
Wilson, Ellen J., and Peter H. Reill
  2004   *Encyclopedia of the Enlightenment.* revised edition. New York: Book
          Builders Inc.
Wokler, Robert
  2007   "Rites of Passage and the Grand Tour." In *Finding Europe: Discourses on
          Margins, Communities, Images*, edited by Anthony Molho and Diogo Ra-
          mada Curto. Oxford: Berghahn Books, Pp. 205-222.
Wolff, Larry and Marco Cipolloni
  2007   *The Anthropology of the Enlightenment.* Stanford: Stanford University Press.

Chapter 4

"A Genuine Victorian Oddity": Harriet Martineau's Fiction

MARILYN COHEN

My business in life has been to think and learn, and to speak out with abso-lute freedom what I have thought and learned.[1]
She was born to be a destroyer of slavery, in whatever form, in whatever place, all over the world, wherever she saw or thought she saw it.[2]
No true woman can be happy without some sort of domestic life; without hav-ing somebody's happiness dependent on her...[3]

A recurring theme among scholars of Harriet Martineau is that despite her re-nown as England's premier woman of letters in the early nineteenth century, she is relatively neglected and her writings are considered obscure. Most of her books are out of print. Although feminist scholars have reinstated Martineau to sociology's founding canon, I argue that she should also be recognized as a founder of a radical, critical, feminist anthropology. The reasons are many: establishing qualitative research methods, her determination to link social sci-ence research with social justice activism, her perspective on work as fundamen-tal to humanity and society, her early analysis of race, class, and gender as social constructions, and their myriad intersections in the public and domestic do-mains. While men were distanced by their gender from contact with the mainte-nance of daily social life, women were confined to the domestic sphere where they cultivated close observation, introspection, and analysis. Martineau under-stood that as a woman she had access to private domestic life, a sphere more difficult to investigate than the public and often neglected by men.[4] Martineau's fiction anticipates the genre of domestic realism that is rich with information of interest to anthropologists.

Martineau believed that social progress, which followed well-defined stages, would result from strengthening individual character through education. She wrote successfully across a range of disciplines including political economy, sociology, history, and fiction for adults and children and was committed to directing her formidable analytic talents toward educating the working and middle classes. Unlike the aristocracy, whose lives were characterized by lavish consumption and leisure pursuits, the middle class stressed hard work, domestic moderation, and rational thinking.[5] Although most of Martineau's writing consisted of nonfiction (social analysis, journalism, history, travel books, autobiography) she first established her reputation as a writer by producing short tales to illustrate the principles of political economy, taxation, and the poor laws. With the exception of her successful *Illustrations of Political Economy* and *Deerbrook*, Martineau's fiction has attracted little scholarly attention since nonfiction better suited her direct empirical writing style. In fact, Martineau was well aware of her artistic limitations. Readers familiar with the brilliance of nineteenth century English novelists will realize that Martineau lacks the artistry of Jane Austen (the role model for *Deerbrook*), or the integrative intellectual genius of George Eliot (influenced by *Deerbrook*) whose years of historical study in preparation for a novel blended seamlessly with her artistry. Martineau, who later in life was attracted to Comtean positivism and translated Comte's writing, was a writer whose expository style suited the new empirical holistic science of society.

Martineau experienced writing as a vocation, not as a choice. "Authorship has never been with me a matter of choice ... Things were pressing to be said; and there was more or less evidence that I was the person to say them."[6] Her literary career challenged the Victorian gender binary of men wielding the powerful pen in the public domain while women's literacy, like their sewing needle, was confined to the home. Expert at both the "womanish" skill of needlework and the "mannish" skill of writing, her "need of utterance" was "so compelling that its expression required articulate and inarticulate modes alike." As Valerie Sanders states, Martineau was considered by her contemporaries to be "masculine in a womanly way," a gender thaumatrope. A critical reformer, Martineau's goals were to make her writing accessible to the general public ("my great pupil, the public") and thereby be useful.[7]

For Martineau, the relative attainment of "happiness" or liberty in a society can be evaluated by how powerless groups such as women, prisoners, or the poor are treated. She dedicated much of her life to abolitionist movements in Great Britain and the United States and to identifying issues relating to women's lives and work. She anticipated the contemporary anthropological perspective on race as a social construction, the intersections among race, gender, sexuality and colonialism, and the symbolic linkages among gender identity, domestic division of labor, and material home spaces. Martineau was equally convinced that gender was a social construction and she anticipated the feminist theoretical argument that class consciousness is gendered. Central to her investigations was the question: "Are women present, and under what law of liberty?"[8] Martineau can be regarded as a liberal feminist before the letter. Her writings continue to have relevance for global feminism since she stated that one determinant in estimating the degree of liberty in any society is the status of women.

Martineau was "a pioneer in using the prism of work to render a spectrum on society."[9] Much of her analytical writing focused on women's domestic work and their low waged work as domestic servants, governesses, seamstresses, and textile operatives, to expose their exploitation, myths, and instigate needed change. She was among the first, following Daniel Defoe and Mary Wollstonecraft, to recognize the structural similarities between slaves and women. For Martineau, although women's agency is constrained by gender domination, it remains active, varied, and significant to the economy and society.[10]

Harriet Martineau (1802-1876) was born in Norwich, England, to Thomas and Elizabeth Martineau. The Martineau's were Unitarians, a particularly intellectual sect of Dissenters who deemphasized the significance of a personal God in favor of living by God's principles. They questioned religious dogma and many were political radicals involved in myriad reform movements including the abolition of slavery. Unitarians believed all were worthy of salvation with benevolent concern extended to the helpless and weak.

For Martineau freedom of thought and education extended equally to women. In an early article on "Female Education," Martineau argued that women had the same mental endowment as men.[11] Martineau was primarily educated at home; like all women of her time, she was barred from attending university. However, due to the favorable attitude of her parents regarding educating girls, she and her sister received several years of formal schooling at a boy's grammar school and she benefited from the college education of her brothers.

Norwich was a prosperous industrial town and Thomas Martineau was a small-scale textile manufacturer, who provided a comfortable middle-class standard of living for his family. However, by 1824, the transformations characteristic of industrial capitalism resulted in the demise of the Martineau family's business and a sharp decline in their standard of living and much of Norwich. After a bad investment and Thomas Martineau's death in 1826, the business collapsed in 1829. "These experiences made 'political economy,' as the emerging science of economics was then known, a prime topic of discussion in her home, a topic that would be her initial entry into social science writing."[12]

Martineau described her childhood, as the sixth of eight children, as unhappy, frustrating, and deprived of maternal nurturance.[13] She was sickly and by the age of twelve had permanently lost most of her hearing. Martineau's main coping strategy was reading, studing, and writing and she developed early a "lifelong habit of disciplined self-education and writing."[14] After the collapse of the family business and the sudden death of her fiancée, Martineau's deafness justified her remaining at home to earn a living by sewing and writing rather than as a governess.[15] The loss of the family's gentility and her choice to remain single provided Martineau with the freedom she cherished to write and travel.

> But for that loss of money, we might have lived on in the ordinary provincial method of ladies with small means, sewing and economizing, and growing narrower every year ... by being thrown, while it was yet time, on our own resources, we have worked hard and usefully, won friends, reputation, and independence, seen the world abundantly abroad and at home, and, in short, have truly lived instead of vegetated.[16]

By 1830 Martineau was writing everyday at her desk from seven-thirty until two in the afternoon and she continued to fulfill her "need of utterance" for fifty-four years.[17] She considered writing a masculine achievement and demonstrated her competence in masculine rhetoric. In her autobiography Martineau asserted, "I am probably the happiest single woman in England."[18]

Early Fiction: Intersections among Liminality, Didacticism, and Necessarianism

Little did her liberal-minded parents dream that their permissiveness in allowing Harriet access to books would enable her to become a genuine Victorian oddity; a self-supporting yet respectable single woman, an internationally influential professional writer, and a strong-minded free-thinker unafraid to challenge such entrenched cultural institutions as aristocratic privilege, parliamentary law, organized religion and the medical establishment.[19]

Victor Turner's concept of liminality is useful in analyzing Harriet Martineau's "odd" marginal life and career as a writer. For Turner, "the attributes of liminality or of liminal personae ('threshold people') are necessarily ambiguous ... Liminal entities are neither here nor there; they are betwixt and between the positions assigned and arrayed by law, custom, convention, and ceremonial." The essence of liminality is "choice," "multiplicity," "release from normal constraints."[20] Martineau was well aware of her release from the normal constraints of middle class Victorian women and she wove liminal characters into her fiction, several of which were autobiographical.

By 1827, at age twenty-five, Martineau began to earn money as a writer, using her own name. She initially wrote short stories about machine breaking and wages, entitled *The Rioters* and *The Turnout*, unaware that she was "meditating writing on Political Economy."[21] In 1827 she wrote a longer tale analyzed here entitled, *Principle and Practice—The Orphans*, a precursor to the *Illustrations of Political Economy* (1832-1834), where the story served as the vehicle for Martineau's values concerning education, hard work, and family devotion. Martineau's father's business fluctuated, and was "never a very enriching one." As rational Unitarians, her parents chose "to let us know precisely the state of their affairs, and to hold out to us ... the probability that we might sooner or later have to work for our own living, daughters as well as sons."[22] Throughout her life, Martineau remained convinced in the restorative qualities of hardship, hard work, and useful service. "Work took on first moral and then sociological dimensions, so that it became, for her, synonymous with autonomy, emancipation, and selfhood."[23]

"I propose to give a plain unaffected narrative of the exertions made by a family of young persons, to render themselves and each other happy and useful in the world."[24] These words open *Principles and Practice*, a story that rejected romanticism in favor of a new conception of realism. The story features orphans, a liminal category of persons, who faced the substantial challenge of coping with the death of their parents. Orphans appear frequently in Martineau's fiction, perhaps reflecting her self-image "as an unmothered child."[25] Similar to her own family, this story illustrates how catastrophic the death of the wage earner was to a family whose finances were already stretched. After Mr. Forsyth's death, his children had no near relatives and inherited "nothing but the good principles and industrious habits which his care and affection had imparted to them."[26]

Martineau held a deep respect for women's domestic work, which she considered to be a natural inclination and vocation. She believed that good housekeeping skills, characteristic of middle and working class women, required keen intelligence, mature judgment, and a willingness to place the welfare of the family above one's self. "An orderly domestic life is necessary to the life satisfaction of any worker. Knowledge of home nursing, cooking, cleaning, and hygiene ... were part of the necessary domestic skills."[27] In *Principles and Practice*, Jane, Mr. Forsyth's eldest girl of sixteen, is the character who personifies these qualities and skills. At sixteen, Jane is a liminal female adolescent. After her mother's death, she had been her father's friend and housekeeper and possessed a remarkable mature judgment, sound religious principles, along with an anxious emotional disposition, not uncommon among adolescents.

When we meet Jane after the loss of her father, she was anxious and "oppressed by the thought that the only prospect before her, was a melancholy one of long years of struggles against poverty, and all the grievous evils of dependence."[28] As was normative, Jane is very close to her brother Charles, age fifteen, as was Martineau to her younger brother James, the strongest passion of her life.[29] Charles' male liminality is tied to his transitional status as an emerging breadwinner, the heir to his father's business. He had been under his father's watchful eye and carefully trained. Charles' "active, enterprising disposition, full of hope and cheerfulness ... his acquired habits, his sense of responsibility, joined with his strong affection for his sisters, made him the object on which Jane fixed her best hopes for the future prosperity of the family."[30]

Mr. Barker, the family's close friend and executor, temporarily took in the children after the funeral. He openly informed Jane that their yearly income would be only 80-90 pounds a year, or less than two pounds a week, a sum that spelled poverty. He agreed to Jane's request that the children, Isabella, Harriet, and Alfred, remain together, but Charles, the future breadwinner, would have to leave for London to work for a friend of his father in a merchant's warehouse. Jane and the other children would live in a small house owned by her father that could be made ready shortly with little expense. Their nursemaid Hannah wished to remain and would assist Jane as housekeeper. Jane, who had taught her younger sisters, would be employed as a day governess for Mrs. Everett while her sisters and Alfred went to school. Charles was unable to return home from London for two years. Since Jane and Charles were separated, Martineau, an avid letter writer, uses the epistolary technique to construct their close relationship.

Martineau anticipated sociologist Anthony Giddens' functionalist concept of structuration. Routines enable individuals to maintain control over their daily lives, personalities, and the stability of social institutions.[31] There are many parallels between Jane and Martineau, whose need for structured routine and useful work enabled her to tame her own childhood anxieties, develop her personal capacities, and free herself from dull idleness and ennui. Like Martineau, who coped with feelings of maternal deprivation by lavishing attention on her younger siblings James and Ellen, Jane was loving, and fully committed to the well-being of her younger siblings. She carefully scheduled her days rising before six o'clock to study for two undisturbed hours, essential to her development as a teacher. At 8:00am the family assembled in the parlor for prayers and Scripture reading before breakfast. Before work at 9:00am Jane walked her younger siblings to school and gave household directions to Hannah. After returning from work at 3:00pm, Jane had dinner and sat down to her needlework. The younger children learned their lessons until tea time, and after they all walked if the weather allowed. They would then read until 9:00pm when the younger ones went to bed. Jane sewed again until 10:00pm, walked around the house with Hannah "to see that all was safe and as it should be" and then she went to bed. Like Martineau, "Jane was an excellent workwoman [sewer], and her sister Isabella had been in the habit of assisting her, by keeping her own clothes in very good order."[32] Like Martineau, Jane recognized the importance of balance—useful physical work and regular exercise to her "vigour of mind," of regular social interactions with her siblings, of prayer to the tranquility of her mind, and the necessity of regular peaceful sleep.[33] Under Jane's excellent management during the first year, the household spent only fifty-six pounds. The remainder and Jane's salary paid for the younger children's education.

In her analysis of female industry, Martineau focused on teachers, a typology of occupations open to middle class women that included school mistresses, family governesses, day governesses like Jane, and special teachers of the arts. "Martineau regarded the occupation of governess, while requiring a good strong character and disposition and diligent, dedicated work, as an interesting and rewarding, if not remunerative, profession." School mistresses, were at the top of Martineau's typology of teachers since they enjoyed greater control over their work than governesses, greater personal satisfaction, and no health liabilities.[34] Martineau questioned the assumption that anyone could teach children. The main causes of anxiety among governesses were lack of preparation, fatigue, anxious or demanding parents, and controlling children. Jane was dedicated to preparation and was sensitive to how Mrs. Everett treated her and evaluated her competence.

After Isabella returned from London, where she spent two years developing her "remarkable" talents at writing and drawing, she and Jane moved to a new larger home and opened their own day school. Expenses were paid for by a ten pound raise in Jane's salary, twenty pounds a year sent from Charles to assist with Alfred's schooling, and the promise of pupils from Mrs. Everett and her friends. The sisters opened the school with ten pupils who attended between

9:00am-3:00pm, securing the afternoon and evening for their own continuing education. Jane and Isabella, now independent, asserted to Charles:

> We feel as if a great weight were taken off our minds, now that we are at liberty to use our powers for our own support, instead of being burdensome to others. You have long known and enjoyed this feeling; to us it is new and inexpressibly delightful. For the future we have no fears, and no further desires than to go on living as we are living now, only with the additional satisfaction of seeing that our endeavours to be useful are not in vain.[35]

Ceaseless activity, didactic purpose, and determined independence were central principles in Martineau's life.

In this early story Martineau's emerging liberal feminism is grounded in women's independence. Women, like men, require moral principles, an "enlightened mind" through education, and rational preparation for continuous useful work inside and outside of the home.[36] Since the teaching professions generally precluded marriage, the sibling bond remained primary and they lived together until Alfred would come of age at fifteen to begin his training in London at the merchant's warehouse. Although Martineau admired domesticity, her female characters remained single, as did she, living with her nieces and maids at the Knoll in Ambleside. Single women as liminal personae were freer than married women to attain autonomy, to write, travel, and engage in public life.

Thereafter, Martineau's success as a writer emerged from her interest in political economy, and her dedication to translating these principles for the common person. She was motivated to write twenty-four tales to popularize the influential theories of Smith's laissez-faire doctrine, Ricardo's attack on the Corn Laws, Malthus's *Essay on Population,* and Bentham's greatest happiness principle, an "unlikely female enterprise."[37] The chief sources of her ideas were Joseph Priestly's philosophical concept of necessarianism and James Mills' *Elements of Political Economy.* Martineau fused the tradition of didactic tales (Hannah Moore) with Jane Marcet's *Conversations on Political Economy* (1816), a textbook written for young people that demonstrated to her the possibility of popularizing theoretical concepts through realist fictional narrative intended to persuade readers of their truth.[38] Martineau's contribution was both literary and sociological: "It struck me at once that the principles of the whole science might be advantageously conveyed ... by being exhibited in their natural workings in selected passages of social life."[39]

The "phenomenally successful monthly volumes" of the *Illustrations of Political Economy* eliminated all anxiety about employment or money for Martineau who proved herself to be a good story teller.[40] Their intense, albeit short-lived, popularity, with sales by 1834 reaching 10,000 volumes, extended to readers of all social classes.[41] Thereafter, according to Deirdre David, Martineau functioned as an "organic intellectual" whose "talent for powerful popularization" and ardent desire to educate her adult and child readers by exemplification was linked with her goal of "auxiliary usefulness."[42] She followed a rigid formula of composition beginning each tale with researching the leading topic and organizing the didactic material that would comprise the "Summary of Principles" at the end of each monthly number. The characters were crafted to personify issues; the plots and dialogue to advance the lessons that illustrate how the lives of people and communities are determined by forces beyond their control. By popularizing principles that she assumed to be immutable and necessary to progress, Martineau facilitated the hegemonic process. She was convinced that by elevating the understanding of common people, they would recognize their function in the new capitalist system where classes would work together for mutual benefit. Classical political economy was a new cosmology, a hegemonic world-view, that offered structure and "relief from the anxiety produced by the new contingencies and uncertainties this form of capitalism produced." Like myths, Martineau's tales offered a "stable unifying philosophy by which to interpret a given subject matter" or social practice.[43] Like propaganda, the tales offered a "scheme for propagating doctrines."[44]

One of her best-known tales, *Demerara*, which addressed slavery in Barbados, will be examined here to illustrate Martineau's early thinking on the issues of waged work verses slavery and the social construction of race. When *Demerara* was published in 1832, public opinion in England had turned decidedly against slavery with the British Parliament outlawing the system in 1833. Slavery had always been a distant reality for the average British citizen, taking place outside its boundaries in the West Indies or American South. In pre-Civil War America, the climate was profoundly different, since slavery was central to the country's political economy and southern way of life. Slavery was a fervently discussed topic on both sides of the Atlantic and Martineau's fame as the author of *Demerara* preceded her trip to America in 1834. Abolitionists heralded her arrival: "The apologists for slavery in this country are thoroughly alarmed ... The author of *Demerara* is a formidable personage in the Southern States ...You are received with the most marked attention, writer as you are of the best antislavery tale ever written, while a New England man who should have written that work would have been ... indicted and imprisoned."[45] Indeed, many feared for Martineau's safety during her travels in America and subsequently as she received hate mail after her return to England.

In *Demerara*, Martineau employs both logic and passion to shock readers about slavery, particularly English readers who had no direct empirical experience of the system. In the Preface she states: "SLAVERY is a topic which cannot be approached without emotion. But ... perceiving ... that the most stirring eloquence issues from the calmest logic, I have not hesitated to bring calculations and reasonings to bear on a subject that awakens the drowsiest, and fires the coldest."[46] *Demerara* begins with a "culture shock device." Mr. Bruce, the plantation owner, welcomes his twenty-one year old son and daughter to Barbados from England. They are immediately appalled by the pervasive ennui bred by slavery. Work for Martineau, "allows the exercise of personal capacities and facilitates development, at the same time that it expresses certain basic human rights—freedom, equality, self-fulfillment."[47] Slavery debases work and dehumanizes both the slaves and slave owners who "tyrannize their slaves yet live in perpetual fear of retaliatory insurrection"[48] Blacks, "made to live in sunshine," were rendered "sluggards" by slavery even when the weather is "delicious" and conducive to work.[49] Martineau demonstrates throughout *Demerara* that the laziness of slaves is a response to slavery rather than an inherent racial short-coming. Still, she does not consider intransigence as a legitimate method of resistance to slavery.

Through Alfred, the young heir to Mr. Bruce's plantation, Martineau illus-trates a key principle of political economy that paying wages for free labor is the antidote for laziness. Alfred, a middle class Victorian man, is eager to apply his education and learn all he can about his prospects in Barbados. Alfred rapidly developed a deep dislike for slavery after observing it. Growing impatient with the "slow and indolent manner" of slaves when compared with the focused dis-patch of paid agricultural laborers on English plantations, Alfred snatches up a hoe thrown down by a slave and finishes "more in half an hour than any slave near him since sunrise."[50] The apathy among slaves was even worse on another plantation, Mr. Mitchelson's sugar cane fields, where slave gangs were treated with more cruelty.

> Alfred thought ... how poor is the purchase of a man. It is the mind that gives the value of a man ... and the mind cannot be purchased—only that small portion of it which can be brought under the dread of the whip and the stocks. Where the man is allowed the possession of himself, the purchaser of his labour is benefited by the vigour of his mind through the service of his limbs: where man is made the possession of another, the possessor loses ... all that is most valuable.[51]

Alfred's experiment to prove that paying wages would increase productivity was to employ slaves as wage laborers to fix Mr. Mitchelson's burst mill-dam. Mitchelson's surveyor suggested that English laborers would complete the re-pairs in twelve to fifteen days, while slaves would take sixty. Alfred, the manly Englishman, boldly asserted that his employed men would complete the repairs in twenty. "The main feature of Alfred's plan was to pay wages. He collected the men, told them what they had to do and expect, promised them warm cloth-ing in case of their working early and late, showed them the ample provision of meat, bread, and vegetables he had stored at hand, marched them off." When the work was half done, Alfred's father Mr. Bruce "was struck with the appearance of activity so unusual in that region." The employed slaves talked among them-selves, sung, and cheerfully executed their work until after sunset.[52] Slavery wastes money capital for their owners due to negligence, insurrection, and theft on the part of the slave. "Instead of capital being reproduced, it is 'sunk' and an 'incalculable amount of human suffering' endured for the sake of 'wholesale waste of labour and capital.'"[53]

Martineau insisted that the brutality of slavery destroyed love undermining marriage and family, institutions sacred to most Victorians. Slave women were prevented from legitimate marriage and sexually exploited for breeding purposes. Although slaves formed romantic ties and marriages, these unions had no legal rights and obligations. "if the man gets free, the woman cannot go with him ... if anybody buys her, her husband may not follow her unless his master allows it. They cannot do their children any good. They cannot make them free, nor save them from labour, nor help them to get justice."[54] Love was emotionally precarious "because a black must first be a slave and than a man. A white woman has nobody to rule her but her husband, and nobody can hurt her without his leave: but a slave's wife must obey her master before her husband; and he cannot save her from being flogged." Children "as often get a kick as a kind word ... they are carried away where their father shall never see them again."[55]

In *Demerara* the central right of all individuals, the right to act autonomously as a moral being is denied by slavery, a form of domination. Martineau asserts a moral principle that no man has the right to own another as property and a radical principle that the responsibility for slavery lies squarely with the state who gives it legislative protection.[56] Political economy provided the logic for the abolition of slavery: a free trade in sugar would banish slavery, since competition must induce an economy of capital and labor by substituting free waged labor.[57] "Martineau's best world is one which employer and employee work reciprocally ... that is work should be a mutual affair between employer and employee, part of community life, in which individuals express their relation to and responsibility toward one another."[58]

Between Impartiality and Ethnocentrism

Martineau's *Illustrations* provided her with "sufficient financial security, confidence, and reputation to allow more independent thought."[59] In need of change, Martineau took advantage of an opportunity open to her as a liminal persona: the freedom to travel. She set sail for America in 1834 producing three books from the experience of traveling extensively for two years: *How to Observe Morals and Manners* (1838), *Society in America* (1836-1837), and *Retrospective of Western Travels* (1838). These books establish Martineau as the first modern sociologist. The first book is a pioneering sociological text that stresses the need for systematic objective observation and outlines qualitative research methods. The second applies these methods during two years of travel.[60]

Martineau's social science was both ahead of its time and firmly rooted in it. She stated that "the appropriate orientation for the observer is 'impartiality,' a proscription against ethnocentrism" and a "prescription for independent standards of judgment and the practice of sympathetic understanding."[61] In *How to Observe Morals and Manners*, Martineau recognized that "the mind of the observer ... is as essential as the material to be wrought."[62] After identifying what the observer wants to know, she then outlined the "requisites the traveler ought to make sure that he is possessed of before he undertakes to offer observations on the Morals and Manners of a people." These include "untrammelled and unreserved" sympathy (empathy) and liberality of judgment when observing different ways of life.[63]

These "requisites" to exclude "philosophical and national" prejudice approach cultural relativism. "Every prevalent virtue or vice is the result of the particular circumstances admist which the society exists. The circumstances in which a prevalent virtue or vice originates, may or may not be traceable by a traveler. If traceable, he should spare no pains to make himself acquainted with the whole case. If obscure, he must beware of imputing disgraces to individuals."[64] Liberality of judgment "dissolves prejudice and casts a full light upon many things which cease to be fearful and painful when they are no longer obscure."[65] Reflecting on mummy pits and animal sacrifice in ancient Egypt in 1848:

> If I had been on the banks of some South African river, seeing a poor naked savage at his Fetish worship, I must have tried to learn what idea ... was at the bottom of his observance; and here, where I knew that men had read the stars, and compassed invisible truths of geometry, and achieved unaccountable marvels of art, and originated, or transmitted, the theologies of the world, I could not despise them for one set of tenets and observances which remained unexplained.[66]

Martineau's objectivity did not imply value neutrality. She simultaneously held strong convictions about liberty or freedom from domination and the direction of human progress that could lead to ethnocentrism. "While the reader is convinced of Martineau's sincere humanitarianism, there remains the undeniable elevation of nineteenth century Christianity and British civilization over all that preceded it."[67] Like Defoe, a century before, indigenous peoples were often portrayed as "savages," or exotic others. Martineau writes of Native Americans: "a solitary Indian might be frequently seen standing on a heap of stones by the roadside, or sleeping under a fence. There is something which rivets the eye of the stranger in the grave gaze, the lank hair, the blanket-wrapped form of the savage, as he stands motionless."[68] The nomadic Lapps in Norway, were treated disparagingly in the children's story *Feats on the Fiord.* "A deputation of Lapps came from the tents, bringing reindeer venison, and half of a fine Gammel cheese ... Erica had time to pour out a glass of corn-brandy for each of this dwarfish party, in token of thanks, and because it is considered unlucky to send away Lapps without a treat ... The Lapps, as being dirty and despised, were got rid of as soon as possible."[69]

Martineau accepted the necessarian view that the universe is governed by natural laws. Cultural evolution follows a linear progression from paganism to Christianity, polygamy to monogamous marriage, and nomadic hunting to settled farming and commerce. The Oneida Indians near Oneida Castle in New York State were "declared to be reclaimed from idolatry" as a result of the newly built Episcopal Church.[70] Norwegian Pre-Christian beliefs were "superstitions" responsible for needless anxiety and fear, unlike Christianity with its belief in one benevolent God.[71] Polygamy, observed in Egyptian harems during

Martineau's travels in the Middle East in 1846-1847, was considered "a hell upon earth."[72] Indigenous people are infantile, and need to be instructed in religious, economic, and social matters so that they can develop and mature.[73]

Anomalies and Feminist Intersectionality

This mindset that vacillated between objective observation and ethnocentrism, set the stage for Martineau's inquisitive observation, a qualitative research method involving "pedestrian traveling," learning the language so that questions can be asked "with an open heart and frank manners," the interpretation of "things," and the records of institutions that objectify collective morals and manners.[74] *Society in America* (1834-1836, book 1837), the companion to the methodological *How to Observe Morals and Manners*, is "the first book on the methodology of social research in the then still unborn disciplines of sociology and anthropology."[75] It is based on two years of extensive travel and inquisitive observation in the United States and delineates Martineau's strategy to analyze the relationship between morals and manners. Like many subsequent sociologists and anthropologists, Martineau assumed that a society's central values and myths were major influences determining its institutional structure.[76]

Of interest here are Martineau's ideas regarding the social construction and intersection of race and gender. These structures of inequality were the most serious anomalies in American society. The glaring contradiction between the moral founding principles that all men are born free and equal and that rulers derive their just powers from the consent of the governed, stemmed from the exclusion of women and slaves from participation in the democratic process. This exclusion resulted from both being denied the right to property and personal independence, deemed necessary for citizenship by the founding fathers.[77]

Fundamentally, the organization of work differed in the North and South. In the South, the elite, who performed no work, exercised absolute control over "the servile" class, owning as private property their bodies and all that they produce. Under such circumstances, slave labor could not "realize human potential, nor could it require or reward independent thought or personal initiative." By contrast, the North was a meritocracy where all young men need to work hard to earn the means to educate themselves and to establish themselves in their professions. Since all men were created equal, labor was not degraded and laborers were not excluded from intellectual ideas. "All laborers shared the rights and responsibilities of citizens."[78]

In both the South and North, women were excluded not only from the franchise but also from the kind of productive economic activities that would qualify them, like white men, to exercise political rights. In the south all labor, unwaged domestic and waged was devalued, resulting in white women focusing their attention on acquiring accomplishments that would make them desirable to men on the marriage market. In the North, women participated in the "blessing of work" directing their attention to "the material maintenance of her home and family." However, their work was reduced to household drudgery since women were excluded from most occupations and from education that would expand their experiences.[79]

As in *Demerara*, Martineau painted a vivid picture of the ways that slaves were dehumanized, work degraded, family life made impossible, and morality ignored under the slave system. She rejected prevailing racist arguments as a justification for slavery. "In both the North and the South she found examples of Negroes who, given the opportunity, demonstrated real abilities. This proved to her that the Negro like other men was capable of the highest human attainments." Racism allowed white Southerners to displace their guilt. "It is an old truth that we hate those whom we have injured."[80]

Martineau's accounts of the intersections among race, class, gender, and sexuality in the American South anticipated scholarly themes in the field of gender, sexuality and imperialism (see John Pulis's discussion of "creolizing" and David Surrey's discussion of Twain's "Roxy" in this volume). She focused on the nature of social relations between white women and enslaved black and interracial women and confronted the then taboo issues of miscegenation between white men and enslaved black women. Guided by the concept of domination, Martineau challenged the unequal race and gender-based power relations that facilitated and shaped Southern white men's "licentiousness" or privileged sexual access to slave women's bodies.

Hilary Beckles states that although black male slaves were initially preferred, slave owners quickly realized that the entry of black women allowed for the "natural reproduction of slavery" as a cheaper alternative to slave trading. The sexual possession and forced fertility of enslaved black women by their white masters represented the wider racial domination at the core of the institution of slavery. Enslaved black women also allowed slave managers to "meet the social demands of favoured male slaves." Slave women were targeted as sexual objects by both hegemonic white and marginalized black masculinities. In contrast, "the white woman was constitutionally alienated from slavery and represented the embodiment and conveyor of social freedom." Enslaved men "possessed the distinct privilege of being able to father free-born children."[81] Martineau was acutely aware of the patriarchal power held by white men over black and white women, and of the race-based domination of hegemonic white over marginalized black masculinity since white male slave owners could break up slave families at will. However, she does not address the sexual domination black women suffered by enslaved black men.

Sexual control and matrilineal inheritance of slave status were essential to the construction of racial boundaries and categories. Liminality produced danger and fear when the color markers of free verses slave among mixed race children were ambiguous. "A southern planter said ... that the very general connexion of white gentleman with their female slaves introduced a mulatto race whose numbers would become dangerous if the affections of their white parents were permitted to render them free. The liberty of emancipating them was therefore abolished, while that of selling them remained."[82]

Concrete expressions of enslaved women's struggles were diverse ranging from intransigence in relation to work, running away, refusing to procreate at expected levels, infanticide, abortion, poisoning their mistresses and sexual relations with white men to better their material and social conditions and to prevent the perpetuation of slavery.[83] Martineau recounted a case of poisoning:

> A lady of fortune carried into her husband's establishment, when she married, several slaves, and among them a girl two years younger than herself, who had been brought up under her, and who was employed as her own maid. Mrs. ... had been unusually indulgent to this girl, having allowed her time and opportunity for religious and other instruction ... One night, when the girl was undressing her, the lady expressed her fondness for her, and said: 'When I die you shall be free;'—a dangerous thing to say to a slave only two years younger than herself. In short time the lady was taken ill with a strange, mysterious illness which no doctor could alleviate. One of her friends, who suspected foul play, took the sufferer entirely under her own charge, when she seemed to be dying. She revived; and as soon as she was well enough to have a will of her own again, would be waited on by no one but her favourite slave. She grew worse ... At last, the friend excluded from her chamber every one but the physicians; took in the medicines at the room door from the hands of the slave and locked them up. They were all analyzed by a physician, and arsenic found in every one of them ... There was never a case of more cruel, deliberate intention to murder ... What was done? ... The lady sold her.[84]

Martineau, unable or unwilling to see the resistance to slavery beneath this attempted murder, advocated the gallows.

Female slaves with fair skin or of mixed race were more successful in extracting benefits including legal freedom from white slave owners. Martineau was no exception. Her fascination with and empathy for mixed race girls and women reflected the European cultural connections among whiteness, beauty, intelligence, and civilization and their repugnance toward miscegenation. While in New Orleans, Martineau became interested in an eight year old "mulatto child" named Ailsie, who she described as "perfectly beautiful ... quick, obedient, and affectionate to a touching degree." Ailsie's father was a white gentleman outside of the family and her mother the family's black cook. The cook's black husband hated Ailsie and threatened to kill her. She was then sold to Mr. and Mrs. Newbreen, "one of the wisest and best of American women." After Mrs. Newbreen's death, Martineau feared for Ailsie's future since Mr. Newbreen could not protect her. "None but a virtuous mistress can fully protect a female slave, and that too seldom." Mr. Newbreen wrote to "entreat me to take charge of the girl." Martineau agreed to adopt Ailsie, then twelve years old, bring her to England as her maid and to educate her. She rejected Newbreen's offer of a yearly allowance "because my friend's money was derived from slave-labour, and I would not touch it." Despite Martineau's preparations for Ailsie's arrival, Newbreen's mother-in-law, Ailsie's legal owner, refused consent and demanded her return. "In her ripening beauty she was too valuable to be given to me. For what purposes she was detained ... there is no need to describe ... I have never heard of her since."[85]

Martineau wrote extensively about the beauty and racialized sexual oppression of the "mulatto and Quadroon" women she encountered in New Orleans.

> The Quadroon girls of New Orleans are brought up by their mothers to be ... the Mistresses of white gentlemen. The girls are highly educated, externally, and are as beautiful and accomplished a set of women as can be found. Every young man early selects one, and establishes her in one of those pretty and peculiar houses ... in the Ramparts. The connexion now and then lasts for life; usually for several years ... when the time comes for the gentleman to take a white wife, the dreadful news reaches the Quadroon partner. The Quadroon ladies are rarely or never known to form a second connexion. Many commit suicide; more die broken hearted ... Every Quadroon woman believes that her partner will prove an exception to the rule of desertion. Every white lady believes that her husband has been an exception to the rule of seduction. What security for domestic purity and peace can there be where everyman has had two connexions, one of which must be concealed ... where the conjugal relation begins in treachery.[86]

Anthropologist Ann Stoler argues:

> The colonial politics of exclusion was contingent on constructing categori legal and social classifications, designating who was "white," who was "native" could become a citizen rather than a subject, which children were legitimate property and which were not ... Social and legal standing derived not only from color, but from the silences, acknowledgements, and denials of the social circumstances in which one's parents had sex.[87]

Quadroons were liminal personae. Their skin color was deliberately racially ambiguous and they were given an education similar to white women. However, their status was as mistress not wife, and they were slaves like their mothers. "Miscegenation signaled neither the absence nor presence of racial prejudice in itself; hierarchies of privilege and power were written into the condoning of interracial unions, as well as into their condemnation."[88] Martineau illustrates:

> A southern lady... had possessed a pretty mulatto girl, of whom she declared herself fond. A young man came to stay at her house, and fell in love with the girl. 'She came to me,' said the lady, 'for protection, which I gave her.' The young man went away, but after some week, returned saying he was so much in love with the girl that he could not live without her. 'I pitied the young man,' concluded the lady, 'so I sold the girl to him for 1,500 dollars.' The degradation of women is so obvious a consequence of the evils disclosed above.[89]

For Martineau, "two hellish practices, slavery and polygamy" were inextricably linked.[90]

> There is no occasion to explain the management of the female slaves on estates
> where the object is to rear as many as possible, like stock, for the southern market; not to point out the boundless licentiousness caused by the practice; a practice which wrung from the wife of a planter, in the bitterness of her heart, the declaration that a planter's wife was only 'the chief slave of the harem'... the female slaves were to become mothers at fifteen.[91]

The American experience radicalized Martineau and gave her courage of conviction to fully identify and support the abolitionist cause. Transcending "auxiliary usefulness," in *Society in America* "she espouses with force and clarity racial equality, the emancipation of the slaves, the abolitionist cause, the rights of women, and the need for equalization of property."[92] Through moving personal narratives that include violence and sexual exploitation, Martineau's accounts of slavery reflect her willingness to speak her mind on extending democratic principles to all.[93]

Historical Fiction and an Ethnographic Fairytale

Between 1839 and 1844 Martineau was ill, yet continued to write prolifically including *The Hour and the Man* (1841), a historical novel based on Toussaint L'Ouverture, the black liberator of Haiti, and *The Playfellow* (1841), an enormously popular series of children's adventure stories. Martineau's literature for children was an integral part of her ardent desire to instruct her readers.[94] Martineau's lifelong dedication to the abolition of slavery, drew her to Haiti, a free republic, the first to abolish slavery and to Toussaint L'Ouverture, the movement's Commander-in-chief. "I speedily made up my mind to present that genuine hero with his actual sayings and doings (as far as they were extant) to the world."[95]

In the appendix Martineau presented the printed sources she used to establish historical accuracy regarding Touossaint's life, death, and the revolutionary wars for Haitian independence. Following Hayden White, Martineau's subjective evaluations of this "objective" evidence, a reflection of her own social context, inextricably shaped the novel's emplotment. She reached her own conclusions about Toussaint's character, rejecting frequent depictions of him in existing sources as "savage in warfare; hypocritical in religion—using pity as a political mask; and in all his affairs the very prince of dissemblers."[96] Instead, Martineau constructed Toussaint as gentle and compassionate, citing as evidence his kindness to animals and his strict no retaliation rule as a general and Commander-in-chief. Martineau believed that Toussaint's religion was genuine since he evinced "the spirit of piety from his infant years, finding in it the consolations required by a life of slavery, and guided by it in a course of the strictest domestic morality, while surrounded by licentiousness."[97] She viewed Toussaint as a modest man since he rejected making himself a sovereign and remained loyal to France until convinced of French incompetence and ignorance. His key concerns were conciliation and establishing credibility among all sides. For the other characters Martineau relied on verisimilitude. Nearly all actually existed, but she needed to invent much about them. "The only character designed to be fully and faithfully accordant with history is that of Toussaint."[98]

The novel opens in 22 August, 1791, in the town of Cap Francais in the French colony of Saint Domingo after leaders in Paris had passed a decree that granted mulattoes the privileges of French citizens including suffrage, and seats in the parochial and colonial assemblies. When the decree arrived at Cap Francais, whites and the governor of the colony denounced it. The white gentry were determined to make their own laws for the colony in defiance of the King of France.

On the Breda estate near Cap Francais lived the novel's hero, Toussaint Breda, a slave working for his kind-hearted master Monsieur Bayou. Toussaint, as interpreted by Martineau, is a liminal persona. First, although he is a slave, he is devoted to and loyal to his master. Second, although he is a slave, he lived in his own cottage with his wife and five children rather than in the slave quarter since he had recently been promoted to overseerer, a reward for his hard work. Third, unlike most slaves who were denied literacy, Toussaint was taught to read by his master Bayou. He is an avid reader and self-educated man, skills that later served him well. Fourth, Toussaint is a religious Catholic, whose moral code was incorruptible, unlike many slaves whose circumstances led them to debased behavior and hatred of whites. Given Martineau's views concerning polygyny and rampant marital infidelity on slave estates in the American South, it is inconceivable for her to choose a hero who was not living in a monogamous marriage, who was not self-educated, hard-working, or religious. Toussaint considered both the white rebellion against the French King and the black rebellion against their white masters to be great sins. When the Breda estate is threatened, Toussaint and his wife Margo whole-heartedly assisted with the arrangements for Bayou's safe passage out of the colony on a cargo boat to America.[99]

Martineau asserted that free slaves could and should determine their own lives. Without a master, Toussaint, like other blacks whose masters had fled, was an autonomous man who could use his reason, education, and morals to guide himself, his family and fellow blacks toward freedom, independence, and progress. Initially, Toussaint agreed to fight alongside blacks only to remain loyal to the French King and defend the colony for France. He abhorred murder and insisted that he be allowed to protect other whites. Toussaint joined with the Spanish allies of the French and was made a colonel for their black troops. However, in his tent, Toussaint confessed to Father Laxabon that his liminality produced deep anxiety: "How shall I appear before God—I who have ever been guided, and who know not whether I can guide myself—my master gone—my employment gone—and I, by his will, a free man, but unprepared, unfit?"[100]

Toussaint's strong moral fiber is contrasted with Monsieur Papalier, an example of licentious married white men who sexually exploited enslaved black women. Papalier's "favorite" was Therese, a young "negress" who bore his child and whose beauty "was celebrated all over the district" by whites and blacks.[101] When Toussaint, Bayou, and Papalier find the terrified Therese and her baby hiding by the side of the road after the burning of Papalier's estate, Toussaint is reluctant to allow his daughters to interact with her. Therese's sin of sexual impropriety renders her a pariah. Papalier condescends to Toussaint:

> I am sorry to see you set your girls above their condition and their neighbors. There is no harm about poor Therese. Indeed she is very well educated; I have had her well taught; and they might learn many things from her, if you really wish them to be superior. She is not a bit the worse for being a favourite of mine; and it will be their turn soon to be somebody's favourite, you know ... They are ... very fine girls for their age.

Toussaint refused to listen to such toxic speech. Although Therese was educated, like the Quadroons of New Orleans, Papalier was strongly against blacks learning to read and none on his estate were literate. "Bayou was a fool to allow it. I always told him so. When our negroes get to read like so many gentlemen, no wonder the world is turned upside down."[102]

Later that night when they all escape to safety on the estate of Toussaint's brother Paul, the cries of Therese's baby endanger them. "A strong hand wrenched the child from her grasp in the black darkness." The frantic mother asked for her child to be returned or to be left behind to find it. Papalier refused: "I should never see you again; and I cannot spare you. It is sad enough to have lost the child." Therese suspected that it was Papalier, the baby's father, who killed the baby, instigating an enduring hatred. Later in the novel, Therese refused to leave with Papalier for Paris where his daughters reside. Instead she immediately freed herself of gendered race domination by agreeing to marry Jacques Dessalines, who proposed to her to express his love for her and all oppressed blacks.[103] After their marriage, when Jacques and Therese meet with Toussaint Breda, by then a general of the black troops, he agreed to let Therese live with his wife Margot and his daughters at the Breda estate. Therese, now a married woman who atoned for her sin to God, is pure and fit to be Madame Dessalines, the loving wife of Jacques, a fictive daughter to Margo, and friend to his daughters Aimee and Genifrede. At the end of the novel, when Papalier lay dying nursed by Therese, he still addressed her as his slave, proclaiming how he cannot spare her, despite her change in status and power to grant his daughters the security he desired. When Therese inquired if Papalier had killed her baby, he replied, "I do not say that I ... did not allow it. But I did not do it." Although Papalier knew the killer, he refused to tell Therese, and she resolved never to seek this knowledge.[104]

Papalier informed Toussaint about the decree of the French revolutionary Convention that had confirmed and proclaimed the liberty of the blacks to be accepted as citizens and the colony as part of France. Realizing that he was now on the wrong side, Toussaint confessed to Father Laxabon that he would give up his Spanish command.

> Father, I feel that the hour may be come for the negro race to be re-deemed; and that I, a common man, may so far devote myself as not to stand in the way of their redemption. I feel that I must step out from among those who have never admitted the negroes' claims to manhood. If God should open to me a way to serve the blacks better, I shall be found ready.

Toussaint left the Spanish camp and "henceforth, the city, the colony, the island, and after a time, all Europe, rang with the name of Toussaint L'Ouverture."[105]

After independence, Toussaint, as Commander-in-chief, is no longer liminal. Residing at the palace in Port-au-Prince, Toussaint and his family reflect the progress and prosperity that inevitably results from the elimination of race domination. Through Toussaint Martineau conveys her conviction that race is a social construction. Toussaint recognized that the period after independence was liminal both for blacks and for his country's economy. As their leader Toussaint endeavored to promote peaceful interactions among formerly antagonistic groups, "by weaning their [blacks] minds from thoughts of anger, and their eyes from the sight of blood" and by promoting industry and agriculture.[106] He re-stored displaced whites to their estates partly because of prior ownership and his concern for economic development. "By circumstances—not by nature—the whites have been able to acquire a wide intelligence, a depth of knowledge, from which the blacks have been debarred. I desire for the blacks a perpetual and friendly intercourse with those who are their superior in education."[107] Toussaint circulated lists of the unclaimed estates in the colony, France, and the United States.

Monsieur Bayou, Toussaint's former master, returned and attempted to ex-press his love and gratitude. When Bayou hastened to embrace Toussaint, he asserted his full transformation from former slave to Commander-in-chief. "Gently sir," said the Commander-in-chief, drawing back two steps. "There ... can be no familiarity with the chief of a newly redeemed race." Toussaint de-sired for Bayou, one of the "good old masters," to take a leadership role among white estate owners in the economic development of the Breda estate using well disciplined free laborers.[108]

When Toussaint conducted Bayou to greet Madame L'Ouverture and his daughters, they too have transcended liminality and accept his gifts of friend-ship. In conditions of freedom, the "animated sweetness of the negro counte-nance" emerged. Madame L'Ouverture, was still motherly and busily employed with her needle, but tempered by a gratified matronly grace. Daughters Genifrede and Aimee were both "wonderfully improved in beauty," especially Genifrede, in love with her first cousin Moyse, Paul's son, who worships her.

In her was seen by the European who attended the levee of that day, what the ne-gro face and form may be when seen in their native climate, unhardened by deg-radation, undebased by ignorance, unspoiled by oppression—all peculiarities of feature softened under the refining influence of mind, and all peculiarities of ex-pression called out in their beauty by the free exercise of natural affection.[109]

Therese, loved by Madame as a daughter, was even more beautiful than Genifrede, and even more beautiful than she was as a girl. Although her girlish-ness, sensitivity, and animation were gone, "her carriage was majestic, her coun-tenance, calm and its beauty now refined by the life of leisure and the con-sciousness of rank ... her husband now a general in Toussaint's army."[110]

Deep racial divisions nevertheless continued to tear at the social fabric of Saint Domingo, posing challenges for governance and social relations in Tous-saint's family that shape the remainder of the novel. Toussaint blamed slavery for all of the challenges to peace in Saint Domingo. "We negroes are ignorant, and have been made loose, deceitful, and idle, by slavery."[111] In France, exiled white planters such as Papalier, who hated Toussaint and black independence, had the ear of Bonaparte arousing his jealousy. In Saint Domingo whites, "made tyrannical and unjust by being masters," believed the blacks to be "ambitious, rebellious and revengeful." Toussaint's nephew Moyse, a general, never lost his deep hatred for whites and persuaded his love, Genifrede, to hate them. Moyse's poisonous hatred led to his execution for disobeying Toussaint. Moyse's death, divided the family: both Moyse's lover Genifrede and his brother Paul, Moyse's father, disengaged from Toussaint. At the novel's end, after his overthrow, de-parture from Saint Domingo, imprisonment and death in a French prison, Tous-saint's cellmate Mars Plaisir despairs: "these whites think that we blacks are created to be serving, serving always." Toussaint humbly replied: "And they are right. Their mistake is in not seeing that the same is the case with all other men."[112]

During her long illness, Martineau also wrote *The Playfellow* consisting of four books written for children. *Feats on the Fiord*, the third book, will be ana-lyzed here as an early example of ethnographic fiction. Although Martineau never visited Norway, it possesses many of the structural and stylistic elements of a traditional ethnography tempered by Martineau's idiosyncratic combination of objective rational observation and didacticism. *Feats* is less didactic than the *Illustrations*, employing the fairy tale trope where the leading man proves him-self worthy of winning his bride. Martineau interjects her didacticism when comparing Norwegian indigenous religious beliefs, viewed as irrational, conser-vative "superstitions," with Christianity, the belief system associated with pro-gress. Martineau's theoretical approach is that culture (morals) mediates all material needs and complex belief systems shape social interactions (manners) between people and their physical environments.

Set in Norway in the 1740s, Martineau begins with vivid descriptions of the ecology and geography. Social and economic life are structured by the "the strange mixture of land and sea"—the towering cliffs along the coasts, the fiords, bays, mountains, meadows—and the northern seasonal climate—long, cold, snowy winters with short stints of daylight alternating with short mild summers when the sun never fully sets. Martineau stresses Norway's beauty both in winter, where the land and sea are encased in ice and snow, and in summer when the snow melts, the sun shines, and all of nature is lush with grasses, trees, flowers, and wildlife.[113]

Martineau follows with detailed information about subsistence practices which are structured both by the limitations of the environment and the gender division of labor. Agriculture consisted of grains, vegetables, and fruits that could be grown in the short windy summer season and pasture to feed horses, cows, and goats for seven months. A cyclical transhumant pattern of life prevailed with animals in summer being driven up the mountain to graze on pastures until the first frosts. There at the "seater" herdsmen and dairywomen live on the mountain with the herds and "enjoy the mode of life extremely."[114] Milk and dairy products, particularly butter and cheese, were produced by the women. Men hunted wild game throughout the year.[115] Each year in winter a large fair took place where peasant men would purchase or barter for goods that they did not produce. These included reindeer meat, their skins and manufactured articles by nomadic Lapps and traveling Russian merchants.[116]

While men attended this yearly fair, "it was Madame Erlingsen's business to calculate how much of all these foreign articles would be required for the use of her household for a whole year; and, trusting to her calculations ... her husband came home from the winter fair heavily enough laden with good things." In Norway accurate household calculations by the wife needed to include hospitality norms during visits and annual Christmas feasts when corn-brandy, tobacco, coffee, and sugar would be consumed in large quantities.[117] Households included servants, apprentices, and journeymen and women were responsible for all domestic labor.

Anthropologists analyze the economic interconnections between nomadic hunter-gatherers and settled agricultural societies in particular regions where goods and sometimes labor were/are exchanged. The Lapps, nomadic reindeer herders, are mentioned throughout the story. They are portrayed as a savage society where the undersized nomadic people live in dirty tents. Lapps are looked down upon by settled Norwegians of all social classes who never socialize with them beyond charity or periodic exchanges of reindeer meat and skins. When the anticipated visit from the Bishop includes his willingness to enter a Lapp's tent to assist in curing a sick child, all are shocked.[118] Martineau grants to Lapps the shrewd self-interest of scavengers who benefit from their close observation of peasant ritual behavior. The "superstition" of those residing at the seater clouds any knowledge of this symbiosis. Erica and other dairymaids appease the mountain-demon by leaving the first Gemmel cheese on the soft ridge moss.

> If she [Erica] had had the curiosity and courage to watch for a little while, she
> would have seen her offering carried off by an odd little figure, with nothing

very terrible in its appearance; namely a woman about four feet high, with a flat face, and eyes wide apart, wearing a reindeer garment like a waggoner's frock, a red comforter about her neck, a red cloth cap on her head, a blue worsted sash, and leather boots up to the knee: in short, such a Lapland girl as Erica would have given a rye-cake to as charity, but would not have thought of asking to sit down, even in her master's kitchen; for the Norwegian servants are very high and saucy toward the Lapps who wander to their doors. It is not surprising that the Lapps who pitch their tents on the mountains should like having a fine Gemmel cheese for the trouble of picking it up; and the company whose tents Erica had passed on her way to the seater, kept a good look-out upon all the dairy people round, and carried off every cheese meant for the demon ... What would Erica have thought of had she beheld this fruit of so many milkings and skimmings, so much boiling and pressing, devoured by greedy Lapps in their dirty tent?[119]

Martineau uses marriage and its public rituals to establish a sense of community, rights and privileges, and close social bonds. Among the rural Norwegians there were two ceremonies associated with marriage: one when the couple is engaged and the other when they are married. "In Norway, this betrothment gives the couple a certain dignity beyond that of the unengaged, and more liberty of companionship, together with certain rights in law. This makes up to them for being obliged to wait so long as they often must before they can marry." Servants typically worked for and lived with the same family for life, caring for them in their old age, and waiting years to marry "till some houseman dies or removes" when they inherit the farmer's house. After marriage they remain in that house for life. The long wait to marry was understood as a preparation for marriage, increasing the likelihood of happiness and compatibility.[120]

In *Feats*, the young betrothed woman is the beautiful, hardworking, yet superstitious and anxious Erica, a dairymaid at the Erlingsen farm, and her lover Rolf who served as houseman for an old couple Peder and Ulla. Their winter betrothal festival began at two, "when the short daylight was gone." Guests wrapped in furs arrived at the Erlingsen's large house by boats on the fiord and by sledge. "All were glad to have arrived safely, to be greeted warmly and to be ushered into the great room where all was light, warm, and cheerful." *Hors d'oeuvres* were served and domestic industry implements cleared away to make room for dancing. Older men lit their pipes and talked or played cards in a smaller room while the young men selected their dance partners. "The dance was led by the blushing Erica ... All the women in Norway dance well, being practiced in it from their infancy, as an exercise for which the leisure of their long winter, and the roominess of their houses afforded scope." After dancing the company and men of the household sat at the supper table while the women served them "piles of fish," "joint after joint of reindeer venison," "preserved fruits and berries, eaten with thick cream." The last dish was sweet cake. "Long was the supper, and hearty was the mirth around the table."[121]

It was customary in rural Norway to offer a slice of cake and ale at festival times and at Christmas to the spirit Nipen. Erica, riddled with superstitions learned from her mother as a child, and confirmed by her mother's untimely death frozen in a forest recess, was anxious that Nipen not be offended. "Everybody knows who lives in the rural districts of Norway, about Nipen, the spirit that is always so busy after everybody's affairs, about the Water-sprite, an acquaintance of everyone who lives beside a river or lake, about the Mountain-Demon, familiar to all who lived so near Sulitelma," and "a race of fairies or magicians living underground, who are very covetous of cattle."[122] The young Lutheran pastor Kollsen, dismayed by these pagan beliefs, is determined to abolish them quickly.

The tension between pagan "old customs" and Christianity is illustrated by the tormented Erica, whose slavish devotion to "selfish and revengeful spirits" imprisons her emotionally. Those closest to her, the Erlingsens and Rolf, repeatedly attempt to persuade her that peace of mind can only come from belief in one just God.[123] Erica's conversion comes only after the kindly Bishop of Tronyem explains to her how the old myths and legends arose from the human need to explain the world around them.

> And how did this old religion arise?—Why, the people saw grand spectacles every day, and heard wonders whichever way they turned; and they supposed that the whole universe was alive. The sun as it traveled they thought was alive, and kind and good to men. The tempest they thought was alive, and angry with men. The fire and frost they thought were alive, pleased to make sport with men.

Among the rural people, whose oral traditions were strong, children grew up hearing the old songs and stories about demons and sprites. "And when the child is grown to be a man or woman, the northern lights shooting over the sky, and the sighing of the winds in the pine-forest, bring back these old songs, and old thoughts about demons and sprites; and the stoutest man trembles." The Bishop was certain that eventually mothers would sing to their babies about Jesus and men would no longer be afraid, confident that God the Father was with them. The Bishop's gentle words and gestures persuade Erica that "everything that happens is done by God's own hand."[124]

The kind Bishop of Tronyem married Erica and Rolf before leaving Nordland and the story has a fairytale ending: a beautiful bride, glittering crown, happy bride-groom, soothing music, the hearty cheers of neighbors, and the Bishop's kindly welcome of Erica to the altar. "Go; and peace be on your house."[125]

An Anthropology of the Home and Domesticity

Themes relating to home, community, marriage, and domesticity are central to Martineau's domestic romance novel *Deerbrook*. Previously Martineau's fiction was, an "empirically-grounded thought experiment."[126] *Deerbrook* was Martineau's experiment with writing a novel drawing solely on her imagination for the "morally suspect" purpose of "the manipulation of readers to no other end other than the excitement of feeling."[127]

Feminist scholars argue that although *Deerbrook* was influential as a precursor of domestic realism (George Eliot, Elizabeth Gaskell, and Charlotte Bronte), it is a frustrating novel because it lacks artistry and authorial authority, and the plot and female characters are conventional. In *Deerbrook*, Martineau largely acquiesced to Victorian hegemonic gender constructions characteristic of nineteenth century middle class culture. The feminist critiques that enliven Martineau's travel writings and sociological investigations into women's work are largely missing.[128]

Marriage was the central institution reproducing asymmetrical gender relations in Victorian England, as it was in the early modern period. Men at marriage assumed economic and legal responsibility for their wives and future children becoming protective and authoritative. Men controlled courtship and marriage proposals since they needed to have the resources to support a wife.[129] Women also assumed full adult status at marriage. The role of wife was essentially as helpmeet and women were seen as domestic by nature. Wives were bound to provide their husbands with domestic and sexual services and husbands could sue wives who refused to provide these. Spinsterhood was considered a failure, and many women were pressured to marry when they would have preferred to remain single.[130]

Both household and family in the English middle class were flexible in their composition including extended kin and non-kin. For example, one after another of the daughters of brother Thomas Martineau, a Birmingham brass manufacturer, lived with their aunt Harriet as companions.[131] "Specific categories of age, gender and function were seen as necessary to staff a family. If these were not filled biologically, surrogates were found."[132]

In industrial capitalist societies, "it is the material culture within our home that appears as both our appropriation of the larger world and often as the representation of that world within our private domains."[133] Capitalism not only separated the spaces associated with home and work, but also separated space from place, since more people were distant from home places. Capitalism, as Marx argued, separated time and space, with time assuming dominance; the ability to "annihilate space" by technological innovations in the ability to move people, commodities and information through space. Time, coded masculine, is associated with linear movement, history, progress while space, coded feminine, is associated with circular rhythms, stasis, passivity, enclosure. Localism is symbolically similar to the home, with both theoretically explained in essentialist ideological terms. Home places and spaces are essentially feminine, reliable, and authentic, like the women whose stable identities and roles are constructed and constrained in them.[134] Home places have deep emotional and symbolic meaning that shape the social relations associated with space and place.

Martineau was a pioneer of the home and domesticity as research contexts. She anticipated the recent anthropological analyses of how gender identities are constructed through housework and the material and sensory environment of the home.[135] Recent anthropological analyses show that the home can be both a stable foundation for kinship and domestic life and the setting for mobility and change. In *Home Truths*, Sarah Pink challenges the theoretical gender binary that interprets the home and housework in essentialist terms that reproduces gender dichotomies and denies women's agency. Pink's agentic perspectives, that emphasize the heterogeneous and negotiated aspects of constructed gender identities in the home, are consistent with those of Martineau who clearly recognized the agency of women involved in housework; their skills were essential to the health, happiness and financial stability of their households.

Pink treats the home as a creative domain, "a space where each individual ... could articulate her or his unique gendered self in negotiation with the sensory, social, cultural, and material environment in which she or he lived."[136] Housework is associated with the everyday repetitive performance of tasks that aim to maintain a result or equilibrium. All human activities, even the most mundane, can be expressive and performative in relationship to other ongoing emotional narratives in daily life, serving as ways to resist as well as reproduce hegemonic gender constructions. The home is a complex configuration of identity that is closely interwoven with an individual's project of self and/or a couples' project of us. Projects of home are evolving requiring on-going imagination and interaction with existing resources—economic, material, social, and sensory.[137]

Deerbrook is of anthropological interest since it is a novel about Victorian rural locality, home, domesticity, and "dailiness." According to Vineta Colby, this novel is pioneering to the genres of domestic realism and to the sociological novel that developed over the next quarter century. Domestic realism shifted the focus from the aristocracy to the middle class, was anti-romantic, glorified the values of domesticity, and emphasized the imperatives of duty, self-sacrifice, and endurance. Novels of social community focused on the close interdependence of the residents with individual character shaped by the community. In *Deerbrook*, as in domestic realism generally, "its particular focus is the community's women, whose exclusion from the productive economy necessarily reinforces their provincial isolation from the national narrative of scientific, economic, and political progress that is the novel's implicit point of appeal."[138]

The novel opens with the anticipated arrival by the Grey family, living in the pretty village of Deerbrook, of the Miss Ibbotsons, Hester, age twenty-one and Margaret, age twenty of Birmingham, recently orphaned after the death of their father, a cousin of Mr. Grey's. As in *Principle and Practice*, the orphaned sisters are liminal, in limbo. Mr. Grey was their nearest relation and "he had invited them to visit his family while their father's affairs were in course of arrangement, and till it could be discovered what their means of living were likely to be." Mrs. Grey and her eldest daughter Sophia, age sixteen, are sitting in the drawing room sewing, usefully waiting. As expected in a small rural community: "all Deerbrook had been informed of their expected arrival."[139]

Upon their arrival, Hester, Margaret, and their maid Morris were quickly given "an account of the society of the place." The Greys are Dissenters, and

considered by the bookseller who supplied their bookclub to be "rather intellectual people," traits that reflect Martineau's upbringing and values.[140] It was
expected when extended kin were visiting for locals to call to meet their acquaintance, and anticipating this normative practice, Mrs. Grey informs the
reader along with the sisters of the principal families and characters—Edward
Hope, the Levitts, Enderbys, and the antagonistic Rowlands.

In the nineteenth century, a young woman's physical appearance was critically important to her chances of attracting a husband. Margaret is considered
reasonably attractive, but Hester is very beautiful. One of the central characters,
Edward Hope, stopped by on business soon after Hester and Margaret's arrival.
Given Hester's beauty, Mrs. Grey begins to imagine a match between Hester
and Hope. Hope, whose surname signifies what he represents to Deerbrook and
to the novel's central characters, is the local medical man, and a great favorite of
the Greys. Hope and other medical men, were progressive intellectual leaders in
small towns and rural areas. "I see you know something of the predilection of
villagers for their apothecary, how the young people wonder that he always
cures everybody; and how the old people could not live without him; and how
the poor folks take him for a sort of magician; and how he obtains more knowledge of human affairs than any other kind of person." From the perspective of
Philip Enderby, an educated man who resides in London, Mr. Hope, "no ordinary case of a village apothecary" is the "great boast of the place."[141]

The bond between sisters was often the strongest in Victorian women's lives.
Margaret possessed an ideal feminine disposition: devoted, open, intuitive, with
the ability to read her sister Hester's every mood by her facial expressions. Hester, on the other hand, is jealous, moody, and prone to self-rebuke of her im-
properly disciplined imagination, believing herself to have a wicked jealous
temper that Margaret frequently attempts to assuage. "If I were to lose you,
Hester, there are many many things that would be shut up in me for ever ... Do
you believe this Hester? ... Then you will never again doubt me ... You cannot
imagine how my heart sinks when I see you are fancying that I care for someone
else more than for you."[142]

The morning after their arrival Hester and Margaret meet Miss Maria Young,
the children's governess. Ann Hobart argues that Maria Young is the "novel's
most striking innovation" inaugurating a series of fictional governesses, "single
women of reduced means, strong sensibilities, and no very tempting exterior"
and sociological concern with the occupation.[143] There are significant parallels
between the liminal Maria Young and Martineau. Martineau lived her life as a
Victorian oddity, and at mid-century, governesses were at the margins of gentility and work, guardians of and threats to middle-class values and norms.[144] Martineau's didacticism regarding "redundant" single women, their employment,
and the particular circumstances faced by Victorian governesses, like her own
sister Ellen, were given voice through Maria Young. Both Young and Martineau
are single, and openly weigh the social limitations and possibilities for women
who do not assume their primary roles as wives and mothers.[145] "Women who
have what I am not to have, a home, an intimate, a perpetual call out of them-

selves, may go on more safely, without any thought for themselves than I ... but ... the blessing of a peremptory vocation, is to stand me instead of sympathy, ties and spontaneous action."[146] As women at the margins, both Young as governess and Martineau as a writer are keen observers of other people's lives. Financial necessity forced both to earn a living due to the death of their fathers, one as a governess, the other as writer, after a comfortable childhood. Both were somewhat formally educated, yet somewhat cut off from society due to physical disabilities inflicted in childhood—Martineau is deaf and Young is lame after a tragic accident. Both loved to sew. Maria Young's students, too young to appreciate the art of needlework, were astounded that she "could sit sewing, as fast as her needle could fly, for the whole afternoon ... and that some of her pleasantest hours were those which she passed in this employment."[147] Like Martineau, who conquered her own unhappiness as a child by creating structured routines, Young believes happiness is rooted in "the conquest of circumstances" that flows from learning what to expect rather than freedom of choice. Maria Young gives voice to the key goal of domestic realism: depicting life as it really exists. Few governesses would enjoy their work since they suffered too many social and economic deprivations. "Do you suppose that one's comfort lies in having a choice of employments? My experience leads me to think the contrary ... I am disposed to think that the greatest number of happy people may be found busy in employments that they have not chosen for themselves, and never would have chosen."[148] Maria Young, like Martineau, longs to educate and Margaret agreed to be taught "the bright field of German literature" by her. They become close friends often arousing Hester's jealousy.

Deerbrook is noisy with the din of social connections and gossip orchestrated mostly by women "who are always busy looking into one another's small concerns." Romance and marriage are central concerns that are not easily controlled, but for Martineau, an individual's romantic passion is controllable. It can and should be resisted and overcome in certain circumstances.[149] Two romantic love triads are central to the novel and both involve the concealment of passion. Maria Young loves Philip Enderby, but he loves Margaret Ibbotson, her best friend in whom she never confides her love. Hester Ibbotson loves Edward Hope, but he too loves Margaret who he described in a letter to his brother as "pure existence ... infinite simplicity, from which all selfishness is discharged, and into which no folly can enter."[150] Hope, unfortunately, is pressured by Mrs. Grey to marry Hester and Margaret, as was customary for sisters who had never been parted, lived with them creating intense psychological strain for Hope. He is determined that Margaret should remain unaware of his erotic affections for her. Margaret loves Philip Edendery who suspects that she loves Hope. Margaret, who had always longed for a brother, devotedly maintained her sibling bond for both Hopes until leaving to marry Philip Edendery at the end of the novel.

The triad of Edward, Hester and Margaret is of particular anthropological interest since it illustrates sororate marriage in the English context. In England it was normative for a wife's younger sister to live with the married couple. She became like a sister to her brother-in-law, calling him brother, and like a second wife assuming specific domestic duties in the home. These relationships could have erotic overtones as in the case of Edward Hope (or Charles Dickens). If the wife died, it was not uncommon for the husband and his sister-in-law to marry, the benefits of which to the continuity of the family were many. The legal prohibition against the sororate in 1835 (repeal of the Deceased Wife's Sister Clause of the Marriage Act) was "passionately debated from the 1830s" and, thereafter, friendly relations with sisters-in-law were slightly suspect. Hope maintains the harmony of his household by controlling his sexual attraction to Margaret.[151]

Martineau's view that romantic love should be freed from the silly, vain, and often heart-breaking "art of wooing" to reflect the serious realities of married life and homemaking are given voice through Margaret. In the chapter "Preparing for Home," Martineau states how the preparations for Hester's marriage were synonymous with furnishing the Hopes' new home to represent their new conjugal status. Over a century later, anthropologist Levi-Strauss similarly stated that the house is the objectification of the marriage relationship. Anthropologists Maurice Bloch and Chang-Kwo Tan have applied this theory to the Zafimaniry of Madagascar and the Paiwan of Taiwan. Among the Zafimaniry, "The creation of the house and marriage are viewed as two sides of the same thing; the building and decoration of the house is bound up with the transformation of conjugal relations from fluid to thing-like, as solid and concrete as the wooden central post of a house." For the Paiwan, "the married couple is the core of kinship, and is identified with the house they build together in an enduring marriage." Wives decorate the rooms with great attention to color, furniture, and fragrance to create an atmosphere conducive to the physical and psychological rest and renewal of their hardworking husbands.[152]

Martineau's description of the Hopes' new home is rich with material and sensory details that signify the couple's permanent conjugal relationship, their bright future, and reflects her respect for women's agency in establishing domestic intimacy.

> furnishing a house is a process of high enjoyment when it is the preparation of a home for happy love. The dwelling is hung all round with bright anticipations, and crowded with blissful thoughts, spoken by none, perhaps, but present to all. On this table, and by this snug fireside, will be the cheerful winter breakfast to go forward, when each is about to enter on the gladsome business of the day; and that sofa will be drawn out, and those window-curtains will be closed, when the intellectual pleasures of the evening, the rewards of the laborious day begin. Those ground-windows will stand open all the summer noon, and the flower stands will be gay and fragrant; and the shaded parlour will be the cool retreat of the wearied husband, when he comes in to rest from his professional trials. There will stand the books destined to refresh and refine his higher tastes; and there the music with which the wife will indulge him. Here will they first feel what it is to have a home of their own, where they will first enjoy the privacy of it, the security, the freedom, the consequence in the eyes of others, the sacredness in their own. Here they will first exercise the graces of hospitality, and the responsibility of

control. Here they will feel that they have attained the great resting-place of their life. [153]

Great care was given to furnishing the attic for their devoted servant Morris, and to Margaret's bed chamber, one of the prettiest rooms in the house.[154] When Margaret shows the new house to Maria Young, Martineau conveys her belief that women are naturally domestic.

> Women do inevitably love housekeeping, unless educational or other impediments interfere with their natural tastes. Household management is to them the object of their talents, the subject of their interests, the vehicle of their hopes and fears, the medium through which their affections are manifested, and much of their benevolence gratified. If it be true, as has been said, that there is no good quality of a woman's heart and mind which is not necessary to perfect housekeeping, it follow that there is no power of mind of affection of the heart which may not be gratified in the course of its discharge.[155]

For Martineau strong human emotions should be contained within normative bounds. Hester's and Margaret's income from their father's estate was seventy pounds per year. Margaret's financial contribution of fifty pounds to the Hopes' household expenses and meeting her own personal expenses assured her independence, a healthy compliment to her amiable even temper. When distressed, Margaret took long solitary walks, as did Martineau, with "thick shoes, umbrella and muff, guarded against everything that might occur overhead and under foot."[156] Hope, the breadwinner, is even tempered, a loyal husband, and unwavering in his support of the household that depends on him despite his early disappointment in Hester and his initial experience of his marriage as bondage. Due to her "agitation of spirits," Hester has difficulty disciplining her emotions so that she can fulfill her duty of creating a happy domestic environment.[157]

In fact, Hester does not rise to the occasion until Hope faces real financial hardship. In small rural places, landlords exerted considerable political influence, and many of the inhabitants were uneducated. Medical men could become entangled in the narrow ideas, confining norms, and limited perceptions in small rural communities where it was expected that they remain outside of politics. Hope's practice declined rapidly after his decision to vote for a candidate in the county election not supported by the landlord Sir William Hunter and after vicious slanders spread by Mrs. Rowland about doctors like Hope robbing churchyards of bodies for dissection purposes. Many of Hope's patients who formerly worshipped him, succumbed to ignorant delusion and sought a new doctor, and Sir William barred him from practicing at the almshouse.

This social context for Hester's psychological transformation reflects Martineau's conviction that hardship is valuable to human development, as evidenced by her own life. The loss of Hope's patients plunged the household into poverty. Margaret, confident in her sister's ability to cope with the coming adversity, assured Hope that "I fear nothing for her but too much prosperity."[158]

Indeed, adversity for the Hope household deepened as most of Deerbrook withdrew from their society. The sisters' growing competence in domestic management bring emotional rewards, particularly for Hester. For Martineau useful selfless labor is therapeutic and Hester grows happier, more amiable, and effectively supportive of the husband she dearly loves. As a result Hope grows to love and trust Hester. Hope's therapy and salvation results from committed duty to his family and community.[159]

> Hester was so much happier, so reasonable, so brave, admist her sinking fortunes, that Margaret could scarcely have been gayer than in plying her needle by her side ... Morris and they were so completely in one interest, Edward was so easily pleased, and they were so free from jealous dependants, that they could carry their economy to any extent that suited their conscious and convenience. One superfluity after another vanished from the table; every day something which had always been a want was discovered to be a fancy; and with every new act of frugality, each fresh exertion of industry, their spirits rose with a sense of achievement, and the complacency proper to cheerful sacrifice.[160]

The birth of the Hope's baby boy brought great joy to all and everyone doted on Hester. "With what zeal did Margaret apply herself, under Morris's teaching, to cook Hester's choice little dinner! Yes to cook them. Margaret was learning all Morris's arts from her."[161]

At the end of the novel, Martineau orchestrates the vindication of the noble Edward Hope and his household after a drought and fever epidemic ravage Deerbrook. Superstition, fortune-tellers, charms, and quacks, believed by the ignorant who fell ill, gave way to the compassionate scientific healing offered by Hope. The three families, the Greys, Enderbys, and Rowlands make amends through marriage ties and "thus united, the representatives of science, commerce, and industry gain ground against aristocratic power."[162]

Only Maria Young remains "out of the game" a liminal persona with no suitor or good job. Maria, as a spokesperson for women's employment, maintains that her independence is satisfying and "that there are glimpses of heaven for me in solitude."[163] She rejects Margaret's anxiety on her behalf as she prepares for her marriage to Philip and future life in London. Nevertheless, like the majority of redundant women, "Maria is left solitary, ill, and uncertain about financial prospects ... Such a fate—whatever its consolations—could hardly be chosen, only enforced."[164]

Conclusion: Governess to Great Britain

Anyone seeking to analyze Harriet Martineau's writing will be overwhelmed by her prolific "need of utterance" and by the breadth of her intellect. Martineau's purpose for writing was to educate children and adults about the important moral ideas and issues of her time and to affect social change through instruction. Martineau's social science was critical and radical in that her research and analysis emerged from her moral conceptions of justice, liberty, and happiness. Her critical perspective also emerged from her liminal marginal position as a Victorian oddity—a fully autonomous single woman who earned her living as a writer, a male profession, who traveled extensively and spoke her mind with total freedom.

Martineau's guiding theoretical framework for the study of society, as stated in *How to Observe Morals and Manners*, is that a society's normative behavior (manners) is inseparable from its collective ideas (morals). This framework guided her observations and analysis of life in *Society in America* during two years of travel. It is also evident in her fiction, especially her early fiction that functioned as a didactic tool to illustrate the "fixed" laws that govern human social life. Drawn initially to philosophical ideas associated with the emerging capitalist hegemony Martineau's *Illustrations of Political Economy* were explicitly didactic, illustrating the principles of political economy for the middle and working class. Although her initial role was functioning as an organic intellectual, illuminating this new hegemony and soothing anxiety over the new capitalist mode of production, Martineau was convinced that the origins of domination (race, class, gender) were social rather than natural and could be changed in contrast to Social Darwinism that emerged in the mid-nineteenth century. Martineau was equally committed to the Unitarian-derived ethic of personal responsibility, a morality that can only emerge under conditions of liberty, hard work, and selfless service to others as illustrated in *The Hour and the Man* and *Deerbrook*. This contradictory tension between necessarian "immutable laws" and Unitarian inspired critical agency, present in her writing, provided the dialectic fueling her intellect.

Marx offered the most powerful argument regarding the significance of creative human work, linking it to species-being, and Martineau's perspective on work as "the nexus of self and society" was in full accord with this fundamental materialism.[165] She had a deep respect for women's work and devoted much of her energy to its history, variety, significance to the economy and society, and the hardships and limitations faced by women workers due to patriarchal ideas and practices. Pointing to a reality as relevant today as it was in the mid-nineteenth century, she asserted that women were a permanent category of wage earners and the need for "female industry" increases as their dependence on men decreases.[166] Much of her writing emphasized the necessity of useful work for all, and those classes she admired, the middle and working classes, were those who worked hard outside and inside the home. Martineau believed that the physical exertion, structured routine and agency associated with work allowed individuals to overcome hardship, achieve emotional stability, and experience personal satisfaction and growth.

The significant dimensions of domination that dehumanized work or excluded categories of people from working were slavery, class exploitation, and gender discrimination. Slavery was a virulent form of domination thoroughly offensive to Martineau's morals and she spent her life as an active abolitionist. In *Demerara* she turns to political economy—the free market in labor—for a rational argument against this system that affected her so deeply at an emotional level. She stated that owing people as property dehumanizes slaves and owners as human beings; it degrades their work, their family ties, their religious beliefs, their sense of decency, and capital is wasted due to resistance to work, ignorance, and fear of rebellion.

Martineau consistently understood race as a social construction. Rejecting biology as the determinant factor explaining behavioral differences, she assumed that if the social context of slavery were to be abolished, free blacks could be the equal of free whites in every respect. She illustrated this conviction in *The Hour and the Man*, which portrayed the transformation of Toussant Breda, the slave to Toussant L'Ouverature, the liberator and Commander-in-chief of Haiti. She was also aware that the liminality of newly freed slaves was socially determined; they were free to develop their human potential, but limited by the forced ignorance and degradation they previously endured.

Martineau was an early formulator of feminist intersectionality theory. She was aware of the significant differences in experience between male and female slaves, male and female slave owners and free white women and enslaved women of color. In *Society in America*, Martineau's intersectionality is evident in her portrayals of how race, class, and gender connect in the triple exploitation of enslaved women's bodies. She repeatedly condemns in the strongest terms the sexual exploitation (licentiousness) of enslaved black women by white men who rape them and form extramarital ("polygamous") relations with them producing interracial offspring. When female, these offspring were highly eroticized objects, as illustrated by Quadroons. To Martineau, slavery and polygyny are interdependent and she condemns both in the harems of Egypt during her travels there and on the plantations in American South. Martineau was also aware of how race divided women; observing the exploitative relationship that existed between white women, who were oppressed by their husbands and idle lives, and the black female slaves who served them. Although Martineau was willing to recognize that some mistresses became attached to favorite slaves and treated them kindly, she pointed out the structural similarities between slave workers owned as property and idle elite southern white women who "exist in a condition of unofficial bondage to her husband, no more than a sexual ornament and agent of his pernicious values."[167] Although Martineau was aware of how race divided masculinities, she stopped short of analyzing the gender domination existing between enslaved men and women rooted in the reproduction and transmission of slave status through women and the stability earned by sexually gratifying favored slave men.

Gender domination presented more contradictions for Martineau as a Victorian woman intellectual than did slavery. To Valerie Sanders, Martineau is a "Janus" figure, both aggressively feminist and strongly influenced by Victorian domesticity. Rejecting women's intellectual inferiority, Martineau took from the rationality and individualistic perspectives of the Enlightenment, Unitarianism and Utilitarianism the belief that all women have the right to develop their potential and she consistently opposed educational and economic discrimination. Martineau's respect for women's contributions to domesticity is evident in her fiction. She anticipated Virginia Woolf's ardent feminist recognition that in the "trivial" details of private domestic life: housework, childcare, and home furnishings, we discover ways of life and that scholarly neglect of the "small" domestic domain was the result of misogyny.

However, "Martineau's experience of domestic life was mixed; a consistently difficult relationship with her mother, serious quarrels with most of her siblings, never interested in marriage, and only later in life able to set up a household on her own terms."[168] Ann Hobart summarized Martineau's ambiguous liberal feminism:

> On the one hand, she characterizes women's exclusion from the productive economy—and the ideology of gendered duties that upholds it—as the cause of both their political subordination and their moral and intellectual debility. On the other, she represents the sexual division of labor, in which the energies and resources of women are subordinated to men's as "natural" consequences of sexual difference to which the general good requires that women submit.

Martineau's feminism is more evident in her morality and "her energetic invention of her womanly Victorian self."[169]

Class domination also posed challenges for Martineau who did not see the exploitative contradiction between social classes as a structural feature of capitalism. Labor and capital are interdependent and essentially cooperative. She accepted as immutable the "laws" of population, the market, and private property. Low wages were the result of too many laborers competing for the same jobs or due to diminishing capital or profits, not private property or the profit motive. Nevertheless, Martineau was in favor of labor unions to enable workers to negotiate from a position of strength with their employers. The optimal situation emerged from the elimination of class domination through mutual respect.

When Martineau was contributing to the new science of society from 1834, her methods, perspectives, and theories were as applicable to the new discipline of anthropology. Although it took until 1998 for sociology to fully recognize Martineau as a founder, she remains invisible to anthropology despite her pioneering contributions to inquisitive observation and objectivity, despite her theoretical focus on the relationship between morals and manners in a society and despite her unwavering concern with structures of inequality. Martineau was stepping "off the verandah" in her travels nearly a century before Malinowski. Similar to other nineteenth century scholars, Martineau was a product of her historical context: a middle-class, Victorian, English woman who embraced the superiority of British culture and social life. Similar to other nineteenth century scholars she believed in lawful linear progress that can be measured. Martineau's yardstick was human liberty and happiness. Her rejection of value neutrality, open commitment to social reform, and the elimination of domination provides an early model for the critical reflexive anthropology practiced today.

Notes

1. Harriet Martineau, *Harriet Martineau's Autobiography* (Boston, Ma.: Houghton, Osgood and Co., 1879), 101-102.
2. Florence Nightingale quoted in Deborah Anna Logan, *The Hour and the Woman* (Dekalb: Northern Illinois University Press, 2002), 78.
3. Harriet Martineau quoted in Leonore Davidoff and Catherine Hall, *Family Fortunes* (Chicago: University of Chicago Press, 1987), 186.
4. Patricia Madoo Lengermann and Gillian Niebrugge, *The Women Founders* (Long Grove, Ill.: Waveland Press), 42-43; Vineta Colby, *Yesterday's Woman: Domestic Realism in the English Novel* (Princeton: Princeton University Press, 1974), 34.
5. Davidoff and Hall, *Family Fortunes*, 21, 26.
6. Logan, *The Hour*, 9.
7. Logan, *The Hour*, 77; Valerie Sanders, *Reason Over Passion: Harriet Martineau and the Victorian Novel* (New York: St. Martin's Press, 1986), 168; Shelagh Hunter, *Harriet Martineau: The Poetics of Moralism* (Aldershot: Scolar Press, 1995), 37.
8. Harriet Martineau, *How to Observe Morals and Manners* (London: Charles Knight and Co., 1838), 65.
9. Susan Hoecker-Drysdale, "Words on Work: Harriet Martineau's Sociology of Work and Occupations—Part I: Her Theory of Work," in Michael R. Hill and Susan Hoecker-Drysdale, eds., *Harriet Martineau: Theoretical and Methodological Perspectives* (New York: Routledge, 2003), 99.
10. Lengermann and Niebrugge, *Women Founders*, 43; Hunter, *Harriet Martineau*, 173. See also Reeves, this volume.
11. Davidoff and Hall, *Family Fortunes*, 185.
12. Lengermann and Niebrugge, *Women Founders*, 24-25.
13. Ainslie Robinson, "Playfellows and Propaganda: Harriet Martineau's Children's Writing," *Women's Writing* 9 (2002): 407.
14. Lengermann and Niebrugge, *Women Founders*, 25.
15. Davidoff and Hall, *Family Fortunes*, 185.
16. Logan, *The Hour*, 14.
17. Deirdre David, *Intellectual Women and Victorian Patriarchy* (Ithaca, NY.: Cornell University Press, 1987), 27-28; Elaine Freedgood, "Banishing Panic: Harriet Martineau and the Popularization of Political Economy," *Victorian Studies* (Autumn 1995): 38.
18. Martineau, *Autobiography*, 102; Linda H. Peterson, "Harriet Martineau: Masculine Discourse, Female Sage," in Thais E. Morgan, ed. *Victorian Sages and Cultural Discourse: Renegotiating Gender and Power* (New Brunswick: Rutgers University Press, 1990), 171-172, 175.
19. Logan, *The Hour*, 12.

20. Victor Turner quoted in Robert Daly, "Liminality and Fiction in Cooper, Hawthorne, Cather, and Fitzgerald," in Kathleen M. Ashley, ed. *Victor Turner and the Construction of Cultural Criticism* (Bloomington: Indiana University Press, 1990), 70-71.

21. Martineau, *Autobiography*, 103.

22. Martineau, *Autobiography*, 98.

23. Hoecker-Drysdale, "Words on Work," 100.

24. Harriet Martineau, *Principle and Practice – The Orphan Family* (London: Messrs. Houlston and Stoneman, 1827), 1.Robinson, "Playfellows and Propaganda," 407; Hunter, *Harriet Martineau*, 22; Sanders, *Reason*, 8. Defoe's Moll Flanders is another liminal orphan.

25. Martineau, *Principle and Practice*, 2.

26. Hoecker-Drysdale, "Words on Work," 104; Sanders, *Reason*, 180.

27. Martineau, *Principle and Practice*, 2.

28. Davidoff and Hall, *Family Fortune*, 351.

29. Martineau, *Principle and Practice*, 2.

30. Sarah Pink, *Home Truths* (Oxford, UK: Berg, 2004), 142.

31. Martineau, *Principle and Practice*, 5: Logan, *The Hour*, 36-77.

32. Martineau, *Principle and Practice*, 6; Hoecker-Drysdale, "Words on Work," 106.

33. Susan Hoecker-Drysdale, "Words on Work": Harriet Martineau's Sociology of Work and Occupations—Part II: Her Empirical Investigations," in Michael R. Hill and Susan Hoecker-Drysdale, eds., *Harriet Martineau: Theoretical and Methodological Perspectives* (New York: Routledge, 2003), 143-144.

34. Martineau, *Principle and Practice*, 64; Hunter, *Harriet Martineau*, 3.

35. Martineau quoted in Davidoff and Hall, *Family Fortunes*, 186; Hunter, *Harriet Martineau*, 199.

36. Elisabeth Sanders Arbuckle, Review, "Political Economy and Fiction in the Early Works of Harriet Martineau," *Victorian Studies* (Spring, 2002): 517; Davidoff and Hall, *Family Fortunes*, 185; David, *Intellectual Women*, 40, 41.

37. Martineau, *Autobiography*, 105; Claudia Orazem, *Political Economy and Fiction in the Early Works of Harriet Martineau* (Frankfurt: Peter Lang, 1999), 19, 61-67, 197.

38. David, *Intellectual Women*, 40; Orazem, *Political Economy*, 97.

39. Freedgood, "Banishing Panic," 36; Sanders, *Reason*, x; Colby, *Yesterday's Woman*, 216.

40. David, *Intellectual Women*, 30-31.

41. David, *Intellectual Women*, 31; Freedgood, "Banishing Panic," 33, 34, 36; Orazem, *Political Economy*, 19, 61-75; Sanders, *Reason*, 10.

42. Robinson, "Playfellows and Propaganda," 396; Hunter, *Harriet Martineau*, 156; Sanders, *Reason*, 31-56.

43. Maria Weston Chapman quoted in Deborah Anna Logan, "Introduction: The Theory and Practice of Society in America," in Deborah Anna Logan, ed., *Harriet Martineau: Writings on Slavery and the American Civil War* (Dekalb: Northern Illinois University Press, 2002), xiii.

44. Harriet Martineau, *Demerara, Illustrations of Political Economy*, Vol. II (London: Charles Fox, 1834), vi-vii.

45. Hoecker-Drysdale, "Words on Work," 103.

46. Logan, "Introduction," xii.

47. Martineau, *Demerara*, 6.

48. Martineau, *Demerara*, 8-9.

49. Martineau, *Demerara*, 29-30.
50. Martineau, *Demerara*, 66-69.
51. Martineau, *Demerara*, 143.
52. Martineau, *Demerara*, 60.
53. Martineau, *Demerara*, 60.
54. Martineau, *Demerara*, 61.
55. Martineau, *Demerara*, 143; Logan, "Introduction, xii.
56. Martineau, *Demerara*, 143.
57. Hoecker-Drysdale, "Words on Work," 109.
58. Lengermann and Niebrugge, *Women Founders*, 26.
59. Lengermann and Niebrugge, *Women Founders*, 37; Hunter, *Harriet Martineau*, 183.
60. Lengermann and Niebrugge, *Women Founders*, 33.
61. Martineau, *How to Observe*, 11.
62. Martineau, *How to Observe*, 20.
63. Martineau, *How to Observe*, 27.
64. Martineau, *How to Observe*, 13-14, 17, 20. Mark Twain held similar views. See Surrey this volume.
65. Harriet Martineau, *Eastern Life, Present and Past*, Vol. 2 (London: Edward Moxon, 1848), 50-60; Hunter, *Harriet Martineau*, 134.
66. David, *Intellectual Women*, 72.
67. Harriet Martineau, *Retrospective of Western Travel* (Armonk, NY: M.E. Sharpe, 2000), 33.
68. Harriet Martineau, *Feats on the Fiord* (London: Charles Knight and Co., 1841), 100.
69. Martineau, *Retrospective*, 31; Hunter, *Harriet Martineau*, 6.
70. Martineau, *Feats*, 75.
71. Martineau, *Eastern Life*, 148.
72. Robinson, "Playfellows and Propaganda," 400.
73. Martineau, *How to Observe*, 63.
74. Seymour Martin Lipset, ed., "Harriet Martineau's America: An Introductory Essay," in *Harriet Martineau, Society in America* (New Brunswick, NJ: Transaction Books, 1981), 7.
75. Lipset, "Martineau's America," 10.
76. Ann Hobart, "Harriet Martineau's Political Economy of Everyday Life," *Victorian Studies* (Winter, 1994): 229.
77. Hobart, "Political Economy," 230.
78. Hobart, "Political Economy," 232.
79. Lipset, "Martineau's America," 33.
80. Hilary McD. Beckles, "Taking Liberties: Enslaved Women and Anti-slavery in the Caribbean," in Clare Midgley, ed., *Gender and Imperialism* (Manchester, UK: Manchester University Press, 1998), 138-140.
81. Martineau, *Society in America*, 226. Martineau returned to these concerns thirty-five years later: "… to remedy the instability caused by white fathers emancipating their own light complexioned mulatto offspring rather than selling them. The consequence was the formation of the notorious Colonization Society—the hopeless device of the slaveholders for the deportation of their surplus 'hands,' and especially of those most troublesome …" See "William Lloyd Garrison and the Liberator," *London Daily News*, 9 January 1866, quoted in Logan, *Writings on Slavery*, 122.
82. Beckles, "Taking Liberties," 146-147.

83. Martineau, *Society In America*, 221-222.
84. Martineau, *Retrospective*, 113-114; *Autobiography*, 435-36.
85. Martineau, *Society in America*, 225-226; Lengermann and Niebrugge, *Women Founders*, 55-56.
86. Ann L. Stoler, "Making Empire Respectable: The Politics of Race and Sexual Morality in Twentieth-Century Colonial Cultures," in Louise Lamphere, Helena Ragone, and Patricia Zavella, eds. *Situated Lives: Gender and Culture in Everyday Life* (New York: Routledge, 1997), 374.
87. Stoler, "Making Empire," 391.
88. Martineau quoted in Lengermann and Niebrugge, *Women Founders*, 56.
89. Martineau, *Eastern Life*, 159.
90. Martineau, *Society in America*, 226.
91. Lengermann and Niebrugge, *Women Founders*, 27.
92. Lengermann and Niebrugge, *Women Founders*, 57-58; David, *Women Intellectuals*, 59.
93. Robinson, "Playfellows and Propaganda," 395-396.
94. Martineau, *Autobiography*, 446; Clare Midgley, *Women Against Slavery* (London: Routledge, 1992), 179.
95. Harriet Martineau, *The Hour and the Man: An Historical Romance* (Teddington, UK: The Echo Library, 2008), 335.
96. Martineau, *The Hour*, 336.
97. Martineau, *The Hour*, 342.
98. Martineau, *The Hour*, 8, 26, 34.
99. Martineau, *The Hour*, 37.
100. Martineau, *The Hour*, 22.
101. Martineau, *The Hour*, 28-30.
102. Martineau, *The Hour*, 32-33, 66-67.
103. Martineau, *The Hour*, 294.
104. Martineau, *The Hour*, 52, 58, 77.
105. Martineau, *The Hour*, 81.
106. Martineau, *The Hour*, 88.
107. Martineau, *The Hour*, 89.
108. Martineau, *The Hour*, 83.
109. Martineau, *The Hour*, 84.
110. Martineau, *The Hour*, 162-163.
111. Martineau, *The Hour*, 317.
112. Martineau, *Feats*, 1-2.
113. Martineau, *Feats*, 49.
114. Martineau, *Feats*, 42.
115. Martineau, *Feats*, 2-3.
116. Martineau, *Feats*, 3.
117. Martineau, *Feats*, 101.
118. Martineau, *Feats*, 93.
119. Martineau, *Feats*, 3, 8-9.
120. Martineau, *Feats*, 5, 6, 10.
121. Martineau, *Feats*, 4, 72.
122. Martineau, *Feats*, 75.
123. Martineau, *Feats*, 105-107.
124. Martineau, *Feats*, 111-112.

125. Michael R. Hill and Susan Hoecker-Drysdale, "Taking Harriet Martineau Seriously in the Classroom and Beyond," in Michael R. Hill and Susan Hoecker-Drysdale, eds. *Harriet Martineau: Theoretical and Methodological Perspectives* (New York: Routledge, 2003), 19.

126. David, *Intellectual Women*, 75.

127. Logan, *The Hour*, 201, 232; David, *Intellectual Women*, 75.

128. Davidoff and Hall, *Family Fortunes*, 324. See Reeve's discussion of Moll Flanders, this volume.

129. Jane Lewis, *Women in England 1870-1950* (Sussex, UK: Wheatsheaf Books, 1984), 3, 75, 120.

130. Davidoff and Hall, *Family Fortunes*, 206.

131. Davidoff and Hall, *Family Fortunes*, 282, 322.

132. Daniel Miller, "Behind Closed Doors," in Daniel Miller, ed., *Home Possessions* (Oxford, UK: Berg, 2001), 1; David Morley, *Home Territories* (London: Routledge, 2000), 23, 29.

133. Doreen Massey, *Space, Place, Gender* (Minneapolis: University of Minnesota Press), 1-9, 179.

134. Miller, "Closed Doors," 15.

135. Pink, *Home Truths*, 1.

136. Pink, *Home Truths*, 4, 45-47.

137. Hobart, "Political Economy," 240; Colby, *Yesterday's Woman*, 212, 230, 236.

138. Harriet Martineau, *Deerbrook* (London: Penguin Books, 2004), 9.

139. Martineau, *Deerbrook*, 13.

140. Martineau, *Deerbrook*, 37-38. See Davidoff and Hall, *Family Fortunes*, 261-263 for a discussion of the ranked divisions in the medical profession in nineteenth century England.

141. Martineau, *Deerbrook*, 22; Colby, *Yesterday's Woman*, 241-243.

142. Hobart, "Political Economy," 242.

143. Hobart, "Political Economy," 243; Sanders, *Reason*, 61.

144. Hobart, "Political Economy," 242.

145. Martineau, *Deerbrook*, 47.

146. Martineau, *Deerbrook*, 42; Colby, *Yesterday's Woman*, 254-255; Sanders, *Reason*, 62.

147. Martineau, *Deerbrook*, 29; Sanders, *Reason*, 63-66.

148. Martineau, *Deerbrook*, 39.

149. Martineau, *Deerbrook*, 97-98; Sanders, *Reason*, 78.

150. Davidoff and Hall, *Family Fortunes*, 351; Colby, *Yesterday's Woman*, 244-245; Sanders, *Reason*, 69-70.

151. Chang-Kwo Tan, "Building Conjugal Relationships: The Devotion to Houses amongst the Paiwan of Taiwan," in Daniel Miller, ed., *Home Possessions* (Oxford, UK: Berg, 2001), 149, 159-162; Colby, *Yesterday's Woman*, 246-247.

152. Martineau, *Deerbrook*, 163.

153. Martineau, *Deerbrook*, 180.

154. Martineau, *Deerbrook*, 183.

155. Martineau, *Deerbrook*, 307; Sanders, *Reason*, 59, 74-75.

156. Hobart, "Political Economy," 244.

157. Martineau, *Deerbrook*, 309; Colby, *Yesterday's Woman*, 248.

158. Hobart, "Political Economy," 246.

159. Martineau, *Deerbrook*, 420.

160. Martineau, *Deerbrook*, 496.

161. Hobart, "Political Economy," 247; Sanders, *Reason*, 61.

162. Martineau, *Deerbrook*, 599.

163. Hobart, "Political Economy," 247-248.

164. Lengermann and Niebrugge, *Women Founders*, 43; Hoecker-Drysdale, "Words on Work," 103.

165. Hoecker-Drysdale, "Words on Work," 101.

166. David, *Intellectual Women*, 60.

167. Davidoff and Hall, *Family Fortunes*, 186; Sanders, *Reason*, 168, 178, 184; Hunter, *Harriet Martineau*, 203.

168. Hobart, "Political Economy," 239.

References

Arbuckle, Elisabeth Sanders
    2002   Review, "Political Economy and Fiction in the Early Works of Harriet Martineau." *Victorian Studies*, Spring, Pp. 517-519.
Beckles, Hilary McD.
    1998   "Taking Liberties: Enslaved Women and Anti-slavery in the Caribbean." In *Gender and Imperialism*, ed. Clare Midgley. Manchester, UK: Manchester University Press, Pp. 137-157.
Colby, Vineta
    1974   *Yesterday's Woman: Domestic Realism in the English Novel.* Princeton: Princeton University Press.
Daly, Robert
    1990   "Liminality and Fiction in Cooper, Hawthorne, Cather, and Fitzgerald." In *Victor Turner and the Construction of Cultural Criticism.* ed. Kathleen M. Ashley. Bloomington: Indiana University Press, Pp. 70-85.
David, Deirdre
    1987   *Intellectual Women and Victorian Patriarchy.* Ithaca: Cornell University Press.
Davidoff, Leonore, and Catherine Hall
    1987   *Family Fortunes: Men and Women of the English Middle Class, 1780-1850.* Chicago: University of Chicago Press.
Freedgood, Elaine
    1995   "Banishing Panic: Harriet Martineau and the Popularization of Political Economy." *Victorian Studies*, Autumn, Pp. 33-53.
Hill, Michael R., and Susan Hoecker-Drysdale
    2003   "Taking Harriet Martineau Seriously in the Classroom and Beyond." In *Harriet Martineau: Theoretical and Methodological Perspectives*, eds. Michael R. Hill and Susan Hoecker-Drysdale. New York: Routledge, Pp. 3-22.
Hobart, Ann
    1994   "Harriet Martineau's Political Economy of Everyday Life." *Victorian Studies*, Winter, Pp. 223-251.
Hoecker-Drysdale, Susan
    2003   "Words on Work": Harriet Martineau's Sociology of Work and Occupations— Part I: Her Theory of Work" and "Part II: Her Empirical Investigations." In *Harriet Martineau: Theoretical and Methodological Perspectives*, eds. Michael R. Hill and Susan Hoecker-Drysdale. New York: Routledge, Pp. 99-152.
Hunter, Shelagh
    1995   *Harriet Martineau: The Poetics of Moralism.* Aldershot: Scholar Press.
Lengermann, Patricia Madoo, and Gillian Niebrugge
    2007   *The Women Founders: Sociology and Social Theory 1830-1930.* Long Grove: Waveland Press.
Lewis, Jane
    1984   *Women in England 1870-1950: Sexual Divisions and Social Change.* Sussex, UK: Wheatshaft Books.
Lipset, Seymour Martin

1981   "Harriet Martineau's America: An Introductory Essay." In Harriet Martineau. *Society in America*, ed. Seymour Martin Lipset. New Brunswick, NJ: Transaction Books.

Logan, Deborah Anna
1984   *The Hour and the Woman: Harriet Martineau's "Somewhat Remarkable" Life*. Dekalb: Northern Illinois University Press.
2002   "Introduction: The Theory and Practice of Society in America." In Harriet Martineau. *Writings on Slavery and the American Civil War*, ed. Deborah Anna Logan. Dekalb: Northern Illinois University Press, Pp. ix-xxiv.

Martineau, Harriet
1827   *Principle and Practice – The Orphan Family*. London: Messrs. Houlston and Stoneman.
1834   *Demerara, Illustrations of Political Economy*, Vol. II. London: Charles Fox.
1834   *Poor Laws and Paupers Illustrated*. London: Charles Fox.
1834   *Illustrations of Taxation*. London: Charles Fox.
1835   *Society In America*. New Brunswick, NJ: Transactions Books [1981].
1838   *How to Observe Morals and Manners*. London: Charles Knight and Co.
1838   *Retrospective of Western Travel*. Armonk, NY: M. E. Sharpe [2000].
1839   *Deerbrook*. London: Penguin Books [2004].
1840   *The Hour and the Man*. Teddington, UK: The Echo Library [2008].
1841   *Feats on the Fiord*. London: Charles Knight and Co.
1848   *Eastern Life, Present and Past*. 3 vols. London: Edward Moxon.
1879   *Harriet Martineau's Autobiography*. 3 vols. London: Elder.

Massey, Doreen
1994   *Space, Place, and Gender*. Minneapolis: University of Minnesota Press.

Midgley, Clare
1992   *Women Against Slavery: The British Campaigns, 1780-1870*. London: Routledge.

Miller, Daniel
2001   "Behind Closed Doors." In *Home Possessions: Material Possessions Behind Closed Doors*, ed. Daniel Miller. Oxford, UK: Berg, Pp. 1-19.

Morley, David
2000   *Home Territories: Media, Mobility and Identity*. London: Routledge.

Peterson, Linda H.
1990   "Harriet Martineau: Masculine Discourse, Female Sage." In *Victorian Sages and Cultural Discourse: Renegotiating Gender and Power*, ed. Thais E. Morgan. New Brunswick: Rutgers University Press.

Pink, Sarah
2004   *Home Truths: Gender, Domestic Objects and Everyday Life*. Oxford, UK: Berg.

Orazem, Claudia
1999   *Political Economy and Fiction in the Early Works of Harriet Martineau*. Frankfurt: Peter Lang.

Robinson, Ainslie
2002   "Playfellows and Propaganda: Harriet Martineau's Children's Writing." *Women's Writing*. Vol. 9, Pp. 395-412.

Sanders, Valerie
1986   *Reason Over Passion: Harriet Martineau and the Victorian Novel*. New York: St. Martin's Press.

Stoler, Ann L.
  1997   "Making Empire Respectable: The Politics of Race and Sexual Morality in
          Twentieth-Century Colonial Cultures." In *Situated Lives: Gender and
          Culture in Everyday Life*, eds. Louise Lamphere, Helena Ragone, and Patricia
          Zavella. New York: Routledge, Pp. 373-399.
Tan, Chang-Kwo
  1999   "Building Conjugal Relations: The Devotion to Houses amongst the Paiwan
          of Taiwan." In *Home Possessions: Material Culture Behind Closed Doors*,
          ed. Daniel Miller. Oxford, UK: Berg, Pp. 149-172.

Chapter 5

Mark Twain's Weapon of Mass Destruction: "The Human Race Has Only One Really Effective Weapon and that Is Laughter"

DAVID SURREY

The report of my death was an exaggeration
Mark Twain[1]

Maybe yes and maybe no. Certainly when Mark Twain made this statement in 1897 he was correct. Indeed, ahead of him lay some of his most biting commentary, especially on the three-headed monster of racism, social class, and imperialism. In many ways he was also wrong. Much of Twain's role as a social commentator was and is, if not dead, lost as we tend to repeat the very inequities that he so strongly opposed. The targets of Twain's pen still thrive; that he was a champion against them, however is not how he is generally remembered. If Twain is read today, it is usually either *Tom Sawyer* or *Huckleberry Finn*. While these are two of the most frequently banned books in history, they are actually less contentious than Twain's other works.

My incorporation of literature in social science courses began over thirty years ago. I have repeatedly found that fiction engages students by providing what can be viewed as lively ethnographies of the cultures and time periods that we are exploring. Reading and exploring fiction builds a critical foundation from which students can then advance more excitedly than with traditional social science readings. Indeed, in contrast to the richness of fiction, the view that many social science cultural descriptions are deadly prevails. Literature provides a much more engaging entrance for our students who subsequently often find the social science literature richer.

This chapter explores how Mark Twain's work can be used to complement social science literature to engage students with questions of race, social justice, class structure, and imperialism in nineteenth and early twentieth century culture. My central argument is that this nineteenth and early twentieth century writer had a vision that lives on due to its relevance, and provides a set of lens for today's students to better understand history and the present.

Unless their education overlapped with one of the times these books were banned, our parents, our generation and our children generally read *Huckleberry*

Finn or *Tom Sawyer* (or the *SparkNotes*) in high school. However, if completed, the depth of these readings rarely goes beyond questions such as: Was Twain a cracker? Was his use of language appropriate or racist? Where were the strong women? While this chapter does not provide a literary analysis of Twain's texts, I focus on how contemporary faculty can rely on Twain to provoke students about social issues of the past that continue to haunt us in the present. Twain's combination of biting humor with characterizations of social reality in the nineteenth and early twentieth century provides a formula for delivering his message that is a familiar one today. In my classes, students can conjure up Twain as a (deeper) version of George Carlin, a (less smug) Jon Stewart, an (even more, if possible) sarcastic Maureen Dowd, a (relatively) stable Dave Chappelle, and a (slimmed downed) Michael Moore. Just as the spirit of Twain can be found in these contemporary social critics, the targets of his criticism can be found in the updated practices of water boarding prisoners, the prison industrial complex, widening inequality gaps, gentrification, and "No Child Left Behind."

The chapter is organized into four overlapping sections. The first is domestic relations and I primarily use *Pudd'nhead Wilson* to examine racial attitudes and class structure. The second is censorship. I demonstrate how all of the political spectrums have responded to Twain's social critiques with banning and censorship. I will try to explore why and how Twain's works have been banned. What makes those in power so fearful of his work is another part of the dialogue that accompanies the uses of his writings. The third is overseas travel. I mainly draw on Twain, the relatively light-hearted observer of how Americans behaved and observed while overseas, as reflected in essays and speeches that he fashioned into *The Innocents Abroad*. The fourth, imperialism, reveals the elder Twain as an angry, betrayed, anti-imperialist as evident in several works including *A Defense of General Funston* and *King Leopold's Soliloquy*. Each section describes the time period in which the texts are written or written about and the contemporary repetitions of these same issues. Each section demonstrates how the readings can be used in college classes. A note of caution is needed regarding pedagogy. Sometimes the exercises are successful and sometimes they are flops. It is important to thoroughly prepare students. If or when an exercise fails, the failure is a learning experience for both students and instructors. Indeed the class discussions and controversies that emerge out of the readings never cease to reinforce to me how much Twain's work is needed today. Twain was a cross-century, trans-national provocateur. It is time to remember the power of his words, and reconsider how he might be invited into our classrooms today.

Part I: The Tragedy of Pudd'nhead Wilson

A better title, perhaps, would be "The Decline and Fall of Mark Twain;" for, looking at it solely as a piece of literature, there is no denying, that his much-advertised serial is tremendously stupid ...

*"Pudd'nhead Wilson" is more than stupid. So far as it has ap-
peared—to the end of the second installment, that is—it is at once
malicious and misleading. So much so, indeed, that involuntarily one
recalls the gentleman who, it was said, "went to his memory for his
wit, and his imagination for his facts."*
Martha McCulloch Williams, February 1894[2]

*... the Missouri village in which the scene is laid, is so vividly real-
ized in its minutest details; and the people, in all their fatuous prejudice and stolidity, are so credible and authentic. So steeped in the local atmosphere, that the illusion becomes perfect, and we swallow the
melodrama without a qualm ...*
Hjamar Hjorth Boysen, January 1885[3]

Puddn'head Wilson was completed just three years before Plessy v. Ferguson, twenty-four years after Darwin's *Origins of the Species* and twenty-nine years after the formal end of slavery. The novel provides a colorful ethnography of a small, rural, pre-civil war community. As a text, the book opens doorways for discussions about the overt, *de jure*, institutionalization of racial discrimination in the pre- and post-slavery eras of the nineteenth century, facilitating conversation about the covert capillaries of modern racism. Twain provides evidence of how Social Darwinism was justified in the nineteenth century, including the internalization of prejudices by those dominating and those dominated. The novel reveals, at the same time, the compelling resistance against prevailing power structures.

With the comfort and distance of time and history, *Puddn'head Wilson* enables classroom conversations about race, segregation, and state imposed violence that are more difficult to engage when we start with contemporary examples of the same dynamics. Twain's writing forces a conversation about representation. We engage in frequently difficult debates over Twain's extreme characterizations of both whites and blacks, including language usage. For those not familiar with the novel, or who need a brief refresher, you can either read it now —it is a quick 150 pages— or indulge in the injustice below with my superficial summary. Before beginning the reader should note that some of the quotations from the novel are Twain's version of the slave dialect. This use of his vernacular has been, and remains, controversial, including in my own classrooms. This will be explored later in the chapter.

The timing of the book is critical to understanding its value. Written at the height of Jim Crow, when slavery was legally over but not forgotten, its pre-civil war setting exposes post-civil war attitudes—attitudes that to some extent echo today. It is also written at time when Darwinism was being corrupted into Social Darwinism to justify racial hierarchies, social class, and social labeling. The latter are used here to explore how a person is defined by the stereotypes imposed internally and externally.

The story is set in pre-civil war Dawson's Landing, Missouri. Dawson's Landing is a very thinly disguised, slightly more southern version of Mark Twain's (Samuel Clemens) native town of Hannibal, Missouri. The plot winds its way through circuitous routes to a murder trial where the title character, Puddn'head Wilson, successfully earns an acquittal for his clients through the innovative use of the infant science of fingerprinting. In exposing the true murderer, Wilson reveals a racial switching of two babies scheme that has fooled the town for two decades. To get to the climax at the trial, Twain uses the life narratives of the main characters to reflect his views of the kaleidoscope of United States culture. There is just enough believability in the tale, and more than enough sarcasm, to hold the readers.

Roxana (Roxy) is a sixteen year-old slave who is one-sixteenth black by blood. Thus, at the time the novel takes place, she is legally a slave and legally black. Roxy and her mistress give birth to sons on the same day. Roxy's baby is fathered by one of the wealthiest white citizens in town, thus making the baby one-thirty second black. The father will have no part of the baby who, with or without his acknowledgment, by law is considered a slave and black since slave status was matrilineal. Roxy's looks are white but in dress, speech, behavior, and self-perception, she is a slave. Both Roxy and her mistress' sons also look white. At their birth, Roxy is immediately charged with raising her mistresses' baby, and expected to neglect the needs of her own child.

Knowing her biological son's certain dismal future, Roxy at first intends to kill herself and her baby, an option not unknown among slave women. Thereafter, she has a more sophisticated plan to switch the babies. Thus her legally enslaved son, now to be known as Thomas à Becket Driscoll, is raised as heir to the York Leicester Driscoll fortune. Her mistresses' son, now condemned to live out the life of a slave, is known as Valet de Chambers. Had events not overtaken both sons, the one called Tom would have had a long life of privilege and freedom. The one called Chambers was destined for a life of misery and abuse by virtue of nothing other than Roxy's exchange of cradles. "Tom got all the petting, Chambers got nothing. Tom got all the delicacies, Chambers got mush and milk, and clabber without sugar. In consequence Tom was a sickly child and Chambers wasn't. Thomas was 'fractious,' as Roxy called it, and overbearing; Chambers was meek and docile."[4]

Throughout his text, Twain uses the desk calendar of Puddn'head Wilson to introduce appropriate framings of his characters or events. For example, April 1: "This is the day upon which we are reminded of what we are the other three hundred and sixty-four—Puddn'head Wilson's Calendar."[5] Here we learn about the title character. David "Puddn'head" Wilson is the eventual, accidental, hero who is responsible for exposure of the Roxy's scheme. A lawyer and from the East, two crimes in themselves in Dawson's Landing, he earned his unfortunate nickname shortly after arriving in town. Wilson commented on a barking dog saying, "I wish I owned half of that dog ... because I would kill my half."[6] For that remark, until the climax of the text, Wilson is marginalized as an incompetent boob. Wilson also has what is considered a very strange habit. He is determined to fingerprint every inhabitant in town, white and black, at various stages of their lives. Although this further enhances his reputation as a fool, it is not a habit he will surrender.

The imposter Tom learns and hides his secret as an adult. He has grown to be selfish, spoiled, greedy, and eventually a murderer. Although we do not see much of him in the novel, the unfortunate young man raised as Chambers, remains a slave, enduring his place, including horrible physical abuse by Tom. In the end, the secret of their true identities is revealed. Their roots emerge after the man known as Tom is exposed for murdering his uncle, who was also his benefactor. That he is a murderer is one problem, but the heavier burden for Tom is that he is found to be one thirty-second black. The real Tom, despite his inheritance and permitted acceptance, cannot adapt to the white community. Tom, although known and accepted his entire life by the white community, is literally sold "down the river" as a slave.

The social structure of the town, with vividly colored black and white personalities, is presented as a rigid product of societal attitudes, laws, norms, and behaviors, but twisted and secured by genetics, violence, rape, and abuse. Twain insists that readers contend with the horrors of the power of nurture over nature, class over humanity, and prejudice over insight.

I now turn to how the novel serves as an escort to provocative conversation in the contemporary classroom. Roxy (one-sixteenth black ancestry) provides Twain with his vehicle to explore the violent and arbitrary racial classification systems in place in the pre-Civil War South. He raises questions about race as both a physical or cultural marker. Although the Supreme Court in Plessy v. Ferguson in 1896 was to (further) establish the legality of the one-drop rule, this time at one-eighth, the percentage really did not matter. This would be again verified almost fifty years later in 1944 when in Korematsu v. U.S., the Supreme Court vindicated interning the Japanese, this time at one-sixteenth non-white. Twain takes this absurd, yet structurally violent reality, even further with Roxy's one-thirty second black child of a one-sixteenth black woman, with a white father, being legally declared a slave. Or was that Thomas Jefferson and some of his children?

While Twain is provocative by 1893 standards, some of my students in the ensuing debates out-Twain Twain by criticizing him for not directly bringing sex without choice, rape, into the equation. A lack of parallel passion for women, slave or free, black or white, is a critique that raises valuable discussion points on why these topics are generally avoided by Twain.

Connecting and contesting bloodlines, Twain provides the contradictions that are ignored (and at the heart of) in Dawson's Landing and that still confront us today. He adds further depth to the discussion by placing race in the context of economic reality. He writes: "to all intents and purposes Roxy was as white as anybody, but the one sixteenth of which was black outvoted the other fifteen parts and made her a negro. She was a slave, and salable as such."[7]

Twain tells us that Roxy's "complexion was very fair, with the rosy glow of vigorous health in the checks ... her eyes were brown and liquid, and she had a hearty suit of fine soft hair." Her physical appearance, however, is trumped by culture as "her head was bound about with a checkered handkerchief."[8] If clothing was not enough to show her slave status, Roxy's speech was also that of a slave. Linguistic markers reveal the "true" legitimate basis for disenfranchisement. In responding to Wilson's praise of the beauty of the yet to be switched Tom and Chambers, Roxy tells Puddn'head: "it's pow'ful nice o' you to say dat, ca'se one of em ain't on'y a nigger."[9] Roxy is a white woman by physical appearance but by deference, dress, external law and custom, internalized attitude, and speech is a slave.

These sections richly season the text, providing excellent discursive launching pads for discussions beyond slavery. Students can begin to explore the mechanisms, motives and consequences of stereotyping and discrimination. Students take up these questions from their own biographies of being victims, witnesses, and sometimes perpetrators of such practices. What often emerges from these discussions is how the labels become rationales for deprivation and control as well as the naturalizing of social hierarchy. In Dawson's Landing, we see how to both blacks and whites in the town, the proper English speaking, well-dressed, whites, deserved to be on top, and those on the bottom belonged there.

We then turn to a deeper discussion of how Social Darwinism justified slavery, Jim Crow discrimination and, as we will see later, imperialism. It can also lead to an examination of how a belief in meritocracy justifies seemingly neutral legislation such as "No Child Left Behind." Social Darwinism clothed as equity of opportunity is firmly embedded in the high stakes standardized testing regimes of today, resorting and legitimating the class and race hierarchies of access to higher education. Results of these life-defining measurements of students today are clearly tied to income that is still clearly tied to race.

The next logical step in our class discussion has become our forty-fourth president, Barack Obama. Why is he our first "black" president, when he can trace his entire mother's side to Western Europe including Moneygall, Ireland? His first "white" ancestor arrived in the colonies in 1640. A popular YouTube video, the Irish Obama, by Hardy Drew and the Nancy Boys, place Obama's arbitrary racial labeling in perspective with such lines as: "His granddaddy's daddy came from Moneygall, a small Irish village, well known to you all ... He's as Irish as bacon, and cabbage and stew. He's Hawaiian, he's Kenyan and American too."[10]

Commentators, usually those on the right who are taking a break from birth certificate searches, are also confounded by the lack of any "dialect" in Obama's speech. If the outwardly white looking Roxy is black the moment she opens her mouth, why is physically black Obama not white the moment evolving ideas emerge out of his mouth? My students are heatedly drawn into this discussion as they disclose how they are both labeled externally by their own speech patterns and are judged by their peers if they indeed "go middle class" in their diction.

Roxy becomes a powerful vehicle to consider the racial issues of her day and ours. She permits a safe entry into serious discussions on the arbitrariness of race and the subtexts of labeling. A first generation Italian/Irish student may burst out why he only identifies as Irish-American or Italian American or simply an American. On the other hand, a third generation Irish/Pakistani student will talk about how, whether she likes it or not, she is considered a Pakistani-American, or still only a Pakistani, or a terrorist. The conversation addresses profiling as well as exploring why some groups have the privilege of losing the hyphen versus those who have no choice but to dangle precariously from it.

Roxy also illustrates how the beliefs of inferiority and superiority are not merely external but also internalized. To her, her own child is "on'y a nigger." Although this son is switched into the white world from infancy forward, to her his adult flaws have nothing to do with his privileged station in life or the way he was raised, but rather are due to the fact that he has one-thirty second black blood in him. She muses: "Thirty one parts o' you is white, en on'y part of nigger, en dat po' little one part is you yo' soul."[11]

The fake Tom, despite having lived virtually his entire life as a privileged white, has incorporated the racist ideology into the core of his being. Upon learning his true identity, although it is a secret shared only by Roxy and himself, he thinks: "a nigger. I am a nigger. Oh, I wish I were dead."[12] Or when Roxy tells him to kneel before her or she will tell his identity he muses: "I've knealth before a nigger wrench ... I have struck bottom this time. There's nothing lower."[13] The newly revealed Tom cannot help but carry out the expected behavior of blacks that had been engrained so deeply into him as a white man. When Tom believed himself to be white, he was exceptionally cruel to blacks, including Chambers, who he had been raised with. Twain writes that now if Tom,

> met a friend, he found the habit of a lifetime had in some mysterious way vanished—his arm hung limp, instead of involuntarily extending the hand for a shake ... And the "nigger" in him was surprised when the white friend put out his hand for a shake with him. He found the "nigger" in him involuntarily giving the road, on the sidewalk, to the white and rowdy loafer. When Rowana [a white woman], the dearest thing his heart knew, the idol of his secret worship, invited him in, the "nigger" in him made an embarrassed excuse and was afraid to enter and sit with the dread white folks on equal terms ... He said to himself that the curse of Ham was upon him.[14]

The attitudes of both Tom and Roxy can be better comprehended with the introduction of theories on internalized racial oppression. Specifically I have applied what Fanon would call racialized self-hatred[15] or what Du Bois would call double consciousness.[16] First generation, or generation 1.5 students (born raised by immigrant parents), often shamefully admit how they judged or were silent when their parents were judged by the majority attitudes of their cultures.

Twain adds even more depth to the power of these internalized perspectives. The real Tom, who as Chambers was raised a slave, is incapable of claiming his rightfully privileged position. He is not denied his new place by the white community, but by what has been internalized into his very being. He "suddenly found himself rich and free but in a most embarrassing situation ... He could neither read nor write, and his speech was the basest dialect of the Negro quarter. His gait, his attitudes, his gestures, his bearing ... were the all the bearing of the slave." Worse than these external markers for the Tom formerly known as Chambers, is his internal compass. For the new Tom "Money and fine cloths could not mend ... The poor fellow could not endure the terrors of the white man's parlor ... the family pew was a misery to him."[17] He too is trapped by internalized conditioning imposed by race where labels shape reality.

A discussion of internalization goes beyond the cultural life of nineteenth century Missouri. One exercise I often use with my college students based on these sections of the novel is cultural switching. Students are asked to imagine being dropped at the cradle into another culture. How could they and would they act? How would they be perceived? By starting with fiction as the safe mustache, students explore the roots of their views of both their own culture and that of the one they pick. Usually in this example class trumps race, where inner city students place themselves in families in more affluent suburbs and tend to follow different life trajectories. Conversely, the comparatively wealthier suburban students pick even more affluent suburbs with the same results.

Returning to nineteenth century Missouri, Twain reveals that the greatest fear among the slave community, based in reality, was being "sold down the river." While not minimizing the day-to-day horrors of slavery, this potential of being torn away from one's family and sold into harsher conditions hovers thick in the air. Once sent down the river, even if the slaves were to survive the harsher conditions, it was very unlikely that they would ever see their children, parents, wives or husbands again. The final trigger for Roxy to switch the babies was her fear of seeing her biological son shipped to the deeper south, thereby breaking the mother-child connection. She apologizes to the real Tom by saying: "I's so sorry for you honey: I's sorry, God knows I is- but what kin I do ... Yo' pappy would sell him [her real son] to someone, sometime, en den he'd go down de river." [18]

When Roxy reveals Tom's true identity to him, he initially threatens her so that she will stay silent. But she successfully turns the table, holding the threat of Tom being sold into slavery and sent to the deep south. "You's a nigger!—bawn a nigger en a slave!—en you's a nigger en a slave dis minute; en if I opens my mouf ole Marse Dricoll'll sell you down de river befo' you is two days older den you is now!"[19]

Again relying on Wilson's desk calendar, Twain is happy pointing out the sanctimonious hypocrisy of leading citizens: "When I reflect upon the number of disagreeable people who I know have gone to a better world, I am moved to lead a different life—Puddn'head Wilson's Calendar."[20] Twain then introduces York Leicester Driscoll. Driscoll suspects at least one of his slaves is stealing.

He tells the slaves that if the thief does not come forward, he will sell them all down the river. This fear prompts them all to step forward and confess. At that point, Driscoll majestically states: "I will sell you here although you don't deserve it. You ought to be sold down the river."[21] Through such a presumed act of kindness as selling the slaves in town rather than down the river, Twain reveals the perverse power relations between master and slave, referring to Master Driscoll as "a fairly humane man to slaves and other animals."[22] The meaning of going down the river has been so engrained in whites and blacks that Driscoll sees himself, and is seen by the slaves, as a magnificent man as "The culprits flung themselves prone ... and kissed his feet ... for like a god he had stretched forth a mightily and closed the gates of hell."[23]

Twain leaves little doubt that the acceptance of the black family, even the mother-child connection, is absent in the white community. Black women are seen to be most valuable as breeders, who have been frequently raped by their owners. If they are allowed to retain their children, fathered either by whites or blacks, these children are not seen as a reason to stop being available day or night to serve the needs of their masters. Roxy was fortunate only in the sense that her child was the same age as her mistress' son. This gave Roxy some opportunity to have time with her son. Still she had to dress the boys differently, feed them differently and beg for resources for the real Tom if both children were in distress. This violent slashing of the mother-child bond is, of course, not fiction. Frederick Douglass painfully describes it in his autobiography. Douglass' mother was put back to work virtually immediately after giving birth. He wrote that he "did not recollect to ever seeing mother by the light of day."[24]

Despite the superficial belief that slaves accepted their status, Twain does not come close to the trap of framing slaves as accepting a passive subservience to whites. Indeed, Roxy is feisty, clever, daring, and subversive in her resistance. Switching babies, even though it meant a life of servitude for the real Tom, was the ultimate act of revolt. So convinced that her resistance was justified, Roxy has virtually no sympathy for the true Tom. The fake Tom shows no sympathy either. Only once, when Roxy rebukes her biological son, is there even lip service to the sufferings of the other: "En dat po' boy dat you's be'n a-kickin' en a-cuffin today is Percy Driscoll's son en you master."[25]

Twain invites us to consider how breaking the law can be viewed as an act of resistance or social justice. He casts Roxy as more than willing to steal from white families. She not only helps the faux Tom in his exploits of stealing from whites to pay off his gambling debts, but she quickly takes over the key role in planning these endeavors. Twain asks readers to juxtapose law and justice. Twain insists that readers recognize the uneducated Roxy as far more clever than the overeducated imposter. Roxy also demands a cut of the take. Her rational is "T'ain't no sin—white folks have done it."[26] Or, upon sipping the master's whisky, she states: "it is prime—I'll take it along."[27]

In *Mark Twain Social Critic*, historian Philip Foner cites passages from several Twain novels that express the untold history of active black resistance to the white autocracy. Foner argues: "Twain justifies all measures they [slaves] took against oppression."[28] In a passage in *Puddn'head Wilson*, Twain elaborates the slaves' rationale for thefts against the masters by stating that slaves were "perfectly sure in taking this trifle from the man who daily robbed him of an inestimable treasure—his liberty—any great sin that God would remember against him in the Last Great Day."[29] Foner notes that in contrast to the historic moment when the novels were written, "Twain's novels proclaimed to the world that the Negro never accepted slavery, had fought for his freedom, and was entitled to enjoy the full fruits of democracy."[30] Later Foner explores how Twain's slave characters, in stark contrast to their deploring conditions, embodied a collective and existential humanity lacking in the white community. In a discussion of Jim in *Huckleberry Finn* and Roxy in *Puddn'head Wilson*, Foner notes that in "both novels he showed that the Negro slave, through brutalized, was a human as lovable and as admirable as any man."[31]

Roxy also understands the blinders that whites place over their eyes, as if anticipating the protagonist in Ellison' *Invisible Man*. Ellison's main character is seen by whites only as "A matter of the construction of their inner eyes, those eyes with which they look through their physical eyes upon reality." Ellison's man uses the mask of the generic black man to avoid surveillance of the white world. To Ellison's character, the ironies of invisibility reflect a partial blessing for it "is sometimes advantageous to be unseen."[32] Similarly Iris Carter Ford describes how Dizzy Gillespie successfully employed invisibility when arrested in Texas in the 1950's. He simply told the police he was Louis Armstrong. It worked—one black entertainer was as good as another for the booking.[33] History is filled with brilliant, ironic and strategic exploitations of invisibility by blacks to avoid, contest or undermine racism. What is unusual is that Twain was a white man writing in the 1800s, who understood at least some of the strategies used to subvert racism by Blacks in the nineteenth century.

Roxy also demonstrates the power of invisibility. At one point she conceives a plan for Tom to sell her up the river. Roxy had been freed years earlier when the first Master Driscoll had died, but Tom needed money and Roxy wanted her cut. Tom, while not averse to selling his own mother, questioned whether this ploy would be effective since Roxy was well known to be free. Roxy responds: "I's a nigger, en nobody ain't gwine to doubt it dat hears me talk."[34] She is right and that part of the scheme worked. Tom then double-crossed her by actually selling her down the river, but that is another problem that the smarter Roxy was able to solve.

In the final analysis, most agree invisibility is never an advantage. Ellison articulates well the social, political and psychological trauma induced by systemic invisibility: "you often doubt that you really exist. You wonder whether you aren't simply a phantom of other people's minds."[35] Fanon echoes this in his discussions of "Black Masks" when he writes of being "suddenly abraded into non-being" as his person identity is stripped into "an object."[36] Ronald Takaki stresses the dehumanizing effect of this throughout our history. Slaves were rarely provided a last name in official documents, or given their masters' names, to deny their heritages or families. Takaki again demonstrates the systematic forced invisibility endured by Filipino, Japanese and Chinese Hawaiian plantation workers in the late nineteenth century who were called by numbers not names.[37] Yet it is Roxy who is most articulate when she tells Tom his true identity: "En his (Chambers) name's Tom Driscoll, en you ain't got not fambly name, beca'se niggers don't have em!"[38]

These passages open the door for lively classroom discussions of what is seen and what is invisible in different cultural contexts, and what strategic interventions young people and elders deploy to get by, get over, and get through. Students are asked how labels have rendered them invisible or, conversely how they have used labels to create generalized others. The ensuing debates of the advantages and disadvantages of invisibility are very rich. The first time I used this, an affluent white student stated that minorities were not the only ones who are invisible. Just as I thought she was to be lunch for the rest of the class, she added that unlike other groups, she can get away with just about anything in her college classes because her invisibility is one of privilege. I learned something that day.

Beneath her speech, beneath her desperation, beneath her dress, beneath her plots, and beneath her dehumanization, Twain uses Roxy to reveal another dimension of oppression. He observes: "When angry count to four, when really angry, swear—Puddn'head Wilson's Calendar."[39] Roxy is mad. She is mad at her treatment as a woman. She is mad at being a slave. She is mad that she cannot be a mother to her own son. She is mad that her biological son grows into the white oppressor. The full force of Roxy's anger explodes when she confronts the fake Tom with his true identity. Roxy makes him kneel before her. Twain lets Roxy vent as the "heir of two centuries of unatoned insult and outrage and seemed to drink in deep draughts of satisfaction." Roxy states with sarcasm to the kneeling Tom, "tine nice you white gen'l'man kneeling down to a nigger wrench! I's wanted to see dat jes once befo' I's called. Now, Gabr'ek, blow de hawn. I's ready."[40] Later Roxanna rebukes her son for disrespecting her by calling her by the slave term Roxy— "Dat's one thing you gots to stop, Valet de Chambers. You can't call me Roxy, same as you my equal. Chillen don't speak to dey mammies like. You'll call me ma or mammy."[41]

One famous slave owner, over 100 years before Twain, recognized the explosive nature of the institution of slavery. Thomas Jefferson wrote to James Monroe in 1793 his fears of a slave revolt: "It is high time we should foresee the bloody scenes which our children certainly, and possible ourselves have to wade through." In 1820 Jefferson acknowledged that holding on to slavery was a doomed proposition similar to having "the wolf by the ears, and we can neither hold him nor safely let him go."[42] This anger is something we might expect to understand with the hindsight of the twenty-first century, but few would have understood it and fewer would have dared to write about it in the nineteenth or eighteenth centuries.

Twain sketches the raw, even grotesque expressions of contradictory consciousness that evokes complex discussions among students about ideologies past and present, politically imposed, and psychologically ingested. In many ways Roxy has engrained much of the ideology of the day. She embodies the belief that Tom is bad because of that one-thirty second ratio. Tom presents this as "the nigger in him," feelings that emerge immediately upon his learning his "true" identity. On the other hand, Roxy also reveals a powerful political and psychological resistance to a history and structure of racialized and gendered oppression; she switches babies and she demands respect revealing a pride, a strength and a refusal that is impossible to ignore.

Twain ends the novel with the fake Tom being sold down the river. The thirty-one thirty-second white Tom has been lawfully and morally converted to property. He is no longer a person. As property he could not be convicted of murder, but he could generate a profit. Indeed, the community's outrage was not about the murder but rather over the fact that his owners "had already lost sufficiently in being deprived of his services." Twain uses the fate of Tom to parody the hypocrisy of society. He concludes the book by writing "If 'Tom' were white and free it would be unquestionably right to punish him—it would be no loss to anybody; but to shut a valuable slave for life—that was quite another matter ... As soon the Governor understood the case, he pardoned Tom at once, and the creditors sold him down the river."[43] The novel's conclusion provokes class discussions that can be directed in a variety of directions. It certainly gives a reality to the Dred Scott decision, where the Supreme Court ruled in 1857 that slaves are property not people. This brings the students back to the pernicious consequences and exposes the cultural and economic roots of United States slavery.

Puddin'head Wilson is a text that can be taught as a discursive platform for interrogating racism, classism, and sexism—then and now. The novel can also be used as nineteenth century ethnography to reflect on the law, science, economics, and psychic damage of slavery and racism. Finally, the book painfully holds a mirror to contemporary society, forcing us to acknowledge how, why, for whom, and on whom, today's economy requires an unprotected, seemingly compliant, highly exploitable underclass.

Part II: Banning, Censorship, and Political Correctness

Right here I wish to ask why it is that the Southern man who has an honest and descent pride in the fact that he comes of good stock fares so ill at the hands of certain literary gentlemen?... I make, here and now, my protest against this injustice. I cannot comfort myself with the belief that he has sinned ignorantly against half his countrymen.
Martha McCulloch Williams, 1894[44]

*Twain, it should be remembered, was endeavoring to accurately de-
pict the prevailing social attitudes along the Mississippi River Valley
during the 1840; accordingly he employed in both novels [Huckle-
berry Finn and Tom Sawyer] a linguistic corruption of 'Negro; in
reference to African American Slaves, and tagged the villain in Tom
Sawyer with a deprecating racial label for Native Americans ...*

Alan Gribben, 2011[45]

While some people rocked boats, Twain challenged the sailors, the fleet, the shipbuilders, and their financers. In turn they tried to silence him with censorship and by purging the vocabulary of *Tom Sawyer* and *Huckleberry Finn*. The first quote is by a contemporary of Twain's claiming his unfairness in describing the white culture of the south. The second is from the introduction to a 2011 edition of *Tom Sawyer* and *Huckleberry Finn*, where the editor substitutes the words nigger and injun with politically correct albeit culturally misleading terms. Twain's targets and those he made uncomfortable, then and now, fought back.

Perhaps Twain's greatest gift to classroom discourses are the controversies that arose at the time of his publications and continue today. The *Adventures of Huckleberry Finn* was first published in 1884 and then banned in 1885. It is the fourth most banned book in United State's history. *Puddn'head Wilson* has endured a similar fate and also remains on many censored lists today. The fact that conservatives and progressives, including, at times, the N.A.A.C.P., are among those promoting the ban, reflect how deeply Twain was able to cut into the core of our society.

Ralph Waldo Emerson, a defender of Twain, was among many who predicted that strategies of censorship would backfire when he wrote that "Every burned book or house enlightens the world; every suppressed or expunged word reverberates through the earth from side to side."[46] A case in point began when *The New York Times* in November 1906, reported on a typical rational for banning a Twain book. The Charlton, Massachusetts Public Library removed *Eve's Diary* from the shelves because it represented Twain's satiric interpretation of the story of Adam and Eve: "WORCESTER, Mass. —"Eve's Diary," by Mark Twain, a copy of which is among 100 books recently bought for the Charlton Public Library, has been barred by Frank O. Wakefield, one of the Trustees."[47] (This story has a happy ending as 105 years later the library restored all 100 of these books).[48] Twain's reaction to those he referred to as the "freaks of Charlton's Library" can be found in his comments to a friend regarding the ban in 1907: "But the truth is, that when a library expels a book of mine and leaves an unexpurgated Bible lying around where unprotected youth and age can get hold of it, the deep unconscious irony of it delights me and doesn't anger me."[49]

Many critics have asserted that Twain wrongfully and dangerously painted a generic version of whites as evil, slave owning, rapists, and buffoons. As an example, as soon as serialized chapters of *Puddn'head Wilson* began appearing in *Century Magazine* in 1893, they came under attack. The review by Williams quoted at the beginning of both this and the previous section was published after the first eight chapters had appeared in the magazine. William's disgust is evident in her characterization of the volume as stupid ... malicious and demeaning and that Twain slanders southern society. She was particularly incensed that Twain granted credibility to the belief slave women bore many children by white masters. She also accuses Twain of leading people to question if there are "in the South any pure blacks at all, or any pure-blooded whites?"[50] Williams also critiques Twain's repeated scenes of selling slaves, especially down the river. She says: "setting wholly aside the human affection that often sustained between white and black, few men were so foolish as to inconvenience themselves by entire change of ménage, without the most imperative necessity." Williams defends the myth of slaves' fondness for those who enslaved them. She also ignores that selling slaves, and the threat to sell them, were significant means of control and economic exploitation, and amplifies instead the fantasy of one big happy, multi-racial family.[51]

While Williams was not alone in her immediate criticism of *Pudd'head Wilson*, the book was also positively reviewed at the time of its publication by a significant number of writers. Hjamar Hjorth Boysen (1895) defended Twain's portraits of the South as realistic: "the scene is laid, is so vividly realized in the minutest details." In contrast to Williams' dismissal of *Pudd'nhead Wilson* with her remembrances of harmonious relationship between whites and slaves, Boysen honors Twain's analysis, acknowledging that he "has an ample fund of experience to draw upon ... shaping remembered truth into artistic coherence."[52]

Twain has had major supporters, but he is, undoubtedly, his own biggest advocate. Note the verb "is" rather that "was." In the *Autobiography of Mark Twain*, Vol. 1, which he cleverly arranged to be released in 2010, 100 years after his death, Twain settles many scores. This book continues his sarcastic, ironic, and boldly outspoken views about issues that persist today. For our purposes, we need not entertain this 600-page assault about the betrayals of Twain's truth, justice and the American way. We can catch the flavor of Twain's responses with the following exchange that was belatedly published in the *New York Times* in 1935.

New Mark Twain Letters Reveal He Poked Fun at Huck Finn Banned Humorist Vigorously Defended His Boy Heroes When Huckleberry and Tom Sawyer Were Criticized at Brooklyn Library as No More 'Course' Than Unexpurgated Bible.

Two hitherto unpublished letters by Mark Twain which echo a national controversy waged thirty years ago over Tom Sawyer and Huckleberry Finn were made public yesterday for the first time by Asa Don Dickinson, head librarian at Brooklyn College. Twain's letters were sent to Professor Dickinson in response to the librarian's appeal for the author to defend his two beloved characters from the onslaughts of an official of Brooklyn Public Library, who charged that the two characters were "bad examples for youth."

The controversy began in 1905 when a young woman, superintendent of children's department, insisted that *Huckleberry Finn* and *Tom Sawyer* be removed from the children's room because of their "coarseness, deceitfulness and mischievous practices." Professor Dickinson strongly disagreed and sent a letter to Twain acquainting him of the librarian's action.

Mark Twain's Defense

The creator of *Tom Sawyer* and *Huckleberry Finn* immediately sent back this reply:
21 5th Avenue Nov. 21, '05.

Dear Sir:

I am greatly troubled by what you say. I wrote *Tom Sawyer* & *Huck Finn* for adults exclusively, & it always distressed me when I find that boys and girls have been allowed access to them. The mind that becomes soiled in youth can never again be washed clean. I know this by my own experience, & to this day I cherish an unappeased bitterness against the unfaithful guardians of my young life, who not only permitted but compelled me to read an unexpurgated Bible through before I was 15 years old. None can do that and ever draw a clean sweet breath again on this side of the grave. Ask that young lady—she will tell you so.

Most honestly do I wish I could say a softening word or two in defense of Huck's character, since you wish it, but really in my opinion it is no better than God's (in the Ahab & 97 others), & the rest of the sacred brotherhood.

If there is an Unexpurgated [Bible] in the Children's Department, won't you please help that young woman remove Tom & Huck from that questionable companionship?

Sincerely yours, S. L. Clemens

I shall not show your letter to any one—it is safe with me."[53]

The practice of banning books leads to class discussions about who decides to ban and who is banned? While many of us complain that students do not read enough, it is rare that I have a student who has not read at least one of the books, including the Bible, that often have been banned in his or her lifetime. Students are outraged and better prepared to discuss Twain and the politics of censorship.

Focusing on politically correct language, as the Roxy's quotes in *Puddn'head Wilson* illustrate, Twain employs a vernacular he knew from his own experiences with pre-civil war Missouri slave dialect. To some critics this depicts the slaves as ignorant, perpetuating negative stereotypes. Twain's frequent use of the word nigger, 219 times alone in *Huckleberry Finn*, is used as an example of his demeaning or stereotyping blacks. Today Alice Walker and Maya Angelou are among many contemporary writers who have received virtually the same criticism, as does the use of the n-word in rap music.

Twain's defenders maintain that the dialect, including the dreaded n-word, reflects the cultural norms of the time. They argue that cleaning up the language would misrepresent the lives and relationships Twain was exploring. To the critics, Jim's use of language in *Huckleberry Finn* is demeaning, perpetrating an ignorant stereotype. Yet Twain's contemporary Booker T. Washington states that he "succeeded in making his readers feel a genuine respect for 'Jim'... [who] exhibited his sympathy and interest in the masses of the negro people." Much later, Ralph Ellison further argued: "in freeing Jim, Huck makes a bid to free himself of the conventionalized evil taken for civilization." To Ellison, Twain had to understand Jim in terms of how Jim would have understood himself to rid himself of the constraints of societal prejudices.[54]

Twain, cutting across time, has been praised and damned for his portraits of African-Americans and whites, in their demeanor, language, ethics and relationships. Among Twain's supporters, besides Washington, one will find W. E. B. Du Bois, T. S. Eliot, Ernest Hemingway, at times, the N.A.A.C.P., Ralph Ellison, Toni Morrison, Zora Neal Hurston, and James Baldwin. While Twain's use of the language may be painful, without it Twain's texts might not exert such a powerful force in literature, history, or anthropology. As Jeff Nichols, executive director of the Mark Twain House and Museum in Hartford states: "The word [nigger] is terrible, it's hurtful, but it's there for a reason ... it's there to convey the language and attitudes of Missouri in the 1840's."[55]

Detractors label Twain as racist for depicting blacks as Sambo or minstrel-type characters, especially through language. While many civil rights advocates have praised Twain, civil rights groups, including at times, the N.A.A.C.P., libraries, the New York City Board of Education, and Louisa May Alcott have advocated the banning of Twain's works. Beginning in 1955, one year after Brown v. Board of Education, the move to ban Twain from schools was justified as a civil rights issue, arguing that offensive language in texts could model and legitimate negative language for youth; that the language was hurtful to not only blacks but also to whites, and that Twain's books, including *Huckleberry Finn* and *Puddn'head Wilson*, raised issues that would ignite dangerous dynamics in some classrooms.

In 2011, Professor Alan Gribben of Auburn University developed what he proposed as a solution to the dilemma of the language in *Tom Sawyer* and *Huckleberry Finn* with the publication of a sanitized version of the texts. His changes included replacing "nigger Jim" with slave Jim and "Injun Joe" to Indian Joe. Gribben writes in his introduction:

> The n-word possessed, then as now, demeaning implications more
> vile than almost any insult that be applied to other racial groups.
> There is no equivalent slur in the English language ... I always re-
> coiled from uttering the racial slurs spoken by numerous characters,
> including Tom and Huck. I invariably substituted the word "slave"
> for Twain's ubiquitous n-word whenever I read any passages aloud.
> Students and audience members seemed to prefer this expedient, and
> I could detect a visible sense of relief each time, as though a nagging
> problem with the text had been addressed.[56]

Gribben, who has forty years of experience in teaching Twain, is right when
he claims there is a great deal of discomfort around Twain's language. I am
uncomfortable as our many of my students. But isn't that the point? Does not
this discomfort, which is Twain's way of challenging the conditions of the
world, encourage the debate, the dialogues, needed to evoke changes in attitudes
and behaviors? A reaction piece to Gribben in *The Economist* summarizes the
issue clearly when the author states that one cannot:

> fully appreciate why 'nigger' is taboo today if you don't know how it
> was used back then, and you can't fully appreciate what it was like to
> be a slave if you don't know how slaves were addressed. The 'visible
> sense of relief' Mr. Gribben reports in his listeners is not, in fact, de-
> sirable; feeling discomfort when you read the book today is part of
> the point of reading it.[57]

I initially thought that Gribben's edited versions were another post-death
release written by Twain himself as a way to mock his critics. The awkwardness
of Gribben's version, the bite, and yes the discomfort, removed from Twain's
dialogue and the idea that one should write, and teach, comfortable versions of
books designed to make us uncomfortable is a plot Twain would have been
proud to conceive himself.

Gribben is correct in acknowledging that Twain's dialogue will evoke tensions. My students—across racial, ethnic, class and gender groups—often become quite vocal in their reactions to Twain. This is something instructors
should be both prepared for and embrace. Indeed I now use the Gribben controversy as part of the preparation to read Twain. We also have to trust (and prepare) ourselves, and our students, that the classroom is exactly the place where
these issues can and must be discussed. The debate, which remains inclusive, is
how do we write to describe others without repeating the harmful labeling effects of language.

Challenged historically and today, Twain's publications have become iconic
texts situated at the crossroads of a complex and contested question; what is the
purpose of education? Should our classrooms be designed to expose injustice,
provoke radical critical thinking, inquire about how an alternative society might
be organized, and challenge the status quo, or are our classrooms designed to

justify what is, diminish dissent, stifle debate, and facilitate consensus even if that means white-washing history and present injustice?

Part III: Twain as the Not So Innocent Abroad

Twain was born prior to the Civil War in an isolated hamlet on the banks of the Mississippi in a nation that had yet to define itself. In his lifetime, this sleepy nation transformed from agricultural to industrial. It consolidated its powers from sea to shining sea. By the last fifteen years of Twain's life, the United States also emerged as an awkward international bully. Twain's writings reflect, and contest, these developments. In his words: "I am an anti-imperialist. I am opposed to having the eagle put his talons on any other land."[58]

Initially Twain's fiction and non-fiction commentary on other nations, focused on perceptions of a world far bigger than most Americans could imagine. His writings circled around the question of how we, in the United States, fit into this broader world. His non-fiction writing took the form of newspaper and magazine articles sent home as well as speeches and letters, written through the eyes and pen of Sam Clemens, son of Hannibal, Missouri. His fictional works developed characters referenced in these articles, re-created as vehicles for how Americans viewed others and how they viewed us. Some of the most compelling texts include *Following the Equator, A Tramp Abroad, A Connecticut Yankee in King Arthur's Court*, and most powerfully, *The Innocents Abroad.*

In the last fifteen years of his life, there is a significant shift in Twain's writing, from comparatively light critiques of Americans abroad to bold outrage at the growing imperialism of the United States as a world power. An increasingly bitter Twain, while on the surface still extremely funny, was no longer laughing. His writing was a weapon to advance bitter attacks on national policies. This rhetorical turn is expressed most forcefully in *A Defense of General Funston* and *King Leopold's Soliloquy.*

Twain never lost his Hannibal, Missouri perspective. Nor did he lose his ability to critique it. "'I am a free-born American, sir, and I want everybody to know it!' He did not mention that he was a lineal descendant of Balaam's ass; but everybody knew that without his telling it."[59] Contradiction and hypocrisy were the currency of his texts, as we saw in his mocking analysis of the race and class structure of Dawson's Landing. When overseas, Twain was equally centered in and critical of his origins. In the 1869 *The Innocents Abroad*, the characters Twain creates for his ship, the Quaker City, are those he knew well. Through their bumbling naiveté we are introduced, for better or worse, to Americans' distorted views of Europe, Africa, and their ultimate goal the Holy Land, as only sheltered, myopic citizens would view these wonders.

The Innocents Abroad was Twain's first full-length book, published eight years before *Tom Sawyer* and fourteen years prior to *Puddn'head Wilson*. An expansion and fictionalization of his speeches and newspaper articles about his global tours, in *The Innocents Abroad* the journalist Twain views his fellow travelers as the main attractions. Twain describes these travelers as pilgrims in honor of their ultimate destination of the Holy Land and through their journey readers visit sites such as the Eiffel Tower, the Coliseum in Rome, the Gibraltar, and Jerusalem.

The true stars of this book are, of course, the Americans themselves, or more accurately, their provincial misperceptions of historic sites. Thus, the Sphinx is not viewed as a rich historical monument but rather as: "The block must have been as large as the Fifth Avenue Hotel." Again, "each side of the Pyramid of Cheops is about as long as the Capitol at Washington."[60] Every school board today that has slashed its foreign language budgets should familiarize themselves with Twain's observation of American language abilities: "In Paris they just simply opened their eyes and stared when we spoke to them in French! We never did succeed in making those idiots understand their own language."[61] In the Holy Land, the ultimate destination of their journey, the references are still focused on the tourists' American experience and worldview: "Palestine is only from forty to sixty miles wide. The State of Missouri could be split into three Palestines, and there would be enough material for part of another—possibly a whole one." Or the "celebrated Sea of Galilee is not so large a sea as Lake Tahoe (I measure all lakes by Tahoe)."[62] Twain travels afar to document how Americans distort the opportunity to engage "difference" and return their line of vision to a nationally narcissistic comparison providing an opportunity for classroom discussions of worldviews and ethnocentrism.

Twain also takes shots at the pomposity of United States theatre critics, writers, and tour guides (all of the latter on this trip are named Forrest), and they are presented as giving generic tours based only on what tourists wanted to hear. For instance, the Coliseum in Rome is described through mid-nineteenth century American eyes:

> the man of fashion who could not let fall in a casual and unintentional manner sometime about 'my private box at the Coliseum' could not move in the first circles. When the clothing-store merchant wished to consume the corner grocery man with envy, he brought secured seats in the front row and let the thing be known. When the irresistible dry goods clerk wished to blight and destroy, according to his native instinct, he got himself up regardless of expense and then took some other fellow's young lady to the Coliseum, and then accented the affront by cramming her with ice cream between acts. [63]

While in the Coliseum, Twain "discovers" in the ruins "the only playbill of that establishment." The reader is presented with a message phrased in contemporary terms that only Americans would understand (or misunderstand), regarding the monumental events that occurred in this wonder of the world. He writes to his nineteenth century audience on the other side of the Atlantic with a familiarity that spoofs our values.

Notwithstanding the inclemency of the weather, quite a respectable number of the rank and fashion of the city assembled last night to witness the debut upon the metropolitan boards of the young tragedian who has of late been winning golden opinions in the amphitheaters of the provinces. Some sixty thousand persons were present, and but for the fact that the streets were almost impassable, it is fair to presume that the house would have been full. His august Majesty, the Emperor Aurelius, occupied the imperial box.[64]

The Infant Prodigy performed wonders. He overcame his four tiger whelps with ease, and with no other hurt than the loss of portion of his scalp. The General Slaughter was rendered with a faithfulness to details which reflects the highest credit upon the late participants in it ... A matinee for the little folks is promised for this afternoon, on which occasion several martyrs will be eaten by the tigers.[65]

Sections such as this are valuable teaching tools on several levels. First, they provide a history lesson, through obviously satirical lenses, on Ancient Rome's public spectacles. Second, they present the nineteenth century audience with some insights into what Americans value. Third, for my classes, they provide the basis for a writing exercise where students consider how and why their parents or grandparents might write about the music they listen to, thus exposing them to the connection between perspective and social context when describing events in different cultures or historical times.

Twain satirizes how Americans conduct themselves abroad. He views and represents the United States as a provincial nation that exports country bumpkins, innocent versions of the younger Clemens himself, who have a difficult time comprehending differences; who refuse to see what is before their eyes and thus homogenize difference into sameness. In the Holy Land, he satirizes the elevated status provided for the Mary and Joseph relationship. He comments that one would expect Mary to have some elevated status: "But really here the man rides and the carries the child ... and the woman walks. The customs have not changed since Joseph's time. We would not have in our house a picture of Joseph riding and Mary walking; we would see profanation in it."[66]

Perhaps as a preview of American imperialistic impulses, Twain has his individual tourists constantly taking, consuming, claiming, stealing, and hording that which belongs to others. They pilfer relics, including slices of the Coliseum, Gibraltar, and the Sphinx:

One of our well meaning reptiles—I mean relic-hunters—had crawled up there and was trying to break a "specimen" from the fact of this most majestic creation the hand of man has wrought. But the great image contemplated the dead ages as calmly as ever, unconscious of the small insect that was fretting at its jaw. Egyptian granite that has defied the storms and earthquakes of all times has nothing to fear from the tack-hammers of ignorant excursionists—highwaymen like this specimen.[67]

Even an inability to adjust a watch is worthy of Twain's commentary. One of Twain's key pilgrims could not figure out how to adapt his watch as the ship changed time zones. Rather than taking responsibility, the tourist complained about the watch itself: "This is a swindle ... Why this watch. I bought her in Illinois—gave $150 for her—and I thought she was good. And, by George, she is good onshore, but somehow she don't keep up a lick here—gets seasick maybe."[68] These experiences resonate well with students. Ironically, since my students reflect a very diverse population, they will use Twain as a platform for humorous yet sometimes painful anecdotes about their immigrant or migrant parents to describe cultural misunderstandings. I ask students, immigrant and not, to describe an instance when they felt culturally embarrassed by their parents. Their answers include lack of English fluency, ignorance of American customs, dress, and norms that do not apply in the American context. I then ask them when their behavior culturally embarrassed their parents. Students' answers include lack of fluency in their first language, ignorance of customs, lack of religious knowledge or observance, and rejecting the family business as a career. Again, students learn the connection between context and perceptions.

Twain, however, had stopped laughing. As events forced his unit of analysis to shift from tourism to imperialism, the humor became bitter, the amusement moved to anger, and his acceptance of the emergent United States shifted to intolerance: "It is by the goodness of God that in our country we have those three unspeakably precious things: freedom of speech, freedom of conscience, and the prudence never to practice either."[69]

Part 4: Imperialism: *Following the Equator* and *King Leopold's Soliloquy*

Twain lived during the time when the United States government was completing the destruction of the remaining Indian nations and, with our European allies, viciously and aggressively carving up the world. Particularly bothersome to Twain was how the guise of Christianity and civilization were the ideological cover stories for conquest, genocide, and economic exploitation. The collective imperial efforts of the United States and Europe kept God very busy at the dawn of the twentieth century.

The Spanish-American War led to the United States seizing Cuba, Puerto Rico, and the Philippines. While these conquests were justified in the name of freeing these countries from the Spanish, there was fierce opposition from those who America declared to be liberated. Among those who were especially resistant to American efforts to "free" them were the Filipinos, who endured Christianization through torture, ranging from water boarding to blatant genocide. After we "liberated" them from Spain, the Filipinos resisted for years that ultimately decimated their culture and cost the lives of approximately 300,000 people. Virtually at the same time in South Africa, the British were placing 40,000 Boers in detention camps, including women and children. To back up these consolidation efforts, the British sent 450,000 troops. In China, justified by the slaying of close to 250 outsiders, imperialist spheres of influences were carved out, employing 18,000 troops from eight nations.[70]

While Twain was more vilified for his opposition to United States and European imperialism than he was for his critiques of America, he also attracted more allies in these struggles such as the Anti-Imperialist League, where he served as an officer. Twain's efforts to use the League as a platform to rally against injustice were recognized almost a century later by British-Pakistani historian Tariq Ali in response to the 2003 United States' invasion of Iraq: "The model of what needs to be done by today's dissenters was established in the last year of the 19th century. Mark Twain, shocked by the chauvinist reaction to the Boxer Rebellion in China and the U.S. occupation of the Philippines, sounded the tocsin. The problem, he argued, was imperialism."[71]

Twain, often a loner, found allies in the Anti-Imperialist League. The League was founded in 1898 in Boston in opposition to the Spanish-American War. It had a diverse membership including Jane Addams, W. E. B. Du Bois, Ambrose Piece, Andrew Carnegie, former president Grover Cleveland, John Dewey, Samuel Gompers, Henry James, William James, and William Graham Sumner. Indeed the adage "my enemies' enemy is my friend" united many of them. The unity of this group is an educational topic in itself. I have had my students role play some of these luminaries in an effort to understand how their opposition to foreign polities would lead such a diverse group to unite against imperialism. Sadly this powerful group had very limited effect on slowing the pace of United States' dominance in the world.[72]

Twain's contribution to the cause against expansionist policies was through his writing and speeches. His fictional "*A Defence of General Frederick Funston*," a real life "hero" of the Spanish-American and Philippine-American wars, traces American foreign policies back to the revered images of George Washington. This short missive was released on Washington's Birthday in 1902. Twain separates what he admired about Washington from the Washington (as well as the God), who were used as rationales for imperialism. In this satirical heroic elevation of Funston, Twain effectively demonstrates the misappropriation of Washington's image, deployed as a foil for the brutality of those ravaging the Philippines: "Did Washington's great value, then, lie in what he accomplished? No; that was only a minor value. His major value, his vast value, his immeasurable value to and to the world and to future ages and peoples, lies in his permanent and sky-reaching consciousness as an influence."[73]

Twain felt that Washington's real gift to the nation was the standard that we would not follow other nations in violating democratic principles with the oppression of others. Thus he ridiculed those who raised the stature of the Funstons to Washington's level of heroism. Twain, with obvious sarcasm, wrote that: "the proper inborn disposition was required to start a Washington; the acceptable influences and circumstances and a large field were required to develop and complete him. The same with Funston."[74] In other words, Twain feared that the peddlers of imperialism would successfully elevate Funston to the stature of Washington for generations to come, from school children to the military. "This competition [with Washington] has already begun ... there are now public-school teachers and superintendents who are holding up Funston as a model hero and Patriot in the schools."

> If this Funstonian boom continues, Funstonism will presently affect the army...Funston's example has bred many imitators, and many ghastly additions to our history: the torturing of Filipinos by the awful "water-cure," for instance, to make them confess—what? Truth? Or lies? How can one know which it is they are telling? For under unendurable pain a man confesses anything that is required of him, true or false, and his evidence is worthless. Yet upon such evidence American officers have actually—but you know about those atrocities which the War Office has been hiding a year or two; and about General Smith's now world-celebrated order of massacre—thus summarized by the press from Major Waller's testimony: "Kill and burn—this is no time to take prisoners—the more you kill and burn, the better—Kill all above the age of ten—make Samar a howling wilderness!" [75]

History tells us that Twain was clearly right about the dangers of war, and their long lasting results. The water boarding interrogations exposed in the twenty-first century involving the United States were military grandchildren of the Philippine war toolkit. Waller's "testimony" anticipates General Curtis LeMay, who in Vietnam advocated "bombing them back to the stone age." LeMay would have been at home in Funston's army.

Two years after publishing "Funston," Twain used a similar strategy when he produced the even more biting *King Leopold's Soliloquy*. In 1876 Belgium's King Leopold II declared himself head of the International Association for the Exploration and Civilization of Central Africa. By the time Twain published his expose, up to eight million of the twenty million targets of this civilization had died. Others had been made examples, with amputations of hands and feet; men were castrated, women were raped, and children put into forced labor.[76]

Twain takes the liberty of speaking for King Leopold; crafting a defense of Leopold's actions, articulating a rhetorical tirade against those who had the nerve to attack him. The soliloquy begins with a shocked Leopold throwing down his critics' pamphlets, banging a table, cursing and then kissing his cross. His shock is not caused by the exposure of his brutal behavior, but rather that his efforts to civilize with Christianity have been misunderstood.

> In these twenty years I have spent millions to keep the press of the two hemispheres quiet, and still these leaks keep occurring ... Grant

them true, what of it? They are slanders all the same, when uttered against a king ... They [his critics] tell it all: how I am wiping a nation of friendless creatures out of existence by every form of murder ... how every shilling I get costs a rape, a mutilation or a life. But they never say, although they know it, that I have labored in the cause of religion at the same time and for all the time." [77]

Leopold responds to a pamphlet that describes his cruelty:

Lying about on the grass ... were numbers of human skulls, bones, in some cases complete skeletons from which the skulls were missing. [quote of survivor] "the soldiers shot so many we grew tired of burying, and very often we were not allowed to bury ... Each time the corporal goes out to get rubber, cartridges are given to him ... for every one used he must bring back a right hand ... the soldiers kill the children with the butt of the gun."[78]

[Leopold] ... provides nothing in return but hunger, terror, grief, shame, captivity and massacre ... That is their style! I furnish "nothing"! I send the gospel to the survivors; these censure-mongers know it, but would rather have their tongues out then mention it. I have several times required my raiders to give the dying an opportunity to kiss the sacred emblem; and they obeyed me.[79]

Twain's soliloquy was vilified by his political targets, including the heavily invested Rockefellers, the United States Government, and a Cardinal in the Catholic Church. Sadly it could have been written today, simply by substituting the Military Industrial Complex, Halliburton, and former Vice President Dick Cheney.

Most of my students, through no fault of their own, know next-to-nothing about the political agendas of the Spanish-American War, particularly the aftermath in the Philippines. Even fewer know about humanistic costs of colonializing Africa. The impoverishment of Africa seems only a far away tragedy, self-imposed, futile, not structured by global politics, historically designed and economically beneficial to the West. Twain opens their eyes and very frequently their curiosity to learn more. In these texts, Twain provides a prophetic mirror to our nation's becoming an imperial power. The students' initial view of this process is a generous, gracious, and sacrificial struggle taken up for liberty, democracy and freedom. As our students would say, Twain keeps the term Manifest Destiny real. The United States expanded then and now in the name of God, democracy, profit, and to protect the people from the evils of themselves. We are still in the business of saving nations, protecting them from themselves, to expand our own definition of democracy and to increase our own wealth as profits earned overseas are not heavily taxed. Ultimately, Twain feels that the Christian God as constructed in the United States, is the root of evil, both nationally and internationally. In 1900 Twain wrote in the *New York Herald*: "I bring you the stately matron named Christendom, returning bedraggled, be-smirched, and dishonored from pirate raids in Kao-Chou, Manchuria, South Africa, and the Philippines, with her soul full of meanness, her pocket full of boodle, and her mouth full of pious hypocrisies."[80] Twain had little patience for the hypocrisies of religious justification of slavery or imperialism. He frequently mocks the moral cover the church provides for immoral individual or national acts:

> It [a wing of Notre Dame in Paris] was built by Jean Sans-Peur, Duke of Burgundy, to set his conscience at rest—he had assassinated the Duke of Orleans. Alas! Those good old days are gone, when a mur-derer could wipe the stain from his name and soothe his trouble to sleep simply by getting out his blocks and mortar and building an ad-dition to a church.[81]

I use Twain's views of religion as a classroom opportunity to expand on the evils done in the name of religion. Domination has long been justified by the belief that god or gods are squarely behind those in power. Twain was right to expose the misuse of religion at the end of the nineteenth century and he would be right today. Conversely I also use Twain's views as a springboard to examine the positive role of religion in terms of social change. Teaching, as a Jew, at a Jesuit University, gives credence to both a discussion of inclusive liberation theology as well the hypocrisies within religious orders. The Civil Rights and Anti-War movements would have been less successful without religion; less necessary had it not been for religion.

Conclusion

Mark Twain evolved from making us laugh at ourselves to bitterly attacking our commitment to imperialism. Along the way, he exposed a nation to the injustic-es of slavery, the hypocrisies of social class stratification, and a national inabil-ity to see or accept others. Along most of the way, he taught us how to have a good time in life. Twain's writings confirm that history has the annoying habit of repeating itself. The Twain of the nineteenth and early twentieth century is relevant in too many areas today. He identified grave wrongs domestically. He saw innocents turned into imperialists overseas. A social critic whose wisdom carries over time and place, he enraged and engaged our ancestors, our contem-poraries, and those in between in discussions of who we have been, who we are, and who we could be.

Yet there is one final piece to Twain's legacy that I invite my students to understand. Mark Twain was an uncompromising idealist who believed in the United States. He saw in our history virtues that had been betrayed, but would eventually right the ship. Twain firmly believed that the virtues of the Washingtons would prevail over the evil of the Funstons:

> The nation will speak; its will is law; there is no other sovereign on this soil; and in that day we shall right such unfairnesses as we have done. We shall let go our obsequious hold on the rear-skirts of the sceptred land-thieves of Europe ... hands recleansed in the patriotism of Washington, and once more fit to touch the hem of the revered Shade's garment and stand in its presence unashamed. It was Washington's influence that made Lincoln and all other real patriots the Republic has known; it was Washington's influence that made the soldiers who saved the Union; and that influence will save us always, and bring us back to the fold when we stray.[82]

Twain was disappointed and angry, but ultimately trusted Americans. In *Puddn'head Wilson,* he asserted that our nation would have to take the long way home to learn who it is, or should be: "It would be wonderful to find America but it would be more wonderful to miss it."[83] America had to grasp which values had been lost to in order to gain them back. Twain's prescription was to learn about others to learn about ourselves, a quintessentially anthropological perspective. In *The Innocents Abroad,* he summarized this point in one powerful sentence: "Travel is fatal to prejudice, bigotry, and narrow-mindedness, and many of our people need it on these accounts."[84] Even today, few have matched his extensive travels, domestic and abroad, with his accompanying introspective critique.

I end this chapter on a personal note. Sam, yes we are both from Missouri, so I can be familiar—you are an idealist. Too bad, Mr. Clemens, I know you have an image to protect, but you blew your cover. In your *Autobiography* you wrote: "I still believe, in spite of everything, that people are truly good at heart."[85] Sorry Sam, although you had to be dead for 100 years before you allowed this book to be released, you finally let the cat out of the bag. You knew we could to better. Otherwise you would have stayed on the Mississippi. Thanks.

NOTES

Acknowledgments

I would like to thank generations of my students for thirty years of feedback. Telessia Williams was especially helpful on *Pudd'nhead Wilson* with her passionate input that did not always equate with agreement.

1. The wording of this quote varies but a handwritten document has been produced in which Twain actually says exactly: "the reports of my death are greatly exaggerated." http://www.twainquotes.com/index.html<Dictionary.com

2. Martha McCulloch Williams, "Re Puddn'head Wilson," *Southern Magazine* (February 1894), 99.

3. Hjamar Hjorth Boysen, "Two Humorists," *Cosmopolitan* (January 1895), 378-379.

4. Mark Twain, *Pudd'nhead Wilson and Those Extraordinary Twins* (New York: Barnes & Noble, 2005 [1894]), 23.

5. Twain, *Pudd'nhead Wilson*, 129.

6. Twain, *Pudd'nhead Wilson*, 8.

7. Twain, *Pudd'nhead Wilson*, 12.

8. Twain, *Pudd'nhead Wilson*, 12.

9. Twain, *Pudd'nhead Wilson*, 13.

10. Hardy Drew and the Nancy Boys, "The Irish Obama," 2008. http://news.bbc.co.uk/2/hi/americas/us_elections_2008/7718583.stm (accessed March 15, 2009).

11. Twain, *Pudd'nhead Wilson*, 87.

12. Twain, *Pudd'nhead Wilson*, 55.

13. Twain, *Pudd'nhead Wilson*, 50.

14. Twain, *Pudd'nhead Wilson*, 56.

15. Frantz Fanon, *Black Skin, White Masks* (New York: Grove Press, 1952); Frantz Fannon, *The Wretched of the Earth: A Negro Psychoanalyst's Study of the Problems of Racism & Colonialism in the World Today* (New York: Grove Press, 1961).

16. W. E. B. Du Bois, *The Souls of Black Folk* (Boulder: Paradigm Publishers, 2004 [1903]).

17. Twain, *Pudd'nhead Wilson*, 140.

18. Twain, *Pudd'nhead Wilson*, 19.

19. Twain, *Pudd'nhead Wilson*, 51.

20. Twain, *Pudd'nhead Wilson*, 77.

21. Twain, *Pudd'nhead Wilson*, 15.

22. Twain, *Pudd'nhead Wilson*, 14.

23. Twain, *Pudd'nhead Wilson*, 16.

24. Frederick Douglass, *Narrative of the Life of Frederick Douglass, An American Slave Twin* (New York: Macmillan Higher Education, 2002 [1845]), 2.

25. Twain, *Pudd'nhead Wilson*, 51. See Cohen, this volume for additional discussion of resistance strategies among women slaves.

26. Twain, *Pudd'nhead Wilson*, 19.

27. Twain, *Pudd'nhead Wilson*, 49.

28. Philip S. Foner, *Mark Twain Social Critic* (New York: International Publishers, 1972 [1958]), 281.

29. Twain, *Pudd'nhead Wilson*, 15.

30. Foner, *Social Critic*, 281.

31. Foner, *Social Critic*, 402.

32. Ralph Ellison, *Invisible Man* (New York: Vintage Books, 1980 [1952], 3-6.

33. Iris Ford Carter, "The Travel and Travail of Negro Showpeople," *Anthropology and Humanism* 26, issue 10 (June 2001): 41.

34. Twain, *Pudd'nhead Wilson*, 99.

35. Ellison, *Invisible Man*, 4.

36. Fanon, *Black Skin, White Masks*, 109.

37. Ronald Takaki, *A Different Mirror* (New York: Little, Brown and Company, 2008 [1993]), 54-54, 238-240.

38. Twain, *Pudd'nhead Wilson*, 51.

39. Twain, *Pudd'nhead Wilson*, 55.

40. Twain, *Pudd'nhead Wilson*, 48.

41. Twain, *Pudd'nhead Wilson*, 52.

42. Takaki, *A Different Mirror*, 71.

43. Twain, *Pudd'nhead Wilson*, 140.

44. Williams, "Re Puddn'head Wilson," 99-101.

45. Alan Gribben, "Editor's Introduction: Reuniting Two Companion Books," in *Mark Twain's Adventures of Tom Sawyer and Huckleberry Finn*, The NewSouth Edition (Montgomery: NewSouth Press, 2011), 9.

46. Ralph Waldo Emerson, "Compensation Essay," in *Columbia World of Quotations* (New York: Columbia University Press, 1998 [1841]).

47. "Bar Mark Twain's Book," *New York Times*, November 4, 1906, 1.

48. Abby Goodnough, "Century After It Was Banned, Place of Honor for Twain Tale," *New York Times*, September 21, 2011, A14.

49. Goodnough, "Century," A14.

50. Williams, "Re Puddn'head Wilson," 101.

51. Williams, "Re Puddn'head Wilson," 99, 101.

52. Boysen, "Two Humorists," 378-379.

53. "New Mark Twain Letters Reveal He Poked Fun at Huck Finn Ban" *New York Times*, November 2, 1935.

54. Peter Sawlen, "Is Huck Finn Racist" http://www.salwen.com/mtrace.html, 2012 (accessed October 27, 2012).

55. Jeff Nichols, "Interview," Quoted by United Press International, January 6, 2011.

56. Gribben, "Introduction," 8.

57. G.L. "There weren't any niggers, then," The Economist Blog, http://www.economist.com/blogs/johnson/2011/01/sanitising_huckleberry_finnJJJanuary 7, 2011 (accessed August 15, 2012).

58. Stefan Heym, "Introduction," in *Mark Twain's King Leopold's Soliloquy* (New York: International Publishers, 2006 [1905], 16.

59. Mark Twain, *The Innocents Abroad* (New York: Signet Classics, 2007 [1869]), 69.

60. Twain, *Innocents Abroad*, 490-492.

61. Twain, *Innocents Abroad*, 506.

62. Twain, *Innocents Abroad*, 366, 388.

63. Twain, *Innocents Abroad*, 205.

64. Twain, *Innocents Abroad*, 206

65. Twain, *Innocents Abroad*, 208-209, 211, 212.

66. Twain, *Innocents Abroad*, 368.

67. Twain, *Innocents Abroad*, 492.

68. Twain, *Innocents Abroad*, 28.

69. Mark Twain, *Following the Equator* (New York: Oxford University Press, 1996 [1897]), 195.

70. Foner, *Social Critic*, 326-329.

71. Jim Swick, *Confronting Imperialism: Essays On Mark Twain and the Anti-Imperialism League* (West Conshohocken, Pa.: Infinity Publishing, 2007), ix.

72. Swick, *Confronting Imperialism*, ix-xiii.

73. Mark Twain, "A Defence of General Funston," *North American Review* (February 22, 1902): 1.

74. Twain, "A Defence," 3.

75. Twain, "A Defence," 3-4.

76. Foner, *Social Critic*, 11-27.

77. Mark Twain, *King Leopold's Soliloquy* (New York: International Publishers, 2006 [1905], 32, 35-37.

78. Twain, *Leopold's Soliloquy*, 45-47.

79. Twain, *Leopold's Soliloquy*, 51-52.

80. Howard Zinn, *A Peoples History of the United States* (New York: HarperPerennial, 2005 [1980]), 321.

81. Twain, *Innocents Abroad*, 92.

82. Mark Twain, "A Defence," 4.

83. Twain, *Pudd'nhead Wilson*, 139.

84. Twain, *The Innocents Abroad*, 512.

85. Mark Twain, *Autobiography of Mark Twain: The Complete and Authoritative Edition*, Volume 1 (Berkeley: University of California Press, 2010), 365.

References

Boysen, Hjamar Hjorth
    1895   "Two Humorists." *Cosmopolitan.* (January): 378-379.
Carter, Iris Ford
    2001   "The Travel and Travail of Negro." *Anthropology and Humanism.* Volume
           26, Issue 10 (June): 35-45.
Drew, Hardy and the Nancy Boys
    2009   "The Irish Obama." http://news.bbc.co.uk/2/hi/americas/us_elections_2008/
           7718583.stm (accessed March 15).
Douglass, Frederick
    2002   *Narrative of the Life of Frederick Douglass, An American Slave Twin.*
           New York: Macmillan Higher Education [1845].
Du Bois, W. E. B.
    2004   *The Souls of Black Folk.* Boulder: Paradigm Publishers [1903].
Ellison, Ralph
    1980   *Invisible Man.* New York: Vintage Books [1952].
Emerson, Ralph Waldo
    1998   "Compensation Essay" in Columbia World of Quotations. New York: Col-
           umbia University Press [1841].
Fanon, Frantz
    1987   *Black Skin, White Masks.* New York: Grove/Atlantic Press, [1952].
    1961   *The Wretched of the Earth: A Negro Psychoanalyst's Study of the Problems*
           of Racism & Colonialism in the World Today. New York: Grove Press, Inc.
Foner, Philip S.
    1972   *Mark Twain Social Critic.* New York: International Publishers [1958].
G. L.
    2011   "There weren't any niggers, then" The Economist Blog, http://www.
           economist.com/blogs/johnson/2010/01/sanitising_huckleberry_finn
           January 7, 2011 (accessed August 15, 2012).
Goodnough, Amy
    2011   "Century After It Was Banned, Place of Honor for Twain Tale," *New York*
           Times, September 21, 2011, 14(A).
Gribben, Alan
    2011   "Editor's Introduction: Reuniting Two Companion Books." In *Mark Twain's*
           Adventures of Tom Sawyer and Huckleberry Finn, The NewSouth Edition,
           Pp. 7-28. Montgomery: New South Press.
Heym, Stefan
    2006   "Introduction to Mark Twain's King Leopold's Soliloquy." In *King Leo-*
           pold's Soliloquy by Mark Twain, Pp. 11-30. New York: International Pub-
           lishers.
New York Times
    1935   "New Mark Twain Letters Reveal He Poked Fun at Huck Finn Ban," *New*
           York Times, November 2, 1935.
Nichols, Jeff
    2011   "Interview." United Press International, January 6, 2011.

Sawlen, Peter
    2012   "Is Huck Finn Racist?" http://www.salwen.com/mtrace.html, (accessed October 27, 2012).

Swick, Jim
    2007   *Confronting Imperialism: Essays On Mark Twain and the Anti-Imperialism League*. West Conshohocken, Pa.: Infinity Publishing.

Takaki, Ronald
    2008   *A Different Mirror*. New York: Little, Brown and Company, [1993].

Twain, Mark
    1901   *Christian Science*. New York: Harper and Brothers [1899].
    1996   *Following the Equator*. New York: Oxford University Press [1897].
    1902   "A Defence of General Funston," *North American Review*. February 22.
    2005   *Pudd'nhead Wilson and Those Extraordinary Twins*. New York: Barnes and Noble [1894].
    2006   *King Leopold's Soliloquy*. New York: International Publishers [1905].
    2007   *The Innocents Abroad*. New York: Signet Classics [1869].
    2010   *Autobiography of Mark Twain: The Complete and Authoritative Edition*, Volume 1. Berkeley: University of California Press.

Williams, Martha McCulloch
    1894   "Re Puddn'head Wilson." *Southern Magazine* (February): 99-102.

Zinn, Howard
    2005   *A Peoples' History of the United States*. New York: HarperPerennial, [1980].

Chapter 6

The Creole Speaks: Daniel, Sandi, and the Other in *Wide Sargasso Sea*

JOHN W. PULIS

Edward Rochester, Antoinette's new husband, is confronted in one of the more enigmatic vignettes in *Wide Sargasso Sea* by an individual known as Daniel.[1] Daniel claims to be a Cosway, the son of Antoinette's father by "another lady," and he approached Rochester seeking what he claimed was his rightful inheritance. Like many West Indian planters, Cosway engaged in "creolizing," a practice in which he fathered children and supported "half-houses" in and around Coulibri, his plantation on the island of Jamaica.[2] It was creole practice for these kin (officially recognized as "moieties" in Jamaica) to congregate around the "great house" at Christmas time to receive gifts (usually money) from their patrons and benefactors. We first learn about these half-houses in Part One when Sandi, Antoinette's "cousin," comes to her rescue in an altercation in Spanish Town, the island capital at that time. Although her assailants were nameless, they were not unknown and were recognized as kith, albeit distant, by Sandi. Daniel's claim was rebuffed by Rochester but his reckoning of history, kinship, and genealogy constitutes a leitmotif in which Jean Rhys addressed a range of issues concerning West Indian society and culture.[3]

Set in Jamaica in the years following the abolition of slavery (1833-1840), *Wide Sargasso Sea* has been acclaimed as a pioneering work of West Indian fiction in which the author anticipated in many ways feminist, post-colonial, and more recent the trends in literary studies.[4] It was first published in 1966, was the last and most successful of several novels published by Rhys, and was released as a feature film in 1995. Rhys was born (1890) on the island of Dominica and the story contains plots and themes that are autobiographical in nature. In *Smile Please*, a memoir published posthumously (1976), Rhys talked about her childhood and family on Dominica and these reminisces are strikingly similar to vignettes in the novel.[5] The novel was conceived as a prequel to *Jane Eyre*, Charlotte Brontë's nineteenth century classic, and the story centers around Antoinette and her mother Annette who are "marooned" on a defunct plantation located in the parish of St. Catherine.[6] Brontë's Bertha is Rhys's Antoinette who marries Rochester in Jamaica and is taken to England where she lives out her days as the mad woman in the attic of Thornfield Hall. Fiction, like all forms of production, is socially constituted and this chapter will approach this story much like an ethnographer conducting fieldwork in an unfamiliar society.[7] Rather than

England, Jane and Thornfield Hall, it will focus on the local and it will enlist figures like Daniel, Sandi, and Christophine as insiders whose subject position provide an alternate and oppositional perspective on a critical juncture in the formation of creole society.[8]

Texts and Contexts

It is not surprising that Rhys chose Jamaica rather than Barbados, Saint Kitts, or Trinidad as the setting for her novel. The island was taken from Spain in 1655 and was transformed into the crown jewel of the British West Indies by a loose association of planters, merchants, and privateers.[9] This association developed into an elite whose hegemony has been referred to as a "plantocracy." They organized plantations, parceled the island into parishes and counties, and convened a legislature known as the House of Assembly.[10] The Assembly became the vehicle through which the plantocracy wrested an unprecedented degree of autonomy from the metropole. The laws they enacted established the legal basis for a civil or more properly patriarchal society empowering the few with a mandate to control all aspects of insular life.[11] Known as the "Slave Acts," this legislation mediated authority through a series of codes and statues based on color and legitimated a political culture, a licentious form of behavior known as "creolizing."[12]

The private world of European salons became, as Patricia Mohammed, Jennifer Morgan, and Barbara Bush suggest, the creole world of Anglo eroticism, fantasy, and desire.[13] Sexuality was a transfer point and hegemony was mediated through networks that included European men and women, captive and free Africans, and an intermediate strata known as "people of color." The codes disseminated patriarchy through "whitening" or pseudo-legal codifications of identity. There were eight color-coded identity formations (mulatto, quadroon, musteephino, et al.) and the progeny of European men (free) and African women (enslaved) were born into a caste-like hierarchy and were awarded privileges based on "degrees of whiteness." Class was complemented by race, color became a marker of rank and status, and the Island developed the pyramidal white, brown, black social structure typically associated with the British West Indies.[14] African features were demonized and people of various shades and pigmentations were denied the "rights and privileges" of their European kin and kith. They could not engage in political processes, inherit estates valued more than two-thousand pounds (Jamaican), and were subjected to the "most cruel and inhuman of punishments."[15] Robert Wedderburn, the son of a Scottish planter and an African mother disowned by his father and half-brother, published a series of political tracts in which he referred to plantocracy as a "venal," his father as "abusive," and the enslaved as the object of "lust" born of "brutality."[16]

Antoinette's father may not have succumbed to a "lust born of brutality" but he did nonetheless engage in creolizing. We hear nothing from Cosway himself (he passed away sometime before the narrative begins) and his persona is revealed in bits and pieces as subtext interspersed between the voice of his widow Annette and his daughter Antoinette. We learn from Antoinette in the opening paragraphs that he "belonged to the past" and we hear several pages later via gossip, informal networks of communication, about "old customs," "those women," and how Annette, who was his second wife, "never did anything" to deter his creolizing.[17] Rhys has omitted from her caricature the more heinous aspects of creolizing such as those revealed by Trevor Bernard (*Master, Tyranny, and Desire*) and Douglas Hall (*In Miserable Slavery*) and it becomes readily apparent that Cosway's persona is symptomatic of a bygone era and articulates a theme, albeit glossed and submerged, in most accounts of West Indian history.[18] Although we are not yet introduced to his "other" progeny, we are told by Annette's bridesmaids that his plantation had been "going downhill for years" and that he "drank himself to death" in desperation due in no small part to what was referred at that time as "gradualism," "amelioration," and the inevitable abolition of slavery.[19]

Abolition forever changed the Island. Of the nine-hundred plantations that existed before, less than three-hundred remained operational after the enslaved were emancipated. Many of the less productive were "thrown up" or abandoned, some were purchased by large planters and landless gentry seeking estates, and others, while occupied, went "ruinate" or bankrupt for want of labor and capital.[20] Coulibri falls into the latter category. The great house was occupied but the property had reverted or "gone to bush" typified by Antoinette's sojourns through the back country (crumbling walls) and her ruminations about times gone by (grass covered walkways). Literary scholars refer to these sojourns and ruminations as historical imagination but I think "enactive interpretations" is more appropriate as they were crafted from the personal experience of the author and her extended family.[21] Rhys was the great granddaughter of James Lockhart, a Scottish slave-holder on Dominica, and the ridicule Antoinette endured ("white cockroach") and the angst that she and her mother experienced ("marooned," "feeling safe in bed," "what will become of us") articulate an insider's view of the period.

"The Lockhart's," Rhys noted in her autobiography, "even in my day (early twentieth-century) were never very popular" and these muses and reflections had less to do with the literary or inter-textual, that is, with Rochester, England, and *Jane Eyre*, and more with the extra- or contextual, the local, insular, and creole. Rather than conjure or imagine some unknown past, Rhys drew upon an archive, an orally recounted repository of family and local experiences on Dominica, selected episodes and events for extrapolation, and reinscribed them as vignettes or "thick descriptions" in post-emancipation Jamaica.[22]

Scholars have taken Rhys to task for privileging the subject position of a "white creole" but such criticisms are to my way of thinking misplaced.[23] We must bear in mind that creole and plantation studies were subordinated to narratives of empire until the postwar decades and the author serves here not as an apologist offering lamentations about bygone glories and the "white man's burden" but a participant-observer, alienated, marginalized, and exiled in the metropole, who has resurrected the turmoil, tensions, and struggles of the era.[24] Novelists can and do speak through their characters and in *Wide Sargasso Sea* we hear from multiple interlocutors: white creoles and black creoles, old planters and new planters, Jamaicans and other islanders, each expressing alternate and oppositional "structures of feeling."[25] Christophine, for example, is feared by both blacks and whites because she possessed some innate power (voodoo) carried from Martinique that differed from her compatriots in Jamaica (obeah). Obeah and voodoo, while similar, are by no means synonymous. Obeah (aka obia, obiah, obieah) is a neologism whose origins are to be found among Akan-Ga speaking peoples in area of Africa known then as the Gold Coast. Voodoo (aka, vodo, vodu) is the Francophone counterpart whose origins are to be found among the Aja-Fon speaking peoples along the Slave Coast.[26] Both were deployed by the plantocracy to promote the "civilizing" or pro-slave agenda in London and distort the influence of Africa and Africans on the social, cultural, and political formation of creole society.[27] Christophine's fluency (she spoke French, English, Patois) negated the trope of the "superstitious slave" disseminated by planter-historians like Edward Long, William Beckford, and Bryan Edwards and her comportment (wore a black dress, was "noir," blue-black in color, tied her handkerchief Martinique style) expressed diversity and tension within a purportedly homogenous "black" class.

No happy endings here. The struggle to end slavery was bitter and divisive and it was assumed that all white creoles were adversaries not advocates. Annette marries Mr. Mason but the disdain he expresses about Cora's indifference ("why did she do nothing to help you") and Annette's apathy ("be reasonable, you are the widow of a slave-owner, the daughter of a slave-owner") give us some sense of the rift between the old and new plantocracy.[28] The former protagonists (Anglophile planters, African laborers) were eclipsed by a new alignment of forces and relations epitomized by figures like Mason, old Mr. Luttrell's newly arrived kin, and, of course, Edward Rochester. Whereas the term creole was invented (criar-create/colono-colonist = creole) to distinguish colonist born in Europe from those born in Africa and the New World, it took on a stigma in the decades following emancipation and Rhys not only anticipates the derogatory social status accorded creoles in Victorian society but gives us a sense of its multiple meanings and shifting usage as well.[29]

Kith and Kin

The task of any good story-teller is to make the strange familiar and the familiar strange and Rhys certainly accomplishes this when she introduces her readership to the subtleties and nuances of West Indian kinship. Kinship and family are all-important and play a central role in the narrative.[30] We learn from Antoinette that along with her brother Pierre and her Aunt Cora there were a host of cousins, half-cousins, half-brothers, and other near and distant kin. The blurring and confusion is intentional. On the one hand, it is reminiscent of Dickens and characters like Oliver and Pip who were detached from their biological or families of procreation and were reconfigured as "blood" or kin in fictive or imaginary families of orientation.[31] On the other hand, it was intended to foreground a parallel and similarly hidden network and community in the West Indies. Cosway fathered children and supported half-houses in and around his estate. Just how many is difficult to determine and disentangling the web of kin and kith enabled Rhys to move this heretofore hushed and unspoken history (lust, phobia, eroticism) from the periphery to the center of her accounting. Annette was Cosway's second wife and we are introduced to his "other" progeny toward the end of Part One. Sandi was the son of Alexander Cosway, one of Antoinette's "colored" relatives and the grandson of her father by "another lady" born into one of three half-house families. We presume they were similar in age and their reacquaintance was situated not in the "bush" at Coulibri but in Spanish Town, the island capital at that time.

The shift in setting is not insignificant and is commensurate with abolition, the abandonment of estate work, and migration of the newly emancipated to towns and villages seeking to forge new lives.[32] Whereas Antoinette's earlier travails framed a discussion about the past, her sojourn into post-emancipation society enabled Rhys to expose the legacy or "deep saturation of consciousness" associated with race. Antoinette is confronted on her way to a convent and the derogation cited earlier concerning pigmentation flashed through her mind when she sees and then describes her assailants: "he had a white skin, a dull ugly white covered with freckles, his mouth was a negro's mouth, and he had eyes, like bits of green glass. Worst, most horrible of all, his hair was crinkled, a negro's hair, but bright red, and his eyebrows and eyelashes were red."[33]

Slavery was officially abolished, but like apartheid in South Africa (and Jim Crow in the United States) color became institutionalized, part of the social fabric of post-emancipation society (and this invective is reminiscent of comments vetted some time ago about a performer named "Yello-Man" who was demonized due to albinism). Unlike her caricature of Cosway, which was for the most part measured and restrained, no such chains bound Rhys here and in these brief but potent phrases she exposes the deep saturation of consciousness (race, color, class) bequeathed to the generations that followed. Tia's earlier confrontation and rebuke of Antoinette as a white cockroach expressed one version of this unholy trinity and Antoinette's revulsion at the sight of her assailant another. Rhys does not reference "degrees of whiteness" here but rather the widespread stigma associated with plurality, the mixed or hybrid composition of creole corporal and emotional or psychic embodiment. This theme will surface again in Part Two and is directed at Antoinette who is thought to be similarly "tainted" (with negro blood) by her new husband. Its articulation at this juncture in the story foregrounds the complex linkage between color, class, and stereotype in that her assailant is marked and tainted as threatening and duplicitous with "red negro hair" and "ugly white skin." That Antoinette's repugnance had less to do with biology and more with ideology is exemplified in the paragraph that follows when it was none other than Sandi, her "colored" half-cousin, who comes to her rescue.[34]

Annette's bridesmaids condemned Cosway for promulgating "old customs" and referred to his progeny in derogatory European terminology as "bastards" but these half-house families were officially recognized as "moieties" in Jamaica by the House of Assembly. The word is Latin in origin (*medius* or half) and has been employed by anthropologists to signify a mode of kinship or reckoning in which descent is tracked by several families (usually clans) to a common genealogical ancestor.[35] I can not speak with certainty when the term first entered local jurisprudence, but a cursory review of the *Journals of the House of Assembly of Jamaica* (hereafter *JAJ*) indicates that it was deployed early-on in reference to "people of color." While not enslaved as such, people of color were required to petition the House of Assembly for "the rights and privileges of an English subject, with reservations," and a survey indicates that these moieties were petitioning at the rate of fifty individuals per legislative session and there were four sessions per annum.[36] Once petitioned the Assembly convened a subcommittee empowered to collect evidence, confirm paternity, and award the requisite rights and privileges. Petitioning the Assembly was a costly affair and it was not uncommon for several half-houses to pool their resources and collaborate in their pursuit of rights, privileges, and status associated with teknonymy, that is, creole names, naming practices, and paternity. Take, for example, the petition lodged by Thomas Nicholas Swigle et al.. Swigle was the son of Thomas Nicholas Swigle, esquire and was part of the Hyde-Swigle moiety, two Afro-Jamaican half-houses that included the daughters (two) and sons (three) of Sarah Hyde, a "free mulatto woman," with Thomas Nicholas Swigle and Edmund Hyde, the Earl of Clarendon (former governor and name-sake of Clarendon parish). They petitioned en toto and were awarded rights and privileges in 1774. Swigle was baptized in the Church of England, inherited a portion of his father's estate, and resided in Kingston where he and his wife founded one of the first Afro-Christian congregations on the Island.[37]

Rhys does not tell us if any of Cosway's paterfamiliases filed petitions, achieved recognition, or were awarded privileges. Thinking with their genitals, however, was by no means confined to Jamaica and we assume that the author was well aware of such practices on Dominica. Family and genealogy were all important and Rhys was careful to distinguish her lineage from that of Lockhart, her paternal ancestor. Sandi was Cosway's grandson and the issue of names, naming practices, and paternity, which served as subtext in Part One, is thrust into the foreground and constitutes an arena or zone of engagement in Part Two when we meet another of Cosway's progeny.

Unlike Part One which was narrated by Antoinette, Part Two opens with a backward but by no means self-conscious reflection on recently transpired events by an unidentified narrator. Backward-like glances such as these usually provide a technique for authors to insert a transformative experience in terms of character development and personality formation. Not so here. The language and tone are derisive and desultory and Antoinette's creole naiveté is eclipsed by arrogance, conceit, and condescension wielded by a figure that aspires and seeks recognition as an aristocrat but remains nonetheless landless. Rhys is reported to have said that she kept the narrator nameless as long as possible, in deference no doubt to *Jane Eyre*, and Rhys's caricature does not garner the sympathy that Brontë's does. We are given a glimpse into Rochester's persona when he expresses disdain for the lush tropical foliage and refers to Amèlié, Antoinette's maid-servant, as a "half-caste." Unlike the aforementioned epithets, this designation was not local vernacular and its articulation points to the widespread belief among Anglophiles that despite their white or "clear" skin creoles were marked and tainted in some way, shape, or form by people of African descent. The less vulgar saw this as contagion, the inevitable outcome of life in the tropics or "torrid zone" (a lapse in civilized morals, norms, values) while the blatant referenced the immutable as in caste. "Creoles they may be," Rochester says later, "but they are not English" and the stigma cited earlier concerning hybridity and color is articulated by a priggish character who doubts that any creole could be of "pure English descent."[38]

The shift in language, tone, and narrators is accompanied by a corresponding shift in setting from Jamaica to Dominica. Rhys has exercised a degree of artistic or poetic license here. Annette was a *béké*, the daughter of a slave owner from Martinique, and she inherited an estate (Grandbois, high woods) on the island of Dominica. Dominica was initially occupied by the French (who had seized it earlier from the Spanish), was given to the British as a result of the Seven Years War (1763), and it changed hands several times therafter.[39] The West Indies have been characterized as "the cockpit of Europe" because of the protracted and seemingly endless conflict between rival European nations and it was not uncommon for islands to change political affiliations (along with official languages, flags, and legal systems) with the cessation of hostilities in Europe. The transient nature of affiliations served to bolster and support local customs and it is fair to say that the shift in location inverts the orientation and legitimates creole culture as the yardstick against which metropolitan traditions were compared. Once again, Rhys had first hand knowledge of this as her great grandfather was among those who settled Dominica soon after it was acquired by the British. There is a parallel here worth pointing out, although I could find no precedent in Rhys's autobiography to support it. The New World in general and the West Indies in particular became a destination for "vexed and troubled" Anglos and Lockhart, like Rochester, became landed in a literal sense on Dominica. The thread that links the two is a perception of the islands as a place to recoup lost fortunes, generate new wealth, and realize upward mobility. Mason and Luttrell's newly arrived kin were part of a second wave of "arrivistes" (the West Indian prototype of post-Civil War carpet baggers) that while seeking new found wealth were equally concerned with the rank and status of grandees. These distinctions are vocalized by Rhys when Christophine tells Antoinette that the new people at Nelson's Rest (the plantation adjacent to Coulibri) were not like Luttrell: "Old Mr. Luttrell spit in their face when he see how they look at you."[40]

Whereas Mason infused badly needed capital, Rochester sought to acquire wealth in the New World and invest it in the Old. Rochester was the younger son and was subject to an inheritance practice known as primogeniture whereby his father's estate was passed en toto to his older brother.[41] The origin of this practice dates to the Middle Ages and was part of what ethnologists call a "closed corporate system," an endogamous network of kin and kith designed to preserve wealth, per stirpes, within a specific lineage or patri-clan.[42] Younger sons like Rochester were in affect landless (not disowned like Wedderburn) and were frequently compensated in the form of yearly stipends or per annum incomes from rents, investments, and other family owned enterprises. Primogeniture was the rule not the exception and this caste-like practice was as idiosyncratic to England, class formation, and what became known as the peerage as was recognition of moieties to race, class, hybridity, and the formation of creole society in Jamaica. Whether the Rochester clan qualified as "lords of the earth and stars of the firmament" is open to debate (Daniel described Cosway, his alleged father, as "haughty and proud, he walk like he own the earth"). That Edward was forced to marry-out weighed heavily on his psyche epitomized by his obsession with caste, purity, and creoles tainted and marked with African characteristics. Like metropolitan affiliations, the tensions and struggles of the era were transported along with these migrants and acquiring property was mandatory if Rochester was to achieve his due as a grandee. He could navigate aristocratic social circles but land was a badge and was seminal to the peerage. A local plantation would provide additional income but was not the equivalent of an English manor and marriage was an all-important first step in his climb up the social ladder to realize his ambition.[43]

We learned from Rochester's correspondence that his marriage was arranged by his father (and Mason's son Richard) to end his "shabby maneuvers" (for money) by acquiring a "modest competence" of thirty-thousand pounds from Antoinette. He lamented that he has "sold my soul" and notes as an after-thought that Antoinette "must be seen to" but her fate is of little consequence to his ambition and it is difficult to ascertain if his lamentations are concerned with his modest competence, his father's blessings, or with the fact that this marriage linked him with a woman who was not of "pure English descent," and his progeny, if he anticipated having any, would be marked and tainted as half-castes. (Antoinette's fate was in a way sealed when in a sometimes hostile, sometimes empathetic conversation with Rochester, Christophine asks him to give her some money, leave Antoinette under her care, and return to England alone.)

Rhys conveys these tensions and ambiguities not to elicit sympathy for Rochester but to expose the disdain grandees expressed toward those they consider inferior, their god-given sense of entitlement, and the self-serving nature of genteel etiquette. Love does not conquer all and the erotic is jettisoned by Rhys and replaced by the phobic as Rochester describes his honeymoon suite, the fragrance of flowers, the texture of fabric, and tropical wood of furniture. Rochester's phobia is in many ways the obverse of Antoinette's revulsion and Rhys has accomplished here what few before or since have. We can as scholars discuss the signs and badges of race and class but the essence is elusive and the author has taken us inside a mind-set to expose those deep seated multi-layered interior dimensions. I mentioned structures of feeling earlier and here Rhys, a marginalized and alienated observer exiled in the metropole, foregrounds the olfactory, how genteel sensibilities of aroma, fragrance, and the odorous transformed the erotic into the phobic. While Rochester relents and lives ever so briefly in the moment he succumbs to the dictates of class and retrenches and withdraws behind the emotional and ideological veil of grandee behavior.[44]

The dust has barely settled so to speak when Rochester is confronted with an anomaly unique to the West Indies. His honeymoon, if we can call it that, is interrupted when he encounters Daniel, another of Cosway's progeny. Daniel does not confront Rochester head on as did Christophine but chooses instead correspondence as a strategy or means of communication. This is not of minor importance. Literary theorists have devoted considerable attention to the intertextual dimensions of the novel, but have, for the most part, glossed the importance of literacy and literacy practices as instruments or weapons. It is by no means fortuitous that Rhys recognized them as weapons in the hands of subalterns. Planters in Jamaica learned early-on the maximum that "knowledge is power" and basic skills were denied the enslaved because they fomented resistance and were deployed like machetes, muskets, and poison in slave rebellions.[45] Daniel tells Rochester that he learned how to "read, write, and cipher in Jamaica" and the "good man" on Barbados "teach me more, he give me books, him tell me read the bible every day." The Church of England was the official or Assembly-sanctioned church in Jamaica but Anglican clergy did not extend their ministry to Africans despite the fact that local rectories owned substantial numbers of slaves. That charge fell initially to "catechists" associated with Anglican-sponsored groups like the Society for the Propagation of the Gospel. The Society established schools and lending libraries in Jamaica and elsewhere and catechists attempted to inculcate the "three Rs" but their activities were curtailed by the plantocracy and that task fell to non-conformists (Moravians, Wesleyans, Baptists) who associated literacy with abolition, amelioration, and goal of transforming a superstitious black mass steeped in obeah, vodo and the "black arts" into an educated, civilized, and Christian working class.[46]

If we take leitmotif to mean a recurrent theme then Daniel's correspondence represents an ur-type. Along with negating the stereotype of the illiterate African, it foregrounds literacy as a site of struggle and transformation and Daniel's command over grammar and syntax is superposed to obeah and vodo, the instruments wielded by Christophine on behalf of Antoinette. These were by no means weapons of the weak and their deployment was as logistical and tactical as were the use of muskets, machetes, and poison. Whereas Christophine mixed up libations (bull's blood, wine laced with rum and other herbs) in an attempt to transform cool vacillation into hot passion, Daniel co-opted genteel etiquette, inscribed his weapon in copperplate "BY HAND, URGENT," and had it delivered by a string of agents and accomplices. The formality of correspondence as a way and means stands in juxtaposition to the informality of its delivery. It was drafted by someone unbeknownst to Rochester (but well known to all in the household), a "hermit neighbor" he thinks, and was strategically deposited (by Baptiste) in his coat pocket to be discovered seemingly by chance later in the day. It is safe to assume that the message inscribed in copperplate arrived at Grandbois long before ink and paper and was passed along foot paths by word-of-mouth from one person to another. Those steeped in arts and letters assume that the scriptural is primary and the spoken a tertiary or secondary means of communication. Just the opposite is the case in the Anglophone West Indies where the spoken is considered primary and the scripted secondary.[47] Scholars have referred to this as "mixed-literacies," contexts where alternate and oppositional literacies co-exist and interact in a myriad of ways and we can feel the tension in Daniel's orthography between the written and the spoken much like readers experience the tonality of meter and rhyme in poetry. He tells Rochester that "I take up pen after long thought and meditation," "sat by his [my] window," "words fly past like birds," "and with God's help, I catch some."[48]

How Daniel acquired a domicile on Dominica is open to speculation and he in all probability migrated when the French under Napoleon relinquished possession and sold the island to the British in 1805. It was not uncommon for free people of color to exercise their new found rights and privileges by traveling from island to island in various occupations, and while Rhys makes no mention of Daniel's livelihood, the internal or domestic market was one of few sectors in this slave-based economy open to people of color. The American Revolution disrupted the infamous triangular trade and eliminated the provinces as a source (food products, barrels, etc.) and smaller islands like Dominica became purveyors in what became a brisk inter-island commodity trade.[49] Daniel's house-plot was located down the mountain from Grandbois and his domicile, a multi-room wooden dwelling with a parlor, furniture, and pictures of his family hanging on the wall, was step above the single-room wattle and daub shacks of most islanders, and an indication of material status and rank in society.

This subtext is tangential but critical to the telling of Daniel's story. I mentioned earlier the maxim "the truth is in the telling" (cf. footnote # 7) and by locating Daniel's house near "massacre" (where one brother, Philip, killed his half-brother, Thomas, the Carib son of Sir Thomas Warner, governor of St. Kitts) Rhys recaps key events and reinscribes Daniel's story (however fictional) as meta-narrative, one among many accounts that articulate the spoken or unofficial history of the islands and their peoples. He tells Rochester that he has been deceived by Mason and that he and Antoinette are related. He is the son of Cosway by "another lady" and their father was a "shameless man who died from "madness," as did his father before him. The Cosway's were "wicked and detestable slave-owners since generations" (a local turn of phrase) and "everyone hate them in Jamaica." Daniel is the eldest of all the half-house siblings (legitimate and illegitimate) and he remembers when Cosway's first wife passed away and how "fast" (inappropriate period of mourning) he married again. His biological mother, who was a slave manumitted by Cosway and given a plot of land near Spanish Town, passed away soon after Daniel was born, and he was raised by his god-mother (possibly Sass's, i.e., Disastrous, mother, another of Cosway's "wenches"). While he received the customary "gifts" at Christmas time he adds that the "old devil don't like me" and "I am the most unfortunate and poverty stricken" of the half-house paterfamilias. He says that he once walked five or six hours to visit his father at Coulibri and that Cosway scoffed at the notion of paternity, referred to his mother as a "sly-boot," and parried Daniel's claim with "I can't remember all their names, it's too much to expect of me and I'll eat my hat if there is one drop of my blood in your spindly carcass. Eat it then, Eat. It's you yourself call me Daniel, I am no slave like my mother was."[50]

Anthropologists have spoken about the literary in ethnography and we can invert the orientation here and speak about the ethnographic in the literary. Sly-boot referred to a custom known as a "jacket" whereby a woman (enslaved or free) passed her child off as the progeny (wearing the clothes) of a desired or preferred father in the hope of securing a better future (i.e., Mark Twain's Roxy). Whether or not Daniel and Cosway were father and son begs the question: Cosway manumitted his mother, Daniel was born into freedom, and he received the customary gifts, the signs and badges of paternity, at Christmas time. Alexander, his younger half-brother, was Cosway's favored son and "he prosper right from the start." It seems safe to conclude that unlike the aforementioned moieties these paterfamiliases were not in concert. We learned from a conversation with Amèlié that Alexander owned several rum shops and dry goods stores in Spanish Town and from Daniel that while he is "coloured like me" he "won't speak against white people." He married a "fair (light-skinned)-coloured girl," a respectable family, and his son Sandi was "like a white man, but more handsome than a white man." Lunacy, incest, and hybridity are linked themes and Rhys speaking now through Daniel recounts how Sandi and Antoinette were more just sibs and may have crossed a boundary and transgressed: "I see them when they think nobody see them. I see her when she ..." Antoinette was shameless like her father and her inability to recognize boundaries, taboos, and appropriate behavior was offered as an example of the "madness" endemic to the Cosway family substantiating Rochester's worst fears concerning purity, contagion, the torrid zone, and "clear skinned" Anglophiles who attempted to glossed their tainted ancestry.[51]

Daniel likens Mason's account of Cosway family history to a "nancy story," a fable or tall-tale intended less to entertain and more to dupe and deceive the naive and unknowing about local mores and values. Nancy is the diminutive of Annacy the Spider, the anthropomorphic trickster hero of West African (Akan) folklore who succeeds through cunning, guile, and a good deal of trickery to subvert and triumph over those in more powerful social, economic, and political positions. This is somewhat of a unique inversion and is consonant with Daniel's self-perceived status as a person of color ("I am no nigger like them"), his rejection of obeah, vodo, and "all that devil business" by Christophine (and those he considered inferior), and his irredentist-like claims to Antoinette's modest competence. Although obeah was outlawed early-on it was practiced on a daily basis and remains to this day a seminal part of creole society with both a public and private face. Daniel goes on to say that Christophine "have to leave Jamaica because she go to jail" only to arrive on Dominica where she like Daniel acquired a house-plot. She could not return to Martinique because she was purchased as a wedding gift, a "Negres á talents" or house servant by Cosway for his new wife, and while slavery was initially abolished (1791) it was reinstituted by Napoleon and remained in affect until 1848. (Dominica in this sense becomes a home away from home for both where for a time the possible could still be achieved not like Jamaica or Martinique.[52])

Whereas Mason conjured a "nancy story" and Christophine trafficked in the "black arts," Daniel reinvented himself a folk preacher, an itinerant of sorts who traveled the backcountry spreading the word. There were at the time a slew of itinerant folk preachers, some affiliated with the Afro-Christian congregations established earlier by Moses Baker and George Liele (Windward Rod, Crooked Spring), others with Baptist and Wesleyan chapels (Salter's Hill, Victoria, Stewarts Town et al.), and yet others with so called "native," "spiritual" or Afro-Jamaican congregations that combined various African beliefs (obeah, myal, vodo) with Christianity.[53]

I mentioned names and naming practices earlier and Daniel rejected his given name ("all I get curse from that damn devil my father") and introduced himself to Rochester as Esau. This was not an uncommon transference, especially among those who became members of various Afro-Christian denominations. Acolytes underwent a rebaptism (usually by a spirit), jettisoned their given names and personas, and adopted the personality of biblical, mainly Old Testament, figures such as Isaac and others. That Daniel chose Esau (rather than Cuffee or an African moniker) is significant because his biblical namesake was the first-born son of Isaac (and Rebecca) who lost his birthright to Jacob, his younger brother.

Daniel's resurrection as Esau "shadowed" or fulfilled prophecy and his transference on a personal level is consonant with a way of reading scripture known as "biblical figuralism." Biblical figuralism is a type/anti-type mode of interpretation in which Old, and to a lesser extent New, Testament figures and prophecies were complemented and fulfilled in the present in this case by people of African descent exiled in the New World.[54] Each passage in the Authorized or King James Version (excluding the Apocrypha) was reduced to a numbered heading, each heading was accompanied by an annotation that discussed its importance, and members were given a monthly reading calendar in which they read both the Old and New Testaments over the course of a year (hence the local adage, "a chapter a day keeps the devil away").

Subalterns not only speak but are agents and Daniel epitomizes what Radway and Certeau call "resistant readers" in that he selected or "poached" passages from the text and translated the meanings and messages inscribed on the page into his own personal and historical experience.[55] Like Esau, he was cursed by that "damn devil my father" and we assume by this that he was denied his birthright because unlike Alexander and Sandi his son and namesake who were marked with "clear" skin Daniel was tainted, "that yellow bastard" Christophine says to Rochester. Similar to the stigma associated with expatriates, Rhys anticipated rhythms and events that unfolded as she crafted this story. Daniel's transference not only resonates with those known in the nineteenth-century as "native-Baptists" but with their twentieth-century counterparts as well, the loose aggregation of house and mansions that recognized the divinity of Haile Selassie.[56]

Cosway's demise severed the link but not the obligation, and along with Rochester's right to Antoinette's inheritance (supported by common law) Daniel's claim contests the subordination of creole custom to Anglo jurisprudence. This points to the thorny relation between metropole and dependency, core and periphery, mother country and colony. The umbrella of English common law extended in principal to British colonies, but this was not the case in practice, and the ambiguity between the creole custom and Anglo jurisprudence became a source of endless conflict and debate. If, for example, slavery was deemed illegal in the mother country by the Somerset case how then could it persist in the colonies? If primogeniture was the norm and Daniel the eldest, how then and by what means was he denied his birthright? After all, he received the requisite signs and badges of paternity and Rochester's modest competence was accordingly his. I mentioned bastards earlier and the clash, struggle, and confrontation here is one of custom, tradition, and reconciling oppositional modes of kinship, Anglo, Creole and African. Daniel argues "I have my rights" and his argument is given credence by passage in 1813 of an act that allowed half-house progeny to inherit their benefactor's estates, if so willed. Rochester approached Antoinette about Daniel's claim and she asserted that they were not in fact siblings. His surname was Boyd and she explained that Daniel hated her and all white people and told lies about us (the Cosway clan). Rochester learned from Christophine that "it all lies. The more he do (Cosway), the more they hate him. The hate in that man Daniel, he can't rest with it."[57] The issue of conflicting modes and inheritances is compounded by the fact it was Mason not Cosway who left half of his estate to Antoinette (and the other half to his son Richard) and it was Mason not Annette who enabled Christophine to acquire a house-plot on Dominica. Daniel's claim is rebuffed and his ministrations, we learn as denouement in the introduction to Part Three, come to naught. Although Rochester travels back to Jamaica to settle his accounts with Mason, he learns upon arrival in England that both his father and brother have passed away (leaving their estate to him) while he and Antoinette were enroute and his ambition is realized in an ironic turn of events by providence.[58]

The past has often been characterized as a foreign country and Rhys has brought a critical juncture alive through these characters, muses, and vignettes much like what Dickens, Austen, and others have done in the metropole. Fiction yes, in that there was no Cosway, no Coulibri, and no Antoinette, however the imaginative, especially Parts One and Two, has more to do with what Hanks ("Text And Textuality"), Bauman and Briggs ("Poetics & Performance"), and other performance-centered approaches call "contextualization." The text in ethnographic, as opposed to other types of close reading, is the beginning not the end of analysis and performance-centered readings approach novels, fiction, and other "truth in the telling" accounts much like the score in musical transcription in that signs and annotation inscribed on the page offer some insight into the accompanying performance. *Wide Sargasso Sea* was the last and most success-ful of several novels and Rhys leveraged her position as a marginal and alienat-ed creole exiled in the metropole into that of an astute and perceptive partici-pant-observer. Her choice and rendering of lived experiences, muses and reflec-tions, encounters and altercations, episodes and events, was neither arbitrary nor formulaic and buried or submerged within them is an artful and meticulously crafted meta-narrative of West Indian history, culture, and performance.

Rhys has provided us with an insider's perspective on a turbulent era. On the one hand, she has opened a window on an embryonic creole nationalism, a class or proto-class in the process of emergence, black but no longer African, released from the shackles of slavery but not yet free, experiencing the growing pains and struggles that would burst on the scene in the post-war fifties, sixties, and seven-ties following breakup of the Empire. On the other hand, moving beyond the color line permeates the story and its characters, be they Anglo, Creole or Afri-can. If we build and expand upon Brathwaite's analogy of Rhys and *Wide Sar-gasso Sea* with Helen of the *Iliad* ("Helen of Our Wars") then I think it is fair to say that Helen's "shadow" has fulfilled prophecy and Rhys has spoken for all people of color and we would do well if we stepped outside our subject positions and adopted the posture of a creole.

Notes

1. Unless stated otherwise, all references, paraphrases, and quotes refer to the Norton Critical Edition, *Wide Sargasso Sea/Jean Rhys; Background & Criticism*, ed. Judith L. Raskin (New York: W.W. Norton & Company, 1999). The above cited vignette is located in Part Two, 57-59, 76, where Daniel asks Rochester for £500 to cease and desist spread-ing gossip about Antoinette and her family.

2. For "creolizing" see Philip Wright (ed.), *Lady Nugent's Journal of Her Residence in Jamaica from 1801 to 1805* (Kingston: IOJ, 1966 [1839]), "Introduction," xii-xxxii, and 117; for patriarchy, promiscuity, and licentiousness, see Barbara Bush, *Slave Women in Caribbean Society* (London: James Curry, 1990), 11-23; Verne Shepherd, Bridget Brereton, and Barbara Bailey (eds.), *Engendering History: Caribbean Women in Histori-cal Perspective* (Kingston: Ian Randle, 1995), Introduction, xi-xiii; Jennifer L. Morgan, "Some Could Suckle over Their Shoulder": Male Travelers, Female Bodies, and the Gen-

dering of Racial Ideology, 1500-1770," *William & Mary* 54 (1997): 168-90; Patricia Mohammed, "But most of All mi Love Me Browning': The Emergence in Eighteenth and Nineteenth Century Jamaica of the Mulatto Woman as Desired," *Feminist Review* 65 (2000): 22-48.

3. I understand leitmotif to mean a series of interrelated and recurrent themes. See Raskin, *Jean Rhys*, 2; Veronica Marie Gregg, *Jean Rhys' Historical Imagination* (Chapel Hill: University of North Carolina Press, 1995), Ch. 1, 5-10; Francis Wyndham, "Introduction," in *Wide Sargasso Sea/Jean Rhys*, 3-8; and Susan Thomas, *The Worlding of Jean Rhys* (Westport, CT.: Greenwood, 1999), "Introduction," 1-3 and especially page 4 for motifs, tropological patterns, narrative strategies, and thematics.

4. See Raskin, "Preface," *Jean Rhys*, ix-xiii, and Thomas, *Worlding*, Ch. 8. By anticipate I mean laid the groundwork for and established a pattern of scholarship for those that followed. These various readings and approaches, Freudian, Lacanian, Marxist, feminist, and post-colonial are complementary and not exclusionary or hierarchical.

5. Jean Rhys, *Smile Please: An Unfinished Autobiography*, foreword by Diana Hill (New York: Harper & Row, 1975), 3-5, 25-9, 149-50, and Raskin, "From *Smile Please*" in *Jean Rhys*, 149-52 for autobiography. The author was born Ella Gwendolen Rees Williams on Dominica and Jean Rhys was one of several pen names or pseudonyms.

6. St. Catherine was one of fourteen parishes in Jamaica at the time or setting of this novel. It was one of the seven original precincts established after the British seized the island in 1655. Spanish Town or St. Jago de la Vega was the original Spanish capital.

7. The maxim "the truth is in the telling not in the telling of the truth" is appropriate here and my understanding of fiction as socially constituted and discursive is based on Raymond Williams, "Literature," in *Marxism and Literature* (New York: Oxford University Press, 1977), 45-55. By discursive I am following Richard Bauman and Joel Sherzer (eds.), *Explorations in the Ethnography of Speaking* (New York: Cambridge University Press, 1989 [1974]), 3-6, 417-19, 433-53; Richard Bauman and Charles L. Briggs, "Poetics and Performance as Critical Perspectives on Language and Social Life," *Annual Review of Anthropology* 19 (1990): 59-88; and Dell Hymes, *Foundations in Sociolinguistics* (Philadelphia: University of Pennsylvania Press, 1974), 83-118. See also Thomas, *Worlding*, Chapter One, "Jean Rhys and Dominican Autoethnography," 9-10 for autoethnography. Although currently in vogue, autoethnography predated postmodernism. Suffice it to say that ethnography is not a nihilist or solipsistic encounter between an abstract other and equally abstract self, but a form of knowledge that differs from the speculation of philosophers and the archival excavations of historians. See William Roseberry and Nicole Polier, "Tristes Tropes: Postmodern Anthropologist Encounter the Other and Discover Themselves," *Economy and Society* 18 (1982), and R. Beals, "Reflections on Ethnography in Morocco," *Critique of Anthropology* 15 (1995) for critiques of postmodernism and autoethnography.

8. Subalterns not only speak, but are agents and accomplices in an ongoing struggle. See Thomas, *Worlding*, 12 and Gregg, *Historical Imagination*, 104, for a similar understanding and a critique of Spivak. See Carine M. Mardorossian, "Shutting up the Subaltern: Silences, Stereotypes, and Double-Entendre in Jean Rhys's *Wide Sargasso Sea*," *Callaloo*, 22, no. 4 (1999): 1071-90, and Coral Ann Howells, Review of *Jeans Rhys' Historical Imagination* in *Yes*, 27 (1996): 294-95 for the centrality of creole or subaltern voices in the novel. My understanding of alternate and oppositional, and dominant, residual, and emergent as working or analytical constructs is based on Williams, *Marxism*, Part II, "Culture Theory," Sections 6 "Hegemony," 7, "Traditions, Institutions, Formations, and 8, "Dominant, Residual, Emergent," 108-36.

9. For composition of the invasion force see S. A. G. Taylor, *The Western Design: An Account of Cromwell's Expedition to the Caribbean* (Kingston: Institute of Jamaica, 1965), Ch. 1. For a reappraisal of the standard narrative of conquest, see James Robertson, "Stories and Histories in Late-Seventeenth-Century Jamaica, in Kathleen Monteith and Glen Richards (eds.), *Jamaica in Slavery and Freedom: History, Heritage, and Culture* (Kingston: University of the West Indies Press, 2002), 25-51.

10. For legal and constitutional history see George Metcalf, *Royal Government & Political Conflict in Jamaica: 1729-1783* (London: Royal Commonwealth Society, 1965); Frederick G. Spurdle, *Early West Indian Government* (New Zealand; N. P., 1962); and Frank Wesley Pitman, *The Development of the British West Indies* (New Haven: Archon Books, 1967 [1917]). See also Clinton Black, *The Story of Jamaica* (London: Collins, 1968); Lowell Ragatz, *The Fall of the Planter Class in the British Caribbean* (New York: Octagon, 1928); Richard Dunn, *Sugar and Slaves: The Rise of the Planter Class in the English West Indies* (New York: Norton, 1972); Richard Sheridan, *Sugar and Slavery: An Economic History* (Baltimore: Johns Hopkins University Press, 1974); and David Watts, *The West Indies: Patterns of Development, Culture, and Environmental Change since 1492* (New York: Cambridge University Press, 1990) for sugar production, the plantocracy, and overviews of the British West Indies. For overviews of Jamaican bibliography see the dated but still useful Frank Cundall, *Bibliographica Jamaicensis* (London: Institute of Jamaica, 1902) and *Historic Jamaica* (London: Institute of Jamaica, 1915).

11. See Philip Curtin, *Two Jamaicas* (New York: Atheneum, 1975), Ch. 2; Edward Brathwaite, *The Development of Creole Society in the Jamaica, 1770-1820* (London: Oxford, 1972); and Susan Dwyer Amussen, *Caribbean Exchanges: Slavery and the Transformation of English Society* (Chapel Hill: North Carolina, 2007), for 33-9 for overviews and discussions.

12. See *Journal of the House of Assembly of Jamaica* (hereafter *JAJ*), Vol. V (1761), 311 for the "slave codes," legislation passed as a result of a slave rebellion (1760) that outlined rights and privileges, and penalties for the enslaved majority and a group known as free people of color. Afro-Jamaicans were placed in a color/caste continuum (i.e., mulatto, mustee, sambo) in various degrees of racial characteristics: white or European to African, black, and enslaved. Free people of color were required to register with local vestries on a yearly basis and to petition the House of Assembly for "rights and privileges."

13. Creolizing was the operative term. See Wright, *Lady Nugent*, "Introduction," xii-xxxii, 117. For patriarchy, promiscuity, and licentiousness see Bush, *Slave Women*, 11-23, Shepherd, Brereton, and Bailey, *Engendering History*, Introduction, xi-xiii; Morgan, "Some Could Suckle," 168-90; Mohammed, "But most of All," 22-48, and Joan Dayan, "Codes of Law and Bodies of Color, *New Literary History* 26 (1995): 283-308, for race, gender, and eroticism.

14. George Beckford and Michael Witter, *Small Garden and Bitter Weed* (Morant Bay: Maroon Publishing House, 1982); Orlando Patterson, *Sociology of Slavery* (Kingston: Sangster, 1973 [1967]); and Kathleen E. A. Monteith and Glen Richards, *Jamaica in Slavery and Freedom* (Kingston: University of the West Indies Press, 2002) for class and social structure.

15. For the relationship between law, repression, and spectacle see Diana Paton, "Punishment, Crime, and the Bodies of Slaves in Eighteenth Century Jamaica," *Social History*, 34 (2001), and *No Bond But the Law: Punishment, Race, and Gender in Jamaican State Formation, 1780-1870* (Durham: Duke University Press, 2004), 31-52. For the use of ritual, spectacle, and the dismemberment of the dead as a means of control see

Vincent Brown, "Spiritual Terror and Scared Authority: The Power of the Supernatural in Jamaican Slave Society," in Edward Baptist (ed.), *New Studies in the History of American Slavery* (Athens: Georgia, 2006), 179-210, and the early but still relevant Agnes Whitson, *The Constitutional Development of Jamaica* (Manchester: Manchester University Press, 1929), Ch. 1; Elsa Goveia, *The West Indian slave Laws of the 18th Century* (New Haven: Yale University Press, 1970); Braithwaite, *Creole Society*, Appendix VII, 338-42 for an overview.

16. For Robert Wedderburn see the collection of his letters, pamphlets, and speeches published by Ian McCalman, *The Horrors of Slavery and Other Writings by Robert Wedderburn* (New York 7 Princeton: Markus Weiner, 1991), 1-42.

17. These excerpts are from pages 9-11.

18. See Trevor Burnard, *Mastery, Tyranny, and Desire: Thomas Thistlewood and his Slaves in the Anglo-Jamaican World* (Chapel Hill: North Carolina, 2004), 19-22; Saidiya V. Hartman, *Scenes of Subjection: Terror, Slavery, and Self-Making in Nineteenth-Century America* (New York: Oxford University Press, 1997), Part I, "Formations of Terror and Enjoyment," 17-79, especially 26-29; and Robert Dirks, *The Black Saturnalia: Conflict and Its Ritual Expression on British West Indian Slave Plantations* (Gainesville: University of Florida Press, 1987), Ch. 1.

19. Excerpted from pages 16-17. See William Green, *British Slave Emancipation: The Sugar Colonies and the Great Experiment 1830-1865* (Oxford: Clarendon Press, 1976*)*, "Amelioration," 99-105, for gradualism and the abolition.

20. See Barry Higman, *Slave Population and Economy in Jamaica 1807-1834* (Cambridge: Cambridge University Press, 1976); "The Spatial Economy of Jamaican Sugar Plantations: Cartographic Evidence from the Eighteenth and Nineteenth Centuries," *Journal of Historical Geography* 18 (1987); "The Internal Economy of Jamaican Pens, 1760-1830," *Social and Economic Studies* 38 (1989); *Jamaica Surveyed: Plantations Maps and Plans of the 18th- & 19th-centuries* (Kingston: Institute of Jamaica Publications, 1988); Roderick McDonald, *The Economy and Material Culture of Slaves* (Baton Rouge: Louisiana State University Press, 1993), Chs 1 & 3 for old and new frontier, provision grounds, and satellite plantations. For plots, plans, and historical geography, see Higman, *Jamaica Surveyed*, 261-73, *Slave Population*, Ch. 1, and *Montpelier, Jamaica: A Plantation Community in Slavery and Freedom, 1739-1912* (Kingston: West Indies Press, 1998), Ch. 4 & 5, p. 118, 128; *Plantation Jamaica, 1750-1850: Capital and Control in a Colonial Economy* (Kingston: West Indies Press, 2005), Ch. 7, 194-97.

21. For historical imagination, see Gregg, *Jean Rhys*, Ch. 2, "The 1840s to the 1900s: the Creole and the Post slavery West Indies," 82-106; see also Thomas, *Worlding*, 9-10, and Rhys, *Smile Please*, 13-19. See also Williams, *Marxism*, 192-98, for a similar understanding of "authors," "enactive interpretation," and "text-works."

22. My understanding of intra-, extra-, entextualixation is based William Hanks, "Texts and Textuality," *Annual Review of Anthropology* V.18 (1988): 95-127 and refers to the ways the various ways oral (and written) texts are connected, linked, or related to a social and cultural world. My understanding of close reading as a form of analysis that links literary with social, cultural, and historical analysis is based on E. P. Thompson, *Witness Against the Beast* (New York: The New Press, 1993); Williams, *Marxism*; and Betsey Erikkila, "Ethnicity, Literary Theory, and the Grounds of Resistance," *American Quarterly* 47 (1995): 563-94. Thick description was the phrase first employed by the philosopher Gilbert Ryle and was later borrowed by Clifford Geertz, *The Interpretation of Cultures* (New York: Basic Books, 1973), chapter 1, and applied to the way ethnographers describe non-Western activities and practices. See also Williams, *Marxism*, 192-98, for a similar understanding of "authors," "enactive interpretation," and "text-works." I may be violating some conventions here but interpolation, transliteration, employment,

and narrative sequencing are strategies that are not confined to text-based practices. By narrative I mean, following Tedlock (1987) and Finnegan (1992), a testimony or text-like work (oral or written) that was circulated within a given speech community. See also Rhys, *Smile Please, 25.*

23. For critiques and overviews see Raskin, "Preface," ix-xii; Wyndham, "Introduction," 3; Caroline Rody, "Burning Down the House," 217; Edward Kamau Brathwaite, "A Post cautionary Tale of the Helene of our Wars," *Wasafiri* 22, 69-78. For revisions of the white creole who can not speak for others see Mardorossian, "Shutting Up," 1071 and especially note 3, 1088. I disagree with some who suggest that Rhys was complicit, unaware, or by virtue of her color and class position as a white Creole, could not grasp the plight of either poor black or white West Indians. There are instances in which these characters and personas are both complicit yet oppositional to what many call a dominant colonialist-imperialist discourse. Rhys was not, despite her genealogy (and skin color), a member of the plantocracy and her marginality and alienation provided her with a critical vantage point or subject position. I first read *Wide Sargasso* as an undergraduate and later as a graduate student preparing for field work in Jamaica.

24. See Gregg, *Jean Rhys*, 25-26, for a survey of literature of the era and its relationship to what she calls the dominant colonist-imperialist discourse. See also Thomas Holt, *The Problem of Freedom: Race, Labor, and Politics in Jamaica* (Baltimore: Johns Hopkins University Press, 1992); Paul B. Rich, *Race and Empire in British Politics* (Cambridge: Cambridge University Press, 1990); Obika Gray, *Radicalism and Social Change in Jamaica 1960-1972* (Knoxville, TN: University of Tennessee Press, 1991); and Lawrence James, *The Rise and Fall of the British Empire* (New York: St. Martins Press, 1994), for the social, political, and ideological struggles of the era and the formation of alternate and oppositional discourses. I cannot speak with certainty, but it is unlikely that Rhys would not have been privy to Malinowski, functionalism, ethnography, and the emerging field of social anthropology given its anti-colonial leanings. See Talal Asad, "The Concept of Cultural Translation in British Social Anthropology," in James Clifford and George Marcus Clifford (eds.), *Writing Culture: The Poetics and Politics of Ethnography* (Santa Fe, NM: School for Amercian Research, 1986). See also E. Valentine and Jeffrey Peck, *Culture and Contexture: Explorations in Anthropology and Literary Studies* (Berkeley: University of California Press, 1996), for a discussion of the politics of cultural translation. Rhys in this sense adopted a position that very closely approximates that of a traditional participant observer. See Barbara Tedlock, "From Participant Observation to the Observation of Participation," *Journal of Anthropological Research* 47 (1991) and D. Tedlock, "Questions Concerning Dialogical Anthropology," *Journal of Anthropological Research* 43 (1989) for both an historic overview and a survey of issues, trends, and debate in dialogical anthropology. As Tedlock has commented in "Questions," 326-27 critical approaches to ethnography have a long genealogy. See Stanley Diamond, "The Politics of Field Work," in *In Search of the Primitive* (New Jersey: Transaction Books, 1974) and Bob Scholte, "Toward a Reflexive and Critical Anthropology," in Dell Hymes (ed.), *Reinventing Anthropology* (New York: Random House, 1969) for early and still relevant calls for a critical ethnography. See also Frederic Jameson, "Regarding Postmodernism," *Social Text* 17 (1987) and John Beverley, *Against Literature* (Minneapolis: University of Minnesota Press, 1993) for a similar understanding of the relation between fiction and nonfiction.

25. For structures of feeling see Williams, *Marxism*, 128-35. These characters and personas are in this sense in the process of [re] formation, expressing their own points of view during a critical or transitory juncture in the West Indian history.

26. For definitions of obeah, also spelled obi, obiah, see Cassidy, *Jamaica Talk*, 241-4, and Cassidy and LePage, *Dictionary*, 89, Richard Allsopp, *Dictionary of Caribbean English Usage* (Kingston: University of the West Press, 2003), 413, and see also Jerome Handler and Kenneth M. Bilby, "On the Early Use and Origin of the Term 'Obeah' in Barbados and the Anglophone Caribbean," *Slavery & Abolition* 22 (2002): 87-100. The word obeah has a complex provenance that is related to its origin and political history. Edward Long, drawing upon comparative mythology (cf. Bryant's, *Mythology*, V. I, 48 and 475) attributed the origins of the term to the Egyptian "ob" or "aub" meaning serpent worship (1774, V. II, 421) and this meaning and understanding of African semantics and word-formation as cultural diffusion rather than invention was paraphrased by one planter-historian after another (e.g., Bryan Edwards, Hasketh Bell) and was supplemented by contemporary ethnography by Joseph J. Williams in the 20th-century (cf. *Voodoos and Obeahs in Jamaica* (New York: Dial Press, 1932); *Psychic Phenomena of Jamaica* (New York: Dial Press, 1934). Whereas Williams draws upon the ethnography of A. B. Ellis and R. B. Rattray to cite the African or Ashanti term "obayifo," meaning witch or wizard, as a cognate-origin, he nonetheless agrees with the diffusionists and concludes (cf. *Voodoos and Obeahs,* 110, Note #3) that the term ob constitutes not an African or a New World creation but a "Hebrewism" that originated with the ancient Canaanites. Rather than a "Hebrewism" (and what Long paraphrased as the Egyptian ob), there is evidence to suggest an alternate etymology, not from the Ashanti as such, but from the Akan-speaking people such as Fetu, Fanti, and the polities along the Gold Coast. Handler and Bilby are correct in asserting that the emphasis witch and witchcraft is unguarded and has been accepted un-reflexively and distracted alternate etymologies and possibilities. Since the Ashanti were not in direct contact with Europeans during the early phases of European encounter it is, I submit, from the coastal Fetu, Fanti and related dialects forms from which the term originates. See Monica Schuler, "Myalism and the African Religious Tradition in Jamaica," in Margaret Crahan & Franklin Knight (eds.), *Africa and the Caribbean: the Legacies of a Link* (Baltimore: Johns Hopkins University Press, 1979); *Alas, Alas, Kongo: A Social History of Indentured African Immigration into Jamaica* (Baltimore: Johns Hopkins University Press, 1980); Alleyne, *Roots of Jamaican Culture,* Ch. 2, and Joan Dayan, *Haiti, History, and the Gods* (Berkeley: University of California, Press, 1995), for history as ritual as applied to Haiti and Jamaica, and Maureen Warner-Lewis, *Central Africa in the Caribbean* (Kingston: University of the West Indies Press, 2003) for Kongo cultural influence. For general histories see A. B. Ellis, *The Tishi-Speaking Peoples of the Gold-Coast* (Netherlands: Oosterhout, 1966 [1887]); J. D. Fage, *A History of West Africa* (London: Cambridge University Press, 1969); Eva L. R. Meyerowitz, *The Early History of the Akan States of Ghana* (London: Red Candle Press, 1974); J. D. Fynn, *The Fante of Ghana, 1600-1874* (Legon: University of Ghana, 1989) and *Asante and its Neighbors, 1700-1807* (Evanston: Northwestern University Press, 1971); and for Akan, Fanti, and Tishi-related dialects see J. G. Christaller, W. Locher, and J. Zimmerman, *A Dictionary of English, Tishi, Ahra; Comprising as dialects Akan (Asante, Akem, Akuapem, etc.) and Fante; Akra (Accra) connected with Adangme; Gold Coast, W. Africa* (Basel: Basel Missionary Society, 1874). See also Paul Gilroy, *The Black Atlantic* (Cambridge, MA.: Harvard University Press, 1993); John K. Thornton, *African and Africans in the Making of the Atlantic World* (New York: Cambridge, 1992); Linda Heywood and John Thornton Central Africans, Atlantic Creoles, and the Foundations of the Americas (NY: Cambridge, 2007); Linda Heywood and P. E. H. Hair, "Outthrust and Encounter: An Interpretative Essay," in Cecil H. Clough & P. E. H. Hair, *The European Outthrust and Encounter: The First Phase 1400-1700* (Liverpool: University of Liverpool Press, 1994), 43-75. For definitions and overviews of the Atlantic World,

the European-African encounter, and modernity see Thornton, *African and Africans*, Ch. 1, *Central Africa*, 1-3; Linda Heywood, *Central Africa and Cultural Transformation in the American Diaspora* (New York: Cambridge University Press, 2001) xii; Hair, "Outthrust and Encounter," 43-75, A. Teixeira and P.E.H. Hair, *East of Mina: Afro-European Relations on the Gold coast in the 1550s and 1560s* (Madison, WI: University of Wisconsin, 1988), 3-33; Robin Law, *The Slave Coast of West Africa: 1550-1750: The Impact of the Atlantic Slave Trade on African Society* (Oxford, UK: Clarendon, 1991), 1-13; and John D. Fage, A History of West Africa (London: Cambridge, 1969), 50-89 for the area known as Upper Guinea, Lower Guinea, Angola, and the Kongo in the sixteenth and seventeenth centuries. See Thomas Astley, *A New General Collection of Voyages and Travels Consisting of the Most Esteemed Relations, which have been hitherto published in any Language in Four Volumes* (London: printed for Thomas Astley, 1745-1746), V. II, Books III & IV, 374-698, for an account produced during the eighteenth century.

27. As Brathwaite has noted in *History of the Voice* (Port of Spain, Trinidad: New Beacon Books, 1984), Ch.1, the West Indies produced two distinct but interrelated narrative traditions: one codified in the printed accounts of colonial historians, missionaries, and travelers and a second in a spoken or oral tradition of the enslaved. Obeah was codified in the latter but created by the former. For literary histories and novels see Alan Richardson, "Romantic Voodoo: Obeah and British Culture," in Margarita Fernandez Olmos, and Lizabeth Paravsini-Gebart (eds.), *Sacred Possession: Vodu, Santeria, Obeah, and the Caribbean* (New Brunswick, NJ: Rutgers University Press, 1997), 171-95; see also Jean D'Costa, "Oral Literature, Formal Literature: The Formation of a Genre in Eighteenth-Century Jamaica," *Eighteenth-Century Studies*, 27 (1994): 663-76; Thomas W. Kriese, *Caribbeana: An Anthology of English Literature of the West Indies, 1657-1777* (Chicago: University of Chicago Press, 1996); Keith A. Sandiford, *The Cultural Politics of Sugar: Caribbean Slavery and Narratives of Colonization* (New York: Cambridge University Press, 2000); Karin Williamson, *Voices of Slavery* (Kingston: West Indies Press, 2008); Elsa V. Goveia, *A Study of the Historiography of the British West Indies to the End of the Nineteenth-Century* (Washington, DC: Howard University Press, 1980); Gordon K. Lewis, *Main Currents in Caribbean Thought* (Baltimore: Johns Hopkins University Press, 1983); and Susan Legêne, "From Brooms to Obeah and Back: Fetish Conversion and Border Crossings in Nineteenth-Century Suriname," in Patricia Spyer (ed.), *Border Crossing: Material Objects in Unstable Places* (New York: Routledge, 1998), 35-59 for obeah and vodu.

28. See page 16.

29. Words, like all human inventions, are socially constructed. See Cassidy and LePage, *Dictionary*, 56, and Cassidy, *Jamaica Talk*, 23, for etymology; Richard Dunn, *Sugar and Slaves*, 45 for Barbados; Brathwaite, *Creole Society*, 32; and Long, *History of Jamaica*, 406 for Jamaica. See Thomas Astley, *A New General Collection of Voyages and Travels Consisting of the Most Esteemed Relations, which have been hitherto published in any Language in Four Volumes* (London: printed for Thomas Astley, 1745-1746), V. III, 376 for use of the term creole in reference to West Africa in the eighteenth century. The word is a contraction, a semantic narrowing of the Portuguese criar and colono, colonize and colonists, and referred initially to those creoles born in Africa and later in the Americas. It was infused with power and status and it was deployed early on in the West Indies to distinguish local processes of social, cultural, and political formation from those that had occurred elsewhere. Meanings, of course, are socially constructed and, similar to obeah and vodu creole underwent a number of linguistic or semantic processes. In eighteenth century Jamaica it was deployed to distinguish those who were born on the Island, or elsewhere in the Caribbean, from those who were born in the

Old World while at the same time it was deployed to differentiate an elite who resided in England, cultivated sugar, and owned several thousand acres of land from a class of small farmers who resided on the Island, engaged in the production of minor commodities, and who owned smaller parcels. See John Holm, *Pidgins and Creoles, V. I. Theory and Structure* (Cambridge: Cambridge University Press, 1988), Ch. 3, especially pp. 100-103, for semantic narrowing/broadening and their implications for word formation. See Mariam K. Slater, *The Caribbean Family: Legitimacy in Martinique* (New York: St. Martins Press, 1977), 57-59 for béké and other color-coded designations.

30. See Raskin, *Jean Rhys*, 14; Gregg, *Historical Imagination*, 135; Wyndham, "Introduction," 3-8; and Thomas, *Worlding*, 12 for a similar understanding of the centrality of kinship, genealogy, and family.

31. I am thinking here of *Oliver Twist* and, to a lesser extent, *Great Expectations* where Oliver and Pip become members of re-imagined or fictive families. The theme was of major importance to Dickens and is an undercurrent in most of his novels.

32. See Holt, *Problem*, Part Two, 115-68, Douglas Hall, *Free Jamaica 1838-1865* (New Haven: Yale University Press, 1959); and Green, *British Slave Emancipation*, Ch. 8 for the transition from slave to free labor and migration from estates to villages and towns. I am using classic terminology here and reference biological as family of procreation and affine as family of orientation.

33. See pages 29-30.

34. *Ibid.*

35. The term moiety, meaning half, was deployed by the Assembly in its investigation of kinship, genealogy, the awarding of "rights and privileges" to free people of color. See Long, *History*, Vol. 2, 261; Brathwaite, *Creole Society*, 168; and Paterson, *Sociology of Slavery* 159-66, for the color caste classification codified in the law.

36. See John W. Pulis, "Important Truths" and Pernicious Follies:" Texts, Covenants, and the Anabaptist Church of Jamaica," in Kevin Yelvington (ed.), *Afro-Atlantic Dialogues: Anthropology in the Diaspora* (Santa Fe, NM: School of Amercian Research, 1999), 193-210.

37. For the Hyde-Swigle petition see *JAJ* Vol. V, 588.

38. For the torrid zone and fear of hot climates see Karen Kupperman, "Fear of Hot Climates in the Anglo-American Colonial Experience," *William & Mary* 41 (1982): 213-40.

39. For Dominica, see Knight, *Caribbean*, 50-51; Watts, *West Indies*, 249-53; Dunn, *Sugar and Slaves*, 15-17; Eric William, *Capitalism and Slavery* (Chapel Hill, University of North Carolina Press, 1944); and Carl Bridenbaugh, *Vexed and Troubled Englishmen, 1590-1642* (New York: Oxford University Press, 1968).

40. See page 15; Bridenbaugh, 1968, and Williams, 1944.

41. For primogeniture see G. M. Trevelyan, *English Social History* (New York: David McKay, 1942), Ch. 1; *Chaucer's England*, 1-28; and David Cannadine, *The Decline and Fall of the British Aristocracy* (New York: Anchor Books, 1990), Prologue, 16-25.

42. For lineage, endogamy, and what ethnologists call closed corporate kinship see Carol Ember and Marvin Ember, *Anthropology* (New Jersey: Prentice Hall, 1990), 326-71. By per stirpes I am following Anglo jurisprudence to mean blood or descent tracked via patri-lineal reckoning.

43. Cannadine, *Decline*, 8-15.

44. Structures of feeling is an analytical concept that helps us understand, and its descriptive or ethnographic analog here is the olfactory and odorous, the sense of smell. Rhys moves from the abstract to the corporeal and grounded Rochester's revulsion in the

senses. See Jonathan Benthall and Ted Polhemus (eds.), *The Body as a Medium of Expression* (New York: E. P. Dutton, 1975).

45. My understanding of literacy and literacy practices is based on Brian Street, *Literacy in Theory and Practice* (London: Cambridge University Press, 1983) and James Collins and Richard Blot (eds.), "Introduction," in *Literacy and Literacies: Power, and Identity* (New York: Cambridge University Press, 2003), 1-4, 9-12, for activities in which the printed or scriptural is called into play. As Collins (1995) has commented (cf. "Literacy and Literacies," *Annual Review of Anthropology* 24, 1995: 75-93), studies of literacy have tended to equate readers as victims and the reader-text interface as a passive rather than an active process. For rebellions see Orlando Patterson, "Slavery and Slave Revolts: A Socio-historical analysis of the First Maroon War," *Social & Economic Studies*, 19 (1975): 289 335; *Sociology of Slavery* (Kingston: Sangster, 1973 [1967]); Richard Hart, *Black Jamaicans' Struggle Against Slavery* (Kingston: Institute of Jamaica, 1977); *Slaves Who Abolished Slavery: Vol. 1 Blacks in Bondage* (Kingston: Institute of Social & Economic Research, 1980), *Slaves Who Abolished Slavery: Vol. 2 Blacks in Rebellion* (Kingston: Institute of Social & Economic Research, 1985).

46. For an overview of Anglican activity see Sylvia Frey and Betty Wood, *Come Shouting to Zion* (Chapel Hill: University of North Carolina Press, 1998), Ch. 3, The Anglicans. See also, Gordon, *God Almighty*, 8-9; Brathwaite, *Creole Society*, 20-25; Stewart, *Religion and Society*, Ch. 1 for Anglicans. See *JAJ*, Vol. 12, 732. The Anglican rector of St. Elizabeth received an annual sum of £300 for the maintenance and upkeep of the rectory in Lacovia. When the parish seat was transferred to Black River in 1788, a petition was forwarded requesting additional "public monies" to construct the new church, rectory, and burial place. These facts and figures are in *Lambeth Palace Papers* [hereafter *LPP*], Vol. 18 (reel 17), Jamaica, 9th November 1752, 57; "A list of the Parishes of Jamaica with the yearly value of the Livings, 1752." In toto the various parishes were assessed at £ 6,390, per annum quite a sum for the Church. See also *LPP*, Vol. 10 (reel 9), 115, for a listing of the ministers by parish (17) and church dated 18 April 1715; see *LPP*, Vol. 17, 1724, 175; "A Catalogue of books sent 1st April 1724 to Mr. Barrett missionary to Jamaica..."; see also p. 179, "Instructions Sent with Mr. Barrett with Reference to the Negroe slaves and his library." For correspondence from Jamaica see *Records of the Society for the Propagation of the Gospel in Foreign Parts*, Letters, Series B, 1701-86, Vol. 17 (reel 17), Jamaica, p. 282, letter dated Spanish Town (the capital), December 2(?) 1707. See Morgan Godwyn, *A Supplement to the Negro's and Indian Advocate* (London: J. D., 1681), 9, 10; and *Trade preferred before Religion* (London: B. Took, 1685), 1-3 for Mammon. See John C. Van Horner, *Religious Philanthropy and Colonial Slavery* (Urbana: University of Illinois Press, 1985), Ch. 1 for an overview of Anglican mission-societies and the Associates of Dr. Bray.

47. By subordinate I mean following Michel Certeau, *The Practice of Everyday Life* (Berkeley: University of California Press, 1984); and Janice Radway, Reading the Romance (Chapel Hill, NC: University of North Carolina Press, 1994) a process whereby readers draw upon the same tactics or methods as in everyday life to "poach" or take what they want from texts. See also Shirley Heath, *Ways with Words* (New York: Cambridge University Press, 1983); Geneva Smitherman, *Talkin and Testifyin: The Language of Black Americas* (Detroit: Wayne State University, 1977) for a similar understanding and see Roger D. Abrahams, *The Man-of-Words in the West Indies* (Baltimore: Johns Hopkins University Press, 1983), 1-21, "Patterns of Performance in the West Indies." Daniel considered himself a man of words.

48. Excerpted from pages 54-59. See Collins and Blot, *Literacy and Literacies*, 10, and Ch. 6, "Colonial Legacies," 121-55 for a similar understanding of orality, literacy,

and the text as a score of the spoken; Richard Bauman and Charles L. Briggs, "Poetics and Performance as Critical Perspectives on Language and Social Life," *Annual Review of Anthropology* 19 (1990): 59-88, a set of interrelated social and linguistic activities; Williams, *Marxism*, 192-98 for a similar understanding of "authors," "enactive interpretations," and "text-works." All words possess a phonetic or sound-structure that is "felt" when articulated or expressed in reasoning and each word produced a distinct rhythm or vibration, that is, a meaning that was both felt and heard. Rhys here has attempted to capture, to codify those unique West Indian rhythms in print. See especially Abrahams, *Man-of-Words*, Chapter Five, "A Performance centered approach to Gossip," 77-86. See Wolfgang Iser, *The Act of Reading* (Baltimore: Johns Hopkins University Press, 1977); Jonathan Boyarin (ed.), *The Ethnography of Reading* (Berkley: University of California Press, 1992); Jack Goody, *The Interface Between the Written and the Spoken* (London: Cambridge University Press, 1987); and Walter Ong, *The Presence of the Word* (New Haven and London: Yale University Press, 1967) for mediations between the written and the spoken. Orthography aside, Daniel's letter represents, in my sense of the term, an "enactive interpretation. Along with conveying the importance of literacy and the tension between the two as means of communication, Rhys has attempted to capture and codify a soundscape, the lyricism and poetics of creole as a spoke language. In this respect she anticipated or prefigured what Brathwaite and others call "nommo." If we allocate fault here it has do with Rhys' orthography; mi was the operative pronoun not I as de/I for the plural, but she has captured the idiomatic in creole speech patterns.

49. See Holt, *Problem*, Ch. 10, "the banana trade..." and Appendix 1, "migration," 403; Barry W. Higman, *Plantation Jamaica, 1750-1850: Capital and Control in a Colonial Economy* (Kingston: West Indies Press, 2005), Chs. 1; *Montpelier, Jamaica: A Plantation Community in Slavery and freedom, 1739-1912* (Kingston: West Indies Press, 1998); and Sidney Mintz and Douglas Hall, *The Origins of the Jamaican Internal Marketing System* (New Haven: Yale University Publications in Anthropology Number 57, 1960). For the internal market see Richard Sheridan, "The Crisis of Slave Subsistence in the West Indies during and after the American Revolution," *William & Mary* 33 (1976): 618 and Selwynn H. H. Carrington, "The American Revolution and the British West Indies' Economy," *Journal of Interdisciplinary History* 17 (1987): 823-502 for the Amercian revolution and the commodity trade.

50. See page 74.

51. Excerpted from page 75. See Kupperman, "Fear of Hot Climates," 220 for lunacy, madness, and the tropics. See Richard Bauman, *"The Story in the Story: Meta narration in Folk Narrative,"* in Richard Bauman (ed.), *Verbal Art as Performance* (New York: Dover, 1988), 24-30 for meta narration, the folkloric practice of telling a story inside of or in relation to another tale. I may be violating some conventions here but interpolation, transliteration, emplotment, and narrative sequencing are strategies that are not confined to text-based practices and Rhys has positioned Daniel's story as meta-narrative or supplement to traditional accounts of West Indian history and the formation of creole culture.

52. See Walter Jekyll, *Jamaican Song and Story, Annacy stories, Digging Tunes, and Ring tunes* (New York: Dover, 1966[1904]), Part One, Annacy Stories," 17-152. For African origins see Roger Abrahams, *African Folktales* (New York: Pantheon, 1983), Part III, "Tales of Trickster," 153-212; and Roger Abrahams and John Szwed, *After Africa* (New Haven: Yale University Press, 1983), Ch. 3, Annacy Tales," 108-130. See Olaniyan, *Scars of Conquest,* 9 for the importance of diaspora, exile, and return as recurring themes; Mimi Sheller, *Consuming the Caribbean: From Arawaks to Zombies* (New York: Routledge, 2000); Susan Legêne, "From Brooms to Obeah and Back," 35-59 for

obeah, vodu, zombies and others; and Watts, *The West Indies*, 234 for Martinique and slavery.

See Lucille M. Mair, *A Historical Study of Women in Jamaica, 1655-1844* (Kingston: West Indies Press, 2006) and Rhoda Reddock (ed.), *Interrogating Caribbean Masculinities: Theoretical and Empirical Analyses* (Kingston: West Indies Press, 2004) for masculinity; and Richard D. E. Burton, *Afro-Creole: Power, Opposition, and Play in the Caribbean* (Ithaca, NY: Cornell University Press, 1997) for creole, creolization, Jamaica Talk, Jonkonnu (also John-Canoe, Junkunnu), obeah, myal, native-Baptist, and the formation of creole as opposed to other types of social formations in the New World.

53. See Pulis, "Important Truths" and Pernicious Follies," 210 for reading, literacy, and conversion. See also Gerald Davis, *I Got the Word in Me and Can Sing It, You Know It* (Philadelphia: University of Pennsylvania Press, 1985); Gerard Loughlin, *Telling God's Story: Bible, Church History, and Theology* (Cambridge: Cambridge University Press, 995); Albert Raboteau, *A Fire in the Bones* (Boston: Beacon Press, 1995); Smitherman, *Talkin and Testifying*, Ch 4, for the chanted sermon and old time preaching and Richard Bauman, "The Story in the Story: Meta narration in Folk Narrative," in *Verbal Art as Performance* (New York: Random House 1977), 61-80. While similar citing-up differs in that it mediates between and subordinates the text and printed word to the spoken. By mediate I mean following Williams, *Marxism*, 95-106, and Theophlius Smith, *Conjuring Culture* (New York: Oxford, 1992), 123-24, a process whereby readers draw upon the same tactics or methods as in everyday life to "poach" or take what they want from texts. For a similar understanding of orality, literacy, and reading see Iser, *The Act of Reading;* Boyarin, *The Ethnography of Reading;* Jack Goody, *The Interface Between the Written and the Spoken* (London: Cambridge University Press, 1987); and Walter Ong, *The Presence of the Word* (New Haven and London: Yale University Press, 1967) for mediations between the written and the spoken.

54. Biblical figuralism or typology is a form of interpretation, a type/anti-type method in which biblical or text-based types are linked to post-biblical persons, places, and events. It differs from other forms and methods, such as allegory, in that each type/anti-type dyad complements, rather than replaces, the other, so that one signifies, represents, and fulfills the other. For a more detailed discussion see Hans Frei, *The Eclipse of Biblical Narrative* (New London: Yale University Press, 1974); Northrop Frye *The Great Code* (New York: Harcourt & Brace, 1982); Henry Louis Gates, *The Signifying Monkey* (New York & London: Oxford University Press, 1988); and Smith, *Conjuring Culture*, for modes of figuration. See Loughlin, *God's Story*, above for an interesting discussion of how Rev 10: 9-10 (eating the text) became associated with the Eucharist and Christian understandings of transubstantiation. By identify or transference I mean in this case how Daniel how saw through the eyes of biblical actors; inserted himself into the text and constructed an inter/extra-textual world. By narrative sequencing I mean the way biblical verses or "chant[cant]-phrases," i.e., text-based plots and sub-plots were removed from texts, reinscribed with meaning, and woven into a living testament of African culture and history. See Smitherman, Chapter 5, "Black Modes of Discourse," in *Talkin*; Cooper, Chapter 7, "Chanting Down Babylon," in *Noises in the Blood* (Durham, NC: Duke University Press, 1993); Gates, Chapter 4, "The Trope of the Talking Book," in The Signifying Monkey; and H. Adlai Murdach, "Displacing Marginality: Cultural Identity and Creole Resistance," in *Research in African Literatures*, 25 (1994); Tejumola Olaniyan, "Agones: The Constitution of a Practice," in *Scars of Conquest/Masks of Resistance* (New York: Oxford University Press, 1995); and especially Betsy Erkkila, "Ethnicity, Literary Theory, and the Grounds of Resistance," *American Quarterly* 47 (1995): 572-75, for point of view, double-voicing, and historical identities in black discourse.

55. For poaching and resistant readers see Certeau, *Practice*, and Radway, *Reading the Romance*, whereby readers draw upon the same tactics or methods as in everyday life to "poach" or take what they want from texts. See also Smitherman, Chapter 5, "Black Modes of Discourse"; Cooper, Chapter 7, "Chanting Down Babylon"; Gates, "The Trope of the Talking Book"; Murdach, "Displacing Marginality"; Olaniyan, "Agones"; and Erkkila, "Ethnicity, Literary Theory," 572-75.

56. See page 94.

57. See page 85.

58. See page 105.

References

Abrahams, Roger
  1983 *African Folktales.* New York: Pantheon.
  1983 *Man-of-Word in the West Indies.* Baltimore: Johns Hopkins University Press.
Abrahams, Roger, and John Szwed
  1983 *After Africa.* New Haven: Yale University Press.
Alleyne, M.
  1997 *Roots of Jamaican Culture.* London: Pluto.
Allsopp, Richard
  2003 *Dictionary of Caribbean English Usage.* Kingston: University of the West Indies Press.
Amussen, Susan Dwyer
  2007 *Caribbean Exchanges: Slavery and the Transformation of English Society.* Chapel Hill: University of North Carolina Press.
Asad, Talal
  1986 "The Concept of Cultural Translation in British Social Anthropology." In *Writing Culture: The Poetics and Politics of Ethnography,* James Clifford and George Marcus, ed. Pp. 141-64. Santa Fe, NM: School for American Research.
Astley, Thomas
  1745 *A New General Collection of Voyages and Travels Consisting of the Most Esteemed Relations, which have been hitherto published in any Language in Four Volumes.* London: printed for Thomas Astley.
Bauman, Richard
  1988 "The Story in the Story: Meta narration in Folk Narrative." In Richard Bauman (ed). *Verbal Art as Performance.* Pp. 24-30. New York: Dover.
Bauman, Richard, and Joel Sherzer, eds.
  1989 *Explorations in the Ethnography of Speaking.* New York: Cambridge University Press.
Bauman, Richard, and Charles L. Briggs
  1990 "Poetics and Performance as Critical Perspectives on Language and Social Life." *Annual Review of Anthropology,* 19: 59-88.
Beals, R.
  1995 "Reflections on Ethnography in Morocco." *Critique of Anthropology,* 15: 19-34.
Beckford, George, and Michael Witter
  1982 *Small Garden and Bitter Weed.* Morant Bay: Maroon Publishing House.
Benthall, Jonathan and Ted Polhemus, eds.
  1975 *The Body as a Medium of Expression.* New York: E. P. Dutton.
Black, Clinton
  1968 *The Story of Jamaica.* London: Collins.
Boyarin, Jonathan, ed.
  1992 *The Ethnography of Reading.* Berkley: University of California Press.
Brathwaite, Edward
  1972 *The Development of Creole Society in the Jamaica, 1770-1820.* London: Oxford.
  1984 *History of the Voice.* Trinidad: New Beacon Books.
  1995 "A Post Cautionary Tale of the Helen of our Wars." *Wasafiri,* 22: 69-78.
Bridenbaugh, Carl
  1968 *Vexed and Troubled Englishmen, 1590-1642.* New York: Oxford.

Brown, Vincent
  2006   "Spiritual Terror and Scared Authority: The Power of the Supernatural in
          Jamaican Slave Society." In *New Studies in the History of American Slavery,*
          Edward Baptist, ed. Pp. 179-210. Athens: University of Georgia Press.

Burnard, Trevor
  2004   *Mastery, Tyranny, and Desire: Thomas Thistlewood and His Slaves in the
          Anglo-Jamaican World.* Chapel Hill: University of North Carolina Press.

Burton, Richard D. E.
  1997   *Afro-Creole: Power, Opposition, and Play in the Caribbean.* Ithaca: Cornell
          University Press.

Bush, Barbara
  1990   *Slave Women in Caribbean Society.* London: James Curry.

Cannadine, David
  1990   *The Decline and Fall of the British Aristocracy.* New York: Anchor Books.

Carrington, Selwynn H. H.
  1987   "The American Revolution and the British West Indies' Economy." *Journal
          of Interdisciplinary History,* 17: 823-502.

Cassidy, Frederic
  1961   *Jamaica Talk.* London: Macmillan.

Cassidy, Frederic, and R. B. Le Page
  2002   *Dictionary of Jamaican English.* Kingston: University of West Indies Press.

Certeau, Michel
  1984   *The Practice of Everyday Life.* Berkeley: University of California Press.

Christaller, J. G., W. Locher, and J. Zimmerman
  1874   *A Dictionary of English, Tishi, Ahra; Comprising as Dialects Akan (Asante,
          Akem, Akuapem, etc.) and Fante; Akra (Accra) connected with Adangme;
          Gold Coast, W. Africa.* Basel: Basel Missionary Society.

Collins, James, and Richard Blot, eds.
  2003   *Literacy and Literacies: Power, and Identity.* New York: Cambridge Univer-
          sity Press.

Collins, James
  1995   "Literacy and Literacies." *Annual Review of Anthropology,* 24: 75-93.

Cooper, Carolyn,
  1993   *Noises in the Blood.* Durham, NC: Duke University Press.

Crahan, Margaret, and Franklin Knight, eds.
  1979   *Africa and the Caribbean: the Legacies of a Link.* Baltimore: Johns
          Hopkins University Press.

Crahan, Margaret
  1980   *Alas, Alas, Kongo: A Social History of Indentured African Immigration into
          Jamaica.* Baltimore: Johns Hopkins University Press.

Cundall, Frank
  1902   *Bibliographica Jamaicensis.* London: Institute of Jamaica.
  1915   *Historic Jamaica.* London: Institute of Jamaica.

Curtin, Philip
  1975   *Two Jamaicas.* New York: Atheneum.

D'Costa, Jean
  1994   "Oral Literature, Formal Literature: The Formation of a Genre in
          Eighteenth-Century Jamaica." *Eighteenth-Century Studies,* 27: 663-76.

Davis, Gerald
  1985   *I Got the Word in Me and Can Sing It, You Know It.* Philadelphia: University
          of Pennsylvania Press.

Dayan, Joan
  1995   "Codes of Law and Bodies of Color." *New Literary History*, 26: 283-308.
  1995   *Haiti, History, and the Gods.* Berkley: University of California Press.
Diamond, Stanley
  1974   *In Search of the Primitive.* New Jersey: Transaction Books.
Dirks, Robert
  1987   *The Black Saturnalia: Conflict and its Ritual Expression on British West Indian Slave Plantations.* Gainesville: University of Florida Press.
Dunn, Richard S.
  1972   *Sugar and Slaves: The Rise of the Planter Class in the English West Indies.* New York: Norton.
Ellis, A. B.
  1966   [1887] *The Tishi-Speaking Peoples of the Gold-Coast.* Netherlands: Oosterhout.
Ember, Carol, and Marvin Ember
  1990   *Anthropology.* New Jersey: Prentice Hall.
Erikkila, Betsey
  1995   "Ethnicity, Literary Theory, and the Grounds of Resistance." *American Quarterly*, 47: 563-94.
Fage, J. D.
  1969   *A History of West Africa.* London: Cambridge.
Frei, Hans
  1982   *The Eclipse of Biblical Narrative.* London: Yale University Press.
Frey, Sylvia and Betty Wood
  1998   *Come Shouting to Zion.* Chapel Hill: University of North Carolina Press.
Fynn, J. D.
  1971   *Asante and its Neighbors, 1700-1807.* Evanston: Northwestern University Press.
  1989   *The Fante of Ghana, 1600-1874.* Legon: University of Ghana Press.
Gates, Henry Louis
  1988   *The Signifying Monkey.* New York: Oxford University Press.
Geertz, Clifford
  1973   *The Interpretation of Cultures.* New York: Basic Books.
Gilroy, Paul
  1993   *The Black Atlantic.* Cambridge, MA: Harvard University Press.
Godwyn, Morgan
  1681   *A Supplement to the Negro's and Indian Advocate.* London: J. D.
  1685   *Trade Preferred before Religion.* London: B. Took.
Goody, Jack
  1987   *The Interface between the Written and the Spoken.* London: Cambridge.
Gordon, Shirley
  1996   *God Almighty Make We Free.* Bloomington: Indiana University Press.
Goveia, Elsa
  1970   *The West Indian Slave Laws of the 18th Century.* New Haven: Yale University Press.
  1980   *A Study of the Historiography of the British West Indies to the End of the Nineteenth-Century.* Washington, DC: Howard University Press.
Gray, Obika
  1991   *Radicalism and Social Change in Jamaica 1960-1972.* Knoxville, TN: University of Tennessee Press.
Green, William

1976   *British Slave Emancipation: The Sugar Colonies and the Great Experiment 1830-1865.* Oxford: Clarendon Press.

Gregg, Veronica Marie
1995   *Jean Rhys' Historical Imagination.* Chapel Hill: University of North Carolina Press.

Hall, Douglas
1959   *Free Jamaica 1838-1865.* New Haven: Yale University Press.
1989   *In Miserable Slavery.* London: Macmillan.

Handler, Jerome, and Kenneth M. Bilby
2002   "On the Early Use and Origin of the Term 'Obeah' in Barbados and the Anglophone Caribbean." *Slavery & Abolition,* 22: 87-100.

Hanks, William
1988   "Texts and Textuality." *Annual Review of Anthropology,* 18: 95-127.

Hart, Richard
1977   *Black Jamaicans' Struggle Against Slavery.* Kingston: Institute of Jamaica.
1980   *Slaves Who Abolished Slavery: Vol.1 Blacks in Bondage.* Kingston: ISER.
1985   *Slaves Who Abolished Slavery: Vol. 2 Blacks in Rebellion.* Kingston: ISER.

Hartman, Saidiya V.
1997   *Scenes of Subjection: Terror, Slavery, and Self-Making in Nineteenth-Century America.* New York: Oxford.

Heath, Shirley
1983   *Ways with Words.* New York: Cambridge University Press.

Higman, Barry
1976   *Slave Population and Economy in Jamaica 1807-1834.* Cambridge: Cambridge University Press.
1988   *Jamaica Surveyed: Plantations maps and plans of the 18th & 19th-centuries.*

Holm, John
1988   *Pidgins and Creoles, V. I. Theory and Structure.* Cambridge: Cambridge University Press.

Holt, Thomas
1992   *The Problem of Freedom: Race, Labor, and Politics in Jamaica.* Baltimore: Johns Hopkins University Press.

House of Assembly of Jamaica.
1761   *Journal of the House of Assembly of Jamaica,* V: 311
1792   *Journal of the House of Assembly of Jamaica,* XII: 732.

Howells, Coral Ann
1996   "Review of Jeans Rhys' Historical Imagination." *Yes,* 27: 294-95.

Hymes, Dell
1969   *Reinventing Anthropology.* New York: Random House.
1974   *Foundations in Sociolinguistics.* Philadelphia: University of Pennsylvania Press.

Iser, Wolfgang
1977   *The Act of Reading.* Baltimore: Johns Hopkins University Press.

James, Lawrence
1994   *The Rise and Fall of the British Empire.* New York: St. Martins.

Jameson, Frederic
1987   "Regarding Postmodernism." *Social Text,* 17: 89-122.

Jekyll, Walter
1966   [1904] *Jamaican Song and Story, Annacy stories, Digging Tunes, and Ring tunes.* New York: Dover.

Kingston: Institute of Jamaica Publications.

1998   *Montpelier, Jamaica: A Plantation Community in Slavery and freedom, 1739-1912.* Kingston: University of the West Indies Press.

2005   *Plantation Jamaica, 1750-1850: Capital and Control in a Colonial Economy.* Kingston: University of the West Indies Press.

Knight, Franklin
1990   *The Caribbean.* London: Oxford.

Kriese, Thomas W.
1996   *Caribbeana: An Anthology of English Literature of the West Indies, 1657-1777.* Chicago: University of Chicago Press.

Kupperman, Karen
1982   "Fear of Hot Climates in the Anglo-American Colonial Experience." *William & Mary,* 41: 213-40

Lambeth Palace Papers
1715   Vol. 10 (reel 9): 115
1724   Vol. 17: 175.
1752   Vol. 18 (reel 17), Jamaica, 9th November 1752: 57

Legêne, Susan
1998   "From Brooms to Obeah and Back: Fetish Conversion and Border Crossings in Nineteenth-Century Suriname." In Patricia Spyer (ed.), *Border Crossing: Material Objects in Unstable Place.* Pp. 35-59 New York: Routledge.

Lewis, Gordon K.
1983   *Main Currents in Caribbean Thought.* Baltimore: Johns Hopkins University Press.

Long, Edward
1970   [1760] *History of Jamaica.* London: Frank Cass.

Loughlin, Gerard
1995   *Telling God's Story: Bible, Church History, and Theology.* Cambridge: Cambridge University Press.

Mair, Lucille M.
2006   *A Historical Study of Women in Jamaica, 1655-1844.* Kingston: West Indies.

Mardorossian, Carine M.
1999   "Shutting up the Subaltern: Silences, Stereotypes, and Double-Entendre in Jean Rhys's *Wide Sargasso Sea." Callaloo,* 22 (4): 1071-90.

McCalman, Ian
1991   *The Horrors of Slavery and Other Writings by Robert Wedderburn.* Princeton: Markus Weiner.

McDonald, Roderick
1993   *The Economy and Material Culture of Slaves.* Baton Rouge: Louisiana State University Press.

Metcalf, George
1965   *Royal Government & Political Conflict in Jamaica:1729-1783.* London: Royal Commonwealth Society.

Meyerowitz, Eva
1974   *The Early History of the Akan States of Ghana.* London: Red Candle Press.

Mintz, Sidney, and Douglas Hall
1960   *The Origins of the Jamaican Internal Marketing System.* New Haven: Yale University Publications in Anthropology Number 57.

Mohammed, Patricia
2000   "But most of All mi Love Me Browning': The Emergence in Eighteenth and Nineteenth Century Jamaica of the Mulatto Woman as Desired," *Feminist Review,* 65: 22-48.

Monteith, Kathleen E. A., and Glen Richards
   2002   *Jamaica in Slavery and Freedom.* Kingston: University of the West Indies
           Press.
Morgan, Jennifer L.
   1997   "Some Could Suckle over Their Shoulder:" Male Travelers, Female Bodies,
           and the Gendering of Racial Ideology, 1500-1770," *William & Mary,* 54:
           168-90.
Murdach, H. Adlai
   1994   "Displacing Marginality: Cultural Identity and Creole Resistance." *Research
           in African Literatures,* 25: 34-70.
Olaniyan, Tejumola
   1995   *Scars of Conquest/Masks of Resistance.* New York: Oxford University Press.
Ong, Walter
   1967   *The Presence of the Word.* New Haven and London: Yale University Press.
Paton, Diana
   2001   "Punishment, Crime, and the Bodies of Slaves in Eighteenth Century Jamai-
           ca." *Social History,* 34: 31-52.
   2004   *No Bond But the Law: Punishment, Race, and Gender in Jamaican State
           Formation, 1780-1870.* Durham: Duke University Press.
Patterson, Orlando
   1973   [1967] *Sociology of Slavery.* Kingston: Sangster.
   1975   "Slavery and Slave Revolts: A Socio-historical Analysis of the First Maroon
           War." *Social & Economic Studies,* 19: 289-335.
Pitman, Frank Wesley
   1967   [1917] *The Development of the British West Indies.* New Haven: Archon
           Books.
Pulis, John W.
   1999   "'Important Truths' and 'Pernicious Follies:' Texts, Covenants, and the
           Anabaptist Church of Jamaica." In Kevin Yelvington ed., *Afro-Atlantic Dia-
           logues: Anthropology in the Diaspora.* Pp. 193-210. Santa Fe, NM: School of
           American Research.
Raboteau, Albert
   1995   *A Fire in the Bones.* Boston: Beacon Press.
Radway, Janice
   1994   *Reading the Romance.* Chapel Hill: University of North Carolina Press.
Ragatz, Lowell
   1928   *The Fall of the Planter Class in the British Caribbean.* New York: Octagon.
Raskin, Judith L., ed.
   1999   *Wide Sargasso Sea/Jean Rhys; Background & Criticism.* New York: W.W.
           Norton & Company.
           Records of the Society for the Propagation of the Gospel in Foreign Parts
           1701-86, Vol. 17 (reel 17), Letters, Series B, Jamaica: 282.
Reddock, Rhoda, ed.
   2004   *Interrogating Caribbean Masculinities: Theoretical and Empirical
           Analyses.* Kingston: University of the West Indies Press.
Rhys, Jean
   1975   *Smile Please: An Unfinished Autobiography.* New York: Harper & Row.
Rich, Paul B.
   1990   *Race and Empire in British Politics.* Cambridge: Cambridge University
           Press.
Richardson, Alan

202   John W. Pulis

1997   "Romantic Voodoo: Obeah and British Culture." In Margarita Fernandez Olmos, and Lizabeth Paravsini-Gebart, eds, *Sacred Possession: Vodu, Santeria, Obeah, and the Caribbean.* Pp. 171-95. New Brunswick, NJ: Rutgers University Press.

Robertson, James
2002   "Stories and Histories in Late-Seventeenth-Century Jamaica." In *Jamaica in Slavery and Freedom: History, Heritage, and Culture* Kathleen Monteith and Glen Richards, eds. Kingston: University of the West Indies Press.

Roseberry, William, and Nicole Polier
1982   "Tristes Tropes: Postmodern Anthropologists Encounter the Other and Discover Themselves." *Economy and Society,* 18: 48-72.

Sandiford, Keith A.
2000   *The Cultural Politics of Sugar: Caribbean Slavery and Narratives of Colonization.* New York: Cambridge.

Sheller, Mimi
2000   *Consuming the Caribbean: From Arawaks to Zombies.* New York: Routledge.

Shepherd, Verne, Bridget Brereton, and Barbara Bailey, eds.
1995   *Engendering History: Caribbean Women in Historical Perspective.* Kingston: Ian Randle.

Sheridan, Richard
1974   *Sugar and Slavery: an Economic History.* Baltimore: Johns Hopkins.
1976   "The Crisis of Slave Subsistence in the West Indies during and after the American Revolution." *William & Mary,* 33: 601-25.

Slater, Mariam K.
1977   *The Caribbean Family: Legitimacy in Martinique.* New York: St. Martins.

Smitherman, Geneva
1977   *Talkin and Testifyin: The Language of Black Americas.* Detroit: Wayne State University Press.

Spurdle, Frederick G.
1962   *Early West Indian Government.* New Zealand: N. P.

Stewart, Robert
1985   *Religion and Society in Post Emancipation Jamaica.* Knoxville: Tennessee.

Street, Brian
1983   *Literacy in Theory and Practice.* London: Cambridge.

Taylor, S. A. G.
1965   *The Western Design: An Account of Cromwell's Expedition to the Caribbean.* Kingston: Institute of Jamaica Press.

Tedlock, Barbara
1991   "From Participant Observation to the Observation of Participation." *Journal of Anthropological Research,* 47: 75-91.

Tedlock, D.
1989   "Questions Concerning Dialogical Anthropology." *Journal of Anthropological Research,* 43: 320-52.

Thomas, Susan
1999   *The Worlding of Jean Rhys.* Westport, CT.: Greenwood.

Thompson, E. P.
1993   *Witness against the Beast.* New York: New Press.

Thornton, John K.
1992   *African and Africans in the Making of the Atlantic World.* New York: Cambridge.

Trevelyan, G. M.
1942   *English Social History.* New York: David McKay.
Valentine, E., and Jeffrey Peck
1996   *Culture and Contexture: Explorations in Anthropology and Literary Studies.* Berkeley: University of California Press.
Van Horner, John C.
1985   *Religious Philanthropy and Colonial Slavery.* Urbana: University of Illinois Press.
Watts, David
1990   *The West Indies: Patterns of Development, Culture, and Environmental Change since 1492.* New York: Cambridge University Press.
Whitson, Agnes
1929   *The Constitutional Development of Jamaica.* Manchester: Manchester University Press.
Williams, Eric
1944   *Capitalism and Slavery.* Chapel Hill: University of North Carolina Press.
Williams, Joseph J.
1932   *Voodoos and Obeahs in Jamaica.* New York: Dial
1934   *Psychic Phenomena of Jamaica.* New York: Dial.
Williams, Raymond
1977   *Marxism and Literature.* New York: Oxford University Press.
Williamson, Karin
2008   *Voices of Slavery.* Kingston: University of the West Indies Press.
Wright, Philip, ed.
1966   [1839] *Lady Nugent's Journal of Her Residence in Jamaica from 1801 to 1805.* Kingston: Institute of Jamaica Press.
Wyndham, Francis
1999   "Introduction." In *Wide Sargasso Sea/Jean Rhys.* Judith L. Raskin ed. Pp. 3-8. New York: W.W. Norton & Company.

Chapter 7

Ethnografiction and Reality in Contemporary Irish Literature

HELENA WULFF

In Ireland, the nationalist cultural revival organized by the Gaelic League at the end of the nineteenth century saw the promotion of literature as crucial. Headed by Yeats, the literary movement evolved into a major force in the political process towards national independence. In his influential book, *Inventing Ireland*, literary theorist Declan Kiberd demonstrates that it was during the literary revival that Ireland became a modern nation.[1] Building on the rich literary tradition with classic writers such as James Joyce and Samuel Beckett, there is now an acclaimed generation of contemporary Irish writers. Some of them figure in my anthropological research on the social world of Irish writers and their work.[2] Like other artistic accounts, these literary stories are not direct reflections of what is happening around the writers; they are intricate imaginary commentary, frequently focusing on Irish society. The stories are often political, as well as romantic, and witty. While typically featuring a dark streak, many stories conclude on an unexpectedly hopeful note. Writing about the prominence of Irish writers during the last two centuries, geographer Patrick Duffy interestingly suggests that rather than merely reporting on social reality they, in fact, negotiate multivocal meanings that keep changing.[3]

Contrary to the view of literary critic James Wood stated in *How Fiction Works*, my argument is that much fiction is inspired by real life. In this chapter, I explore literary accounts, primarily novels but also short stories and travel writing, by Éilís Ní Dhuibhne and Colm Tóibín, in terms of ethnografiction, a genre I contextualize in a discussion of the role of literature in anthropology, ethnography versus fiction, and anthropology versus art and science.[4] As writers of ethnografiction, Ní Dhuibhne and Tóibín prepare for their fiction writing through research that includes ethnographic observations, interviews, and archival work. Their stories are often based on two or three real people and events, mixed with one spoonful of fantasy, and an imaginative plot that provides a potential for what could happen. Time and place can be moved around freely in fiction, while ethnography is a more grounded type of reporting of what actually has happened, including accurate accounts of places and time, from a certain theoretical perspective. Both Ní Dhuibhne's and Tóibín´s fiction conform to realist conventions (with the exception of Ní Dhuibhne´s occasional inclusion of fairies). Their stories could have happened—some actually have happened.

In the volume *True Fiction*, Dutch anthropologist Peter Kloos considered the similarities and differences between fiction and anthropology.[5] "Is anthropology a science or is it an art?" he asked rhetorically in the opening line of his introductory chapter.[6] His reply is "that it is both." "After all, any science is a combination of creative imagination, primarily associated with the artist, and methodological rigour, usually believed to be the trademark of the scientist." Separating the texts of science and art into different genres, he sorts literary texts in one category consisting of "the novel, the short story, the poem, the essay." Kloos categorizes anthropology as "monographic account or ethnography, the theoretical treatise, the specialized article, the introductory text, and again the essay."[7] He argues that the novel and the ethnographic account are not easily divided into different genres, as "boundaries between the two are ambiguous." It is likely that, from an artistic perspective, most ethnographies are dull, as Kloos claims, and that from a scientific perspective, novels are considered problematic regarding reliability since they do not offer a report on the research process. Kloos points out that both novels and ethnographic accounts, tend to lack "independent replications."[8] Comparing artistic and scientific representations of reality, Kloos suggests three outcomes: first, the two representations convey the same piece of information; second, the representations diverge leading the scientist to reject the artistic representation as incorrect; and third the artistic rendering displays data that have eluded the scientist. According to Kloos, "novelists have something to offer that is often sadly absent in scholarly work: a sensitivity to important currents and values in actual life ... why is it that scholars often fail to notice these things?" The scientist, on the other hand, provides "systematic and explicit description ... and explanation ... general statements that explain what can be observed: theories, if you like." Kloos concludes that, curiously "an artistic description often rests on what is not said at all!"[9]

Writing about the role of fiction in anthropological scholarship and analysis, Eduardo Archetti distinguished between three types of fiction: "the realistic historical novel that attempts to 'reconstruct' a given period in a given society; the totally imagined story set in a historical period; and the essay devoted to an interpretation of a nation, its characteristics, and creed." As Archetti argued, "some kind of historical and sociological knowledge is important in fiction," which makes the task of writing fiction similar to that of writing anthropology. This is in accordance with Ní Dhuibhne's description of how she works: "short stories come at the spur of the moment, they're not planned. A novel has to be planned, it takes longer, it requires doing research."[10] Archetti anticipated the possibility that a novelist can unintentionally highlight certain cultural topics, while some writers of fiction were trained as academics. This is fiction as "ethnographic raw material, not as authoritative statements about, or interpretations of, a particular society."[11] Archetti's point that "a literary product is not only a substantive part of the real world but also a key element in the configuration of the world itself" is a useful one for the anthropologist to keep in mind.[12]

As the Introduction to this volume illuminates, literary anthropology keeps expanding and now has a substantial history. Victor Turner argued that African ritual and western literature were "mutually elucidating." Clifford Geertz explored the anthropologist as author including Malinowski, Benedict, Evans-Pritchard, and Lévi-Strauss. The influential writing culture debate at the end of the twentieth century was the topic of a recent issue of *Cultural Anthropology* on the occasion of the twenty-fifth anniversary of the publication of *Writing Culture* by James Clifford and George Marcus. Richard Handler and Daniel Segal discuss Jane Austen as an ethnographer of kinship and marriage in her time and social class in England revealing diverse social relationships. In Nigel Rapport's research on the village of Wanet in England, E. M. Forster became a fellow ethnographer, as Rapport juxtaposed Forster's writings to his own findings about the village. The volume edited by Alisse Waterson and Maria D. Vesperi considers anthropological writing for a wider readership. Kirin Narayan's *Alive in the Writing* is a tribute to Anton Chekhov as an ethnographic muse. Finally, in *The Other Shore*, Michael Jackson traces his trajectory as a writer that has opened up opportunities for him to take part in various imaginary communities.[13]

Éilís Ní Dhuibhne: Irish Social Relations from a Woman's Point of View

When researching dance and culture in Ireland, and questions of memory and mobility, I started reading contemporary Irish novels as one way to learn about the society.[14] I discovered Éilís Ní Dhuibhne who is an astute observer of social life, especially from a woman's point of view both historically and in the new Ireland. Irish relations, particularly from a feminine perspective, are at the heart of Éilís Ní Dhuibhne's writings. In addition, Ní Dhuibhne conveys these relations as they unfold in a nation adjusting to the rapid social transformations associated with Ireland's "Celtic Tiger" economy and its dramatic downturn thereafter. As literary scholar Anne Fogarty has remarked, Ní Dhuibhne "more than any other contemporary Irish writer ... explores the gaps between decades of the late twentieth century that appear to be contiguous and shows how the tensions between competing timeframes and value systems are at the basis of the moral and emotional dilemma of her characters. The uncanny familiarity and oddity of the past are central preoccupations of many of her stories."[15]

Trained in Irish folklore, Ní Dhuibhne has an acute awareness of ethnographic detail that makes her portraits of people and their relationships revealing of human life beyond the specific contexts of her fiction. Éilís Ní Dhuibhne can be said to make observations just like an ethnographer while participating in the life around her. "I'm not a sociologist, but I think I have an interest in Ireland and its part in the world," she told me in an interview, and "I care about very specific Irish experiences."[16] Both "relations" and "women's points of view" were, of course, crucial ideas driving anthropology in the middle years of the twentieth century. In her inaugural lecture at the University of Cambridge, Marilyn Strathern famously recalled: "Routing relations through persons became the substance of anthropological empiricism. Whether the relations were intellectual or social, made in fantasy or acted out in daily life, their source in people's interactions was made significant." Relations were understood as "principles of social organization."[17] Women's points of view, were formulated in ground-breaking feminist anthropology publications such as *Perceiving Women* edited by Shirley Ardener and *Toward an Anthropology of Women* edited by Rayna Rapp Reiter.[18]

Ní Dhuibhne's novel *The Dancers Dancing* inspired the active use of Irish fiction as ethnography in my writings. However, this approach was not new. As graduate students in the Stockholm Anthropology Department, we were encouraged to read fiction from our fields, as one way to learn about the places and people we were studying. A number of questions were raised. What exactly can an anthropologist can learn through fiction? What is the relationship between ethnography and fiction? For my study of Irish dance, I found exquisite descriptions of Irish social relations in Ní Dhuibhne's work, especially those of mothers and daughters, and relationships and friendships between teenage girls and sisters, descriptions that extended my findings about tightly-knit family networks. These descriptions inspired new questions, such as the particular position of Irish women who now are under pressure to conform to contradictory ideals from the past and present that I could investigate during interviews and observations. This is a literary anthropology that depends on complementary data from interviews and participant observation with writers in their cultural contexts.

The Dancers Dancing is a rhythmical rendering of a group of adolescent girls who spend the summer of 1972 learning Irish in the Gaeltacht.[19] Just like the Irish language movement initiated by the Gaelic League almost a century before, these classes in the Irish language are combined with learning to dance at a *céilí*, a dance gathering. Fogarty notes that *The Dancers Dancing* is a *Bildungsroman*, "at once an ethnographic fiction and a celebratory tale of sexual and emotional awakening."[20] "Going to the Gaeltacht" is a "seminal teenage experience" in Ireland, but adolescence is universal.[21] The following scene captures adolescent sensitivity as well as tension between tradition and transformation in Ireland: Orla, the protagonist of the novel, who comes from Dublin, is expected to visit her Auntie Annie who lives in the vicinity of the Irish College. Orla is embarrassed by her aunt's odd appearance and by the old-fashioned house where her father grew up, and as a result, she kept postponing her visit. Then, one day towards the end of the stay, Orla summons her courage and tells two of her friends, a girl and a boy, that she is going to see her aunt. To Orla's horror, they want to come with her, and "Orla feels something break inside her head, like the shell of an egg. Her big secret is disintegrating." Nevertheless, the three of them "troop across the yard and into the house. It's dark inside, as in all the old, small-windowed houses. And, despite the lack of sunshine, it's hot in the kitchen, where the range is burning brightly." There they find Auntie Annie and two of their teachers! It turns out that the teachers have visited Auntie Anne before. The woman teacher says admiringly, "isn't this the lovely cosy house?"[22]

> Orla looks at the ticking sunray clock, the uneven rocky floor, the painted dresser stocked with blue plates and an odd assortment of ornaments ... She looks at the bare bulb dangling from a twisted wire in the middle of the ceiling ... Who could find a single thing to praise in this gloomy, old-fashioned ridiculous house? A house that Orla has often wished would burn to the ground and be forgotten for all time.[23]

Aunt Annie greets Orla warmly, and soon they all have tea:

> They eat and drink chatting softly. The warmth of the room increases and the clock ticks loudly on the mantelpiece. Orla finds her sense of well-being burgeoning. The room encloses her like a cradle, warm and old and dark and comfortable. Peace seeps into her soul from the mellow walls, the rocky bed of the floor. Flames flicker in the range, spoons clink against plates, voices rise and fall in meaningless chatter: it is a tune that has been played in this kitchen often before. For hundreds of years. Right in this room.[24]

The man teacher changes the tune. "Time to do some work!" he says, depositing his cup on the table and plugging a tape recorder into the socket." Turning to Orla, he explains that, "Annie is going to tell me some stories," and Orla realizes with a sudden sense of pride that her odd aunt is recognized as an authority on local folklore.[25] The tension that haunted Orla between tradition and modernity, is thus happily resolved here. This resolution can be analyzed as one aspect of how tradition is incorporated into modern life in Ireland, living on in partially new forms, an indicator of how Irish modernity is reconstituted.

The short story "Midwife to the Fairies," also brings out tensions in Ireland's contemporary historical moment, illustrated through a woman's perspective.[26] Here Ní Dhuibhne weaves a folktale into a modern story set in Dublin, which Anne Fogarty says, "in fact, transposes and retells it."[27] The story is about a Dublin midwife who is called late one night to a woman in labor. A woman gives birth to a small, unwanted baby. The midwife informs the new mother that the baby needs to be in an incubator, after which she leaves and tries to forget about the whole event. However, shortly after she learns from a newspaper article that the baby had been found "dead in a shoebox, in a kind of rubbish dump."[28] This story could be interpreted as a straightforward critique of the laws against abortion, which still exist in the Republic of Ireland while, at the same time, the interpolated folktale sections create historical depth. Above all, as Diane Purkiss notes, the story is significant in the ways in which it represents connections between infant death and the world of fairies.[29] For an anthropologist, this is an example of how survivals of traditional beliefs can be found in modern thought and life, both in Ireland, which has a strong folkloric tradition, and in other societies.

According to Ní Dhuibhne, it was the experience of writing a doctoral dissertation on the history of a folktale: Chaucer's "The Friar's Tale," which inspired
her dark novel about fear of nuclear disaster, *The Bray House*.[30] The novel features a Swedish woman archaeologist who comes over to Ireland "with the purpose of reconstructing its culture by carrying out a dig in a countryside devastated by nuclear meltdown," but fails to find the true story.[31] This is fiction as
science fiction, including a meticulous account of a scholarly method of collecting archeological data while steeped in a chilling thriller format. The novel also
engages with one of Ní Dhuibhne's central concerns: "Where is the true story—
in fiction or in scholarship?"[32]

In his comprehensive *Reader on Irish Writing in the Twentieth Century*,
David Pierce presents four main topics of Irish writing: first, "history, politics,
and religion"; second, "the city and the country"; third, "culture and identity"
which includes "folklore and folk tales," "women writers," and "humour"; and
fourth, "the Irish diaspora," and "return" to Ireland.[33] With some exceptions,
notably Lady Augusta Gregory (who, among many other accomplishments,
worked with Yeats in establishing a national Irish theatre), the literary tradition
in Ireland tends to be presented as predominantly male, while, in fact, there were
a number of women who wrote poems, plays, and fiction during the literary
revival in the late nineteenth century. This is revealed in the anthology *Voices on
the Wind*, edited by Ní Dhuibhne.[34] These early women writers shared an engagement with Irish culture, and "like many other writers of the period, their
mission, conscious or unconscious, was to transmit the primary literature and
folklore of Gaelic Ireland to their readers in a diluted form."[35] This was the time
of the cult of the Celt, which entailed certain sentiments that Ní Dhuibhne finds
exaggerated. It is interesting to learn that it was "thoroughly acceptable for
women to write" and that male colleagues "encouraged and admired their female colleagues" who were then able to publish with the leading publishing
houses and take part in the literary establishment.[36] Ní Dhuibhne attributes this
upsurge in women's writing, around the year 1900, to the existence of a lively
cultural climate in Ireland consisting both of international literary and intellectual currents, such as women's suffrage and a search for Irish identity. This favorable climate did not last long, however, and it would take until the 1960s and
1970s for the second literary revival of Irish women writers to emerge.

In 2002 the encyclopedic *The Field Day Anthology of Irish Women Writing
and Traditions: Volumes IV and V* were published.[37] Included are more than
seven hundred and fifty Irish women writers, between 600 A.D. and the year
2000. These two volumes were preceded by three *Field Day* volumes on Ireland's literary history that contained very few women writers, a circumstance
which led to debate in the Irish literary world and eventually to the publication
of the women's volumes. It took eleven years for them to appear and they have
done little to shift the dominant notion of literary history in Ireland as belonging
to men. *The Field Day Anthologies* on Irish women writers substantiates their
existence, as do a number of other publications including *Woman's Part* edited

by Janet Madden-Simpson, *The Female Line* edited by Ruth Hooley, *Wildish Things* edited by Ailbhe Smyth, *Two Irelands* by Rebecca Pelan and *Opening the Field* edited by Boyle Haberstroh, Patricia, and Christine St. Peter.[38]

"My impression was that Irish women hadn't had a voice," Ní Dhuibhne told me, and explained that this is why she started and still writes short stories and novels about women's lives. The idea for her story, "The Flowering," came from a newspaper article about a gifted woman embroideress who was prevented from doing her art when her father died and she had to help support the family. Missing her lace-making caused her to wither away, go mad, and finally die.[39] Ní Dhuibhne's story ends with a reflection about the similarities between the craftsmanship of fiction and scholarship, embroidering, and writing. The story seems to convey an urgent feminist message that women writers who have found fulfillment in writing should be given every opportunity to write. If their inner drive to write is thwarted, their lives will be thwarted also.

Building on autobiographical experiences, Ní Dhuibne's writing depicts her Ireland, which often unfolds against a backdrop of Dublin working class life, as when the Dublin girls in *The Dancers Dancing* go to Irish language class in the Gaeltacht. This accentuates "the relationship between the Irish language and the English language—the cultural schizophrenia—we experience at moments like that," she explained.[40] Of the relationships Ní Dhuibhne creates, the ones between mothers and daughters are especially well-crafted, and are usually narrated through the daughter's perspective. They tend to explore the type of motherly love that warms the daughter when she is away and homesick, which happens now and then to Orla in *The Dancers Dancing* during her summer at the Irish College. Like any close bond, this mother-daughter relationship has many dimensions, even shared mischief. In an entertaining episode, Orla and her mother dress up and have afternoon tea in a fancy hotel, mocking the snobbery of the place. In "The Catechism Examination," which is about a teacher who harasses a slow girl, the narrating girl avoids this distress because, "Mummy tests me every night, in front of the fire, before she reads *Alice in Wonderland*."[41] Some of the women are also daughters in alienated relationships, such as the successful professional woman archaeologist in *The Bray House* who has not seen her mother for many years and who states at the time of her mother's death that, "I'd lost contact with her. For the simple reason that I didn't like her. And the feeling was mutual." Yet, despite their alienation, the mother is constantly on the adult daughter's mind. The daughter admits that the holidays spent with her mother had been crucial as, "the seeds of my anthropological zeal were undoubtedly sown by her, during those many trips to so many different and fascinating lands."[42] At first, there is a sense that the narrator resembles her mother in coldness of character and careerism. As a student, the woman sets out on a brilliant academic career, supported by an older male mentor. When he is retiring, the woman announces that she is applying for his job. He disapproves on the grounds that she is a woman and a less qualified man is appointed. Here the feminist message about unequal career opportunities for women and men is clear.

To what extent siblings can be real friends is disputed in anthropological kinship studies, one relation being ascribed, the other achieved, and voluntary. However, there is no doubt that siblings, especially as children, can be close. Ní Dhuibhne's story "Wuff Wuff Wuff for de Valera," (a play on the children's rhyme, "Vote vote vote for de Valera") reminds the woman narrator of a skipping game and happy playtime with her twin sister in the working class street where they grew up.[43] Having married well into housewifery, the narrator can afford a condescending attitude, looking down as she is looking back: "We had one of those quaint working class childhoods Irish writers are always going on about: scruffy corner shops, luke warm baths once a week, disastrous clothes." Her sister, however, did not have time for such privileged judgment, becoming instead a single parent as a teenager. According to the narrator, "That's why she sort of didn't make it." Her sister ended up working as a civil servant without being promoted.[44] Such differences in class and comfort reveals a sense of competition between the sisters, even in the childhood memory.

Ní Dhuibhne has also published well-crafted academic articles, such as one on "The Irish," where she identifies loquacity as a central characteristic of the Irish:

> A high opinion of the Irish gift for writing and talking is shared by many, especially the Irish themselves. That the Irish are verbally gifted is a *sine qua non* of the image we sell to tourists, but it is probably based on truth. Ireland has produced a high proportion of internationally renowned writers, such as the verbally generous James Joyce and the verbally frugal Samuel Beckett. It is commonly believed that there are more writers per capita in Ireland than in other Countries.[45]

Ní Dhuibhne also notes that a "talent for writing appears in every historical ethnic group. The four Irish authors who have been awarded the Nobel Prize in literature are Shaw, Yeats, and Beckett, Dublin Protestants, and Heaney, a Northern Irish Catholic." She points out that Joyce, surely "the most well-known and influential of all Irish writers," was not a Nobel laureate.

Ní Dhuibhne also reminds us of the absence of Irish women writers in this elite category. In a country where creative wit is highly regarded, Ní Dhuibhne points out that not only writers of literature or plays, but Irish people as a whole "are talkative." Again, there is a significant gender dimension, according to Ní Dhuibhne, since Irish men are considered to be wittier than Irish women: Irish men tell more jokes, and their conversation is full of funny comments and anecdotes. The Irish like to make fun of other people, says Ní Dhuibhne, for speaking and behaving in a different, exaggerated way, or for boasting especially. This ridicule is not presented to peoples' face, but they are typically "laughed at behind their backs." Ní Dhuibhne eagerly adds that, "the Irish like to laugh at themselves, at their sorrows."[46]

I have discussed Éilís Ní Dhuibhne's writings in terms of ethnografiction, as she builds her fiction on what can be seen as ethnographic observations of social life and lore in Ireland. This has accentuated the realism of her fiction. It was through Ní Dhuibhne's work that I first realized the predicament of women in this contemporary moment of social and economic change in Ireland. Although Ireland is now in an economic recession, the "Celtic Tiger" economy brought prosperity and a new cultural confidence. At the same time, the expansion of the economy pressured women as many are expected to have both modern careers and traditional families with husband and children. Ní Dhuibhne's characters are often struggling to combine contradictory ideals of what a woman should be: traditional wife or successful professional; mother or mistress. There is no real reconciliation between these competing demands. In Ní Dhuibhne's novel *Fox, Swallow, Scarecrow*, a social satire of contemporary Ireland, she writes: "Divorce was available in Ireland these days, but it had arrived, strangely enough, at the same time as the big increase in house prices. When people could afford to divorce, it wasn't available, and then when it became available, it became unaffordable. Almost overnight. The free market economy was doing what the Church had done for centuries."[47] Many of Ní Dhuibhne's stories appeal to women readers, because of the first-person woman narrator who speaks to the reader as confidante. This is one reason why I was attracted to Ní Dhuibhne's writings, by feeling an affinity.

Ethnography is often said to be about everyday life, the mundane. Ní Dhuibhne explains: "Stories come to me. People tell me stories. The world is choc-a-bloc with them. I think I have what might seem to some people an inflated sense of the significance of what we call ordinary life. It doesn't seem at all ordinary to me. People's mundane experiences fascinate me."[48] Ethnography and fiction fuses in the ethnografiction of Éilís Ní Dhuibhne's work; a perceptive, witty, and learned woman writing about contemporary Irish relations from a woman's point of view.

Colm Tóibín: Travel, Exile, Catholicism

Colm Tóibín's *oeuvre* can also be understood as ethnografiction. He discusses issues ranging from exile and emigration to Catholicism and homosexuality. In the novel *Brooklyn: A Novel*, an unemployed young woman in 1950s Dublin moves to Brooklyn where she finds work in a department store, trains to become a bookkeeper, and falls in love with an Italian man. The tragic death of her sister, turns the story back to Ireland.[49] *The Master* by Colm Tóibín is based on the life of the American writer Henry James, where his hidden homosexuality is key.[50] As to his travel accounts, I am especially interested in how they phrase contested situations of religion and politics.

With his background in journalism, Tóbín has been a prolific travel writer in a fictionalized form considering issues such as politics and religion. *Bad Blood: A Walk along the Irish Border* is a description of Tóibín's walk from Derry to Newry in the summer of 1986.[51] The historical moment was the aftermath of the

Anglo-Irish Agreement between the United Kingdom and Ireland, a settlement to end the Troubles in Northern Ireland. *The Sign of the Cross* is a series of travelogues that depict journeys Tóibín made between 1990 and 1994 across Europe experiencing various expressions of Catholicism. Ironically, this elapsed Catholic writer is fascinated with faith, pilgrimages, and shrines.[52] In *Homage to Barcelona,* which is a homage to George Orwell and his *Homage to Catalonia,* Tóibín captures the grandeur of the city through his affectionate account. Like Orwell who commented on the Spanish Civil War, Tóibín first came to Barcelona during the political unrest of the 1970s, the public protests against Franco and his subsequent death.[53] Through portraits of people — artists such as Gaudí, Miró and Picasso, and Dalí—Tóibín tells the political and cultural history of Barcelona. He provides delightful descriptions of its art and architecture, churches and museums, cafés and restaurants, markets, and trendy nightclubs. The 1990s was a period when Barcelona became a new world centre for cosmopolitan culture.

"Why do Irish people travel so much?" I asked Colm Tóibín in an informal conversation at a party during my fieldwork in Dublin. "Because they live on an island," he replied. If most people who live on a relatively small island have an urge to travel and see more of the world, in Ireland this urge is coupled with a long tradition of migration that peaked with emigration waves during the Great Famine of the mid-nineteenth century, when two million people were forced to leave the country. Unemployment triggered earlier and later emigration waves. The Irish diaspora is now many times larger than the population of Ireland. Members of the diaspora have returned to Ireland for visits, but return migration had gathered force during the recent period of economic growth. With the current economic recession in Ireland and globally, there is again renewed emigration. As Fintan O'Toole suggests, "emigration and exile, the journeys to and from home, are the very heartbeat of Irish culture. To imagine Ireland is to imagine a journey."[54]

Another recent type of travel that is becoming increasingly common in Ireland, Europe, the United States and elsewhere, is the back-and-forth or transnational mobility between two or three places every year, establishing several homes away from home creating social networks that transcend borders. While based in Dublin, Colm Tóibín regularly spends a few months in Spain and in the United States, for different reasons. In Spain, Barcelona offers him an opera season, while a Pyrenees village, he maintains, is a setting where he can write undisturbed. "It's not about travelling, it's about settling. I have a house in this village. I'm there for two-three months every summer. There are no bars or restaurants. I suppose I could dig or do gardening, but I write. I work every day, in the morning, all day. It's Catalonia, it gets into your system. I read a Spanish newspaper, I listen to the radio.[55] In the United States, Tóibín regularly teaches creative writing and Irish literature as a visiting professor and writer-in-residence at several universities including Stanford, Texas, Princeton, and the New School for Social Research. Ireland features as a matter of course in Tóibín's writings, as do Spain, and the United States, often as nodes in networks of travel. When I asked Colm Tóibín to describe the literary world in Dublin, he exclaimed: "There is no Dublin literary world! Organizations don't matter, don't matter to me. Some writers are in France, the United States, all you want is three writers who share the same jokes ... There is no community, you don't feel it like that. How people know each other is through travelling!"[56]

Nevertheless, writers in Dublin know each other from their university days. Colm Tóibín moves in a circle of friends he has known since they were students. Roddy Doyle, Dermot Bolger, Ann Enright are all international literary writers, and Fintan O'Toole is Dublin based international journalist working both for Irish and foreign newspapers and magazines. In this sense, they are a community with ties to a Dublin literary world.

Like many Irish writers, Colm Tóibín is a true traveller, with a cosmopolitan outlook in accord with Ulf Hannerz's definition. "It is an intellectual and aesthetic stance of openness toward divergent cultural experiences, a search for contrasts rather than uniformity."[57] Tóibín has been travelling since he completed his B.A. degree in History and English at University College Dublin in 1975. In fact, the day after his final exams, Tóibín left for Barcelona where he lived for three years taking an active interest in Catalan culture and politics after Franco's death. Back in Dublin, he took up journalism, and became editor of the current affairs magazine *Magill*, and started writing literary essays. In the mid-1980s, Tóibín left Ireland again, this time heading for South America. He travelled around until he reached Buenos Aires, in Argentina, where he witnessed the trial of the generals after the return of civilian rule. Experiences from this trip fed into his journalism, as did observations from subsequent travels in Sudan and Egypt. Tóibín has written novels, plays, travel books, and numerous literary essays, reviews, and articles on art and politics for newspapers and magazines in Ireland, Britain, and the United States. Many of his essays have been reissued in collected anthologies.

Anthropology implies travel. Typically, the anthropologist travels to another place to do fieldwork, whether commuting to the other side of town or moving temporarily to another country far away. Increasingly, anthropologists find themselves travelling to two, even three places for one study, as the people we study are themselves on the move. Staying in one place risks missing out on an important aspect of the social life we are trying to grasp. It is clear that transnational connections through travel keep growing in number and frequency in many professions, in family ties, and in leisure pursuits such as tourism.[58] Yet, it was not until the 1990s that James Clifford encouraged anthropologists to look for "travelling cultures," while not forgetting a culture's "centres, its villages, its intense fieldsites."[59] Clifford states: "the people studied by anthropologists have seldom been homebodies. Some of them, at least, have been travellers: workers, pilgrims, explorers, religious converts"[60] Clifford argues that travel implies translation. Such cultural translation from one place to another is, of course, what travel writing is about. "Travel has an inextinguishable taint of location by class, gender, race, and a certain literariness." Clifford's description of Victorian bourgeois travellers and their entourage of guides, servants, translators, and carriers heightens our awareness of Colm Tóibín exploring the world as a lone traveller, with an interest in the world from the resident peoples' point of view. There is nothing of the imperial eye as identified by Mary Louise Pratt in Tóibín´s observations.[61]He was raised in the aftermath of British colonialism, in a family that was actively involved in the Irish nationalist struggle including the 1916 rebellion. Being a gay atheist Catholic, travelling was also a way for Tóibín to escape a deeply religious Irish society where homosexuality was still illegal until 1993.

Ireland has been the topic of travel writing since the sixteenth century according to folklorist Diarmuid Ó Giolláin, when Ireland was presented as a "notoriously unsympathetic" place.[62] These early accounts by colonists portray the Irish as an uncivilized race, and called for a "total submission and Anglicization of the Irish." By the late eighteenth century tours were rather common and appreciative accounts also started to appear, where the peasantry are depicted as devout, intelligent, and witty, as welcoming to visitors yet miserably poor. As Diarmuid Ó Giolláin notes, there have been many cross-references between travelogues and scholarly literature, and travel writing keeps providing a source for knowledge of popular culture and custom.[63] In an account by Michael Cronin on travel writing in the twentieth century, Ireland was portrayed as a pre-modern reservoir while the rest of Europe was industrializing and modernizing. Cronin also points to the remarkable development of tourism in Ireland that has attracted many travel writers, both from other countries and Ireland.

Considering travel writing in general and that of Colm Tóibín in particular, Christina Hunt Mahoney asserts that, "Compelling prose is a feature of travel writing, the travel writer's brief is to make the reader long to travel to and experience the essence of a place. Travel writing is meant to have allure, and it is often suitable for reading aloud. It may be written about political trouble spots, dangerous places, exotic locales, or tranquil terrain, but its first requirement is to urge a kinetic, and therefore emotive response."[65] Hunt Mahoney also analyzes Tóibín's style in great detail, finding a poetic, musical structure in his prose, most obvious in his use of "poetic syntax, repetition, and metrical balance."[66] Hunt Mahoney refers to this type of rhythm in prose as cadence. It is likely that it emerges from Tóibín´s interest in classical music, especially opera. He showed me piles of Brahms CDs in his study and talked about how often he plays them, particularly when he writes. Tóibín started writing poetry early, by age twelve the year his father died, and he continued for about a decade. Mostly his poetry has remained unpublished, but it seems to have been a fertile training ground for writing poetic prose.

In *Bad Blood: Walking Along the Border*, which is a literary reportage, Tóibín is on home ground. The point here is, of course, that he encounters political and religious difference along the Irish border as he journeys back and forth between Northern Ireland and the Republic of Ireland. The night before the Twelfth of July (the Protestant celebration involving marches which has a well-known violent past), Tóibín spends in the small village, Ballinamallard, in County Fermanagh in Northern Ireland where preparations were underway for its Orange parade, including a meal of sausage and bread for many people. Tóibín checks into a hotel, and puts himself to bed, but wakes up after midnight by sounds beneath the window. As he listens carefully, he hears a voice denouncing the Pope. Tóbín notes with quiet amusement that the man was not sober. Exhausted from his walking, Tóibín was resting after "drinking in Blake's, swimming in the public baths, and exerting myself as little as possible. I hadn't walked an inch, let alone a mile. Soon I would start walking again, but not yet, O Lord, not yet. Now I was in bed wondering if the man below the window had any idea that up above him was a papist from Wexford."[67]

This book stands out from his other two travel books. Although the individual chapters tell their own tales, they are organized into one long story, reporting on Tóibín's walk from Derry to Newry in the summer of 1986. Despite the political efforts to end the Troubles, tension and fear remained. Tóibín was repeatedly reminded of the situation's complexity when he listened to people from both sides of the community, and observed rituals such as marches and funerals. In one chapter entitled, "Dark Night of the Soul," Tóibín goes on the austere pilgrimage to the island of Lough Derg. The religious theme continues in his next travel book, *The Sign of the Cross*.[68] These travelogues depict a number of journeys he made across Europe between 1990 and 1994, experiencing various expressions of Catholicism in Poland, Seville, Rome, Bavaria, the Balkans, post-Communist Lithuania and Estonia, Scotland, and Ireland. Tóibín has a particular interest in religious pilgrimages and why people undertake these arduous endeavours. On a cheap flight to Lourdes on his way to Barcelona, Tóibín finds himself ironically mistaken for a priest. The hotel in Lourdes is overbooked, and the pilgrims have to share rooms. Not so Tóibín—without a word he is shown to a room of his own. He marvels to himself that the proprietress: "She, too, thought that I was a priest. This worked well and it struck me as I lay in my comfortable bed that it was something I must try again."[69] In the chapter from which the book derived its title, "The Sign of the Cross," the tone is totally different, serious and haunting, as it details how Tóibín, an "elapsed Catholic," to his surprise, is moved to make the sign of the cross in memory of his father during a group therapy session.

When Tóibín travels abroad as a journalist and reports back to Irish, British, or American magazines and newspapers, he performs the work of a cultural foreign correspondent as he translates experiences and events to these diverse readerships. Colm Tóibín is a travel and fiction writer who conveys complex issues of exile, Catholicism, and homosexuality through captivating ethnografiction.

Telling the Truth through Ethnografiction

This chapter on ethnografiction has focused on the relationship between fiction and reality, where fiction emerges as a source for cultural truth. When David Park spins a story about a truth commission in Northern Ireland, he is making a symbolic point rather than a factual one.[70] Although there never was a truth commission in Northern Ireland, there could have been one. Apart from the invented truth commission, everything else in this inside statement on the peace process can be said to be ethnografiction: from portraits of people and their relationships to the way places and politics are described.

There is another frequently mentioned point regarding telling the truth in Ireland. The Irish are indeed famous for being great storytellers, rooted in their rich oral tradition. Storytelling as a skill is honed, especially as young boys grow into men. I was well into my first fieldwork experience before I realized that people in Ireland have a way of saying one thing and meaning the opposite. Such conversational tricks are not often found in literary texts, except in the form of imaginary accounts of what has happened, could have happened, or might happen.

I have made the case for ethnografiction as a genre that can convey information about a society of the same ethnographic quality as a trained anthropologist would identify. But in order to be incorporated into an anthropological understanding, ethnografiction needs to be contextualized in a wider theoretical context. Drawing on my field experience in Ireland, I have suggested that a literary anthropological study benefits from a combined social and a textual analysis. Not only can an anthropologist learn about a society through its literature, the ideal is to be able to bring new data from literature back into social conversation to increase its value, and to discover how key concerns in a society are managed through literature. As a literary anthropologist, I find it useful to get to know a society from an anthropological perspective, not only by reading its literary texts. It is by learning a society's history, culture, and politics that I can understand its key concerns. The insights gained are then helpful when I try to discern which issues recur in literary forms, and why other issues are left out.

This chapter has focussed on two of the writers in my study of the social world of contemporary writers in Ireland: Éilís Ní Dhuibhne and Colm Tóibín. Like many women writers, Ní Dhuibhne is pursuing a woman's perspective, situated in Ireland, and like many women writers, social relations are a defining feature of her work. She considers how Irish women and constructions of femininity are caught between the contradictory forces of tradition and transition, and she explores the familial relationships between mothers and daughters and sisters, both as children and adults.

Considering writing as her career, Éilís Ní Dhuibhne enjoys national fame in Ireland, and a certain international reputation, but she is aware that by keeping the Irish form of her name, she is unlikely to have a major international breakthrough. Éilís Ní Dhuibhne is simply too difficult to pronounce, spell, and thus remember, for most non-Irish speakers. But for her, keeping her Irish name is part of the nationalist project in the Republic of Ireland, still a rather new independent nation. Irish writers who are acclaimed internationally publish mainly with British and American publishers and Colm Tóibín is one of these. His name is also Irish, but easier to pronounce and remember for English speakers. The months he spends abroad every year, in the United States, Spain, and recently in

Britain, have had a positive impact on his international reputation and career. Compared with Ní Dhuibhne, Tóibín sets his stories more often outside of Ireland, even though they might have a link back to Ireland. His ethnografiction is not limited to Irish issues, but when he writes about the politics in Barcelona after Franco or pilgrimage to Lourdes—there are connections to homosexuality and Catholicism in Ireland. Stylistically, Ní Dhuibhne's writings assume a greater familiarity with Irish society, a more local knowledge as Clifford Geertz would have said, than what those of Tóibín. Perhaps this is another factor explaining why Tóibín has a wider international readership.

Notes

Acknowledgments

This chapter is part of the project "Writing in Ireland: an Ethnographic Study of Schooling and the World of Writers," funded by the Swedish Research Council 2007-2009. Methodologically, I conducted the study through participant observation at writers' festivals and retreats, literary conferences, book launches, prize ceremonies, readings, and creative writing workshops (taught by writers in the study). I also spent time with writers informally, and collected additional data from in-depth interviews with them, as well as with publishers, editors, and agents. Literary and journalistic texts by the writers are also central to the study. An earlier version of this chapter was first delivered as The Phyllis Kaberry Commemorative Lecture, International Gender Studies Centre, University of Oxford, May 2006. The present version combines the book chapter Wulff, Helena. "Ethnografiction: Irish Relations in the Writing of Éilís Ní Dhuibhne." In *Éilís Ní Dhuibhne: Perspectives,* ed. Rebecca Pelan (Galway: Arlen House, 2009), and the journal article Wulff, Helena. "Colm Tóibín as Travel Writer." *Nordic Irish Studies,* 9 (2010): 109-116. I am grateful for permissions from *Nordic Irish Journal* and Arlen House to reprint these two articles.

1. Declan Kiberd, *Inventing Ireland: The Literature of the Modern Nation* (London: Vintage, 1996).

2. See Helena Wulff, "Literary Readings as Performance: On the Career of Contemporary Writers in the New Ireland," *Anthropological Journal of European Cultures,* 17 (2008): 98-113; Helena Wulff, "An Anthropological Perspective on Literary Arts in Ireland," In *Blackwell Companion to the Anthropology of Europe,* eds. Ullrich Kockel, Máiréad Nic Craith, and Jonas Frykman (Oxford: Wiley-Blackwell, 2012), 537-550.

3. Patrick Duffy, "Writing Ireland: Literature and Art in the Representation of Irish Place." In *In Search of Ireland,* ed. Brian Graham (London: Routledge, 1997).

4. James Wood, *How Fiction Works* (London: Jonathan Cape, 2008).

5. Peter Kloos, ed. *True Fiction: Artistic and Scientific Representations of Reality* (Amsterdam: Vrije Universiteit University Press, 1990a).

6. Peter Kloos, "Reality and Its Representations." In *True Fiction: Artistic and Scientific Representations of Reality,* ed. Peter Kloos (Amsterdam: Vrije Universiteit University Press, 1990b), 1.

7. All quotations derived from Kloos, *True Fiction,* 1.

8. All quotations derived from Kloos, *True Fiction,* 2.

9. All quotations derived from Kloos, *True Fiction,* 5.

10. Eduardo P. Archetti, "Introduction," In *Exploring the Written: Anthropology and the Multiplicity of Writing,* ed. Eduardo P. Archetti (Oslo: Scandinavian University Press, 1994), 16.

11. Archetti, "Introduction," 17.

12. Archetti, "Introduction," 13.

13. Victor Turner, "African Ritual and Western Literature: Is a Comparative Symbology Possible?" In *The Literature of Fact,* ed. Angus Fletcher. English Institute Series (New York: Columbia University Press, 1976), 45-81; Clifford Geertz, *Works and Lives: The Anthropologist as Author* (Stanford, CA: Stanford University Press, 1988); Orin, Starn, ed. *Current Anthropology,* special issue on 25th anniversary of *Writing Culture,* 2012, vol. 27, issue 3; James Clifford and George E. Marcus, eds. *Writing Culture: The Poetics and Politics of Ethnography* (Berkeley: University of California Press, 1986); Richard Handler and Daniel Segal, *Jane Austen and the Fiction of Culture: An Essay on the Narration of Social Realities* (Tucson: University of Arizona Press, 1990); Nigel Rapport, *The Prose and the Passion: Anthropology, Literature and the Writing of E. M. Forster* (Manchester: Manchester University Press, 1994); Alisse Waterson and Maria D. Vesperi, eds. *Anthropology off the Shelf: Anthropologists on Writing* (Oxford: Wiley-Blackwell, 2009); Kirin Narayan, *Alive in the Writing: Crafting Ethnography in the Company of Chekhov* (Chicago: University of Chicago Press, 2012); and Michael Jackson, *The Other Shore: Essays on Writers and Writing* (Berkeley: University of California Press, 2013).

14. Helena Wulff, *Dancing at the Crossroads: Memory and Mobility in Ireland* (Oxford: Berghahn, 2007).

15. Anne Fogarty, "Preface," In *Midwife to the Fairies* by Éilís Ní Dhuibhne (Cork: Attic Press, 2003), xii.

16. Interview with Éilís Ní Dhuibhne in Dublin, 29th March 2006.

17. Marilyn Strathern, "The Relation: Issues in Complexity and Scale." Inaugural Lecture 1994 by the William Wyse Professor of Social Anthropology (Cambridge: Prickly Pear Press, 1995), 12, 14.

18. Shirley Ardener, ed., *Perceiving Women* (London: Malaby Press, 1975); Rayna Rapp Reiter, ed., *Toward an Anthropology of Women* (New York: Monthly Review Press, 1975).

19. Ní Dhuibhne, Éilís, *The Dancers Dancing* (Belfast: The Blackstaff Press [1999b] 2007a).

20. Fogarty, "Preface," xiii.

21. Nicola Warwick, "One Woman's Writing Retreat: Éilís Ní Dhuibhne," Interview, 2001. (http://www.prairieden.com/front_porch/visiting_authors/dhuibhne.html)

22. All quotations derived from Ní Dhuibhne, Éilís, *The Dancers Dancing,* 221.

23. Ní Dhuibhne, *The Dancers Dancing,* 221.

24. Ní Dhuibhne, *The Dancers Dancing,* 223.

25. All quotations derived from Ní Dhuibhne, *The Dancers Dancing,* 223.

26. Ní Dhuibhne, Éilís, "Midwife to the Fairies." In *Midwife to the Fairies* (Cork: Attic Press, 2003b).

27. Fogarty, "Preface," xi.

28. Ní Dhuibhne, "Midwife," 28.

29. Diane Purkiss, *Troublesome Things: A History of Fairies and Fairy Stories* (London: Penguin, 2001).

Ethnografiction and Reality in Contemporary Irish Literature 221

30. Interview with Éilís Ní Dhuibhne, Dublin, 29th March 2006; Ní Dhuibhne, Éilís, *The Bray House* (Dublin: Attic Press, 1990).

31. Fogarty, "Preface," xi.

32. Interview with Éilís Ní Dhuibhne, Dublin, 29th March 2006.

33. David Pierce, *Irish Writing in the Twentieth Century: A Reader* (Cork: Cork University Press, 2000), 1267-1281.

34. Ní Dhuibhne, Éilís, *Voices on the Wind: Women Poets of the Celtic Twilight* (Dublin: New Island Books, 1995a).

35. Ní Dhuibhne, *Voices*, 11.

36. All quotations derived from Ní Dhuibhne, *Voices*, 16.

37. Angela Bourke, et al. eds., *The Field Day Anthology of Irish Women's Writing and Traditions, Volumes IV and V* (Cork: Cork University Press, 2002).

38. Janet Madden-Simpson, ed., *Woman's Part: An Anthology of Short Fiction By and About Irish Women 1890-1960* (Dublin: Arlen House, 1984); Ruth Hooley, ed., *The Female Line: Northern Irish Women Writers* (Belfast: Northern Ireland Women's Rights Movement, 1985); Ailbhe, Smyth, ed. *Wildish Things: An Anthology of New Irish Women's Writing* (Dublin: Attic Press, 1990); Rebecca Pelan, *Two Irelands: Literary Feminisms North and South* (New York: Syracuse University Press, 2005); Patricia Boyle Haberstroh, and Christine St. Peter, eds., *Opening the Field: Irish Women, Texts and Contexts* (Cork: Cork University Press, 2007).

39. Interview with Éilís Ní Dhuibhne, Dublin 29th March 2006.

40. Interview with Éilís Ní Dhuibhne, Dublin 29th March 2006.

41. Ní Dhuibhne, Éilís, "The Catechism Examination," In *Midwife to the Fairies* (Cork: Attic Press, 2003c), 48.

42. All quotations derived from Ní Dhuibhne, "The Catechism," 46.

43. Ní Dhuibhne, Éilís, "Wuff Wuff Wuff for de Valera." In *Midwife to the Fairies* (Cork: Attic Press, 2003d).

44. All quotations derived from Ní Dhuibhne, "Wuff," 3, 4.

45. Ní Dhuibhne, Éilís, "The Irish." In *Europeans: Essays on Culture and Identity*, eds. Åke Daun and Sören Jansson (Lund: Nordic Academic Press, 1999a), 53.

46. All quotations derived from Ní Dhuibhne, "The Irish," 53, 54.

47. Ní Dhuibhne, Éilís, *Fox, Swallow, Scarecrow* (Belfast: Blackstaff Press, 2007b), 45.

48. Warwick, "One Woman's," 4.

49. Colm Tóibín, *Brooklyn: A Novel* (New York: Scribner Book Company, 2009).

50. Colm Tóibín, *The Master* (London: Picador, 2004).

51. Colm Tóibín, *Bad Blood: A Walk Along the Irish Border* (London: Picador [1987] 2001a).

52. Colm Tóibín, *The Sign of the Cross: Travels in Catholic Europe* (London: Picador [1994] 2001b).

53. Colm Tóibín, *Homage to Barcelona* (London: Picador [1990] 2001c); George Orwell, *Homage to Catalonia* (London: Secker and Warburg, 1938).

54. Fintan O'Toole, "Perpetual Motion." In *Arguing at the Crossroads: Essays on a Changing Ireland*, eds. Paul Brennan and Catherine de Saint Phalle (Dublin: New Island Books, 1997), 77.

55. Interview with Colm Tóibín, Dublin 26th May 2008.

56. Interview with Colm Tóibín, Dublin 26th May 2008.

57. Ulf Hannerz, "Cosmopolitans and Locals in World Culture," In *Global Culture: Nationalism, Globalization and Modernity* ed. Mike Featherston (London: Sage, 1991), 239.

58. Ulf Hannerz, Transnational *Connections: Culture, People, Places* (London: Routledge, 1996).

59. James Clifford, "Traveling Cultures," In *Routes: Travel and Translation in the late Twentieth Century* (Cambridge, Mass.: Harvard University Press, 1997), 25.

60. Clifford, "Traveling Cultures," 19.

61. Mary Louse Pratt, *Imperial Eyes: Travel Writing and Transculturation* (London: Routledge, 1992).

62. Diarmuid Ó Giolláin, *Locating Irish Folklore: Tradition, Modernity, Identity* (Cork: Cork University Press, 2000), 38.

63. All quotations derived from Ó Giolláin, "Locating," 38.

64. Michael Cronin, "Travel writers on Ireland." In *The Enycylopedia of Ireland*, ed. Brian Lalor (New Haven: Yale University Press, 2003), 1074-1075.

65. Christina Hunt Mahoney, "The Poet Tóibín: Cadence, Incantation, Imitation." In *Reading Colm Tóibín*, ed. Paul Delaney (Dublin: The Liffey Press, 2008), 98-99.

66. Hunt Mahoney, "The Poet Tóibín," 98.

67. Tóibín, *Bad Blood*, 53.

68. Colm Tóibín, "Dark Night of the Soul," In *Bad Blood: A Walk along the Irish Border* (London: Picador, [1987] 2001d).

69. Tóibín, "Dark Night," 9.

70. David Park, *The Truth Commissioner* (London: Bloomsbury, 2008).

References

Archetti, Eduardo P.
1994   "Introduction." In *Exploring the Written: Anthropology and the Multiplicity of Writing*. Eduardo P. Archetti, ed. Pp 11-28. Oslo: Scandinavian University Press.

Ardener, Shirley, ed.
1975   *Perceiving Women*. London: Malaby Press.

Bourke, Angela et al. eds.,
2002   *The Field Day Anthology of Irish Women's Writing and Traditions Volumes IV and V*. Cork: Cork University Press.

Boyle Haberstroh, Patricia and Christine St. Peter, eds.
2007   *Opening the Field: Irish Women, Texts and Contexts*. Cork: Cork University Press.

Clifford, James
1997   "Traveling Cultures." In *Routes: Travel and Translation in the late Twentieth Century*. James Clifford, ed. Pp. 17-46. Cambridge, MA: Harvard University Press.

Clifford, James and George E. Marcus, eds.
1986   *Writing Culture: The Poetics and Politics of Ethnography*. Berkeley: University of California Press.

Cronin, Michael
2003   "Travel Writers on Ireland." In *The Encyclopedia of Ireland*. Brian Lalor, ed. Pp. 1074-1075. New Haven: Yale University Press.

Duffy, Patrick J.
1997   "Writing Ireland: Literature and Art in the Representation of Irish Place." In *In Search of Ireland*. Brian Graham, ed. Pp. 64-86. London: Routledge.

Fogarty, Anne

2003   "Preface." In *Midwife to the Fairies* by Éilís Ní Dhuibhne. Pp. ix-xv. Cork: Attic Press.

Geertz, Clifford
1983   *Local Knowledge: Further Essays in Interpretive Anthropology*. New York: Basic Books.
1988   *Works and Lives: The Anthropologist as Author*. Stanford, CA: Stanford University Press.

Handler, Richard and Daniel Segal
1990   *Jane Austen and the Fiction of Culture: An Essay on the Narration of Social Realities*. Tucson: University of Arizona Press.

Hannerz, Ulf
1991   "Cosmopolitans and Locals in World Culture." In *Global Culture: Nationalism, Globalization and Modernity*. Mike Featherstone, ed. Pp. 237-251. London: Sage.
1996   *Transnational Connections: Culture, People, Places*. London: Routledge.

Hooley, Ruth, ed.
1985   *The Female Line: Northern Irish Women Writers*. Belfast: Northern Ireland Women's Rights Movement.

Hunt Mahony, Christina
2008   "The Poet Tóibín: Cadence, Incantation, Imitation." In *Reading Colm Tóibín*. Paul Delaney, ed. Pp. 97-113. Dublin: The Liffey Press.

Jackson, Michael
2013   *The Other Shore: Essays on Writers and Writing*. Berkeley: University of California Press.

Kiberd, Declan
1996   *Inventing Ireland: The Literature of the Modern Nation*. London: Vintage.

Kloos, Peter, ed.
1990a   *True Fiction: Artistic and Scientific Representations of Reality*. Amsterdam: Vrije Universiteit University Press.
1990b   "Reality and Its Representations." In *True Fiction: Artistic and Scientific Representations of Reality*. Peter Kloos, ed. Pp. 1-6. Amsterdam: Vrije Universiteit University Press

Madden-Simpson, Janet, ed.
1984   *Woman's Part: An Anthology of Short Fiction By and About Irish Women 1890-1960*. Dublin: Arlen House.

Narayan, Kirin
2012   *Alive in the Writing: Crafting Ethnography in the Company of Chekhov*. Chicago: University of Chicago Press.

Ní Dhuibhne, Éilís
1990   *The Bray House*. Dublin: Attic Press.
1995a   *Voices on the Wind: Women Poets of the Celtic Twilight*. Dublin: New Island Books.
1999a   "The Irish." In *Europeans: Essays on Culture and Identity*. Åke Daun and Sören Jansson, eds. Pp. 47-65. Lund: Nordic Academic Press.

Ní Dhuibhne, Éilís, ed.
1995b   "Introduction." In *Voices on the Wind: Women Poets of the Celtic Twilight*. Éilís Ní Dhuibhne, ed. Pp. 9-14. Dublin: New Island Books.
2003a   *Midwife to the Fairies*. Cork: Attic Press.
2003b   "Midwife to the Fairies." In *Midwife to the Fairies*. Pp. 22-30. Cork: Attic Press.

2003c "The Catechism Examination." In *Midwife to the Fairies*. Pp. 44-51. Cork: Attic Press.

2003d "Wuff Wuff Wuff for de Valera." In *Midwife to the Fairies*. Pp. 1-8. Cork: Attic Press.

2007a [1999b] *The Dancers Dancing*. Belfast: The Blackstaff Press.

2007b *Fox, Swallow, Scarecrow*. Belfast: Blackstaff Press.

Ó Giolláin, Diarmuid

2000 *Locating Irish Folklore: Tradition, Modernity, Identity*. Cork: Cork University Press.

Orin, Starn, ed.

2012 *Current Anthropology*, special issue on the 25th anniversary of *Writing Culture*, Vol. 27, issue 3.

Orwell, George

1938 *Homage to Catalonia*. London: Secker and Warburg.

O'Toole, Fintan

1997 "Perpetual Motion." In *Arguing at the Crossroads: Essays on a Changing Ireland*. Paul Brennan and Catherine de Saint Phalle, eds. Pp. 77-97. Dublin: New Island Books.

Park, David

2008 *The Truth Commissioner*. London: Bloomsbury.

Pelan, Rebecca

2005 *Two Irelands: Literary Feminisms North and South*. New York: Syracuse University Press.

Pierce, David

2000 *Irish Writing in the Twentieth Century: A Reader*. Cork: Cork University Press.

Pratt, Mary Louise

1992 *Imperial Eyes: Travel Writing and Transculturation*. London: Routledge.

Purkiss, Diane

2001 *Troublesome Things: A History of Fairies and Fairy Stories*. London: Penguin.

Rapport, Nigel

1994 *The Prose and the Passion: Anthropology, Literature and the Writing of E. M. Forster*. Manchester: Manchester University Press.

Reiter, Rayna Rapp, ed.

1975 *Toward an Anthropology of Women*. New York: Monthly Review Press.

Strathern, Marilyn

1995 "The Relation: Issues in Complexity and Scale." Inaugural Lecture 1994 by the William Wyse Professor of Social Anthropology. Cambridge: Prickly Pear Press.

Smyth, Ailbhe, ed.

1990 *Wildish Things: An Anthology of New Irish Women's Writing*. Dublin: Attic Press.

Tóibín, Colm

[1987] 2001a *Bad Blood: A Walk Along the Irish Border*. London: Picador.

[1994] 2001b *The Sign of the Cross: Travels in Catholic Europe*. London: Picador.

[1990] 2001c *Homage to Barcelona*. London: Picador.

[1987] 2001d "Dark Night of the Soul." In *Bad Blood: A Walk Along the Irish Border*. Pp. 30-44. London: Picador.

2004 *The Master*. London: Picador.

2009   *Brooklyn: A Novel.* New York: Scribner Book Company.
Turner, Victor
    1976   "African Ritual and Western Literature: Is a Comparative Symbology Possible?" In *The Literature of Fact: Selected Papers from the English Institute.* Angus Fletcher, ed. Pp. 45-81. English Institute Series. New York: Columbia University Press.
Waterson, Alisse and Maria D. Vesperi, eds.
    2009   *Anthropology off the Shelf: Anthropologists on Writing.* Oxford: Wiley-Blackwell.
Warwick, Nicola
    2001   One Woman's Writing Retreat: Éilís Ní Dhuibhne Interview. (http://www.prairieden.com/front_porch/visiting_authors/dhuibhne.html)
Wood, James
    2008   *How Fiction Works.* London: Jonathan Cape.
Wulff, Helena
    2007   *Dancing at the Crossroads: Memory and Mobility in Ireland.* Oxford: Berghahn.
    2008   "Literary Readings as Performance: On the Career of Contemporary Writers in the New Ireland." *Anthropological Journal of European Cultures,* 17: 98-113.
    2012   "An Anthropological Perspective on Literary Arts in Ireland." In *Blackwell Companion to the Anthropology of Europe.* Ullrich Kockel, Máiréad Nic Craith, and Jonas Frykman, eds. Pp. 537-550. Oxford: Wiley-Blackwell.

Chapter 8

Engaging Students with Fiction, Memoirs, and Film

WARD KEELER

Students enter a classroom today carrying so many instruments with which to distract themselves that simply keeping their eyes looking to the front of the room presents a challenge. I find myself wanting to police them. Yet positive sanctions usually work better than negative ones: rather than forbidding them from using all those gadgets, or at least in addition to telling them not to do so, it behooves me to try to find ways to make them *want* to pay attention to what I put before them. An effective means I have found to accomplish this is to show them that novels and short stories, memoirs, and commercial films all contain compelling anthropological information. Even if reading ethnographic monographs arouses little interest among students, learning how people in other parts of the world live their lives, talk about their world, and think about their social relations does. Fiction, memoirs, and films, all convey that material—to those, at least, who have been shown how to look for it—and do so in a relatively accessible and engaging way.

Students, in other words, are susceptible to what I consider anthropology's strongest drawing card: its ability to satisfy our curiosity about how other people in the world might think and act. Especially since few undergraduates intend to major in anthropology, let alone go on to professional careers as anthropologists, I have come to re-conceive my responsibilities as a teacher of anthropology. Instead of acquainting undergraduates with the most important new work in the field, I ask them to read or watch materials that I think will intrigue them the most: writing and film that will most compellingly play upon the interest they have in other people's lives.

What this means in practical terms is that I assign students very little by way of anthropological texts to read, relying instead on fictional materials—whether literary or cinematic—and memoirs, most of them produced by people from societies far removed from our own. I use class time to draw students' attention to conceptual matters that come up repeatedly in the various materials they encounter. Many students (including some anthropology majors) inform me this

227

technique leaves a more lasting impression upon them than academic journal articles and monographs would be likely to achieve.

In what follows, I do not provide a bibliography of readings that might be used to teach in the way that I outline here. Instead, I wish to illustrate, by discussing just a few titles, how memoirs, fiction, and film, can be used to illuminate important topics in anthropology. I base this account on two courses I teach quite regularly at the University of Texas: a lower division course, "An Introduction to Expressive Culture," and an upper division one, "Cultures of Southeast Asia." In keeping with this volume's focus on how fiction can afford illuminating anthropological insights, I begin with the latter course, since it is the course in which I draw upon written materials, before going on to consider the approach I use for the lower-division one, in which I use commercial films from around the world to teach students how to look with an anthropological eye at mass-mediated fictions.

Southeast Asia through Novels and Memoirs

Contrary to what most students would probably prefer, at least at the outset, I do not rely on short stories when I select readings to assign about Southeast Asia. Short stories are published pervasively in contemporary Southeast Asia, and a fair number have now been translated into English. It would actually be truer to most Southeast Asians' reading experience to assign such stories to my students. Yet I opt for full-length novels and extended memoirs instead, because only in such works do students see a fair segment of a society depicted in real depth. Since it is attending to the all-embracing nature of people's social worlds that distinguishes anthropology from, say, *National Geographic*, I prefer to impose relatively long reading assignments on students rather than settle for brief, more pointed texts. Of course, short stories also make excellent teaching tools, and teachers of lower division college courses or high school may not be able to assign a great number of pages, in which case assigning short stories might turn out to provide a reasonable substitute. Nevertheless, if teachers can still expect their students to read *The Adventures of Huckleberry Finn* (see David Surrey, this volume), there is no reason in principle they can not ask their students to devote as much effort to reading a Southeast Asian text. I would urge teachers to stand firm against our students' supposed brief attention spans. A surprising number of our students have no trouble keeping the pages turning if the pages contain enough good stories to compete successfully with the web and television.

One other prefatory remark is in order. I teach at a large university, but it happens that we have no specialist on Southeast Asian history. I try therefore to give students a sense not just of how Southeast Asia is today but also of what it was like in the past (as far back as the late nineteenth century or as recently as the 1960s and 1970s) and of how the past is implicated in the present. I no longer assign a history textbook, since that would increase their already heavy reading load and make students plow through a text few of them would enjoy (no matter how good for them I told them it would be). In lecture, I provide outline histories of particular places to complement the readings students are doing at any given point in the course, and I draw students' attention to general commonalities in such historical forces as royal efforts to enlarge their spheres of influence, and colonial efforts to impose bureaucratic control over indigenous populations. Students do not come away with a deep grasp of Southeast Asia's history, but I hope they do come to appreciate what some major issues in Southeast Asian history have been.

Malay Villagers

A great many Southeast Asians live on the land, and students should get some sense of what life is like in lowland agrarian villages. James Scott's magisterial *Weapons of the Weak*[1] springs to mind as both a vivid account of a representative (and changing) village and as a powerful contribution to theoretical issues that farmers' lives raise. Nevertheless, I find students respond more enthusiastically to Douglas Raybeck's very accessible *Mad Dogs, Englishmen, and the Errant Anthropologist.*[2] Raybeck is as interested in describing the experience of doing fieldwork as in describing a Malay village, so the text is more an anthropologist's memoir than a straightforward ethnography. Indeed, much that is important about Malay social life gets mentioned but receives only cursory comment. Still, the many good stories Raybeck relates provide excellent material for class discussion, and while the fieldwork on which the book is based was done in the 1960s, most of what Raybeck has to say remains relevant to contemporary Southeast Asian villagers' lives.

Raybeck's often entertaining stories about his and his wife's experiences as new residents of a Malaysian village convey to students what happens when well-meaning but clueless young Americans find themselves on new cultural terrain. Western assumptions about privacy do not obtain; a village's more marginal ("sketchier") figures may be the first to befriend outsiders, to the confusion of the latter and the amusement of everyone else; and participating in illicit behavior (such as petty smuggling operations) goes a long way to making an anthropologist come to be regarded as an insider (in line with what Michael Herzfeld has taught us to call "cultural intimacy").[3] More important themes, concerning such matters as interactional styles, gender, governance, and social standing, are well-illustrated in Raybeck's book by means of anecdotes in which specific individuals act in characteristic ways, that is, in ways that make sense in light of Malay ideological assumptions.

Raybeck is at pains to make clear how much Malay villagers value smooth, conflict-free social relations, what he calls "harmony." The inclination to praise individuals who dissemble irritation and respond to provocative behavior with patience and restraint, and to condemn displays of temper even in the face of outrageous acts, is common to most lowland Southeast Asian societies. It applies to both men and women with equal force. Yet the very validation of discretion and self-restraint makes breaking the rule all the more startling—and effective. Raybeck recounts the story of a young village woman whose destitute parents arranged for her to marry an elderly man for the obvious reason that he was willing to pay an unusually generous bride-price. A few months later, desirous of a divorce but apparently unable to win her husband's consent, the young woman proceeded to pronounce her complaints about his character not in the whispers with which domestic conflict should be expressed but rather in a loud voice as she sat on the porch, upbraiding her husband who remained inside the house! Three days of this behavior won her her divorce. Raybeck relates this story to illustrate the relatively high degree of agency and room to maneuver that Malay women enjoy. The story makes vivid, in a way that the several paragraphs of sociological generalization in which it is embedded cannot, the fact that individuals are rarely helpless in the face of norms and social conventions— certainly not Southeast Asian women, no matter how much received opinion insists that they be modest and self-effacing.

What Raybeck seems not to appreciate adequately is how much hierarchical concerns inform Malay villagers' behavior. He refers often to the Malay concept of *malu*, usually translated "shame" in English (although Clifford Geertz famously translated the Balinese equivalent, *lek*, as "stagefright").[4] He cites a villager, Hussein, who said that he avoided asking someone for a favor if the request was likely to be refused, since a refusal would make him *malu*.

> [Hussein] said that to this date he has not yet asked his nephew for the loan of his car. He says the relationship is part of the reason he hasn't asked: "If a person who isn't a relative refuses something, then you are not too embarrassed and don't take it too hard. But if a nephew refuses, it is very awkward and creates a problem."[5]

The problem here—one that Raybeck does not note—is that Hussein, as an elder relative, enjoyed ipso facto higher standing than his nephew and so should have been accorded respect, and unquestioned access to his nephew's car, as a matter of course. Yet the fact that Hussein's nephew owned a car and he did not already introduced an anomaly in their relative positions. For Hussein then to place himself in the position of suppliant to his nephew would be demeaning, and if his nephew could not be counted on to grant the request, the risk of humiliation was simply too great. Much later in the book, reporting his departure along with his wife from the village, Raybeck mentions that Hussein drove them to the airport in his nephew's car. "You may recall that Hussein had feared to borrow his nephew's car because of the possibility of embarrassment. This was the first time he had done so, and we felt appropriately honored."[6] Raybeck, although aware of the honor accorded him and his wife, seems oblivious to the fact that Hussein could count on his nephew to grant the request because two very high status individuals—the Raybecks—were going to be riding in the car. Providing transportation to the foreign guests reflected well on the standing of both Hussein and his nephew.

Here as elsewhere, Raybeck fails to see, or at least to draw attention to the fact, that much of what he observes about Malay emotions, such as *malu*, which he compares to embarrassment (but which, he adds, "is to embarrassment as tsunamis are to wavelets"[7]), turns on Malay villagers' preoccupation with relative social standing. The same applies to their emphasis on harmony, and to many other patterns Raybeck notes about their social relations. People suffer *malu* when they themselves or others fail to behave appropriately in light of their status relative to others. "Harmony" obtains when everyone knows their place; conflict arises when people disagree as to their standing vis-à-vis one another. Raybeck may sense this point but he does not state it explicitly, leaving it to readers to infer its pervasive significance. At many points, readers must, like alert readers of fiction, put incidents together and trace out their significance without relying on the author to provide explicit comment.

Thai Aristocrats and Nuns

Urban, aristocratic circles are, in Southeast Asia as elsewhere, highly restrictive and unrepresentative by definition. In a way, that is the whole point. But royal courts have long shaped the history and imaginings of lowland societies in the region. Kukrit Pramoj's long and charming novel, *Four Reigns*, makes the preoccupations of that milieu vivid, and if not familiar, at least intelligible.[8] It takes as its subject the life of one aristocratic woman as she experiences the reigns of King Chulalongkorn (r. 1868-1910) and his three successors. From this apparently narrow perspective, the novel dramatizes seismic shifts in Thai history over a period of about sixty years. Kukrit renders the stressful, if exciting, changes in Thai society taking place during this period by following the lives of his aristocratic protagonist, her husband and children, and other kin and acquaintances. Students shriek when I tell them on the first class day that the book is 656 pages long, and the faint-hearted can be seen heading for the door. But few students are immune to the book's period charm and melodramatic narrative once they get started—and the print is large and the pages short, so it is not as daunting a task as it first appears.

Perhaps not surprisingly, the novel's male author portrays the book's central character, Phloi, in conventionally idealizing ways: she is a paragon of Thai womanhood, respectful to her elders, devoted to her husband and children, generous and forgiving even to those who have treated her badly. Well-behaved women, as we know, rarely make history, or for that matter make for interesting stories. But Phloi is not a mealy-mouthed heroine on the order of Esther in Charles Dickens' *Bleakhouse*. Naïve, well-meaning, but insulated from the world beyond aristocratic circles, she is a useful device with which Kukrit can register responses to the changes going on in Thai society.

We watch Phloi come slowly to understand that relations between Thai kings and their subjects are changing. Toward King Chulalangkorn, she evinces absolute devotion and submission. But the awe, verging on dread, with which subjects looked upon—but in fact, never actually at—their monarch was deliberately undermined by Chulalangkorn's successor, Vajiravudh, who went so far as to appear on stage in a performance to which members of the aristocracy were invited. By novel's end, the "democratic revolution of 1932" has radically, if controversially, reduced the monarchy's power, and the young man who returns to Thailand from Europe in 1945 to assume the throne enjoys not so much veneration as the public's solicitous, avuncular regard. Phloi's death in the last pages of the novel coincides with that young king's shocking death in 1946, officially an accident but never satisfactorily explained. (To this day it is a legally actionable offense to suggest it may have been anything else.)

Thai political developments in the first few decades of the twentieth century, wherein younger, Western-educated members of the elite agitated for more progressive forms of governance, are personified in the novel by the differences and conflicts among Phloi's sons. One of them returns from France and joins—to his mother's utter bafflement—the faction pressing for political change, a faction that succeeded eventually in reducing the king's absolute powers during the third of the novel's four reigns (in 1932). That son's elder half-brother (his father's son, by a concubine, whom Phloi generously raises as her own child) allies with the conservative royalist faction that mounts a failed countercoup. Another, younger brother, educated in Great Britain, understands his mother's feelings much better. (It is surely no accident that the more radical brother was educated in France, among heirs to an anti-monarchist revolution, whereas the gentler, more tolerant brother was educated in a society where, in the early twentieth century, the aristocracy retained much of its prestige and authority.) Indeed, the younger brother's fondness for good food, for pleasantly smooth interaction, and for the inconsequential "fun" Thais, including his mother, prize, makes him closer to her emotionally as well as ideologically. Yet in a telling scene, he contests his brother's politics, and points out that if his elder brother holds it against him that he, a younger sibling, should question his opinions, he is failing to apply his egalitarian notions to his own personal relations. This exchange illustrates vividly—by countering—a still widespread inclination among many Southeast Asian parents: to try to instill a sense of hierarchical difference even among full siblings. Only if elder siblings realize, in this view, that they are responsible for their younger siblings' welfare, and younger siblings realize that they, in turn, must offer their elder siblings deference and service, will bonds among them prove long-lasting and resilient. Lacking such feelings, siblings, and brothers especially, are thought likely to compete with one another—and eventually grow apart.

Although Phloi constitutes an idealized portrait of the modest and caring Thai woman, gender receives interesting (if conservative) treatment in the contrast between her and her sole daughter. Phloi, after an initial, ill-fated infatuation, graciously, and indeed happily, entrusts her marriage plans to her elders. They advise her to accept the attentions of a young nobleman who takes a shine to her, and their marriage turns out to be both socially appropriate and personally harmonious. Eventually, Phloi urges her husband to take on a concubine or junior wife, sensing that it would rejuvenate him: here we have a rose-colored rendering of a practice that was, already at the start of the twentieth century, arousing bitter controversy among the Thai newspaper-reading public.[9] Conveniently—this spares the novelist some complications that might otherwise be assumed to ensue—her husband rejects the suggestion. Unlike Phloi, their daughter marries not under the supervision of her elders but rather for love, to her own eventual dissatisfaction and divorce. Readers are left to infer that headstrong young people who are caught up in the allure of the modern (which includes the practice of choosing one's own spouse) risk falling victim to their own impetuousness. Suggesting not just such conservative attitudes but a more disturbingly reactionary streak on the part of the author, there are unpleasant whiffs of racist stereotypes in the novel's intimation that the Sino-Thai son-in-law values profits over kin ties when he tries to make some easy money on the basis of his ailing mother-in-law's need for medicine.

Precisely because *Four Reigns* looks with such sustained nostalgia at an idealized Thai past—more easily idealized because its focus on the privileged few hides from view the poverty and frustrations that have long troubled the lives of Thai commoners—its conservatism points up contrasts between long-standing Thai understandings of appropriate behavior and current assumptions as to what constitutes a good and reasonable life. The novel was enormously popular when it was first serialized in the early 1950s and continues to exert great appeal among middle-class Thais, having been both serialized on television and, more recently, mounted as a musical for the Bangkok stage. Even if the prestige of the Thai monarchy stands under some threat in light of the current crown prince's manifest unpopularity, I suspect that the novel's sepia-tinted depiction of an orderly and resolutely unmodern Thai society will retain its cachet for a while yet.

Not quite an autobiography, but something very close to it, is Sid Brown's remarkable short book, *The Journey of One Buddhist Nun: Even Against the Wind*, the result, she tells us, of an exchange she made with a young Thai Buddhist nun: the latter recounted her life story in Thai in exchange for English lessons.[10] Interleaved with Brown's contextualizing comments, but for the most standing as an unanalyzed, and for that reason all the more intriguing, recollection of how a young woman came to give up life in the world, the book conveys the extraordinary complexity of an ordinary woman's struggle to reconcile spiritual and social needs in a particular family in a particular place. Buddhism, students thereby come to see, constitutes not a set of obscure texts about an abstruse ontology but rather a set of practices, at once constraining and freeing, for those individuals who find its ideals compelling.

Gender concerns come up throughout the text, as the Thai nun, Wabi, relates the onerous burden her kin placed upon her as a woman (not yet a nun), both when she had to take care of her siblings after their father deserted them, and after when her sister had children and presumed upon Wabi to help tend to them.

She must also constantly contend with Thai prejudices against women taking up a religious vocation, rather than marrying and raising children. Not unrelated to this point is the fact that many of the experiences Wabi has in meditation implicate sex: noteworthy are the visits made to her (in visions) of a red-haired foreigner named Joey who is in love with her and wishes to marry her. She refuses him just as she has rejected the attentions of corporeal (as opposed to halucinatory) suitors in the past. Yet this is not just an ethnography of Buddhist nuns; it is also a Buddhist ethnography. Brown relates Wabi's statements, whether about Joey or about other strange experiences, without further comment. We can make what we wish of them, but Brown is not going to apply the depth-psychological analytical tools that many Western readers would be inclined to bring to bear upon them. Indeed, Wabi's account of why she chose to "go forth" as a nun places equal weight on the stresses she experienced as a woman living in Thai society and on the attraction she felt to spiritual pursuits. Brown treats these motivating factors with similar even-handedness.

Two dramatic incidents in Wabi's life do not concern her relations with her kin but rather with other religious women. In both instances, we see that Wabi has felt herself unjustly criticized, and in both instances, her reaction is to become immensely troubled—and to suffer her distress in agonized silence. The second incident hinges on Wabi feeling attacked by a teacher whom she, Wabi, cannot possibly argue with, since a student must never contradict a teacher's words. The extreme nature of her response—she is incapacitated in both cases, and very nearly abandons her religious vocation altogether—would appear to call out for interpretations based upon how the incidents resonated with her early family experience, particularly the troubled relationship she had with her mother. She herself prefers to reflect on the events only with respect to how they entered into her spiritual practice, especially of meditation, a discursive turn with which Brown appears to be fully satisfied. Yet even putting aside psychological musing, which would of course remain speculative, we can note the way that hierarchical constraints shape Wabi's experience. Having felt cared for by her religious superiors and then unjustly attacked, Wabi comes to question the entire Buddhist institution she has made the center of her life. She resolves the crisis only by opting to rely less upon her teachers and her friendships and more upon her own training and schooling. In other words, she opts out of hierarchy, as elaborated in Thai society and in Buddhist institutions, at least to a degree, and so opts out of the reliance upon learned superiors it implies. She does so by reducing her affective attachments. This is a very Buddhist, and very Southeast Asian, move.

Urban and Rural Vietnamese

It was a shock for me to realize a few years ago that more years had passed since the end of the war in Vietnam than had passed since the end of World War II when I was an undergraduate in the sixties. No wonder my students had so little notion of what had gone on! And no wonder they found the passion with which I discussed the war—the defining event of my early adulthood—so puzzling, and maybe even embarrassing. Yet many students are interested to learn about a conflict they have heard about, and which comes in for frequent mention relative to the United State's recent military actions in the Middle East. To make the war more than an unfortunate moment in American diplomatic history, to give it historical and sociological depth, *The Sacred Willow: Four Generations in the Life of a Vietnamese Family*, Mai Elliott's family chronicle, proves immensely useful.[11] Like *Four Reigns*, this is history as lived by members of the urban elite: mandarins, members of the upper reaches of the colonial bureaucracy, successful businesswomen, advisors to the Americans, debutante girls at school, etc. But these are individuals who, when confronted with momentous choices, acted variously, some throwing in their lot with communists, others with the colonizers and their domestic and American replacements, while still others, including the author herself, experienced ever increasing disarray. The effect is to convey an immense panorama with vivid—sometimes astonishing, sometimes harrowing—details. Also like *Four Reigns*, *The Sacred Willow* is very long (and the pages in this case are not short). But it is such a gripping read that some students have told me they stayed up late on weekends to read it.

Because Elliott provides us such rich and frank accounts of her family's history, readers have a chance not only to follow her own remarkable trajectory, from daughter of an elite, French-educated member of the French colonial bureaucracy to wife of an American social scientist, but also to come up with alternative readings of what she reports. It is startling, as well as intriguing, to learn at the very outset that this Cornell-trained, highly literate, and long-term resident of the United States treats a story about the influence of a long-dead ancestor upon several generations of her family's history without a shred of irony or skepticism. It is as though the pair of voices in Sid Brown's book, that of the indigenous believer and that of the foreign researcher, were combined into a single, compelling, and occasionally surprising voice. Some readers may want to challenge Elliott's treatment of her father's collaboration, first with the French colonial bureaucrats and then with the United States-supported, deeply corrupt, and violent Ngo Dien Diem regime, as overly indulgent. Her account of the absolutely unflinching dedication to the nationalist and communist cause that one of her sisters shows, to the detriment, one has to assume, of the young children from whom she was separated for long periods, may strike some readers as idealizing. Yet we are given such a wealth of fascinating material that we should be grateful to Elliott for the chance she gives us to formulate alternative readings of her memoir. Above all, the skill with which she relates the vagaries of so many people's lives makes the terrible consequences of the years and years of war immediate, and deeply chilling.

To complement Elliott's primarily urban perspective, I have used selections from Trullinger's excellent (but sadly, out of print) *Village at War*.[12] Trullinger recounts the experiences of villagers who saw a large swathe of their village taken over to set up a base for the United States' 101st Airborne Division. The narrow focus enables Trullinger to quote individual villagers as they make very clear just what opportunities and what horrors ensue when a horde of American GIs suddenly appears in one's midst. This text is as close as the students come to straightforward social science. It is written in a very matter-of-fact style, but the contents are searingly vivid—and they resonate tellingly, if disturbingly, with the United States' military involvements in Iraq and Afghanistan.

Modernizing Indonesians

Anthropologists, along with most other social scientists, were alerted to the puzzling nature of nationalism, as well as its importance, about thirty years ago, when such authors as Benedict Anderson and Ernest Gellner published their groundbreaking works on the topic.[13] Raybeck's and Kukrit's books make oblique reference to the effects political developments at the national level have in specific people's lives in Malaysia and Thailand, respectively. Elliott's book, by raising the question of just what sort of struggle Vietnamese were engaged in during much of the mid-twentieth century, brings the matter into clearer focus.

What nationalism might mean in a former colony in Southeast Asia is addressed even more pointedly in some Indonesian novels. Pramoedya Ananta Toer's magnificent *Buru Quartet*, a four-volume fictionalized chronicle of an early Indonesian nationalist's life, would be an ideal way to engage the issue, except that its virtues—its complexity and length—rule out its inclusion in any syllabus I can imagine.[14] Having students read the first volume alone (*This Earth of Mankind*) goes a certain way toward introducing important points, particularly how experiencing colonialism can be at once an exciting and a humiliating exercise.[15] But the novel's plotting creaks a little and the drama that drives the action in the first volume reaches no resolution until the end of the following novel (*Child of All Nations*).[16] As a result, I have gone back and forth on whether to include Pramoedya on reading lists. Another Indonesian novel, Mangunwijaya's *Durga Umayi*, which I translated and annotated, provides a brief, wickedly irreverent account of Indonesia's nationalist struggle against its Dutch colonial rulers, an account altogether dismissive of nationalist pieties but one that probably gives a more realistic sense of what any armed conflict looks like on the ground than do grand nationalist mythologies.[17] The novel also describes, in a magical realist style, the tragedies and ironies of Indonesia's postcolonial history by following the adventures of a resourceful woman who makes her way in a highly corrupt, rapidly modernizing society. This conceit of a woman trying to keep her footing despite the sudden shifts in Indonesia's vertiginous history enables the novelist to make bold reference to the horrific, state-sponsored violence against huge numbers of its own citizens that took place in the 1960s, a topic almost all Indonesians, including its intellectuals, have chosen to suppress from memory or at least from public discourse. (Unfortunately, such wars on the part of murderous regimes against their own people have devastated a number of Southeast Asian societies within living memory—and continue apace in Burma at the time of this writing, in late 2012, despite some recent gestures on the part of the Burmese government toward political reform.)

Mangunwijaya sustains the device of his protagonist, Iin's, opportunistic maneuvering to satirize the extravagant consumption, made possible by just as extravagant corruption, of Suharto's New Order, still in place at the time of the novel's original publication in 1991.

Iin, who actually goes by many names and takes on a great many of the roles, licit or illicit, that her society lays open to her as a woman, has choice words of complaint about the double standard that applies to men's and women's activities in Indonesia. Indeed, it is her resentment of her twin brother's greater freedom of movement when they are still children that first motivates her to look beyond the confines of domestic life. In this respect, the novel boasts a feminist agenda. However, a Western scholar of Indonesian literature, Michael Bodden, has published a comparative study of Pramoedya and Mangunwijaya, finding in the former a principled and progressive voice, and in the latter a more conservative one.[18] Specifically, he finds in Mangunwijaya's putatively feminist novel an idealization of women's nurturing role, and so an implicit retention of normative models of what women are "naturally" like. Although I believe that there is much in *Durga Umayi* to sustain that view, what impresses me most about the novel is the way in which Mangunwijaya—himself a committed progressive who stood courageously with the downtrodden throughout the political oppression of the Suharto years—portrays the dilemmas and confusion of people, male or female, who struggle against the circumstances in which they find themselves but have no tools with which to conceive of politics, or social relations, outside hierarchical arrangements.[19] Villagers such as Raybeck describes based on his fieldwork in Malaysia reappear in Mangunwijaya's novel, now rendered in exaggerated, even cartoonish, form, caught up in more extreme and historically consequential events, but still preoccupied with their relative social standing, with their ability to register and elicit deference in accordance with the standing of their interlocutors, and with their vulnerability to the state. Despite their evident flaws, and many moral failings, these characters never elicit Mangunwijaya's censure, only his generous concern.

Mangunwijaya's writing poses real challenges to students' reading skills: some students find the novel's endlessly long sentences, wild shifts in tone, and considerable word play frustrating. But others (often literature majors) prize it above all the other readings. In any case, Mangunwijaya's eclectic style should induce readers to consider how truly cosmopolitan his work is. *Midnight's Children* may well have suggested to him the possibility of writing a national, but anti-nationalist, history in the form of a novel, and perhaps Gabriel Garcia Marquez provided the model upon which he based his use of free indirect discourse. Yet however much Mangunwijaya may have been influenced by foreign models, the novel clearly draws on Javanese aesthetic traditions, including as it does many references to the Javanese shadow play tradition, to give it much of its resonance for Indonesian readers. The melding of different worlds receives fullest, and most paradoxical, expression in the author's nonchalant way with grammar: Mangunwijaya blithely mixes grammatical structures characteristic of Austronesian languages (such as Indonesian, the national language in which the novel is written, and Javanese, the regional language which lurks just below the surface of its prose, since that is the native language of almost all the characters it portrays), with grammatical structures characteristic of Western European languages. This linguistic adventurism enables him to write the long sentences that cause such fertile confusion—and often end with a sudden and ironic sting.

Thinking Comparatively

I have already mentioned certain recurrent themes that matter in the books named above. It is worth singling a few of them out as a recap of topics that matter to any representation of Southeast Asia. Actually, the same topics pertain to any region of the world: what is useful is enabling students to see how they generate consistent patterns in people's behavior in various parts of Southeast Asia.

Gender relations outside the West often look to American students pretty straightforward: we are enlightened in our treatment of women, and people in the rest of the world are not. But reading about Southeast Asia should quickly dispel such easy contrasts. Female ancestors among Mai Elliott's very high status patrilineal forebears are reputed to have been the demur and colorless paragons of virtue essential to every Vietnamese patriline's good name. But her maternal grandmother was an accomplished and remarkably independent businesswoman, far less beholden to patriarchal norms than one might expect. This sort of self-assured, competent, and forthright business woman is familiar to anyone acquainted with Southeast Asia's business circles, and with the vigorous role many women play in them. Phloi, the protagonist of *Four Reigns*, looks more conventionally feminine, and the very idealization of her attitudes and experience explains much of the nostalgic (many would say reactionary) tenor of the novel. Yet her daughter grows up to lay much greater claim to women's right to autonomy, and her actions show that debates about feminism go a long way back in Thai society. The young Thai nun in Smith's book dramatizes a similar conflict between a woman's own desires and her kin's expectations. In the end, she refuses to let the latter trump her spiritual commitments and she leaves her kin behind. Mangunwijaya's female protagonist, part-heroine, part-monster, is capable of courage and mendacity, corruption and naïveté—and perhaps most notably, both egregious moral lapses and real remorse. None of these women simply follows the path some of their respective society's worthies might wish them to take, any more than does the young woman voicing her displeasure on the porch of her home in the Malaysian village where the Raybecks lived.

Because these books bring us close to the experiences of specific individuals, they tend to achieve immediacy at the expense of grand totalizing political and historical generalizations. Nevertheless, they suggest many ways that people in Southeast Asia have addressed the question of how to distribute power in their societies and how to deal with the matter of political succession. Understandings of appropriate governance, that is, whether at the humble level of villages and their immediate surroundings, or at the level of kingdoms or nation-states (or the odd hybrid to be found in today's Thailand), always inflect political and social relations in the societies under review. Raybeck emphasizes the fiercely protective attitudes of Malay villagers, for whom keeping their village free from outside interference matters above all. In *Four Reigns*, Kukrit Pramoj lets us see, if obliquely, how Thais in the early twentieth century started to fight over whether royal authority should go unquestioned or should instead yield to more democratic arrangements. Elliott makes particularly clear how much was at stake in Vietnam's political turmoil, since members of her family operated at high levels of the imperial, French colonial, and American-backed regimes, each of those regimes informed by its own claims to legitimacy, while one of her sisters embraced the leftist view that people should make personal sacrifices in order to better everyone's life chances, and so opted to support the communist forces.

Whether looking at gender, governance, or the tenor of face-to-face interaction, American students grasp many facets of Southeast Asians' lives more clearly when their attention is drawn to how salient hierarchy and social standing are to people living in the region. Members of lowland Southeast Asian societies tend to take disparities in status and power not as lamentable exceptions to an ideologically favored egalitarianism, as Americans often do, but rather as the basis upon which all social relations are organized. As mentioned above, the feeling of "shame," when tracked through many incidents, turns out to arise when someone in any of these societies contravenes hierarchical constraints, as determined by relative age, gender, socio-economic status, official position, etc. It can take some effort to convince American students that they, too, modulate their behavior in accordance with their estimations of their status relative to an interlocutor's. I point out to them that they are likely to feel constrained to show me "respect" if they visit me during my office hours: Southeast Asians do attend to matters of social standing with greater assiduousness and frankness than most Americans do, but the difference is one of degree. Australians, meanwhile, put their egalitarianism into practice more consistently than Americans. I tell students how stunned I was, despite my progressive convictions, when shortly after I started teaching at the ANU an Australian undergraduate addressed me by my first name on the phone before we had even met!

Assuming that the world is fundamentally hierarchical in nature brings many consequences in its wake. That hierarchical difference can be embraced by subordinates as well as superordinates startles many American students. A young Phloi finds solace in her elders' guidance about who she should marry, and later, her husband delights in modeling his behavior and dress on those of a fairly silly monarch. More importantly, dissension about the nature of both gender relations and Thai politics focuses on whether some people (males in the first case, aristocrats in the second) rightfully exercise authority over others by virtue of a fundamental quality, or potency, that they are assumed to possess. Elliott makes it clear that many urban, elite Vietnamese found it very difficult to think of uneducated peasants as people they should be concerned about. As Anderson wrote

about Javanese, Vietnamese, as depicted by both Elliott and Trullinger, look "up" to where power originates, not down to where it grows faint.[20] Pramoedya takes conflicting understandings of what anti-colonial resist-
ance should be based upon, e.g., whether ethnic and religious identifications should determine people's relative prestige and power, and what those under-standings imply about visions for a post-colonial society, as the thread running throughout his tetralogy. Mangunwijaya, more concerned to show how elite actions affect the poor and powerless, lets us see what suffering and moral com-promises are forced upon the weak when the powerful do as they please.

Hierarchy can be summarized as an arrangement wherein social relations are predicated upon mutual interdependence through difference. If males differ im-portantly from females, for example, then it stands to reason that their rights and responsibilities should also differ. It is on the basis of that difference that men and women collaborate and so depend upon each other: it is their mutual inter-dependence that guarantees their continued participation in long-term relations of exchange. And since differences of any kind imply differences in value, men and women enjoy differing degrees of prestige, and men enjoy higher standing than women. Higher standing brings both privileges and constraints. Men's speech, for example, is "important." For that reason, it tends toward the senten-tious and dull, in contrast to women's more mercurial and free-flowing "unim-portant" speech.[21]

In sum, charismatic authority, patriarchal ideology, and deeply felt emotional reactions in Southeast Asia all turn out to make sense in view of an assumption that hierarchy is simply how the world works, that hierarchical difference neces-sarily informs all relationships. The novels and memoirs I have mentioned all provide countless examples of how this assumption applies to specific situa-tions. Each situation generates complications and tensions: that people take hier-archical difference for granted does not mean that they agree on what follows from that fact, that is, on what positions people rightfully find themselves in vis-à-vis each other, only that discussion, or argument, about what is right or virtu-ous or appropriate gets phrased with reference to a set of generally agreed-upon terms. Americans take much more contradictory and ambivalent positions to-ward hierarchy, whether in domestic relationships or larger collective affairs. Raising this point can give rise to a good deal of lively discussion in class. To the extent that this happens, and to the extent that students can be induced to see their own attitudes and behavior in a new light, then they have been made aware of the excitement that studying Southeast Asia in an anthropological mode can generate.

By encouraging students to experience this excitement by reading memoirs and fiction, we can show them how anthropological and literary approaches to human affairs resemble each other. In either case, reading the "data" means de-veloping a repertoire of understandings about people's motivations, goals, and strategies, and about the constraints—material, cultural, historical—within which people live and act. An ethnographic monograph may present us with explicit commentary about such matters; fiction or a memoir may not. Yet in both cases we should try to combine an informed analytic perspective with an intuitive sense of how pieces of the puzzle fit together. An alert reader of fiction and an alert reader of ethnography, then, evince many of the same skills, based upon both a sociological curiosity and a real capacity for human empathy.

Using Commercial Films to Teach Anthropology

Commercial films provide material amenable to an anthropological reading in much the same way that written fiction and memoirs do. In a lower-division anthropology course I teach entitled "Introduction to Expressive Culture," I take advantage of the entertainment value of films to win students over to anthropology's self-reflexive take on both cultural "others" and ourselves.

Nothing appears more "globalized" than film: surely commercial film is an internationally homogeneous genre, deriving all its conventions and styles from Hollywood's "dream machine." So, at least, most American students are likely to assume, particularly in light of how rarely any films of foreign provenance get shown in American theatres. Yet putting well-known Hollywood films alongside commercial films that originate from elsewhere can reveal to students that even so high-tech and modern a genre as the movies turns out to reflect cultural differences. At the same time, questions of representation—idealizing, stereotyping, simplifying, etc.—can be made salient by asking how films represent "others:" not only how Hollywood represents people American undergraduates consider foreign, but even how foreigners, when they make movies, represent those who are foreign to them—which may include us.

Two classic Hollywood films treat of contact zones: John Wayne's *The Alamo* depicts San Antonio in 1836,[22] when citizens of Mexico, both Spanish-speaking residents and more recent, English-speaking, settlers, fought a large army sent up from Mexico City; Disney's *Pocahontas* depicts seventeenth century Jamestown,[23] where Anglo settlers and Native Americans met up. Because I teach in Texas, many of my students have been to the Alamo and so know that it is a small, rather unimpressive building, much more modest than either the film or the importance it holds in Texans' sense of their own history would suggest. But since Wayne's purpose was not to teach his audiences about Texas history but rather about the Cold War conflict between freedom-loving Americans and the benighted victims of dictatorial oppression ("Mexicans" in 1836 and "communists" in 1959), he omits all of the contextual history that would make sense of the actual conflict that ended in massacre. It takes only a summary account of what the nature of the cross-cutting alliances and controversies actually were in early nineteenth century "Tejas" (a part of the Mexican nation, one that Anglo settlers were entering in increasing numbers, to the eventual detriment of both the Spanish-speaking landed elite and their tenant farmers) to demonstrate to students how a narrator plays upon his audience's investments (in "freedom," in free-spirited males' genial camaraderie, in an avuncular male leader's trustworthiness), that is, how he plays upon their cultural assumptions, to win them over to his conservative, and radically simplifying, but for both those reasons, reassuring, perspective. Ironically, fears of Spanish-speaking people entering this region in increasing numbers are now arousing panic—and worries among Wayne's latter-day fans about what changing demographics will mean for the probable outcome of future elections.

Disney's *Pocahontas* illustrates, in its cliché-ridden rendering of Native Americans, how careful Hollywood has become to avoid denigrating representations of racial and ethnic minorities. Native Americans, we are reminded, are "close to nature," committed to their community and kin, and full of traditional wisdom. Snooty English aristocrats, meanwhile, are everything we egalitarian Americans despise, although salt-of-the-earth working-class Englishmen and Scots are a bit of all right. John Smith, we discover at his first appearance, not only has electric blue eyes, a great shock of blond hair, and a swimmer's shoulders, but also, alone of all his colleagues—this is something American viewers are unlikely to note until their attention is drawn to it—speaks with an American accent! So the Disney studio is manipulating audience's responses by playing on widespread conceptions of what "natives" are like, and what our Anglo-American ancestors were like. At the same time, the film-makers are urging us to identify with highly idealized (and not incidentally, physically attractive) protagonists. At the film's conclusion, all concerned turn out to be swept up in racist animosity, except for Pocahontas and John Smith, whose implicit romantic attraction to each other suggests a model of tolerance and understanding we applaud, thereby making us feel good about ourselves. As with Wayne's version of the Alamo legend, Disney's *Pocahontas* radically simplifies the nature of the conflict, reducing a historical encounter that led to the decimation of the region's indigenous population to a straightforward instance of reciprocal racism, easily resolved through the human capacity for romance. Disparities in power, and how they affected outcomes for disparate parties to the encounter, are swept away in favor of a reassuring sense that we, at least, are enlightened, tolerant citizens of a multicultural society, *quod erat demonstrandum.*

The Igloolik film, *Atanarjuat—the Fast Runner*,[24] in pointed contrast to *Pocahontas*, enables students to see how a commercial film can represent members of an indigenous community (in this case Canadian Inuits) as individuals rather than simply as stereotypes. The very fact that it relates a legendary story, and so does not concern itself with the community's contact with Europeans, enables viewers to put ethnic or racial tensions aside for a time. Numerous long takes teach us much about the techniques with which people can make a viable, if always precarious, existence for themselves even in an extremely harsh natural environment. We can only guess about what power follows from donning the walrus-toothed necklace that certain figures fight over, or what authority allows an old woman to banish an extended family from the community at story's end. There is none of an ethnographic film's explanatory voice-over. But in addition to showing what life looks like in an altogether foreign community, the pacing of the film and the concision of its dialogue make a dramatic contrast with Hollywood film-making. Almost exactly the same length as Wayne's *The Alamo*, *Atanarjuat* feels deliberate where the former feels plodding, and it proceeds inexorably toward the legend's dénoument, whereas *The Alamo*'s narrative feels disorganized and dispersed. *Atanarjuat* not only provides a fascinating view of a distant community; it also makes for an altogether unanticipated and ravishing aesthetic experience.

Much more familiar to young viewers in the United States or elsewhere in the world is the style of the Thai action flick *Ong Bak*.[25] Starting with a visually arresting opening that focuses on an athletic contest in a Thai village, the film proceeds at a frenetic pace as it follows a virtuous young martial arts practitioner as he travels to Bangkok and then through a series of fights, chase sequences, and other high-energy scenes. The story line contrasts this young man's ascetic self-restraint, piety, and respect for his betters—his supposedly traditional Thai virtues—with the moral turpitude of corrupt, venal, foreign (Western, Chinese, and Burmese) others, and of Thais who have come under their malign influence. The latter include the hero's own cousin. While the hero remains steadfast and incorruptible throughout the film, his cousin is slowly won back from a fast and dangerous criminal career to Buddhist morality, exemplified most dramatically in his final message of apology, as he nears death, to his parents that he will not be able to win them the merit that accrues to a couple when their son joins the community of monks. Ironically, the film's deeply nativist message—which, among other things, makes young Westerners look violent, deceitful, and incompetent—is conveyed through sophisticated use of international media techniques and an insistent (to me, exhausting) bass beat.

Finally, two films, one immensely popular in South Asia, the other immensely popular in the West, complement each other for the way they address the problem of how people of South Asian descent living in Great Britain will reconcile South Asian attitudes toward social relations, including hierarchical understandings that emphasize filial piety, on the one hand, and on the other, individualist notions predominant in the society in which they find themselves. Not surprisingly, in *Dilwale Dulhania Le Jayange*[26] (hereafter, *DDLJ*), one of the most popular Bollywood films of all time, the cultural conundrum is rendered through the idiom of romantic love. In the Indian/English *Bend It Like Beckham*,[27] romantic love enters the mix, along with young people's aspirations to determine the course of their own lives more generally. In both films, hierarchy is challenged, inasmuch as a South Asian couple's daughter seeks to forge a path other than the one her parents envision for her. In *DDLJ*, the modest and loyal Simran wishes to accede to her father's long-standing plan that she marry his best friend's (arrogant) son, but falls in love despite herself with the apparently irresponsible but charming Raj. In *Bend It Like Beckham*, a young woman becomes enthralled with playing soccer, to the dismay of her mother (who worries about impressions of her modesty, since playing the game means both exposing her legs and playing with boys, and so compromising her chances on the marriage market) and of her father (who cannot overcome his recollection of the racist treatment his earlier experiences playing cricket subjected him to). In *Bend It Like Beckham*, an English family is used as a foil to the South Asian one to brilliant effect: to set up a parallel to the South Asian family's concern about their daughter's inappropriate behavior playing soccer, the English family is made to worry that their daughter is lesbian. Both films portray the girls' mothers as fairly ineffectual or even ridiculous: in these patrilineal South Asian families, and in the English one, too, it is the fathers who matter in the end. And therein lies the two films' most surprising affinity: both films end with the South Asian father becoming reconciled to, and indeed approving, his daughter's wish to follow her dream. In other words, in both films the apparently irresolvable contradiction, between the South Asian validation of filial piety, on the one hand, and the Western validation of individual agency, on the other, yields to a fantasized happy ending wherein no such conflict obtains. Patriarchy remains firmly ensconced in *DDLJ*, inasmuch as Simran passes from the hands of her father into the hands of her future husband. Yet to the extent that Jess, at the end of *Bend It Like Beckham*, also waits upon her father's approval before following her preferred path, taking her to the United States on a soccer scholarship, she leaves at least some of the patriarchal dispensation in place.

These six commercial films appeal to students to varying degrees. *Atanarjuat—the Fast Runner* poses the greatest challenges and generates both the greatest number of complaints and the greatest praise among various students. Yet all of the films mentioned above make it possible to foster an anthropological sensitivity to basic questions we all face: how we will get along among ourselves, and with others. I am happy to report that a few freshmen have been so enthralled with these questions that they have chosen to major in anthropology. More gratifying still is the remark a few students over the years have made at the end of the semester: that they will never watch a movie the same way again. Because stories always implicate social relations, and because anthropologists are necessarily preoccupied—like everybody else—with social relations, films can play on students' interest in their own and other people's ways of solving the problems relationships with other people entail, in order to impart some measure of anthropological insight even into their own lives. This strikes me as the greatest possible contribution anthropology can make to a student's educational experience.

Notes

1. James Scott, *Weapons of the Weak* (New Haven: Yale University Press, 1986).

2. Douglas Raybeck, *Mad Dogs, Englishmen, and the Errant Anthropologist* (Prospect Heights, IL: Waveland Press, 1996).

3. Michael Herzfeld, *Cultural Intimacy: Social Poetics in the Nation-State* (New York: Routledge, 1997).

4. Clifford Geertz, "Person, Time, and Conduct in Bali," in *The Interpretation of Cultures* (New York: Basic Books, 1973), 412-53.

5. Raybeck, *Mad Dogs*, 96.

6. Raybeck, *Mad Dogs*, 223.

7. Raybeck, *Mad Dogs*, 44.

8. Kukrit Pramoj, *Four Reigns*, tr. Tulachandra (Chiang Mai: Silkworm Books, 1998).

9. Scot Barmé, *Woman, Man, Bangkok: Love, Sex, and Popular Culture in Thailand* (Lanham, MD: Rowman and Littlefield, 2002).

10. Sid Brown, *The Journey of One Buddhist Nun: Even Against the Wind* (Albany: State University of New York, 2001).

11. Mai Elliott, *The Sacred Willow: Four Generations in the Life of a Vietnamese Family* (New York: Oxford University Press, 1999).

12. James W. Trullinger, *Village at War: An Account of Conflict in Vietnam* (Stanford, CA: Stanford University Press, 1993 [1975]).

13. Benedict Anderson, *Imagined Communities: Reflections on the Origins and Spread of Nationalism* (London: Verson Press, 1983); Ernest Gellner, *Nations and Nationalism* (Ithaca, NY: Cornell University Press, 1983).

14. Pramoedya Ananta Toer, *Buru Quartet*, tr. Max Lane (New York: Penguin, 1996).

15. Pramoedya Ananta Toer, *This Earth of Mankind*, tr. Max Lane (New York: Penguin, 1996).

16. Pramoedya Ananta Toer, *Child of All Nations*, tr. Max Lane (New York: Penguin, 1996).

17. Y. B. Mangunwijaya, *Durga Umayi*, tr. Ward Keeler (Seattle: University of Washington Press; Singapore: Singapore University Press, 2004).

18. Michael Bodden, "Woman as Nation in Mangunwijaya's *Durga Umayi*," *Indonesia* 62 (October, 1996): 53-82.

19. I discuss this point, and Bodden's analysis, at greater length in "*Durga Umayi* and the Postcolonialist Dilemma," in *Clearing a Space: Postcolonial Readings of Modern Indonesian literature*, eds. Keith Foulcher and Tony Day (Leiden: KITLV Press, 2002), 349-69.

20. Benedict Anderson, "The Idea of Power in Javanese Culture," in *Language and Power: Exploring Political Cultures in Indonesia* (Ithaca, NY: Cornell University Press, 1990), 17-77.

21. See my "Speaking of Gender in Java," in *Power and Difference: Gender in Island Southeast Asia*, eds. Jane Atkinson and Shelly Errington (Stanford, CA: Stanford University Press, 1990), 127-52.

22. *The Alamo*, directed by John Wayne (1960; Santa Monica, CA: MGM/UA Home Video, 2000), DVD.

23. *Pocahontas*, directed by Mike Gabriel and Eric Goldberg (1995; Burbank, CA: Walt Disney/Buena Vista Home Entertainment, 2000), DVD.

24. *Atanarjuat—The Fast Runner*, directed by Zacharias Kunuk, (2001; Culver City, CA: Igloolik Isuma Productions/Columbia TriStar Home Entertainment, 2002), DVD.

25. *Ong-Bak: the Thai Warrior*, directed by Prachya Pinkaew, (2004; Beverly Hills: Magnolia/20th Century Fox Home Entertainment, 2005), DVD.

26. *Dilwale dulhania le jayenge*, directed by Aditya Chopra (1995; Wembley, Middlesex: Yash Raj Films Home Entertainment, 2001), DVD.

27. *Bend It Like Beckham*, directed by Gurinder Chadha (2002; Beverly Hills: 20th
Century Fox Home Entertainment, 2003), DVD.

References

Anderson, Benedict
  1983   *Imagined Communities: Reflections on the Origins and Spread of National-
          ism*. London: Verso Press.
  1990   *The Idea of Power in Javanese Culture. Language and Power: Exploring
          Political Cultures in Indonesia*. Ithaca, NY: Cornell University Press, Pp. 17-
          77.
Atanarjuat—the Fast Runner
  2001   Zacharias Kunik, dir. 172 min. Igloolik Isuma Distributing International.
Barmé, Scot
  2002   *Woman, Man, Bangkok: Love, Sex, and Popular Culture in Thailand*.
          Lanham, MD: Rowman and Littlefield.
Bend It Like Beckham
  2002   Gurinder Chadha, dir. 112 min. Beverly Hills: 20th Century Fox Home En-
          tertainment.
Bodden, Michael
  1996   "Woman as Nation in Mangunwijaya's Durga Umayi," *Indonesia* 62 (Oc-
          tober, 1996): 53-82.
Brown, Sid
  2001   *The Journey of One Buddhist Nun: Even Against the Wind*. Albany: State
          University of New York.
Dilwale dulhania le jayenge
  1995   Aditya Chopra, dir. 189 min. Wembley, Middlesex: Yash Raj Films Home
          Entertainment.
Elliott, Mai
  1999   *The Sacred Willow: Four Generations in the Life of a Vietnamese Family*.
          New York: Oxford University Press.
Geertz, Clifford
  1973   "Person, Time, and Conduct in Bali." *The Interpretation of Cultures*. New
          York: Basic Books, Pp. 412-53.
Gellner, Ernest
  1983   *Nations and Nationalism*. Ithaca, NY: Cornell University Press, 1983.
Herzfeld, Michael
  1997   *Cultural Intimacy: Social Poetics in the Nation-State*. New York: Routledge.
Keeler, Ward
  1990   "Speaking of Gender in Java." In *Power and Difference: Gender in Island
          Southeast Asia*. Jane Atkinson and Shelly Errington, eds. Stanford, CA:
          Stanford University Press, Pp. 127-52.
  2002   "Durga Umayi' and the Postcolonialist Dilemma." In *Clearing a Space:
          Postcolonial Readings of Modern Indonesian Literature*, Keith Foulcher, and
          Tony Day, eds. Leiden: KITLV Press, Pp. 349-69.
Kukrit Pramoj
  1998   *Four Reigns*. Tr. Tulachandra. Chiang Mai: Silkworm Books.
Mangunwijaya, Y.B.

2004   *Durga Umayi*. Tr. Ward Keeler. Seattle: University of Washington Press; Singapore: Singapore University Press.

Ong-Bak: the Thai Warrior

2004   Prachya Pinkaew, dir. 105 min. Beverly Hills: 20th Century Fox Home Entertainment.

Pocahontas
    1995   Mike Gabriel and Eric Goldberg, dir. 81 min. Burbank, CA: Walt Disney/Buena Vista Home Entertainment.

Pramoedya Ananta Toer
    1996   *Buru Quartet*. Tr. Max Lane. New York: Penguin.
    1996   *Child of All Nations*. Tr. Max Lane. New York: Penguin.
    1996   *This Earth of Mankind*. Tr. Max Lane. New York: Penguin.

Raybeck Douglas
    1996   *Mad Dogs, Englishmen, and the Errant Anthropologist*. Prospect Heights, IL: Waveland Press.

Scott, James
    1986   *Weapons of the Weak*. New Haven: Yale University Press.

The Alamo
    1960   John Wayne, dir. 162 min. Santa Monica, CA: UA Home Video.

Trullinger, James W.
    1993   [1975] *Village at War: An Account of Conflict in Vietnam*. Stanford, CA: Stanford University Press.

Index

About the Editor and Contributors

Editor **Marilyn Cohen** is Associate Professor of Sociology and Director of Women's Studies at Saint Peter's University in Jersey City, New Jersey. She holds a Ph.D. in anthropology from the Graduate Faculty/New School University. Her geographical areas of specialization are Great Britain and Ireland and her research has focused on gender, work, athletics, and the transition to capitalism. She is the author and editor of numerous books, articles, and book chapters including: *Linen, Family and Community in Tullylish, County Down, 1690-1914; The Warp of Ulster's Past: Interdisciplinary Perspectives on the Irish Linen Industry, 1700-1920; Reclaiming Gender: Transgressive Identities in Modern Ireland; and No Girls in the Clubhouse: The Exclusion of Women from Baseball.*

Ward Keeler is Associate Professor of Anthropology at the University of Texas at Austin. A specialist in Southeast Asia, the first part of his career was based on long-term fieldwork in Java and Bali, focusing on the performing arts (particularly shadow puppets) and language. More recently, he has been doing research in Burma, looking at the performing arts and music, gender, and Buddhism. He translated and annotated an Indonesian novel, Mangunwijaya's 1991 *Durga Umayi*, to grant readers of English access to an Indonesian public intellectual's brilliant contribution to the literature of anti-colonial and post-colonial history.

Ray McDermott is Professor of Education, and Cultural and Social Anthropology at Stanford University. He takes a broad interest in the analysis of human communication, the organization of school success and failure, and the history and use of various literacies around the world. His work includes studies of inner-city public schools, after school classrooms, and the function of information technologies in different cultures. He is currently working on the intellectual history of ideas like genius, intelligence, race, and capital. Ray's McDermott's current research interests include the political economy of learning, writing systems, educational, and psychological anthropology. He is author of numerous publications including: Herve' Varenne and Ray McDermott, *Successful Failure: The School America Builds*; and Joe Kulpers and Ray McDermott (eds.), *Fine Description: Ethnographic and Linguistic Essays of Harold C. Conklin.*

John W. Pulis is Associate Professor of Anthropology at Hofstra University. He holds a Ph.D. in anthropology from the Graduate Faculty/New School University. His geographical areas of specialization are Jamaica, the West Indies, Africa, and North America. John Pulis's research has focused on the topic of Rastafari and he is the author and editor of numerous publications including: *Moving On: Black Loyalists in the Afro-Atlantic World; Religion, Diaspora, and Cultural Identity: A Reader in the Anglophone Caribbean* and *Gates to Zion: Texts, Voices and the Narrative World of Rastafari.*

Mary-Elizabeth Reeve holds a Ph.D. in anthropology from the University of Illinois and a Masters in Public Health from Yale University School of Medicine. She is a global health practitioner and Director of Global Perinatal Health Programs at the March of Dimes Foundation. Since joining the Foundation in 2000, she developed maternal and neonatal health projects in Latin America, Central and Eastern Europe, and South and Central Asia.

David Surrey is Professor of Sociology, Chair of the Sociology/Urban Studies Department, and Director of Africana Studies at Saint Peter's University in Jersey City, New Jersey. He holds a Ph.D. in Anthropology from the Graduate Faculty/New School University. His academic interests include globalization, desegregation, ethnicity, immigration, housing, urban history, education, and the Vietnam Era. He has written and administered over twenty-five grants and is currently the Director of a large Title V grant at Saint Peter's University – *Strengthening Achievement Among Hispanic and Students of Minority Backgrounds.* He is the author of numerous publications including: *Choice of Conscience: Viet Nam Era Military and Draft Resisters in Canada* (Praeger, 1982) and the co-author of *Keeping the Struggle Alive: Studying Desegregation in Our Town.*

Helena Wulff is Professor of Social Anthropology at Stockholm University. Her research is in the anthropology of communication and aesthetics based on a wide range of studies on the social worlds of literary production, dance, and visual arts. She also has an interest in the anthropology of emotions, media, and the senses. Her current research is on writing and literature focusing on contemporary Irish writers as cultural translators and public intellectuals. Helena Wulff´s books include: *Ballet across Borders: Career and Culture in the World of Dancers*; *Dancing at the Crossroads: Memory and Mobility in Ireland*; *The Emotions: A Cultural Reader; Youth Cultures: A Cross-Cultural Perspective; New Technologies at Work: People, Screens and Social Virtuality;* and *Ethnographic Practice in the Present.* Helena Wulff was editor-in-chief (with Dorle Dracklé) of *Social Anthropology/Anthropologie Sociale*, the journal of the European Association of Social Anthropologists, and Vice President of EASA.